MAHABHARATA
in *Polyester*

HAMISH MCDONALD is Asia-Pacific Editor of the *Sydney Morning Herald*. He has been a foreign correspondent in Jakarta, Tokyo, Hong Kong, Beijing and New Delhi, where he was bureau chief of the *Far Eastern Economic Review*. He has twice won Walkley awards, and has had a report on Burma read into the record of the US Congress. He is the author of books on Indonesia and India, and was made an inaugural Fellow of the Australian Institute of International Affairs in 2008.

MAHABHARATA

in Polyester

The making of the world's richest
brothers and their feud

HAMISH McDONALD

NEW
SOUTH

A New South book
Published by
University of New South Wales Press Ltd
University of New South Wales
Sydney NSW 2052
Australia
www.unswpress.com.au

National Library of Australia
Cataloguing-in-Publication entry
Author: McDonald, Hamish, 1948–
    Title: Mahabharata in polyester: the making of the world's richest
       brothers and their feud/by Hamish McDonald.
    ISBN: 978 174223 158 7 (pbk.)
    Notes: Includes index.
    Subjects: Ambani, Dhirubhai.
       Ambani family.
       Reliance Industries Ltd. – History.
       Businessmen – India – Biography.
       Industrialists – India – Biography.
       Vendetta – India.
    Dewey Number: 338.92

Design Avril Makula
Cover Design by Committee
Cover photo Ambani & Sons: Anil (left) and Mukesh with Dhirubhai
at Maker Chambers IV, Mumbai, soon after they returned from studies
in the United States. (*India Today*)
Printer Ligare

This book is printed on paper using fibre supplied from plantation
or sustainably managed forests.

Contents

Acknowledgments

The Ambani story grabbed me as soon as I landed in India in December 1990 for what turned out to be an enthralling six years, and it still has me in its grip, long after my assignment in New Delhi ended. Dhirubhai Ambani embodied all of the revolutionary capitalism that sympathetic and impatient analysts within the prevailing Western paradigm believed was lurking inside the Indian economy, pressing to be released from bureaucracy. The turbulent election of 1991 resulted in a government that set about unleashing this spirit across the economy. To me, this was the crucial narrative of modern India, behind the more immediate news-making events like caste conflict, Hindu nationalism, Islamist movements, and insurgencies in Kashmir, Punjab and the north-east. Ambani had already pushed out of the subservient position reserved for business, to the point where he had a well-earned reputation as a maker and breaker of governments, and of political and bureaucratic careers. With the economic reforms giving greater access to domestic and global sources of finance, his Reliance group redoubled its rapid growth towards Ambani's target of becoming a petroleum giant. My position reporting for a leading business magazine gave me a ringside seat and, initially at least, personal acquaintance with Ambani and his two sons. Inevitably, the glowing picture of an entrepreneurial hero, so beloved of business magazines, took on more light and shade with detailed study of the Ambani and Reliance story. Still, the relationship of government and big business emerged increasingly as the missing element of popular and academic writing about contemporary India. This book is the result.

It started with a push from Robin Jeffrey, then of La Trobe University, Melbourne, aided by Marika Vicziany of the National Centre for South Asian Studies, Jenny McGregor of Melbourne University's AsiaLink, and the late Ken McPherson of Curtin University's Indian Ocean Centre, for putting together an *ad hoc* fellowship to let me start work. Later, Rodney Tiffin and Jim Masselos of the University of Sydney helped with working space and advice. Navnit Dholakia gave me vital introductions to the Gujarati immigrant communities in London and Leicester. D.B. Patel, of Leicester's Shree Sanatan Mandir, took time out to guide me. Himatbhai Jagani, secretary of Shree Aden Depala in London, welcomed me to this association of former Indian residents of Aden. Other help came from K.D. Patel, C.B. Patel of the Gujarat Samachar, and Ramniklal Solanki of the Garavi Gujarat. In Ahmedabad, Susheel Kothari, formerly of Besse & Co. in Aden, then Reliance, was both hospitable and informative.

In Mumbai, there are many to thank: Manish Mankad, librarian of *BusinessIndia*, S.J. Vasani of Vyapar, Kirtikant K. Kapadia and Kishanbhai Kapadia, of the Swastik Textile Agency, who gave me tea when I walked in off the street and told me about the Pydhonie textile market; Sucheta Dalal and Debashis Basu, now running *MoneyLife*; Pradip Shah; Kanti Bhatt and Sheela Bhatt. In Manipal, Ramdas M. Pai of Manipal Academy of Higher Education. In New Delhi, my thanks to S.R. Mohnot. In Chennai, L. Seshan of the *Indian Express* helped with records of the Gurumurthy investigations. Many other businessmen, members of parliament, lawyers, stockbrokers, merchant bankers, government officials and journalists gave freely of their knowledge about the Ambani story, but would not want to be identified. However, Jamnadas Moorjani, who died in December 2002, can now be mentioned as a wonderful source of information and fair opinion.

Although neither the Ambani family nor Reliance cooperated in this project, the Reliance spokesmen who were my points of contact in earlier times – Yogesh Desai, Tony Jesudason, Jacob John and Deepak Neogi – were always accessible and courteous. When letters from law firms in both Mumbai and Sydney, and court injunctions in India, made it clear that Reliance was opposed to my earlier book *The Polyester Prince* appearing at all, Patrick Gallagher of Allen & Unwin courageously stuck to his publishing plans.

This was not the closing of the book, however, just of a chapter. Dhirubhai Ambani went on to achieve his vision of opening one of the world's biggest oil refineries. Every recovery from previous controversies and scandals had been followed by predictions that his company would become a more 'normal' and predictable corporation taking fewer risks. Yet it became clear that pushing the limits was normal for him. Dhirubhai's sons inherited control of Reliance – and his *modus operandi* – on his death in 2002, but two years later started the bitter feud that divided India's biggest business house. My holidays in India soon turned into research trips for this new book, which has been encouraged by numerous Indians, from India itself and from the diaspora in America, Europe, Asia and Australia, who have contacted me.

Engagement with India is not something that can be turned off by absence. With me, in this lifelong entrancement, has been my wife Penny and our children Alex and Laura, who were born in New Delhi as the first book took shape and for whom India is mother nation. I can only give thanks that they rejoice in India too.

Glossary

BCCI	Bank of Credit and Commerce International
BR	banker's receipt
BSES	Bombay and Suburban Electric Supply Company
CDMA	code-division multiple access
crore	10 million
DGTD	Directorate-General of Technical Development
DMT	dimethyl terephthalate
GDR	Global Depository Receipt
GSM	global system for mobile communications
ICICI	Industrial Credit and Investment Corporation of India
IMF	International Monetary Fund
IOC	Indian Oil Corporation
IPCL	Indian Petrochemicals Ltd
LAB	linear alkyline benzene
lakh	a hundred thousand
lathi	wooden stave, used by police
LIC	Life Insurance Corporation
MEG	monoethylene glycol

NRI	non-resident Indian
NTPC	National Thermal Power Corporation
ONGC	Oil and Natural Gas Corporation
PFY	polyester filament yarn
POY	partially oriented yarn
PSE	public-sector enterprise
PSF	polyester staple fibre
PTA	purified terephthalic acid
PTI	Press Trust of India
RBI	Reserve Bank of India
RCS	Reliance Consultancy Services
REP	Replenishment licence (abbrev.)
RSS	Rashtriya Swayamsevak Sangh (National Volunteers Order)
SEBI	Securities and Exchange Board of India
STC	State Trading Corporation
TRAI	Telecom Regulatory Authority of India
UTI	Unit Trust of India

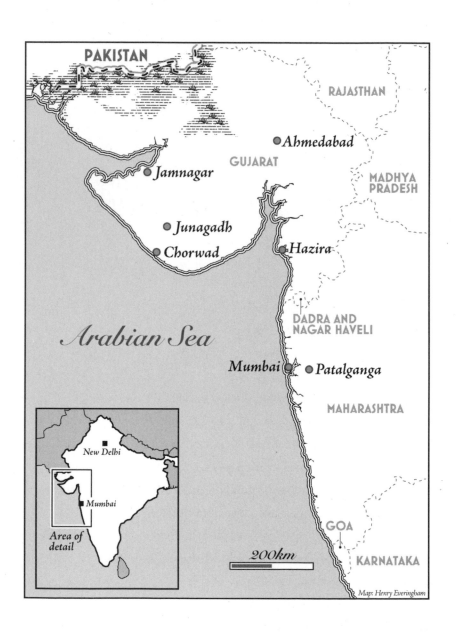

PAKISTAN

RAJASTHAN

●Ahmedabad

GUJARAT

MADHYA
PRADESH

●Jamnagar

●Junagadh

●Chorwad

●Hazira

Arabian Sea

DADRA AND
NAGAR HAVELI

Mumbai● ●Patalganga

MAHARASHTRA

New Delhi

Mumbai

Area of
detail

GOA

200km

KARNATAKA

Map: Henry Everingham

1

Protean capitalist

In January 2007 a Bollywood movie had an unusual launch in three corners of the globe. The full-length Hindi feature film, incorporating the usual song and dance sequences, was shown simultaneously in Mumbai, Toronto and Sydney – thereby claiming to being in the vanguard in the globalisation of Indian popular culture, although in Sydney at least audiences were almost exclusively of Indian origin.

The 'purely fictional' film was titled *Guru* and told of the rise of one Gurukant Desai, son of the local headmaster in the Gujarat village of 'Idhar'. After a spell of trading spices in Istanbul, the ambitious young Guru moves to the textile markets of Bombay, where he lives in a *chawl* tenement with his new wife.

He battles to break into a closed trading circle controlled by an aquiline-featured, wealthy young textile mill owner, prone to golfing in plus-fours and driving about in an open sports car. Intense, active and always looking for loopholes to push through, Guru manages to build up his company, Shakti Trading, diversifying into the manufacture of polyester and raising his capital from adulatory shareholders, to whom he delivers inspirational speeches at mass meetings held in a sports stadium. He wins the friendship of newspaper baron Manikdas Gupta, but the publisher becomes alarmed and insulted by Guru's bribery of his staff – from the peon's polyester safari suit to the editor's new car – and sets Shyam Saxena, a bright young journalist of his newspaper *Swatantra*, to expose him.

Posters summarised the film story as 'Villager, Visionary, Winner'. That the film was meant as more than just entertainment is clear from the 'foreword' that Mani Ratnam wrote for the cover of the digital video recording later put on sale:

> If you are ambitious, if you have dreams, India is the place for you – today. But it wasn't like this always. After independence we were a huge nation, a young nation, where abstinence was respectable, ambition was not, where society took precedence over the individual. Today we have moved from left of centre to the right. When did this happen? How did this happen? Or did it happen in front of us and we couldn't see it? *Guru* is a revisiting of that time, of three decades during which India changed slowly but surely. And the mirror to that change is the life of one man – Gurukant Desai.

The film asserted, sometimes crudely, that Guru was a revolutionary figure, representing a raw new India pushing against the constraints of remnant colonial power structures and nostalgic doctrines. 'I've worked enough for the white man,' says Guru when announcing his decision to strike out in his own business. His dismissive rivals include Parsi business leaders, dressed in the white robes and tall black hats normally worn at fire temples to make the point. 'Neither you nor your *khadi* army can stop me,' Guru declares to newspaper baron Gupta, referring to the home-spun cotton dress of his generation of freedom fighters against British rule. There is a defiant address to supercilious judges looking into the allegations raised by Gupta's newspaper. He tells his shareholders the establishment is against them all 'because we are commoners, middle class'. One of the most contentious figures in contemporary India was being turned into celluloid myth.

Sixteen years earlier, the man being played by one of India's hottest hearth-throb film stars, with music by the famous score-writer A.R. Rahman, had dropped his name on our doorstep in New Delhi. In January 1991 a messenger delivered a card, elaborately embossed with a picture of the elephant-headed deity Ganesh, improbably carried on the back of a much smaller mouse: Dhirubhai and Kokilaben Ambani invited us to the wedding of their son Anil to Tina Munim in Bombay.

The young couple's courtship had been a stormy one. The bride, Tina Munim, was a girl with a past. A film starlet, Tina had had a well-publicised affair with a much older actor before meeting Anil. The groom was the tearaway one of the two Ambani boys. His parents had frowned on the match. Bombay's magnates usually tried to arrange matches that cemented alliances with other powerful business or political families. This one was not arranged, nor did it bring any more than a certain popularity. Hired assailants had been sent with acid and knives to scar Tina's face, so went the gossip (apocryphal: Tina's face turned out to be flawless). Anil had threatened suicide if he could not marry Tina, went another rumour. Finally the parents had agreed.

The father, Dhirubhai, was no less colourful and even more controversial. Ambani had gone into polyester manufacturing in a big way and got huge numbers of Indians to invest in shares of his company Reliance Industries. In India, the home of fine cotton textiles, it seemed that people couldn't get enough polyester. The only constraint on local producers like Reliance was the government's licensing of their capacity or where they built their factories. To increase his capacity, Ambani had become a big political fixer. It was said his executives had been shuttling briefcases of cash to politicians all over Delhi. There had been epic battles, with the press baron Ramnath Goenka of the *Indian Express* and with a textile rival from an old Parsi business house, Nusli Wadia. A year or so earlier, a Reliance public relations manager had been arrested for plotting to murder Wadia. The man had been released, and nothing was moving in the case. Was it genuine or a frame-up? Indian colleagues were not sure: no conspiracy was accepted at face value.

The wedding was going to be big, so big that it was to take place in a football stadium, the same one where Dhirubhai Ambani had held many of his shareholder meetings. But it began in an oddly casual way.

As instructed, in mid-afternoon we went to the Wodehouse Gym-khana Club, some distance from the stadium. There we found guests milling in the street outside, the men dressed mostly in lavishly cut dark suits and showy ties, moustaches trimmed and hair brilliantined. The women were heavily made up, laden with thick gold jewellery and wearing lustrous gold-embroidered silk saris. Anil Ambani appeared suddenly from the club grounds, dressed in a white satin outfit and sequinned turban, sitting on a white horse. A brass band in white, frogged tunics struck up a brash, repetitive march, and we set off in separate phalanxes of men and women alongside the groom towards the stadium. Every now and then, the process would pause while the Indian guests broke into a provocative whirling dance, some holding wads of money above their head. The stadium was transformed by tents, banks of marigolds and lights into a make-believe palace for 2000 of the family's closest friends and business contacts. They networked furiously while a bare-chested Hindu pundit put Anil and Tina through hours of Vedic marriage rites next to a smouldering sandalwood fire on a small stage. Later, the guests descended on an elaborate buffet on tables that took up an entire sideline of the football pitch, starting with all kinds of samosas and other snacks, working through a selection of curries and breads and finishing with fruits and sweets wrapped in gold leaf. The next day the Ambanis put on the same spread – if not the wedding ceremony – at another reception for 22 000 of their not-so-close friends, employees and second-echelon contacts.

The lavishness was eclipsed by bigger displays of wealth in following years, but at the time it was seen as a gesture that Dhirubhai Ambani had made it through the political travails of the previous few years and was unabashed – and certainly not strapped for either cash or friends.

At an interview a month later, Dhirubhai Ambani came limping around a huge desk and sat down at a white leather sofa. Despite the obvious effects of a stroke in a twisted right hand, his mahogany skin was smooth and healthy, his hair plentiful and slicked back decisively in a duck's tail. His attention was unwavering. Disarmingly Dhirubhai admitted to many of the youthful episodes that were the subject of rumours and responded evenly to the criticisms commonly levelled against him. He didn't mind people calling him an 'upstart' or even worse names. It just meant they were trapped in their complacency while he was racing ahead. But the disputes were now 'all history' and the former critics were now all his 'good friends' who bought their polyester and raw materials from him.

'The orbit goes on changing,' he declared airily. 'Nobody is a permanent friend, nobody is a permanent enemy. Everybody has his own self-interest. Once you recognise that, everybody would be better off.'

However, Ambani did point to an unfortunate trait in his countrymen. 'You must know that, in this country, people are very jealous.' It was not like in Hong Kong or other East Asian countries, where people applauded each other's success, he claimed. In India success was seen as the prerogative of certain families. But he didn't really mind. 'Jealousy is a mark of respect,' he said.

The Reliance public relations office continued to be attentive, supplying advance notice of newsworthy events. But the company's history of political and corporate activity had put a sinister shadow across the gleaming success. All through the government changes of 1990 and 1991, the press carried references to a certain 'large industrial house' supporting this or that party or being behind certain politicians. Scores of party leaders, ex-ministers, senior bureaucrats and heads of the big government-owned banks and corporations were said to be 'Ambani friends' or 'Ambani critics'. Mostly it was the friends, it seemed, who got the jobs. At a meeting of shareholders in a big Bombay engineering firm named Larsen & Toubro late in 1991, convened to approve a takeover by the Ambanis, this undercurrent of hostility welled up into a physical mêlée. In the shouting and jostling, the two Ambani sons Mukesh and Anil had to flee the stage. The controversies kept continuing right through the 1990s.

Dhirubhai Ambani attracted adulation or distrust. To his millions of investors, who had seen their share prices multiply, he was a business messiah. To one writer, he was a 'Frankenstein's Monster' created by India's experiments with close government control of the economy. 'There are three Dhirubhai Ambanis,' one of his fellow Gujaratis told me. 'One is unique, larger than life, a brand name. He is one of the most talked-about industrialists, and for Gujarati people he has tremendous emotional and sentimental appeal. He is their ultimate man and has inspired many emulators. The second Dhirubhai Ambani is a schemer, a first-class liar who regrets nothing and has no values in life. Then there is the third Dhirubhai Ambani, who has a more sophisticated political brain, a dreamer and a visionary, almost Napoleonic. People are always getting the three personalities mistaken.'

In a legal chamber lined with vellum-bound case references, a senior lawyer took an equally stark view. 'Today the fact is that Ambani is bigger than government,' said the lawyer in all seriousness. 'He can make or break prime ministers. In the United States you can build up a super-corporation but the political system is still bigger than you. In India the system is weak. If the stock exchange dares to expose Ambani, he tells it: "I will pull my company shares out and make you collapse. I am bigger than your exchange." If the newspapers criticise, he can point out they are dependent on his advertising and he has his journalists in every one of their departments. If the political parties take a stand against him, he has his men in every party who can pull down or embarrass the leaders. He is a threat to the system. Today he is undefeatable.'

Phiroz Vakil, another senior advocate at the Mumbai bar, paused in his tiny chambers in Bombay's old Fort district, stuffing Erinmore Flake tobacco into his pipe, before looking up intently and warning me that people would suspect that writers asking for stories and opinions about Ambani were being used as a stalking horse by the Ambanis themselves to draw out information. For some others, favourable write-ups of the Ambaris in the business media still rankled. 'I suppose you think he's a hero,' said the retired Finance Ministry official and Cabinet Secretary Vinod Pande, down the phone.

Others just seemed too battle-weary. When I telephone the Orkay Silk Mills chairman Kapal Mehra and asked to meet him, there was a long pause. 'I'm afraid that won't be possible,' Mehra said. The former prime minister Viswanath Pratap Singh did not reply to a letter and giggled nervously when I cornered him at a cocktail party in New Delhi. No, he could not possibly talk about any one company, Singh said, easing away quickly into the crowd. Those who did agree to talk for the most part insisted on anonymity: they had to live in India, they explained.

Reliance and Dhirubhai Ambani meanwhile went on to greater fame and fortune – and more controversies. After his death in 2002, the subsequent split of the Reliance group between his sons and their continuing rivalry make the story of this man and his methods pertinent to understanding the return of India to eminence in the world economy.

2

A persuasive young bania

Among all the 550-odd princely rulers left to run their domains in the last years of the British Raj, few were more eccentric than Mahabatkhan, the Nawab of Junagadh. The Nawab's family had run this fiefdom, one of several on the Saurashtra peninsula in Gujarat, since the Mughal warrior Sher Khan Babi founded his own subordinate dynasty in 1690. Two and a half centuries later, this warrior's descendant, best known for his love of dogs, Mahabatkhan had 150 of them, with an equal number of dog-handlers on his payroll and individual quarters for all the canine retinue. The Nawab was the first political target to come into the sights of Dhirubhai Ambani. It was during a movement aimed at overthrowing the Nawab's rule and securing

Junagadh's accession to India during the Partition of British India in 1947 that Ambani, then a teenage high school student, had his first experience of political organisation and his first brushes with authority.

It was the only moment in modern times that Junagadh has figured in the calculations of statesmen. Even today, Junagadh and its surrounds, a region known as Kathiawar, remain one of the quietest, most traditional regions of India and until the end of the twentieth century one of the least accessible in the otherwise busy north-west coastal area of the country.

The land itself is dry, open, arid and stony. The monsoon rains quickly run off down the short rivers and nullahs that radiate from the rocky hinterland and out to the Arabian Sea. The roads are lined with stunted pipul (fig) trees; the stony fields are fenced with straggling rows of cactus. The standard building material is a porous dun-coloured stone cut by saws into ready-made blocks from pits near the seashore. There are few of the modern ferroconcrete extravagances built by the newly rich, or the industrial plants and their residential 'colonies' extending into farmland in other Indian regions.

But if the landscape is monotonous, Kathiawar's people compensate for it with riotous colour where they can. The women drape themselves with cotton scarves tie-dyed in red and orange. The local scooter-taxi is the Enfield motorcycle, grafted to a flat tray resting on two wheels at the back, the handlebars decked with coloured lights, electric horns and whirling windmills. The homes of wealthy merchants are adorned with mouldings of swans, peacocks, flamingos, parrots, elephants, lions and tigers. Massive double doors, twelve-panelled and with heavy iron studs, open tantalisingly on to huge inner courtyards.

A blood-drenched history and complicated mythology are attached to the landmarks and constructions of Kathiawar. On the coast to its west, at Dwarka, is the place where the deity Lord Krishna is said to have died. To the south, the temple of the moon at Somnath is a destination for Hindu pilgrims from all over India. In the steep Girnar hills above the city of Junagadh, long staircases take pilgrims to Jain temples that date back to the third century BC. The city was an important centre for Hindu rulers of Gujarat in the first millennium. Then Junagadh suffered four centuries of sackings until Mughal rule gave it some stability, with Muslim rulers controlling its largely Hindu population. Both its rulers and its people were onlookers in the contest for India's trade among the English, Dutch and Portuguese, whose galleons fought vicious battles off the Gujarat coast. At night, seen from the coastline at the south of Junagadh, processions of navigation lights travel left and right along the horizon. The seaborne traffic between the west coast of India and the Arabian ports goes on as it has for millennia, ever more intense.

Gujarat was the trading hub of ancient India, where Indian cottons and silks were sold to Arabs and later the East India Company in return for silver, gold, incense and coffee from the Red Sea port of Mocha. Gujaratis were prominent in this pre-colonial Indian Ocean trading network, to which India contributed its wealth of cloth, indigo, opium and spices. The small ports of Kathiawar took part in this trade. Diu handled much of Gujarat's trade with Aden in the west and Malacca in the east. Gold, silver, quicksilver, vermilion, copper and woollen cloth would be exchanged for Indian gold and silver embroideries and brocades and for cotton muslins of a fineness expressed by such trade terms as *abrawan* (running water), *baft hava* (woven air) or *shab-nam* (evening dew).

Indian entrepreneurs – in Calcutta the Mawari traders and moneylenders originally from Rajasthan, in Bombay the Parsis (Zoroastrians originally from Persia) – began moving into large-scale industrial production late in the nineteenth century. Smaller traders also took advantage of the peace and stability brought about by the British Empire by taking steamer passages to all corners of the Indian Ocean and South-East Asia and opening small stores and service stations. Most were from Gujarat; a large proportion of them being from Kathiawar, and many of them thus accumulated considerable wealth, the result of rigorous saving, abstemious living and endless hours of work by unpaid family members – an immigrant's success story in many parts of the world. In East Africa, it created a resentment that led to the expulsion of Indian traders and appropriation of their assets after the colonies became independent in the 1960s. The effect was to fling the Gujarati diaspora worldwide, to start the process of capital accumulation again.

Among the Gujaratis, the people of Kathiawar are renowned for their exuberance of speech, inventiveness and commercial drive. 'This is a place of have-nots,' noted Sheela Bhatt, a former editor of the magazine *India Today*. 'It is a barren land, but out of stone they somehow draw out water. The people are so colourful because the landscape is so colourless. They fill their heads with colour. Among Gujaratis, the best language is among Kathiawaris: so many words. Even the trading class will have extraordinary expressions. Kathiawari traders have more vibrant terminology than other traders. They were the first to go out of India for better prospects. Adventure is second nature to them. They have less hypocrisy. All of the other business communities affect modesty to the point of hypocrisy. Dhirubhai Ambani is part of that culture.'

In one sense, Dhirubhai Ambani was born to be a trader, as his family belongs to a Bania caste, a section of the Vaisya category (*varna*) in the traditional Hindu social order whose roles are those of merchants and bankers. This instantly provided a whole network of relationships, a community and social expectations that made commerce an entirely natural and honourable lifetime's occupation. Although socially below the Brahmins (priests and scholars) or the Kshatriya (warriors and landowners) and rarely part of aristocratic elites, the Vaisya castes came to exercise enormous power across India. They marshalled huge amounts of capital, which funded the campaigns of maharajas and nawabs and at times the British trade and military expansion when the budget from London ran short of operational needs. Centuries before the modern banking system, Vaisya shroffs or bankers were the conduits of a highly monetised Indian economy, remitting vast sums around India at short notice through a sophisticated trust system based on *hundi* (promissory notes).

The commercial instincts of Gujarat's Vaisya were encouraged by a convenient interpretation of Hinduism preached by the holy man Vallabhacharya in his wanderings around the region early in the sixteenth century. Another widely followed religious school known as Shaivism (from the god of creativity and destruction, Shiva) had preached that the world was unreal and that an impersonal abstract essence was the absolute reality and truth. The Jain and Buddhist religions, which had sprung from Hinduism, also preached privation, renunciation and destruction of the self. Vallabhacharya saw a personal god who created and sustained life, for whom living life to the full was a form of devotion. His school became known as Vaishnavism, as the focus of devotion was the god Vishnu's playful avatar Krishna, perhaps the most widely adored and human face of the divine among Hindus.

Such a belief naturally appealed to the people of a land richly endowed with opportunity like the central parts of Gujarat. It was a philosophy that justified their way of life and gave a divine purpose to their roles as providers and family members. It also fitted the rising social status of the Banias in Gujarat, overriding the formal *varna* hierarchy:

As Vaishnavism grows, the Varnas decline. We have noticed, for
example, how the Vanias [Banias] have reached a social status as
high as that of the Brahmins themselves. This upsetting of the
balance of the Varnas has been greatly due to economic causes.
The merchant and the financier and the capitalist have, by sheer
force of wealth and power, for a while become dictators over all,
even over the priestly class … A justification of their way of living,
a theory of life and a pathway suited and helpful to the living
of a life engrossed in work and duty as a man, husband, father,
citizen and so on, a hope that such a mode of life as they live is
acceptable to the highest deity – the Gujaratis naturally sought
for all these.[1]

Ambani's particular caste is called the Modh Bania, from their
original home in the town of Modasa north of Ahmedabad before a
migration many centuries ago to Saurashtra. The Modh are one of
three Bania castes in this part of Gujarat, who might eat meals together
but who would each marry within their own caste. They are strict veg-
etarians, and only the men take alcohol. Their practice of Hinduism
follows the Vaishnavite path. But the main object of their pilgrimages,
upon marriage or the start of a new business venture, is a black-faced
idol with a diamond in his chin located in a temple at Nathdwara, a
small town in the barren hills behind Udaipur in Rajasthan. This idol
represents Srinath, an incarnation of Lord Krishna, which was brought
to Nathdwara from Mathura (Krishna's birthplace) by a holy man to
escape the depredations of the fierce anti-Hindu Mughal emperor
Aurangzeb. For reasons that are not clear, Srinath has become the
familiar god of the Modh and other Banias. Portraits based on the
Nathdwara idol are often seen in the offices of Bania businessmen.

In later years, Ambani and his family made frequent visits to the
temple of Srinath, flying into Udaipur airport in his company's executive jet and driving straight up to Nathdwara. In 1994 Ambani built a

large ashram (pilgrim's rest-house) in Nathdwara for the use of visitors. The three-storey building, faced in a pink granite, is dedicated to the memory of his parents.

If the Modh Bania practise piety in the temple and abstemious ways in their homes, they are known as fiercely competitive and canny traders in the marketplace, with no compunction about taking advantage of opportunities for profit. A saying in Gujarat goes: 'Kapale hojo kodh, pan angane na hojo Modh', meaning: 'It is better to have a leucoderma [a disfiguring skin pigment disorder] on your forehead than a Modh as guest in your house.'

Like other Bania castes of the region, the Modh Bania looked far beyond their immediate patch. For centuries it has been a custom for young men to make trading voyages to Arabian ports, building up personal capital over nine or ten years hard work and modest living before returning to marry and take over the family business. Sons inherited family property in equal proportions, with the oldest son assuming the authority of family head.

But all this was a nebulous heritage for Dhirajlal– or Dhirubhai, as his diminutive became – Hirachand Ambani, born on 28 December 1932. His home town was Chorwad, literally meaning 'Settlement of Thieves', although no one seems to remark on that. It is set a mile or so back from the flat Arabian Sea coastline where the Nawab had a two-storey summer palace built of the dun-coloured stone quarried from pits nearby. His father, Hirachand Ambani, seems to have been a diffident trader when he tried his hand at petty commerce, as a wholesaler in ghee (clarified butter, a cooking medium in India). He is recalled by many acquaintances as a 'man of principle', meaning perhaps that he was too goodwilled to be good at making money. He is better remembered as a village schoolmaster in the Nawab's administration. From 1934 to 1936 Ambani senior, a stocky man with dark-brown skin, normally dressed in a white turban, long coat and dhoti, was headmaster of the Chorwad primary school. The industrialist and parliamentarian Viren Shah and his brother Jayan Shah, who also grew up in Chorwad, remember him as a devoted, 'very strict' teacher.

Hirachand Ambani made little money and lived in austere circumstances. The family home still stands in a hamlet called Kukaswada, two or three miles outside the main part of Chorwad. It is a two-roomed stone dwelling with a stamped earthern floor, entered by a low doorway and dimly lit by openings under the eaves. Ambani was married twice, having a son from his first marriage (named Samadasbhai) before being widowed. His second marriage gave him five more children, with Dhirubhai in the middle.

The family's poverty did not keep the Ambanis from contact with better-off members of their social peer group. The Bania occasionally got together for meals or picnics. The Ambani children mixed freely with the Shahs, who were already prospering from a move to the then hub of British commerce in Calcutta, where they set up India's first factory making aluminium cooking pots.

The two houses of the Shah family in Chorwad, Shanti Sadan and Anand Bhavan, were big and rambling in the traditional style. As well as learning all the ways of business, the children were expected to learn various sports, including horse-riding, swimming and athletics, and to take their turn milking the twenty cows and ten buffaloes kept in the gardens. The Shah family had become early followers of Mahatma Gandhi – also a Bania from Kathiawar – and often gave him accommodation in Calcutta. Jayan Shah remembered Dhirubhai, who was about seven years younger than him, coming to Anand Bhavan. Jayan Shah's father took an interest in other people's children, lending them books to read and asking them to do odd jobs around the house. Dhirubhai was welcomed with great affection and returned it with respect. Later,

when he had gone away to work overseas, Shah remembered him drop-
ping by to pay his respects during a vacation back in Chorwad, arriving
with 'great gusto and a feeling of an old relationship'.

The guild-like support of his merchant caste helped Dhirubhai
continue his education after finishing at his father's old primary school.
In 1945 he moved up to Junagadh and enrolled at Bahadur Kanji High
School, which shared with a university college a large yellow stucco
edifice on the outskirts of the city built in 1902 by the nawab of the
time and named after him. Because of his family's poverty Dhirubhai
was admitted as a free student. He found accommodation in a boarding
house funded by the Modh Bania for children of their caste.

The Second World War had largely passed by Kathiawar save for
overflights by military transports and the occasional visit of the new
army Jeeps. The movement for Indian independence had not. On
returning from South Africa, Mohandas Karamchand Gandhi, also
a Bania from Kathiawar, had established his ashram in Ahmedabad,
the main city of Gujarat, and carried out much of his agitation against
British rule in the same region, including the famous 'salt march' to the
sea to protest against the government monopoly of salt in 1930.

His activities were financed by Indian industrialists from the Hindu
trading castes, foremost among them the Calcutta-based Marwari jute-
miller G.D. Birla. His abstemious lifestyle was an extension of their
own ideals, more familiar to them than the Anglicised manners of the
Nehru family. But a real self-interest was also involved. The industrialists also saw in the Bania-born Gandhi a counterforce within the Indian
National Congress – the main secular vehicle of the independence
movement – to the socialist and communist ideas that had taken a
strong grip on the thinking of educated Indians. Although also far from
friendly to big capital, Gandhi's ideas of industrial devolution to the
villages were intrinsically opposed to the proposals for state capitalism

17

and central planning of investment then being promoted by the Left in India as elsewhere in the world.

In Junagadh, the ideas of Gandhi and Sardar Patel, the Hindu nationalist lieutenant of Nehru who was also a Gujarati, cast a strong influence. The Nawab, with a British Resident, Mr Monteith, at his side, was automatically put in defence of the *status quo*. His police force and its detective branch kept a close watch on the independence movement and arrested many agitators throughout the 1940s.

At the Bahadur Kanji school, Dhirubhai was quickly infected by the independence mood. Krishnakant Vakharia, later a leading lawyer in Ahmedabad, was two years ahead of Dhirubhai at the school and met him soon after his arrival in Junagadh. The two took part in a gathering of students to discuss the freedom movement. Vakharia recalled that all were inspired by the nationalist ideals of Gandhi, Jawaharlal Nehru, Sardar Patel and, most of all, the socialist Jayaprakash Narayan, then still in the Congress Party.

The Modh boarding house where Dhirubhai was staying became the headquarters of a new group to push these ideals, which they called the Junagadh Vidyarti Sangh (Junagadh Students' League). The objective was to take part in the national independence movement and Gandhi's *swadeshi* (self-reliant) economic program, which involved boycotting imported factory-made goods in favour of village craftwares, such as homespun cotton (*khadi*). Activities were to include meetings to salute the proposed national flag of India – the saffron, white and green tricolour with the ox-wagon wheel in the middle, which was then the Congress flag – as well as motivation sessions and sports meetings for the other students.

Vakharia became the president of the Sangli, with Dhirubhai and another student called Praful Nanavati serving as secretaries. 'We organised a lot of functions, like saluting the national flag and took a lot of risks,' said Vakharia. 'At one time we printed pamphlets with a photo of Gandhi and with that we approached some leading citizens to be our sponsors – but no one agreed. In Junagadh at that time no one was allowed to even utter "Jai Hind" or "Vande Mataram", or sing national songs. Even wearing khadi made you a suspect in the eyes of the Nawab's CID.'

In 1946 the students learned that Kaniala Munsi, a lawyer and later a leading Congress Party politican and a minister in Nehru's first home-rule government, would be visiting Junagadh. They decided to invite him to address their members in the compound of a boarding house for Jain students. The Nawab's police summoned Vakharia, Dhirubhai and Nanavati and threatened the three with arrest, expulsion from school and trouble from their parents unless they gave an undertaking that no political speech would be given.

Here Dhirubhai showed a spark of his later genius at bringing apparently irreconcilable demands to an accommodation, if through a dubious intellectualism. 'We had said that a literary figure would deliver a speech,' said Vakharia. 'Dhirubhai whispered that there was nothing wrong in giving this undertaking. "We are not going to give the speech. If there is any breach in the undertaking, it's a problem between Munsi and the police."' Munsi came and delivered a rousing speech in favour of early independence.

As 1947 wore on and partition of British India along Hindu/Muslim communal lines became more likely, the political position of the princely states came under great scrutiny. By August, when the transfer of British power was due, all the rulers came under pressure to accede to either India or Pakistan. In most of the more than 550 states, the decision was clearcut because of geographical position, the religion of the ruling family and the predominant religion of the population.

Three difficult cases stood out after 'freedom at midnight' on

15 August: Kashmir, Hyderabad and Junagadh, what the historian H.V. Hodson called 'the joker in the pack'.[2] Junagadh was close to the western side of Pakistan and had a Muslim ruler. But its fragmented territory was interlocked with that of neighbouring Hindu-ruled states and its people were mostly Hindu. Moreover, it contained the great Hindu pilgrimage sites of Somnath and Dwarka. In May 1947 the acting Diwan (the Nawab's prime minister and closest adviser) was Sir Shah Nawaz Bhutto, a politician from Sindh. Bhutto was active in the Muslim League of Mohammad Ali Jinnah, the father of Pakistan, and was himself the father and grandfather of two prime ministers of Pakistan, Zulfikir Ali Bhutto and Benazir Bhutto.

Bhutto kept in close touch with Jinnah and had the Nawab obey his advice to 'keep out under all circumstances until 15th August'. Then, on the day of the transfer of British power, the government of Junagadh announced its accession to Pakistan. Jinnah never actually thought Junagadh would be allowed to join Pakistan. The object of the exercise was to set uncomfortable precedents for Nehru in the more pressing contest for Kashmir and perhaps Hyderabad. If Nehru agreed to a plebiscite in Junagadh, which he eventually did, it would help Pakistan's case for a popular vote in Muslim-majority Kashmir. If the Junagadh ruler's decision was accepted, over the wishes of his people, the same could apply in Hyderabad. If the Indians simply marched into Junagadh, protests against a similar Pakistani use of force in Kashmir would be greatly weakened. Nehru adopted the course of negotiation while throwing a military noose around Junagadh in the neighbouring Hindu-ruled states, which had all acceded to India. Two subordinate territories of Junagadh, the enclaves of Babariawad and Mangrol, were taken by Indian troops on 1 November 1947 without bloodshed.

Meanwhile, Indian nationalists began agitating within and without Junagadh for the overthrow of the Nawab. In Bombay on 25 September they declared an 'Arazi Hakumat' or Parallel Government under the presidency of Samaldas Gandhi, a relative of Gandhi who was editor of the newspaper *Vande Mataram*. From a temporary base in Rajkot, Gandhi kept in touch with supporters inside Junagadh by human couriers simply walking across the open frontiers of the isolated state. Other nationalist journalists called for volunteers to gather in Bhavnagar and other cities close to Junagadh for a non-violent invasion.

The students in the Junagadh Vidyarti Sangh threw their limited weight against the Nawab also. 'We were too scared to carry out physical sabotage like attacking power stations,' said Vakharia. 'So our sabotage consisted of spreading false rumours to cause panic and supplying information back to the provisional government. We used to send someone to Jetalsur or Jedpur in the Indian union to pass on the information.'

In Junagadh, as in many other parts of India, the partition steadily developed a murderous communal nature. Two Muslim communities, called the Sodhana and Vadhana, had taken a militant position in support of accession to Pakistan and mounted big processions through Junagadh, threatening Hindus with retribution if they opposed it. As it became clear that Pakistan was in no position to support the Nawab, Hindus turned on the Muslim minority and massacred whole communities in some outlying villages. Food shortages developed and the Nawab's revenues dried up. As his administration lost its grip, the Nawab decided the game was up and made a hasty departure for Karachi. On 8 November, after an earlier meeting of the State Council, Bhutto asked the Indian Government to take over the state to avoid a complete administrative breakdown, pending an honourable settlement of the accession issues.

The Indian Army moved into Junagadh without incident on 9 November and the communal tension quickly settled down. However,

Vakharia recalls a small communal riot breaking out in Junagadh soon after independence, when some shoe shops belonging to Muslims were looted by Hindus. The students of the Junagadh Vidyarti Sangh went to the area to protect the Muslim shops, but their presence was misunderstood by the police. One of the students was a fellow Modh Bania and boarding-house companion of Dhirubhai named Krishna Kant Shah, who had been born in Kenya and sent back to Junagadh for his education. He was arrested by the police as one of the looters and taken to the lock-up early in the evening. The leaders of the Sangh went to police headquarters and met the police commissioner, named Lahiri, to argue Shah's innocence.

'Dhirubhai [who was then 16] showed a lot of courage in arguing with the police commissioner to defend Shah,' Vakharia said. 'The arguments went on for two or three hours and all of us were threatened with arrest for obstruction of justice. But we were determined we would not go until our colleagues were released. Eventually they decided to let Shah go at midnight.' It was a debt Dhirubhai was to collect from Shah in controversial circumstances more than thirty years later.

The people of Junagadh voted overwhelmingly to join India when a plebiscite was held in February 1948, although Pakistan never recognised it. Dhirubhai returned to his studies and took his matriculation in 1949. Vakharia studied law and continued with his political activity, following Narayan out of the Congress Party into the new Socialist Party in 1948. On graduating in 1951 he moved to practise in Rajkot, then Ahmedabad and eventually returned to the Congress later in an active legal and political career.

With his family still extremely poor, Dhirubhai had no such option. On finishing high school, he had to look for work. At the age of 16, Dhirubhai was physically strong and already possessed of the persuasiveness that was to mark his later business career.

22

It is tempting to look into the culture of the Modh Bania for an explanation of what his critics see as his ruthless business ethics and 'shamelessness'. But many other entrepreneurs have also sprung from the same background in Kathiawar: most would shrink from the manipulation of the government that became part and parcel of the Ambani operation, even at the cost of less success. The answer lies probably in the deep poverty that his family endured as the cost of his father's devotion to a teaching career. While he also learned that life is a web of relationships and obligations, Dhirubhai was fired with an ambition never to become dependent on anyone or to stay long in somebody else's service.

3

Lessons from the souk

Early in the 1950s officials in the treasury of the Arabian kingdom of Yemen noticed something funny happening to their country's currency. The main unit of money, a silver coin called the rial, was disappearing from circulation. They traced the disappearing coins south to the trading port of Aden, then a British colony and military bastion commanding the entrance to the Red Sea and southern approaches to the Suez Canal.

Inquiries found that an Indian clerk named Dhirubhai Ambani, then barely into his twenties, had an open order out in the souk of Aden for as many rials as were available. Ambani had noted that the value of the rial's silver content was higher than its exchange value against the British pound and other foreign currencies. So he began buying rials, melting them down and selling the silver ingots to bullion dealers in London. 'The margins were small, but it was money for jam,' Dhirubhai later reminisced. 'After three months it was stopped, but I made a few lakhs of rupees. I don't believe in not taking opportunities.'[1]

Dhirubhai had gone to Aden soon after finishing his studies in Junagadh at the age of 16, following the long tradition of boys from Bania families in Kathiawar heading for the Arabian trading ports or the market towns of East Africa to gain commercial experience and accumulate capital. A network of personal contacts kept jobs within the same community. Dhirubhai's elder brother Ramniklal, known as Ramnikbhai, had gone to Aden two years before and was working in the car sales division of A. Besse & Co. Founded by a Frenchman named Antonin Besse, the company had developed from trading in animal hides and incense, between the world wars, into the biggest commercial house in the Red Sea area.

Another Gujarati, Maganbhai Patel, from the Porda district, had joined Besse as a junior accountant at the age of 18 in 1931 and was made a director in 1948. He estimates that the company controlled about 80 per cent of the region's commerce soon after the Second World War. It had thirty branches and six to eight ships of its own. It was indeed successful: shortly before his death at the age of 72 in 1948, Antonin Besse made a donation of a million pounds to endow St Anthony's College, Oxford. Thereafter, the company was run by two of his sons, Tony and Peter. It employed more than 10 000 people, of whom about 3000 were Gujaratis hired as clerks, salesmen and middle managers. Susheel Kothari went to work for Besse in 1952 from Wallibhipur in Saurashtra, in a group of fourteen recruits hired after interviews in Rajkot. Besse trusted Indians as honest and loyal, he recalled. While not paid nearly as much as European expatriates, they enjoyed a standard of living that periodically drew complaints from the British colonial administration for forcing up wages generally. On one occasion, Tony Besse had told the Governor to his face that it was 'none of your business what I pay'.

When Dhirubhai left school, his brother Ramnikbhai put in a word for him with Maganbhai Patel. On his next leave in Porda, Patel invited Dhirubhai to come over for an interview. 'My first impression was his way of walking,' recalled Patel, imitating a heavy decisive footstep. 'It was as if time was short and he had to get ahead, to reach a goal.' Patel asked him to read from the *Times of India*, then write a summary in English, a test Dhirubhai passed satisfactorily. He was hired and soon after arrived by steamer in Aden.

As Susheel Kothari noted: 'The first sight of Aden is always a shock.' The oil-filmed blue waters of the port are backed by ominous steep crags of dark-brown rock, remnants of an old volcano, with no sign of vegetation.

Aden had flourished in Roman times as a way station on trading routes between Egypt and India. The opening of the Suez Canal in 1869 revived its importance, and it became a major coaling port for European shipping to Asia and Australasia. From its occupation by a detachment of Indian sepoys sent by the East India Company in 1839, Aden had been an important link in the ties of Britain to its Indian empire. Until 1937, when it was put under the Colonial Office in London, the territory was administered from India. The Indian rupee circulated as its currency until it was replaced by the East African shilling in 1951.

The outpost had been a punishment station for British regiments deemed to have shown cowardice or other offences against discipline while in India. As one of its last governors, Charles Johnston, noted in a memoir, it had been 'the dumping ground, even as late as between the wars, to which regiments sent officers who had got themselves into matrimonial difficulties'.[2] The colony also became the entrepôt for the Red Sea and Horn of Africa, where deepwater ports were few. Between the world wars, the biplanes of the Royal Air Force kept the hinterland quiet by machine-gunning the villages of any unruly Yemeni tribes. Behind this shield of bullets, the middle-man trade flourished. The definitive historian of British rule in Aden, R.J. Gavin, noted:

> Men indeed consisted of a hierarchy of brokers from the heads of foreign firms to the lowest workman or child who offered his labour or hawked in the street … Speculators, hoarders and price rings frequently sent commodity and foodstuff prices rocketing up and down, while moneylenders and dealers dampened the effect of this for the rest of the population at a price which included a claim to social leadership. Acquisitive individualism was mitigated only by ethnic and other local solidarities formed outside rather than within the town.[3]

Aden's economy developed rapidly after the Second World War, but its business milieu still had some of this character when Dhirubhai learnt his basic techniques there in the 1950s.

The spur to Aden's growth was the decision of British Petroleum to build a new oil refinery in Little Aden, another crater jutting into the sea across the bay from the main town. BP's existing refinery in the Gulf port of Abadan had been nationalised by a new Iranian government. The refinery employed up to 11 000 workers at any time during its construction in 1952–54, then had a permanent staff of 2500 housed in a comfortable village. This sparked off a construction boom that saw Aden extend beyond the wastes and saltpans of its causeway, which had been kept clear for defensive reasons in earlier times. Later in the 1950s the British began concentrating strategic reserve forces in Aden from other bases in the Gulf and East Africa. By 1964 Aden had 8000 British military personnel plus dependants – and their demand for housing kept the construction activity going. Aden's population grew from 80 000 in 1946 to 138 000 in 1955.

It became a more modern economy, and air-conditioning amelio-
rated the hot humid weather in the midsummer months. Just before
mass air travel arrived with the first passenger jets, Aden overtook New
York in 1958 to become the biggest ship-bunkering port in the world.
As well as for cargo shipping and tankers, it was a refuelling stop for
elegant liners of the P&O and Orient lines as well as crowded immigrant ships taking Italians and Greeks out to Australia.

Disembarking tourists, brought ashore in launches from the ships
moored out in the roadstead, were immediately surrounded by Arab and
Indian salesmen and touts, desperately offering cheap cameras, fountain pens, transistor radios and tooled-leather items. After making their
purchases and taking a quick taxi tour around the arid town, most visitors were glad to get back to their P&O comfort and security. Aden had
an air of menace, of repressed resentment at its naked display of foreign
military and commercial self-interest. But for the young Gujaratis hired
by Besse & Co., Aden was a kind of paradise, and most recalled their
days there with great affection and nostalgia. 'We felt it was heaven,'
said Himatbhai Jagani, a former Besse employee who had been born
in Aden. 'It was tax free virtually, and we never saw an electricity bill or
rent bill until we left. For fourteen of us in our mess we paid only 400
shillings a month for food. We could save about half our salary. It was
very comfortable – we all missed that life.' Home leave of three months
came after twenty-one months straight work in Aden or at one of the
Besse outposts around the Red Sea.

While most of the British residents lived on the slopes above
Steamer Point, the 15 000 Indians clustered in a few streets of the Crater
district. The Besse & Co. bachelors mess occupied four or five buildings nearby in Aidroos Valley. The Crater had all the features of the
Orientalist watercolours that adorned European drawing-rooms at the
turn of the century, as described by British Governor Charles Johnston:

'Indian merchant families, the women in saris, the men in their white jodhpur-ish get-up, are taking the air, immaculate after the siesta. We drive around a market square with fruit glowing on the stalls and enter a narrow street fairly buzzing with exotic life – pastrycooks, water-sellers, coffeemakers, carpet merchants, all the usual figures of the Oriental bazaar – and pervading the whole thing a strong hot smell of spice.'[4]

The various expatriate communities lived in their own social circles, where, in the way of 'hardship posts', attachments were strong and recalled with nostalgia in later life. The Hindus from India were probably liked the least by the local Arabs – to whom Muslims from India and Pakistan complained about India's incorporation of Kashmir and Hyderabad – but filled a need for white-collar staff that Aden's schools could not meet and had their own social circle, too.

While his brother Ramnikbhai worked in Besse's automotive division, Dhirubhai was assigned to the Shell products division. As a newly arrived youngster he created an early splash, literally, by taking a bet while out helping bunker a ship in the harbour that he could not dive off and swim to shore. The prize was an 'ice-cream party' – which he won, by swimming through waters that had seen occasional shark attacks on swimmers outside the nets of its beaches.

As he developed more familiarity with the trade, Dhirubhai was sent to market Shell and Burmah lubricants around the Besse network, visiting traders in French Somaliland, Berbera, Hargeysa, Assem, Asmara (Eritrea), Mogadishu (Italian Somaliland) and Ethiopia. Some places were not accessible to steamers, so the Besse salesmen would travel by dhow, the traditional wooden sailing vessels of Arabian waters. Lodgings would be extremely rough and the food difficult for the vegetarian Gujaratis.

Dhirubhai was outgoing, robust and helpful to newcomers. He was physically strong and proud of his physique. The other young men tended to be bashful about nakedness in their shared bathrooms, and a common prank was to whip away the towels they wrapped around their waists while crossing the living space in the mess. Dhirubhai would walk around without hiding behind towels. His solid footsteps could be heard from a distance, and his colleagues soon started calling him 'Gama' after a famous Indian *pehelwan* (wrestling champion) of the time. Navin Thakkar, a former colleague at Besse, remembered that Dhirubhai taught him to swim by simply throwing him into the sea, at the swimming place down near the Aden dockyard where they used to go on Saturdays and Sundays.

Dhirubhai delighted in stirring up pandemonium. Old colleagues described it as *bichu chordiya* or 'letting loose a scorpion'. Despite his affability, some of his old colleagues described Dhirubhai as a 'dark character' – not just because of the darkish skin he inherited from his father – but for the ambition and risk-taking he hardly concealed. 'Ramnik was more or less a saintly man,' said one ex-Besse colleague who later went to work for Reliance. 'Dhirubhai was a daring one. He was already advising me to go for business and not to remain in service.'

Dhirubhai's career with Besse was progressing steadily, and the Shell Division was one of the most rapidly expanding areas of company business. By 1956, when the Suez War broke out after Egypt's President Nasser nationalised the Suez Canal, Dhirubhai was managing the Shell refuelling operation at the Aden military base. He was also able to observe construction of the BP oil refinery in Aden, gaining an early insight into the production linkages of the petroleum industry.

In March 1954, at the age of 22, Dhirubhai married, in a match arranged by his mother (his father had died in 1951) but which Dhirubhai himself had supervised. His wife was Kokila (meaning cuckoo), daughter of Ratilal Jasraj Patel, the postmaster in Jamnagar, the port on the western side of Kathiawar. She had grown up in a modest small-town environment, in a row of houses sharing the same long verandah, but had received a sound schooling to high-school level. Her family was not particularly wealthy so it was not a financially advantageous match for Dhirubhai. But 'Kokilaben' (the suffix is an endearment, meaning 'sister') was also a Modh Bania, as the strict caste endogamy of the time demanded, and her character complemented that of Dhirubhai. She was a solid home anchor very much grounded in traditional values and religious piety.

Although he was doing well, Dhirubhai was far from happy with his position as an employee. M.N. Sangvi, who worked alongside Dhirubhai in the Shell division and later went to work for him in India, recalled him as "different" from his workmates: 'I could see he wanted to make something of himself.' His room-mate Susheel Kothari also remembers the ambition. 'Right from the beginning he was determined to do something big,' he said. 'He was never comfortable in service. He was a born businessman.'

After office hours, which finished at 4.30 in the afternoon, Dhirubhai would invariably head for the Aden souk. Initially he just watched the Arab, Indian and Jewish traders in action. Later he began taking positions in all kinds of commodities, particularly rice and sugar, in gambles against rises and falls in prices at time of delivery. Doing business on one's own account was strictly forbidden to Besse employees by the terms of their contract and his older brother Ramnikbhai disapproved, so Dhirubhai would simply say he was 'studying the market'.

Dhirubhai made some profits and learned the fundamentals of business and money. But he also made some near-disastrous mistakes that almost wiped out his capital. On one occasion he suffered a tight financial squeeze when an incoming cargo of sugar was damaged by seawater and his customer refused to accept delivery. Pending settlement of his insurance claim, Dhirubhai had to pass the hat among Besse colleagues for loans to bail himself out.

One particular ally was a Besse employee named Jamnadas Sakerchand Depala, a relative by marriage, who lent Dhirubhai 5000 shillings on this occasion. Depala was close to Dhirubhai and the two usually had lunch together, even after Dhirubhai had married. It was an odd relationship, another attraction of opposites. Depala was not a worldly man and lent money again to Dhirubhai for his 'market studies', but had a strong influence nonetheless. 'Jamnadas was morally in control of Dhirubhai,' said Susheel Kothari, who had been in the same bachelors mess with Dhirubhai. 'If Dhirubhai was drinking too much, no one else could stop him. He'd just swear at them. Kokilaben used to call Jamnadas and Dhirubhai would listen to him.' Jamnadas is said to have made considerable sacrifices for Dhirubhai. On one occasion, Jamnadas and Dhirubhai were reported to Besse management for their private deals and were suspended from service. Jamnadas took responsibility and resigned, allowing Dhirubhai to complete the seven years' service that earned him the right of residence in Aden.

Another story told by ex-Besse staff is that, after leaving the company, Jamnadas continued to invest in rice and sugar deals masterminded by Dhirubhai and lost heavily, to the point of losing most of his capital. Jagani remembers Jamnadas being 'very depressed' around 1961. Whatever the truth of this, Dhirubhai continued to act as though he was in debt to Jamnadas. Some years later, Janmadas returned to India and was given a shop selling textiles for Dhirubhai. After a while Jamnadas stopped coming to work, but Dhirubhai saw that his salary was paid until his death in 1987.

Dhirubhai left Aden in 1958, with his seven years' service and right of residency as a fallback, to try his hand in business back in India.

The house of Besse lasted only another nine years, as long as British rule in Aden, which was being eroded by the sandblast of pan-Arabic nationalism. Some of the transistor radios sold at Steamer Point found their way to the villagers of Yemen, who listened to President Abdul Gamal Nasser's message of Arab nationalism on Radio Cairo. Hit-and-run attacks by rival liberation fronts made Aden unsafe for foreigners. In the second half of 1967, British forces retreated to an ever-tightening perimeter until the rearguard was evacuated by helicopter to naval ships offshore on 29 November 1967.[5] The territory fell unconditionally to the National Liberation Front. It applied its harsh version of Marxism–Leninism, abolishing private property and nationalising most foreign companies. By then the closure of the Suez Canal in the 1967 Arab/ Israel war had cut Aden's bunkering business. Racked by periodic coup attempts and wars with northern Yemen, the new state of South Yemen became an economic backwater and haven for international terrorists – a modern version of the pirates' lair the British first subdued.

Besse & Co. was among the companies appropriated by the new regime. From retirement in France, former director Peter Besse wrote in 1996 that the 'vast trading empire ... of my father collapsed on the arrival of various "People's Democratic Republic" governments. Today nothing is left.'[6]

4

Catching live serpents

At the end of 1958 Dhirubhai returned to India with his wife Kokilaben and first child, a son named Mukesh, born in April 1957. They were expecting their second child (another son, Anil, born in June 1959, to be followed by daughters Dipti, born in January 1961 and Nina, born in July 1962). From all his years with Besse & Co. and all his evenings 'studying the market' he had accumulated savings of just 29 000 East African shillings – then worth about $3000 – which, as his Besse colleague Susheel Kothari had reminded him, would be just 'chutney' back in his homeland.

Dhirubhai was determined to go into business on his own account. At first he looked at Rajkot, the port city of his native Saurashtra facing the Rann of Kutch. Krishnakant Vakharia, by then practising law in Rajkot, remembered that Dhirubhai came to visit. 'He was toying with the idea of a dealership in automobile spare parts there,' Vakharia said. 'I had a friend who was doing just that and who was not doing very well. So I advised Dhirubhai that he should not go into this business and instead of Rajkot he should go to Bombay.'

At Dhirubhai's request, Krishnakant Vakharia, by then practising law in Rajkot, accompanied him down to Chorwad and stayed there a few days while Dhirubhai sounded out friends and acquaintances about ideas and help. He found support in the family of Chambaklal Damani, a second cousin who had been working in Aden for family companies at about the same time that Dhirubhai was there. One business, Madhavas Manikchand, had imported textiles and yarns from India, ran a transit business into Ethiopia and held the agency for Bridgestone Tyres. The other, Anderjee Manekchand & Co., had imported textiles from India and Japan. When necessary Dhirubhai had used the names of these firms during his own after-hours trading.

Damani's father, Madhavlal Manikchand, had closed his businesses in Aden and Ethiopia on retiring in 1957 and decided to put Rupees (Rs) 100 000 into a trading business for his son and Dhirubhai in Bombay. Vakharia saw the agreement concluded in his presence and returned to Rajkot. Dhirubhai and Chambaklal called their new business Reliance Commercial Corporation. The first office was a room of about 350 square feet in Narsinathan Street, in the crowded Masjid Bandar district of Bombay. It had a telephone, one table and three chairs. If the two partners and their initial two employees were all present, someone had to stand.

At first, the business traded spices back to the partners' contacts in the souk of Aden – betel nut and curry ingredients – and shipped some cotton, nylon and viscose textiles to Ethiopia, Somalia and Kenya. But local contacts led them quickly into the frenetic and potentially profitable business of trading synthetic yarns – one of more than sixty commodity markets serving all of India that were located in Bombay, nearly all of them run by Gujaratis. Vakharia had introduced Dhirubhai to a fellow activist in the Socialist Party, a successful yarn trader called Mathura Das Mehta. And Dhirubhai's talented nephew Rasikbhai Meswani (the son of Dhirubhai's older sister) had begun trading in yarns a couple of years earlier.

At the tiny Masjid Bandar office, Dhirubhai began to assemble a team that stayed with him for decades as Reliance grew. It included Meswani, his older brother Ramnikbhai, who had also returned from Aden, his younger brother Nathwarlal (Nathubhai) on completing his education and two former schoolmates from Junagadh named Rathibhai Muchhala and Narottambhai Doshi. Dhirubhai also enlisted the services of old acquaintances from Aden, including Liladhar Golkaldas Sheth, who had been a dealer in textiles, coffee and foreign exchange in Yemen, Burma and Aden (suffering several bankruptcies along the way) before settling back as a foreign exchange dealer in Bombay in the 1950s.

Dhirubhai quickly became a familiar figure around the streets of Pydhonie, the synthetic yarn trading district of Bombay where Gujarati merchants then did their business, sitting on spotless *gaddi* (white canvas floor-covers), entering trades in compendious ledgers and consuming endless cups of tea thick with sugar, spices and hot milk. From late morning until about 4pm, Pydhonie was busy with trading, as dealers made forward trades, trying to guess the future price of yarn of this or that micron size.

If cotton and silk had been the materials of India's textile industry right from the old handloom days to the industrial looms of the early twentieth century, by the 1950s the industry and its consumers were hungry for the artificial threads created by modern chemical science. Nylon, viscose and polyester were cheap, hardwearing, quick-drying and crease-proof and could imitate the textures of both cotton and silk.

The problem for yarn dealers at Pydhonie was not usually to find buyers but to secure supplies. The tightening of industrial controls and import quotas since Independence had choked supply of these 'luxuries' as the economic Brahmins of New Delhi channelled national resources towards new complexes making capital goods such as electrical turbines and steel mills – what Prime Minister Jawaharlal Nehru called the 'temples of modern industry'.

India had one viscose factory, owned by the Birlas, and one government-owned nylon plant. The first polyester fibre plant did not open until the 1970s. These domestic factories supplied only a small fraction of local demand from textile weavers. Smugglers supplied some of this demand, bringing in yarn either by misdeclaring cargoes at regular ports or by simply running small ships to the numerous creeks and beaches of India's west coast. Made-up textiles were also smuggled, via Dubai or Singapore. Indian visitors to Japan's artificial textile industries, then in their great postwar expansion phase, recall seeing vast production of sari-length material, for which there was no legal market in the subcontinent at all.

The other source came from the strictly controlled import licences given to registered exporters of textiles, allowing import of raw materials worth a certain percentage of their export earnings. Like many others, Dhirubhai realised that these import or 'Replenishment' licences (known as REPs) were as good as money, even though some of them were officially not transferrable and imports had to be made by the 'actual user' of the materials. By paying higher margins than any other trader, Dhirubhai soon became the main player in the market for REP licences. The margins were tiny in the trade itself – but his dominance also put him in the position of being able to turn on and off much of the supply of yarn into the Indian market.

Suresh Kothary, whose family business was the importing agency for Du Pont products including textile fibres, chemicals and dyes from 1958 to 1993, and was also active in yarn trading, remembers first meeting Dhirubhai in 1964 at the Masjid Bandar office. Dhirubhai would often drop by at Kothary's shopfront at Pydhonie thereafter, lounging on the white cotton mattress and drinking tea or coffee. They were in effect rivals, as Dhirubhai mostly imported his yarns from Asahi Chemicals in Japan or Ital Viscosa via a long-resident Italian businessman in Bombay, a Dr Rossi, while Kothary handled only the Du Pont product from the United States and elsewhere. But Dhirubhai was a sporting rival, Kothary said: 'He would always say, "This is what I'm going to do, boy!" Whenever he fights an enemy he goes in the open.' Not everyone in the Bombay textile trade would have agreed.

Kothary and many others in the Pydhonie market remember Dhirubhai's intervention in a market crisis in the mid-1960s when spiralling textile prices led government authorities to crack down on 'speculation' in the yarn market by banning forward trading and then arresting traders found to be continuing the practice. 'Consumers must have complained to the government about fluctuations in prices – some people, about a dozen, were arrested in the market,' Kothary said.

The trading community was despondent as their colleagues languished all day in the cells of Picket Road Police Station. Approaches to officials by the Bombay Yarn Markets and Exchange Association got nowhere. Then, late in the evening, Dhirubhai arrived like a storm at the police station, shouting greetings to senior officers and handing out snacks to everyone. Within an hour the arrested traders had been released and complaints against them shelved. Kothary can only guess at the substance of Dhirubhai's intervention. 'The usual – India!' he said.

Dhirubhai also emerged as saviour of the market when an even greater supply crisis occurred in 1967, Kothary recalled. On a report that 'actual user' import licences had been traded and misused, the customs authorities in Bombay under the then Assistant Collector, a Mr Ramchandani, impounded all incoming cargoes of artificial fibres. The government insisted that whoever imported the yarn had to be the manufacturer who wove it into cloth.

According to Kothary, yarn worth about 40 million rupees (then about $5.3 million) was seized. Many traders then defaulted on loans taken out to cover the imports. The entire artificial textile market was paralysed. 'It could have made us all insolvent,' Kothary said. 'This is when I came very closely in touch with Dhirubhai. It was he who saved us all. We fought for about six months. I used to go with him to lawyers day in and day out. We went to Delhi to see Morarji Desai [the then Finance minister]. That was the time I could see he was a wizard. He used all the ways and means.'

The crisis ended as quickly as it started, ostensibly after a one-day hearing of the importers' appeal in the Customs, Excise and Gold (Control) Appellate Tribunal under Justice Oberoi, who found for the appeal. Kothary indicates that an agreement engineered by Dhirubhai was behind the judicial settlement. The details are not revealed, but presumably come under the category of 'India!' also.

On their move to Bombay Dhirubhai and his young family had moved into an apartment on the third floor of the Jai Hind Society building in Bhuleshwar, a very crowded district of shops, markets and residential tenements in the central part of the city. The building is one of the type known as a *chawl* in Bombay: numerous small apartments, often just single rooms, opening on to galleries around a central courtyard, which is set back from the street behind commercial premises. Quite often the toilets and washing facilities are shared at ground level.

Later accounts of Dhirubhai's early career often paint this home as Dickensian in the extreme. The flat, since bought by a later tenant, had two small bedrooms, a living room, kitchen and internal bathroom in 1995. Vakharia, who used to visit the Ambanis for a holiday each Christmas from 1959 to the late 1960s, remembers it being 'quite luxurious' compared to the single rooms many Gujarati families had to occupy in Bombay at that time. Even so, Dhirubhai and his young family, eventually two boys and two girls, lived austerely in surroundings that were crowded, noisy and dirty. The two sons, Mukesh and Anil, who took over day-to-day management of Reliance in the late 1980s, might have had engineering degrees and management studies from American universities, but the lean early years gave them a hungry ambition, unusual for the second generation of a successful Indian business family.

As his confidence grew in his Bombay success, Dhirubhai developed his taste for 'letting loose a scorpion' through practical jokes and whimsy. Vakharia recalls that when he visited Bombay with his new wife for the first time in 1959, he and Dhirubhai were invited home by their senior mentor Mathura Das Mehta. Mehta's wife served the young men mango juice and kept refilling their glasses as soon as they were emptied. Dhirubhai whispered: 'Let's do some mischief.' The two asked for a fourth glass, then kept accepting more. After more than a dozen glasses each, the Mehta kitchen ran out of mangoes and a servant had to be sent to the market to buy more, which were all duly consumed. The Mehtas continued to be friends, 'but they never invited us back for any lunch or dinner at their house', Vakharia said.

Each year, Dhirubhai would make it a point to play an April Fool's joke on an elderly employee named Ghulabchand, an old associate from Aden. For all his experience, Ghulabchand never failed to fall for it. On one occasion, Dhirubhai announced that everyone was invited to dinner across town at an address at Mafatlal Bath. Ghulabchand was sent in a taxi with Vakharia and another member of the office, Raman bhai Patel. At Marine Drive they stopped outside a building and Patel went in to look for a fourth member of the group. After fifteen minutes waiting, Vakharia also went in. Ghulabchand eventually gave them all up and took the taxi to Mafatlal Bath, where he found no one. On returning home, he found Dhirubhai and the others eating a dinner they had warned Ghulabchand's wife to prepare.

Vakharia recalled another prank in 1965. The India/Pakistan War was on, and a blackout had been imposed on Bombay for fear of naval and air attacks by Pakistan. About 10pm Dhirubhai said: 'Let's go out and take a round of the city.' The two drove around the darkened Bombay, with Dhirubhai bluffing police at roadblocks that he was on official business and handing out small tips of ten rupees or so. 'He got saluted all the way,' said Vakharia. 'On the way back we saw some lights in the Japanese consulate, so Dhirubhai went in and told them to douse the lights.'

On yet another occasion, around 11pm on a cold winter night, Dhirubhai announced an immediate picnic. The cook was told to assemble supplies, and Vakharia and the family piled into Dhirubhai's car. Another dozen friends were telephoned and told to rendezvous in their cars. 'We were not told where we were going,' Vakharia said. 'We ended up at Rajeswari, about 50 or 60 kilometres from Bombay, at about 3am. The cold was very severe and we went to a *dharamsala* [pilgrims' lodging] at a hot springs resort. It was meant only for sadhus [ascetic Hindu holy men]. Dhirubhai said we would all sleep there. After half an hour we were still shivering, and Dhirubhai got up and lit a camp fire. When the sun came up we had tea and a bath in the hot springs and cooked kedgeree on the camp fire. We told jokes and sang songs and didn't get back home until late in the afternoon.'

41

Dhirubhai's fast pace caused a rift with his partner Chambaklal Damani in 1965. According to Vakharia, Damani preferred to trade with great caution, leading to constant tension with Dhirubhai, who was a risk-taker. The final rupture came after one clash when, at Dhirubhai's urging, Reliance built up a large holding of yarn in the expectation of a price rise. Damani pressured Dhirubhai to cut back their exposure. So Dhirubhai sold the yarn stockpile – to himself, in secret. Two or three weeks later the price of yarn shot up, and Dhirubhai made a killing. 'Later Dhirubhai told Chambaldal: "I am prepared to share profit with you",' Vakharia said. '"But in future if you do not know the business do not intervene."'

Many others among Dhirubhai's ex-colleagues and trade associates believe the partners were incompatible. 'He takes so much risk that people fear something will go wrong,' said Vradlal Depala, who knew Dhirubhai in Aden. 'But the risks are all calculated. They are not blind risks.'

'Someone advised Dhirubhai's partner that he had made sufficient money – and now should come out,' said Susheel Kothari, an ex-colleague from Besse & Co. who later worked for Reliance. 'Dhirubhai's business is catching live serpents.'

Much later, Chambaklal Damani himself would say only that 'We agreed to separate willingly' or that 'We just became separate as a friend'. But he agreed that the version given by Kothari and others about differences over commercial risk were 'to some extent true'. Damani went into trading in a new company, while Dhirubhai and his brothers paid Rs 600 000 to buy him out of Reliance. Soon after, Dhirubhai moved the office to bigger premises in the more central Court House building at Dhobi Talao, named for the laundrymen who originally worked in the area.

After ten years at Bhuleshwar in 1968, Dhirubhai moved his home out of the *chawl* to a more comfortable flat in Altamount Road, one of the city's elite areas on a hill overlooking the Arabian Sea. The oldest son, Mukesh, later recalled his childhood there with great fondness:

> We were a close-knit family and the four of us – Dipti, Nina, Anil and I – were left to do what we wanted. There were boundaries, of course, but within those, we were not micro-managed … I remember my father never came to our school even once. Nevertheless, he was hugely interested in our all-round development for which he did some amazing things …
>
> In the mid-60s, he put out a newspaper ad for a teacher, but specified that his responsibility would be non-academic; he would have to impart general knowledge. He … selected Mahendrabhai Vyas who taught at the New Era School. Mahendrabhai used to come every evening and stay with us till 6.30–7pm. His brief was our all-round development. We played hockey, football and different kinds of games, watched matches at Cooperage, travelled in buses and trains and explored different parts of Bombay. We went camping and stayed in a village for 10–15 days every year. These experiences have helped us a lot … The two hours with Mahendrabhai every evening were great fun.
>
> A third track running at that time, apart from academics and the fun stuff, was that my father shared with me his passion for business and entrepreneurship from very early on. Even when I was in high school, I used to spend long hours at office on weekends. For my father, life was uni-dimensional. Reliance was his life. Yet, some of my most vivid memories are about spending time with him. However busy he may have been, whatever the pressure, Sunday was for his wife and kids … He was a big nature lover and during our school days, we went to different places every Sunday – we walked through the forest or had a bath in streams.[1]

Fond of driving fast, Dhirubhai had first bought a Fiat car and then moved on to a Mercedes-Benz. Later, in the 1970s, he indulged a taste for flashy automobiles by acquiring a Cadillac, one of the very few in the country then or since. Friends remember him as a dashing figure, the slightly dark skin inherited from his father (the only such characteristic, some say) offset by a white safari suit, the hair slicked back. For a while he put on weight and then trimmed down by taking vigorous dawn walks along the three-kilometre sweep of Bombay's Marine Drive, enlisting friends, colleagues and neighbours as companions.

Within a year of splitting with Damani, Dhirubhai took Reliance into textile manufacturing for the first time. He decided to locate it in Gujarat rather than Bombay because land was cheaper and sent his older brother Ramnikbhai to select a site. Ramnikbhai enlisted Vakharia, then becoming known as a lawyer in Ahmedabad, and the two drove around the state in a small Fiat.

They settled on a plot of 10000 square metres, the last going in a new industrial estate developed by the Gujarat government at Naroda on the fringes of Ahmedabad. Vakharia had got a contact, state Minister for Industries Jaswant Mehta, to approve the purchase and, by a further stroke of luck, the farmers owning 100000 square metres of adjacent land were willing to sell. Dhirubhai had a simple factory built, installed four knitting machines and appointed his brother as plant manager.

Dhirubhai was again lucky in that, around this time, the British hold on Aden was becoming more tenuous. Even ahead of the British withdrawal in 1967, foreign nationals felt threatened by the insurgency mounted by the People's Liberation Front. Many of the Indians working for Besse & Co. decided it was time to go home. So Dhirubhai had a ready-made source of educated managers, accountants and salesmen, drilled to European standards. The word went around that Dhirubhai would find jobs for his old colleagues, and a dozen old hands from Besse & Co. accepted his offer. Most stayed for the rest of their careers.

None of them knew very much about textile production, however, and it was a case of learning by trial and error. As M.N. Sangvi, who left Aden in 1967 and immediately joined Reliance, recalled, 'The first two years, 1966–67, was a very hard time. The product had to be established. We worked from morning to late evening. Dhirubhai was very encouraging and we had a family atmosphere.'

Susheel Kothari, who had returned from Aden in 1966, said that at one point in 1967 it appeared the mill would have to close because Reliance could not sell the cloth it was making. Dhirubhai told Kothari that if the factory had to shut down he should do it gradually and see that no blame attached to his older brother Ramnikbhai. But the Aden hands rallied. After putting in a full shift at the factory in Naroda, from 7am to 3pm, they would spend the afternoons and evenings touring markets around Ahmedabad trying to persuade shopkeepers to stock Reliance fabrics. 'We were determined we should not fail,' Kothari said.

Dhirubhai worked everyone hard, often calling his managers in Naroda at 6am from Bombay before they started out to work. They were expected to solve problems on their own initiative. Dhirubhai himself set the example. Suresh Kothary recalled one incident when spare parts were urgently needed for imported machines at Naroda. Dhirubhai had the parts flown in from Germany, then discovered that no trucks were available for the haul up to Ahmedabad. He bought two trucks, one to carry the parts and one as a back-up, and sent up the consignment. The trucks were then sold in Ahmedabad.

But he was forgiving of honest mistakes, as Sangvi recalled. In one case, Sangvi was overly trusting of some merchants who had placed an order from Patna, the capital city of Bihar in eastern India. Sangvi sent the consignment by rail, collectable on presentation of a payment receipt at a Patna bank branch. The merchants forged the receipt and took delivery from the railway yard. Reliance lost Rs 900 000, a considerable sum at that time, and it took months to recover it. Sangvi said, 'Dhirubhai just told me: "Nathu, nothing to worry – in business, anything can happen. I know you have done it to increase the sales. I am with you and you just concentrate on the business.'''

K.I. Patel, who had been recruited by his relative Maganbhai Patel to Besse & Co. in 1953, returned to India in 1965. Soon after, Ramnikbhai Ambani, with whom he had worked in the Besse automotive division, hired him for Naroda and put him in charge of the knitting machines. Patel knew nothing about them, but was sent to West Germany and Japan later for formal training. He stayed with Reliance until retirement in 1993. 'The years passed before we knew it, we were so busy,' Patel recalled.

The result was steady growth in sales and profits for Reliance. In 1967, the first full year of production at Naroda, the company recorded sales of Rs 9 million, yielding a net profit of Rs 1.3 million. Dhirubhai and his family shareholders refused to take dividends and kept ploughing earnings back into more machines. After a decade of manufacturing, in 1977 Reliance had a turnover of Rs 680 million and profits of Rs 105 million.

In an extensive write-up on the company in August 1979, the *Indian Textile Journal* reported on a massive factory at Naroda occupying 230 000 square metres and employing 5000 staff. It had banks of machines for texturising or 'crimping' artificial fibres to give particular sheens, machines for twisting the polyester and nylon fibres into yarns and machines for weaving the yarns into textiles. The yarns were sold to other Indian textile manufacturers or used in-house.

Most significantly perhaps, Dhirubhai established his own brand

46

name, Vimal (named after a son of his brother Ramnik), by dint of lavish advertising under the slogan 'Only Vimal'. This somewhat snobbish slogan and some well-publicised fashion shows in smart hotels added a touch of class to a product that appealed mainly to less wealthy market sectors. In addition, Dhirubhai had got around the reluctance of established wholesalers and shopkeepers to accept a new brand by creating his own network of shops. Across India, 400 shops were franchised to sell the Vimal brand of polyester materials for saris, shirts, suits and dresses.

In one of the first of many eulogies to appear in the Indian press, the *Textile Journal* noted that Dhirubhai was held in 'high esteem' by his staff, who attributed Vimal's success to his dynamic leadership. 'When the construction of the factory was going on, it is reported, many snakes were seen in the area. According to a popular belief, appearance of snakes is a good omen. Dame Luck certainly seems to have favoured Mr Ambani. Ever since the emergence of Vimal, he has developed the Midas touch.'

5

A first-class fountain

Dhirubhai Ambani remained in Bombay because manufacturing was only one facet of his business. For a decade, the textile plant at Naroda was supportive and subsidiary to his yarn-trading activities. In addition, he was steadily augmenting his skills at breeding money from money and at wielding political and bureaucratic influence on government policies and their interpretation. Dhirubhai was never simply an industrialist, a trader, a financial juggler or a political manipulator, but all four in one.

In his earliest days in Junagadh, Dhirubhai had learned that relationships were the key to unlocking help and that the law could be argued with. 'One thing I have noted with Dhirubhai is that if he starts an acquaintance with someone he will continue it,' said Manubhai Kothary, a president of the textile trade group Sasmira. 'He never throws away any relationship.' Dhirubhai was endowed with a photographic memory for faces and names, and he would try to turn any contact – however fleeting – into a common background on which some affection could be based. His philosophy was to cultivate everybody from the doorkeeper up. For example, Sir Nicholas Fenn, who was British High Commissioner in New Delhi in the early 1990s, was amazed to find Dhirubhai claiming him as an old friend from Aden. In the early 1950s Fenn had been a Royal Air Force pilot flying transport planes through to the Far East and Australia. Dhirubhai had remembered him from refuelling stops at the Shell facility at Aden's airport.

In the India of economic plans and government control of the 'commanding heights' that had developed by the 1960s, a lot of grovelling indeed was required for businessmen to get the clearances they needed. Inevitably the bureaucratic signature needed to move a file from desk to desk came to have a price on it as well. The Congress Party had degenerated from a movement of freedom fighters into a dispenser of patronage, with ministers allocating resources and licences while the bureaucracy worked out ways to make the process look objective.

After becoming established in Bombay, Dhirubhai used to make frequent trips to New Delhi. He frequently went in the company of Murli Deora, a fellow yarn-trader who was then working his way up the Congress Party machine in Bombay. Deora later became the head of the Bombay Municipal Corporation – the city's mayor – then for decades was representative for South Bombay, the area containing the business district and elite apartments, in the Lok Sabha (the lower house of the Indian parliament).

Dhirubhai and Deora used to catch an early flight up to Delhi and park their bags with a sympathetic clerk at the Ashoka Hotel while they did their rounds of politicians and bureaucrats to speed up decisions on import licences. Too poor to afford an overnight stay, they would collect

49

their bags and any messages and fly back to Bombay the same evening. Later, Dhirubhai could afford to keep a room ready at the Ashoka, a government hotel built in a vaguely Mughal monumental style, and eventually appointed a full-time lobbyist for Reliance in New Delhi.

For the lesser bureaucrats, journalists and others who helped to promote the company's interest in various ways, Dhirubhai's standard gratuity was a suit or sari length of material made by his factory. Gradually Dhirubhai also learned the channels for large-scale political donations in the top echelons.

In 1966 Indira Gandhi had become prime minister following the sudden death of Lal Bahadur Shastri, India's leader since the death of her father Jawaharlal Nehru in 1964. With her only ministerial experience being the Information portfolio under Shastri, but a lifetime of watching her father and her late husband Firoze Gandhi in politics, Indira was well versed in Congress Party machinations, although she had a shallow grasp of policies. Power steadily exacerbated a deep psychological insecurity and a melancholic nature that led her to place inordinate trust in unworthy people in her inner circle, as well as on her headstrong youngest son Sanjay.

Among the sweeping economic changes of 1969 was one small legislative amendment that had the effect of entrenching corruption, although its ostensible intention had been the opposite. A section of the Companies Act that allowed directors to make political contributions to any party was repealed in 1969. As one of the officials who supervised the amendment later admitted, this led to political payments by 'black' money. 'Companies had to generate black funds by under/ over invoicing, fictitious sales etc. A pattern of wholesale corruption and large-scale corporate malpractices, through double-accounting, over-invoicing and under-invoicing, came into being, creating massive unaccounted-for and therefore untaxed funds.'[1]

One of the conduits to Indira Gandhi was a private secretary named Yashpal Kapur, a Hindu refugee from the western Punjab in the 1947 Partition who displayed the financially grasping tendencies many members of this community brought to Delhi. In *All These Years*, her memoir of the Nehru and Indira Gandhi years,[2] the well-connected magazine publisher Raj Thapar recalls Kapur and notes that, by 1971, his role had taken on a 'weird' shape. 'Yashpal Kapur, that oily cup-bearer, was growing in stature by the minute and his corruption was becoming legend and his ability to get Indira to sign on the dotted line became the bazaar gossip,' she wrote. Thapar's senior bureaucrat husband Romesh, who early had been a trusted confidant of Indira, felt duty-bound to tell Indira. 'He sought an appointment, went to the office, gave her a run-down of what the average person was thinking, of how the PM's office now harboured a nest of corrupt people led by the favoured Yashpal. She was furious. "You know I would never touch a penny." "Maybe. But you are seen as the queen bee. The others do the collecting."' Thapar went on:

> An unending string of stories were current about Yashpal's power, how he was sought by the high and mighty, how he was well in with Sanjay who was beginning, bit by nibbling bit, to tamper with the administration in his favour. Yashpal was of course no longer in the PM's office. His place had been taken by his nephew, R.K. Dhawan, who was rapidly to assume much vaster powers than his erstwhile uncle and together they were to manipulate patronage in this vast country.[3]

Dhirubhai not only cultivated Yashpal Kapur, says one old acquaintance, 'he practically purchased him'. In due course, the relationship passed on to R.K. Dhawan, who moved eventually from the prime minister's office under Indira and then Rajiv Gandhi into parliament and ministerial portfolios himself.

Over the years, Dhirubhai developed close ties with politicians in many parties. These included such figures as Atul Bihari Vajpayee, senior leader of the Hindu-nationalist Bharatiya Janata Party who became prime minister of a brief minority government in 1996 and later for a momentous six years, and several on the left such as Chandrashekhar, another short-term prime minister in 1990–91. But his strongest connections were always with the Gandhi coterie within Congress, even though he never liked Indira's socialistic policy phase in 1969–70, then later with P.V. Narasimha Rao, who took over the Congress mainstream and prime ministership in 1991.

The links were not always based on money, however. Dhirubhai is widely acknowledged to have been a masterful exponent of his own business visions, which have generally been more far-sighted than those of almost anyone else among India's business leaders. He was quick to grasp that many Indian politicians, officials and bankers could be captivated by intellectual excitement or flattery at being in the inner circle of such an emerging tycoon. Should such individuals later show signs of self-interest or personal financial difficulty Dhirubhai or one of his lieutenants would pick up the signals. A post-retirement job, a business opportunity for a child, indirect funding or a burst of inspired publicity might then result for the person concerned.

Dhirubhai also played on the perception that he was an outsider and 'upstart' who deserved help to break through the glass ceilings of vested interest and privilege in the business community. That there was an inner circle in the 'Licence Raj' – the allocation by New Delhi of licences to set up factories and expand production capacity – was evidenced in 1967 by a report by a Bombay University economist, R.K. Hazare, to the Planning Commission, which revealed that the Birla group of companies had received 20 per cent of the licensed industrial investment approved by the government between 1957 and 1966. The early support given by Ghansyam Das Birla to Mahatma Gandhi had certainly paid off in the independent India ruled by Congress. Writing in 1981 on Birla's 88th birthday, the journalist T.N. Ninan noted that the Birla companies had multiplied from twenty in 1945 to about 150. 'If any industrial house benefitted from the licence-permit raj', wrote Ninan, 'it was the house that Birla built.'[4]

Birla's rapid expansion contrasted with the moderate growth of the Tata group, the Parsi-controlled empire that had grown strongly under British rule. In 1981 the then head of Tata, J.R.D. Tata, told an interviewer: 'I think it wrong for a business to run newspapers [the Birlas had set up the *Hindustan Times*, the strongest paper in New Delhi], wrong for him to play a political role ... But it does seem that others who do not mind mixing politics with business have done extremely well for themselves.'[5]

One of Dhirubhai's earliest backers, the banker and politician T.A. Pai, falls into the category of intellectual sympathiser. Pai came from an extraordinary upper-caste family based in the tiny village of Manipal on the Karnataka coast, far south of Bombay. It is still an out-of-the-way place, on a barren hilltop overlooking a sweep of palm trees and exposed beaches fronting the Arabian Sea. In 1925 the Pai family had established the Syndicate Bank there. By the mid-1960s it was the tenth largest Indian bank, with 190 branches. As well as being bankers, the Pais used their wealth to found a college at Manipal in 1942. It has since grown into one of India's largest private universities, attracting fee-paying students from Malaysia, the Middle East and the West Indies.

The Pais prided themselves on being discoverers and nurturers of talent. A small museum at Manipal is devoted to the family patriarch T.M.A. Pai (older brother of T.A. Pai) and his teachings. One cherished precept: 'A pigmy nourished well can become a giant.' According to

K.K. Pai, a family member who became general manager of the Syndicate Bank, Dhirubhai was introduced to T.A. Pai in the mid-1960s by a former bank employee. The bank was interested in developing its foreign exchange activities and began handling some transactions for the young spice and textile trader. 'Our first impression was that he was very enthusiastic, very enterprising, a man of ideas,' K.K. Pai said. 'From the beginning I had the impression he was a go-getter. He was very persuasive, very convincing in his arguments. He was able to present his case and business proposals very clearly. He gave me the impression he was reliable and knew what he was doing.'

The Syndicate Bank became the main financier for Reliance Textile Industries when it started manufacturing soon afterwards, in 1966, providing much of the Rs 1.5 million needed to buy its first four knitting machines. Another early backer was the Industrial Credit and Investment Corporation of India (ICICI), whose chairman Harkisan Das Parekh, another Gujarati, also took a shine to Dhirubhai's big schemes.

Dhirubhai continued to impress the Pais by his insistence on the best equipment and personnel, as well as his knowledge of the market and its trends. He also made conspicuous donations to educational institutes run by the family. Throughout the late 1960s Dhirubhai kept in close touch with T.A. Pai, making sure he was among the first to call whenever the bank chief visited Bombay from Manipal and to give advance notice of any major initiatives. Pai's nephew Ramdas Pai, who later became president of Manipal Academy of Higher Education, remembers Dhirubhai coming to Bombay's airport in 1968 to greet him on his first trip back from studies in the United States. T.A. Pai in turn promoted Reliance where he could, even to the point of carrying samples of its Vimal-brand material in his briefcase to show others.

The bank continued to be the major lending institution for Reliance even after Indira Gandhi nationalised it and all India's other leading banks and insurance firms in July 1969. Although the Pais were unhappy about losing their asset, family members continued to hold the top executive positions for many years. Their policy of directing credit to small entrepreneurs, agriculturalists and business newcomers – which built up a portfolio of very small but sound loans for the bank – were exactly what Indira had hoped to achieve by the bank nationalisation generally.

Ironically, the government takeover led to the steady bureaucratisation of management and to lending directed by political connections rather than commercial viability. This destroyed the soundness of the Syndicate Bank and all the other twenty nationalised banks. By the end of the 1980s the banks' non-performing assets or bad loans greatly exceeded their capital base by a wide margin and, but for endless capital infusions by the treasury, almost all would have become insolvent. When private sector banking was again encouraged, after the 1991 liberalising reforms, the Pai family took over a small institution based in the south, Lord Krishna Bank. If offered the chance to buy back Syndicate Bank, family members said, they would refuse it.

Immediately after his bank was taken away Indira consoled T.A. Pai by drafting him to apply his ideas as the first chairman of the nationalised Life Insurance Corporation of India. Soon afterwards, he was inducted as a Congress member of the upper house of parliament (the Rajya Sabha, or States' House) to enable him to become her government's Minister of Commerce, handling trade matters. Later in the 1970s Pai became Minister for Industries, which gave him a decisive role in the allocation of industrial licences. He continued as minister during the suspension of democracy under Indira's declaration of Emergency between 1975 and early 1977.

Pai died in 1981, having realised at the end – his relatives say – that his talents had been misused as a respectable cover by the corrupt circle around Indira and Sanjay. 'The enterprise of adventurers always sucks in plain, decent men,' commented the *Indian Express*'s editor, Arun Shourie, not long after Pai's death. 'The number of times men like C. Subramaniam [another of Indira's ministers] and the late T.A. Pai lied on Maruti [Sanjay's car project] far exceeded whatever Mrs Gandhi said about it.'

For Dhirubhai, Pai's elevation meant that, as well as still having friends in a major bank, he now had a friend in a key position to approve import schemes and manufacturing plans. In the early 1970s the immediate pay-off was favourable changes in the import-export regime. Dhirubhai was not a law-breaker but had a creative attitude towards regulation. As one former colleague recalled: 'He would say: "You should not do anything illegal. First of all, the law should be changed."' 'He would not go into anything which was unlawful,' agreed Kothary of the Silk and Art Silk Mills Research Association (Sasmira). 'Everything he did was permitted to do by any other man. But his reading of the system! You have a law, the interpretation which you make – he would take advantage of a particular system in a way which others could not see. By the time other people started anything the government was also waking up and the system would be changed.'

The key to profits in the Indian synthetic textile business through the 1970s was access to supplies of the basic filaments and yarns. Influenced by Mahatma Gandhi's notions of self-reliance and the virtues of home-spun cotton and by a strong lobby of cotton-growers, New Delhi had discouraged use of synthetics – regarding them as a textile for the wealthy.

India already had a few factories making rayon, nylon and polyester. But these domestic sources met only a fraction of the demand, particularly for polyester, as Indians began to appreciate its durability, lustre, colour-fastness and ease of washing. As well as in pure polyester fabrics, the fibre was in demand for blending with cotton at both the large industrial mills and the widely dispersed power-loom workshops. Former colleagues say Dhirubhai resisted any temptation to smuggle in supplies. 'Everyone knew smuggling was there, but Dhirubhai would not want to get involved,' one former Reliance manager said. 'Government support meant too much to him.' Instead, during the 1960s Dhirubhai had steadily become master of the trade in replenishment licences, which were entitlements to import yarn earned by exporters of finished textiles and garments. After the wars with China in 1962 and Pakistan in 1965, India's external trade balances were under strain and the government was ready to entertain more contrived schemes to boost export earnings.

Dhirubhai's coup was to persuade Pai in 1971 to authorise imports of polyester filament yarn (PFY) against exports of nylon fabric. Previously, nylon fabric exporters had earned some rights to replenish their stocks of nylon fibres through imports. Dhirubhai argued that if he could sell nylon or other manufactured textiles (known as 'art silks') at Rs 4.25 a yard, more than double the price stipulated in the old scheme, the exporter should be rewarded by permission to import PFY, which was in greater domestic shortage because local production was far below demand. This resulted in what was called the Higher Unit Value Scheme, which made Dhirubhai a fortune while it lasted. At that time, the domestic price of PFY was seven or more times higher than the prevailing international price. Even if the nylon or polyester exports fetched only a quarter or a third of cost, this was more than offset by the 600 per cent or more profit on the PFY imports.

57

Reliance went into a high-profile export drive, targeting some of the weaker economies of the world. Poland was one focus, with fashion shows being mounted in Warsaw and delegations of Polish trade officials lavishly hosted by Dhirubhai in Bombay. Another was Saudi Arabia, where Dhirubhai had another old Aden colleague, Bharat Kumar Shah, then working as a trader in Jeddah and acting as Reliance's Mid-East 'coordination manager'. Dhirubhai would take out full-page advertisements in the *Times of India* to announce special charter flights taking his export products to foreign markets.

But many senior figures in the textile industry were never persuaded that this export business was anything but bogus. 'If these goods were not saleable at two rupees, how could they sell at four rupees?' one remarked. According to this theory Dhirubhai would have provided his own export earnings, by sending the money out to the ostensible buyer overseas through the illegal foreign exchange channels known as *havala* (accepting the 20 per cent *havala* premium on the official exchange rate). The goods would be sent to a free port such as Singapore or Dubai, to avoid customs duty, then be disposed of at giveaway prices, left to rot on the docks or even dumped at sea. The effective outgoings would be the 20 per cent *havala* premium on the funds sent out and the 60 per cent of the same funds actually spent on buying PFY overseas for import back into India. The returns would be this 60 per cent multiplied by seven or more. The profit would be 425 per cent of the outlay. And, as long as Dhirubhai had the 'export remittance' arriving in his account in Bombay, he could claim credit for doing his bit for India's trade balance.

In an interview with the magazine *BusinessIndia* in April 1980, Dhirubhai said Reliance Commercial Corporation accounted for more than 60 per cent of the exports made under the Higher Unit Value Scheme. 'The schemes were open to everyone,' he said. 'I cannot be blamed if my competitors were unenterprising or ignorant.' Textile trade sources familiar with that era say this was not exactly the case. The adoption of the Higher Unit Value Scheme was not widely publicised in 1971. Dhirubhai had a clear run of one or two years before other exporters began trying to take advantage of the same scheme, or putting up similar proposals for other categories of textile exports. One of these exporters, Bipin Kapadia, later recounted his experience to Bombay police who sought it as background to the sensational murder conspiracy case of 1989 (see chapter 13).

Over two years in the early 1970s Kapadia's family company Fancy Corporation expanded its exports from Rs 2.5 million a year to Rs 15 million on the expectation of receiving import entitlements for PFY from the Commerce ministry's Chief Controller of Imports and Exports. 'On one pretext or another' the authorities withheld the import licences over a 30-month period in 1972–74, causing Kapadia a huge loss. Between 1971 and mid-1975 Kapadia made many trips to New Delhi to plead with officials. At his hotel, Kapadia told the police, 'I used to receive repeated calls on telephone offering me company of women, threatening me of dire consequences, if I were not to leave the persuasion of my import licences.' During one such business trip, Kapadia was approached in the hotel parking lot at night by a knife-wielding man who called out to him. A friend pushed Kapadia out of the way and the man ran off.

In 1974, when some other exporters managed to get PFY shipments coming through and the domestic premium began tumbling, Dhirubhai was blamed by his rivals for instigating a complaint to the Collector of Customs in Bombay, I.K. Gujral, that the others were either importing 'substandard' PFY or under-declaring the value to avoid taxes. Gujral seized all the suspect PFY shipments but did not launch proceedings. It was not until a year later, after Gujral had been replaced by an energetic customs officer named J. Datta, that the customs issued 'show cause' notices to the importers asking them to reply to the complaints. In a one-day hearing on 1 July 1975 Datta listened to the importers and decided in their favour. The goods were released, but the PFY premium tumbled to about 100 per cent and all the importers suffered losses.

The High Unit Value Scheme continued as long as Indira Gandhi's government did. It enabled Dhirubhai to gain dominance over the supply of polyester yarn to India's highly decentralised textile weaving industry, in which more than 70 per cent of capacity is spread over thousands of small-scale power-loom workshops.

Dhirubhai became the major polyester importer in India, from the Italian company Ital Viscosa and C. Itoh & Co.'s Asahi Chemicals in Japan, where his hosts feted the Indian businessman on his buying trips. Later Reliance switched more of its sourcing to the American chemicals firm E.I. du Pont de Nemours & Co. (Du Pont), which had developed technology for a partially oriented yarn (POY) that had a longer useful life than the other companies' POY.

The former Du Pont agent Suresh Kothary recalls Dhirubhai overcoming Du Pont's reluctance to ship to India. 'They said India was not used to containerisation, they didn't want any claims. Dhirubhai said he would never claim. There were then no trucks to take containers from here to Ahmedabad and the roads were bad. Somehow Dhirubhai did it.' The scale of Dhirubhai's imports grew. Around 1978, says Kothari, Dhirubhai heard that Dupont had idle capacity of 300 to 400 tonnes a month at its polyester plant in Germany. 'Dhirubhai booked it all for six months,' Kothari said.

In addition, Reliance also built up to about 50 per cent its share of the lucrative business of crimping, whereby polyester fibre is texturised by passing it through gear-like rollers to impart a waviness to the filament, or coiled to give stretch – attributes that make the yarn more opaque, lustrous and easier to dye. Industries minister Pai over-ruled objections from his department to give Reliance the clearances to quadruple its texturising capacity in 1975.

Two anecdotes are told about Dhirubhai's confident, even brazen, approach to the muttered denigration of his success that inevitably sprang up. On one occasion, a rival yarn trader allegedly spread the rumour that Dhirubhai was going bust. He was indeed short of cash, but went to a public noticeboard in the yarn market and put up a sign inviting anyone he owed money to come and have their advances repaid. No one did.[6] Another story is attributed to D.N. Shroff, president of industry group Sasmira in the 1970s. Market gossip accused Dhirubhai of black marketeering. Dhirubhai asked Shroff to convene a meeting of his association's executive committee, which included many of his critics, then turned up to face it. 'You accuse me of black marketing,' he challenged, 'but which one of you has not slept with me?' All present had bought or sold yarn to Dhirubhai at some stage.[7]

In March 1977 Indira and Congress were swept from power in the elections called immediately after her two years' rule under Emergency powers was lifted. But her government gave Dhirubhai a parting gift. Over the 1976–77 fiscal year (April–March) Dhirubhai had accumulated REP licences both from its own exports and from purchases in the market, worth Rs 30 million. On 7 February, about three weeks after the elections were announced, the government was persuaded to exempt all polyester yarn imports under REP licences issued since April 1976 from customs duty, which was then 125 per cent. It was a gift of Rs 37.5 million to Dhirubhai.

Indira's replacement was the Janata government, a coalition of anti-Congress parties under Morarji Desai, the austere and self-righteous former Finance minister whom Indira had driven from Congress because he had opposed her nationalisation policies in the late 1960s. But, at least to begin with, Dhirubhai fared well under Janata, helped by the good offices of the prime minister's son, Kantilal Desai. On 22 August 1977 the Janata Minister for Commerce, Mohan Dharia, abruptly cancelled the High Unit Value Scheme and allowed any REP licence holder – not just exporters of nylon fabric – to import a specific quantity of polyester yarn.

The premium on licences for PFY crashed from 500 per cent to 50 per cent almost overnight. It was reported a year later by the *Indian Express* that Reliance stepped into the market to acquire licences at this low premium and opened letters of credit for imports totalling Rs 50 million. Then, on 2 September, the Chief Controller of Imports and Exports (in the Commerce ministry) announced another sudden switch of policy. To help 'bona fide users' of PFY secure their reasonable requirements, the linkage of exports of synthetic textiles with the import of PFY was restored with immediate effect. Registered exporters who had entered firm import contracts up to 2 September would be allowed to import directly. But henceforth all other importers would have to take their licences to the State Trading Corporation (STC), which would be the sole channel for imports of yarn.

It was not until March 1978 that the first supplies of yarn began reaching Indian markets through the STC. Over the six months until then, Reliance took delivery of all the PFY supplies for which it had contracted and was able to squeeze a totally captive market. The 'Eleven Day Wonder', as the 22 August–2 September interval came to be called, seemed tailor-made for the benefit of Reliance.

Whether or not bogus exports were made under the High Unit Value Scheme by Dhirubhai has never been proven, and certainly Reliance did make genuine efforts to sell its own products overseas. Its export manager, Rathibhai Muchhala, became a familiar figure around the trade stores of the Gujarati diaspora in East Africa, the Middle East and later the United Kingdom, trying to place stocks of Vimal artificial silks. S.B. Khandelwal, owner of the emporium Sari Mandir (Sari Temple) in Leicester, where many Gujaratis settled after being expelled from East Africa, recalled a visit by Muchhala early in the 1970s. 'They were very anxious to get into export business,' Khandelwal said. 'I took 200 saris on credit. No money was expected upfront. Muchhala said: 'Just say "Shri Ganesh".' (Meaning 'Just for luck'.)

Until around 1977 exports took between 60 and 70 per cent of the fabrics produced at Naroda, Dhirubhai noted to *BusinessIndia* in 1980. That exports ceased to be a significant activity of Reliance soon afterwards indicates that they were propped up by the High Unit Value Scheme and the artificial shortages for PFY created by import controls.

The new environment encouraged Dhirubhai to step up his domestic promotion of Vimal and to expand his franchised exclusive shops to more than 600 by early 1980. Advertisements were plastered across newspapers and billboards. 'Only Vimal offers you exclusive innovations in high-fashion wear', went one, listing such products as Disco Dazzle Sports Jersey or Supertex dress material. It was an advertising expenditure of Rs 10 million a year, then unprecedented in India and more than four times that of established textile producers like Bombay Dyeing. And it worked. In 1979 Reliance Textile Industries raised its sales to Rs 1.55 billion (then $190 million), making it the largest textile producer in the country.

Dhirubhai had meanwhile decided to help bring an end to the Janata government of Morarji Desai. The government had not been particularly friendly to him, after the initial favourable turn in yarn import policy, and Kantilal Desai had become too controversial a figure to be much help. A judicial inquiry set up by Morarji Desai in reply to charges of influence peddling by relatives of ministers did indeed find, in February 1980, a *'prima-face* case for further inquiry' that Kantilal Desai had influenced the government to relax its policy on PFY imports in August 1977. Dhirubhai put his resources behind Indira Gandhi's efforts to split the Janata coalition, which focused on the ambition of the Finance minister, Charan Singh.

It gave Dhirubhai the opportunity to cement a relationship with Indira Gandhi that gave him unrivalled influence over government poilicies. In the murky dealings of 1979 his role was to provide the suitcases of cash needed to induce MPs to take the risk of leaving the government benches and joining the splinter group. In July that year the Desai government fell when Charan Singh's supporters withdrew support in parliament. Charan Singh, pledged support by Indira's Congress, was invited to form a government and demonstrate his support within a month. A vote of confidence was never taken: Indira demanded as a condition that Charan Singh agree to withdraw legislation setting up special courts to try herself and Sanjay for alleged crimes committed during the Emergency. This he was unable to do. In August, the President dissolved parliament and called elections for early January 1980, with Charan Singh as caretaker prime minister.

Suresh Kothary, the Du Pont agent in Bombay, was in close contact with Dhirubhai over this period. 'He used to tell me what was going to happen and it always did,' Kothary said. 'I asked him once: "How do you know? Are you an astrologer?" He laughed and said: "Yes."'

With inflation raging as a result of two years of drought, Indira surged back to power. The first big party staged to welcome her back to government, held at the Ashoka Hotel in New Delhi, was hosted by Congress MPs from Gujarat and paid for by Dhirubhai. Political observers noted that Indira spent more than two hours sitting on the dais receiving well-wishers with Dhirubhai at her side.

Kothary remembers that several times during his turbulent climb to prosperity and influence, Dhirubhai would remark: 'Everything that I have done has been kept in the ground and a first-class fountain has been built over it. Nobody will ever know what I have done.'

6

Guru of the equity cult

Indira Gandhi's return to power opened a golden period for Dhirubhai Ambani. In 1979 his company barely made it to the list of India's fifty biggest companies, measured by annual sales, profits or assets. By 1984 Reliance was in the largest five. Dhirubhai himself had become one of the most talked- and written-about persons in India, gaining a personal following more like that of a sports or entertainment star than a businessman. It was also the period when Dhirubhai made the most rapid part of his transition, in the bitter words of a senior non-Congress politician in 1996, 'from supplicant – the most abject kind of supplicant – to influencer and then to controller of Indian politics'.[1]

Although it was not immediately obvious, Indira's three years in political exile had reinforced a change in her thinking about state intervention in the economy. In large part due to the influence of Sanjay, she was less trustful of bureaucratic direction and more inclined to give the private sector its head.

Indian business leaders were also calling for a drastic relaxation of the licence controls on capacity expansion and diversification vested in the Monopolies and Restrictive Trade Practices Commission. One was J.R.D. Tata, who along with others in the 1940s had willingly laid their heads on the block of state planning. By 1981 Tata was calling on New Delhi to 'unfetter' the big business houses. The intellectual tide had turned in favour of economic liberalisation, although it would not be until a decade later that anything more than tentative policy change was attempted.

In Indira's case, the disillusionment on the economic side was matched by a deeper cynicism in politics. Her second spell as prime minister was marked by callous manipulations, such as the sponsorship of Sikh extremists in the Punjab, and by unapologetic extraction of political funds from businessmen expecting clearances from New Delhi.

Dhirubhai's cultivation of Indira and other Congress figures during the Janata period certainly paid off. In October 1980 Reliance received one of three licences given by the government for manufacture of polyester filament yarn, the location being stipulated as the 'backward' area of Patalganga in the hills of Maharashtra, inland from Bombay. In a field of forty-three contestants for the licences, Reliance beat many larger and longer-established business houses, including Birla. Its licensed capacity of 10000 tonnes a year was by far the largest and, at the time, close to India's entire existing polyester fibre output.

Together with the Du Pont representative Suresh Kothary, Dhirubhai and his eldest son Mukesh had already been to the headquarters of Du Pont at Wilmington, Delaware, and persuaded the American chemicals giant to sell its technology, including a polymerisation process not previously transferred outside the United States. The deal arranged through a New York-based firm called Chemtex Inc. saw Reliance place a $26.7 million order for its first PFY plant. Making polyester is a highly complicated chemical process, involving the reaction of one petrochemical intermediate, either purified terephthalic acid (PTA) or dimethyl terephthalate (DMT), with another, monoethylene glycol (MEG), in processes that involve heat and vacuum, using various catalysts along the way. The resulting polymer, a long molecule, is pumped in a molten state through fine nozzles to produce the filament. It was Dhirubhai's first step in a process of 'backward' or 'upstream' integration that was to bring him many plaudits and a step into the petrochemicals industry, where the scale of business is vastly bigger than in textiles.

As well as an always-open connection to the Prime Minister's office, he now had a friend as Minister of Commerce, the Bengali politician Pranab Mukherjee. His ministry not only helped set trade policy including tariff levels and anti-dumping duties, in conjunction with the Ministry of Finance but also conducted the system of import licences through the powerful office of the Chief Controller of Imports and Exports – whose corridors in New Delhi's Udyog Bhavan were thronged with importunate businessmen and their agents.

At the beginning of 1982 Mukherjee became Minister of Finance, giving him charge of broad economic policy as well as the details of revenue-raising and tax enforcement. The Ministry of Finance also supervised the Reserve Bank of India, the central bank, whose governor is often a recently retired head of the ministry. Through its banking division the ministry also effectively directed the twenty-six nationalised banks through highly politicised board and senior management appointments. It supervised the insurance companies and other financial institutions, such as the Unit Trust of India, and controlled entry to the sharemarkets by Indian companies.

Under a series of secretaries that included Manmohan Singh (later Finance minister in the 1990s and Prime Minister from 2004), R.N. Malhotra, M. Narasimhan and S. Venkitaramanan, the Ministry of Finance engineered a revitalisation of India's capital markets in the early 1980s. The key administrator of this sector was another Bengali, the energetic career bureaucrat Nitish Sen Gupta, who became the ministry's Controller of Capital Issues and Joint Secretary (Investment) in December 1979, just before the return of Indira.

Like his ministry head Manmohan Singh, Sen Gupta had earlier been a diligent builder of the 'Licence Raj'. He had been deputy secretary in the Department of Company Affairs from March 1968, just as government policy was changing from what he has called 'benign aloofness' to 'massive intervention in corporate business', most notably in the nationalisation of major Indian banks the following year. On his arrival at the Ministry of Finance in 1979, his job was partly to set the rules by which companies could raise money by issuing shares or bonds, then to adjudicate the prices they could charge for these offerings. But up to 1979 India's capital markets were quiet places. Stock exchanges had arrived in the major cities as part and parcel of British capitalism in the 1880s. The exchanges were run by cliques of brokers, who set their own rules of trading and rarely punished one of their own for abuse of clients' trust. After periodic busts, the general public had learned to distrust the sharemarket. With only very small percentages of equity being traded actively the managements of listed companies were concerned more with dividend levels than with share prices. The bigger companies went to banks for their finance rather than to the market. Between 1949 and 1979 the average annual total of money raised by Indian companies from capital markets was only Rs 580 million ($71 million at 1979 exchange rates) and the highest in any year Rs 920 million.

By the end of 1983 the amount being raised had jumped to Rs 10 billion a year, with Reliance playing a prominent part in this dramatic increase. Sen Gupta had taken up a study by an Indian economist with the World Bank, D.C. Rao, who suggested greater use of convertible debentures – paper that for a certain period had the character of bonds, earning interest, but which then were converted to shares earning dividends. For investors this meant earnings while the company or project was gestating, with the prospect of equity once it was a going concern. For companies, it offered a way to slash debt after the start-up and to avoid going for loans from financial institutions, who might elect to convert part of the debt to equity and become major shareholders.

Again, Dhirubhai was primed and ready for the new policy. As Reliance expanded its production in the early 1970s, he had begun looking at taking it public in order to raise capital. In 1973 Dhirubhai and members of the Pai family had floated a company named Mynylon Ltd in Karnataka (the Pai family's home state). The intentions remain obscure, for Mynylon's paid-up capital was only Rs 11 000. In July 1975 Dhirubhai took consent of the Karnataka and Bombay High Courts and carried out an amalgamation whereby the tiny Mynylon took over the assets and liabilities of Reliance, which by that time had assets of Rs 60 million. By March 1977 the company had been relocated from Bangalore, capital of Karnataka, back to Bombay and its name changed back to Reliance Textile Industries. For a period that roughly coincided with the Emergency – when T.A. Pai was a powerful minister – Reliance did not formally exist in name. The manoeuvre later became a widely used case study in tax minimisation.

In October 1977 Reliance had gone public, with a public offer of 2.8 million equity shares of Rs 10 each at par taken from the holdings of Dhirubhai and his younger brother Nathubhai. With its shareholding thus broadened to meet listing requirements, Reliance was listed on the stock exchanges in Bombay and Ahmedabad in January 1978. There-after Reliance expanded its equity base through frequent rights and bonus issues to shareholders, while financial institutions converted 20 per cent of their loans into equity in September 1979. But it was through the use of convertible debentures that Dhirubhai made his big splash in the capital markets. Indeed, Dhirubhai had anticipated Sen Gupta's policy with the Series I issue of partially convertible debentures by Reliance in October 1979, raising Rs 70 million. From late 1980 the issues of partially convertible debentures came from Reliance in quick succession, raising Rs 108 million in September from its Series II and Rs 240 million from its Series I the next year and Rs 500 million from Series IV in April 1982.

Dhirubhai capped that by obtaining from Sen Gupta clearance to do what should normally be legally impossible: converting the non-convertible portions of the four debenture issues into equity. By this 'brilliant and unconventional move' (in the words of a magazine jour-nalist) Reliance was able to chop Rs 735 million off its debt book in 1983 and turn it into comparatively modest equity of Rs 103 million, while reserves were raised by Rs 632 million. Instead of an annual interest bill of Rs 96.5 million on debentures, the dividend burden from the extra equity was only around Rs 36 million. This transmutation allowed Reli-ance to continue raising more quasi-debt.

Sen Gupta later denied that he was unduly permissive to Reliance, or that he ever received any benefits from Dhirubhai such as share allotments. 'On my first encounter with him I had to say no,' Sen Gupta recalled. With the third series of debentures, Dhirubhai had put in a request that the holders be entitled to renounce rights attached to their implicit share entitlements. Sen Gupta insisted that the debentures were not shares until converted. But Reliance was highly persuasive. On another occasion, Sen Gupta rejected the premium that Reliance was seeking to put on an issue, on the ground that projected profitability had not been indicated. Without a pro-forma balance sheet for the current year – an extension of results to date – it could not be accepted.

It was 1pm that day; Sen Gupta was due to fly that evening to Bombay for a meeting of his seven-member committee on capital issues the next morning. Obviously it would be impossible to have the paperwork ready for this meeting, he told Reliance. Coming out of the arrivals hall of Bombay Airport at 7pm, Sen Gupta was met by accountants from Reliance and handed a copy of the pro-forma balance sheet and results for each of the seven committee members. 'I had no option but to take up the matter at our meeting,' Sen Gupta said.

By the end of 1986 Dhirubhai had raised an unpreceded Rs 9.4 billion from the public over eight years, including Rs 5 billion from one debenture issue alone. 'In fact this one company, Reliance,' wrote Sen Gupta, 'made significant contributions to the growth of the debenture market in the country through its successive issues of convertible debentures, a new experiment in running a big business undertaking entirely on the resources drawn from the public at large without being backed by any multinational, large industrial houses, or without taking term loans from financial institutions on a significant scale.'[2] It was not entirely true that Dhirubhai did not tap the banks, as we shall see, but his heyday in the capital markets did coincide with the rise of what Indian business magazines came to call the 'equity cult' – and Dhirubhai could rightly claim some of the credit for it.

Between 1980 and 1985 the number of Indians owning shares increased from less than a million to four million. Among those, the number of shareholders in Reliance rose to more than a million by the end of 1985. It was by far the widest shareholder base of any Indian company – and, until the privatisation of major utilities like British Telecom or Nippon Telephone & Telegraph, probably in the world. It was evidence of a popular following that made many politicians – especially in Gujarat where Dhirubhai had earned local hero status – think twice before denying him anything.

Sen Gupta put the sharemarket craze down to the entry of three 'non-traditional' classes of investors. One was the Indian middle class, who had forgotten about their misadventure in the stockmarket in the Second World War. Another was the expatriate Indian communities, prospering rapidly in Britain, North America and South-East Asia after their miserable expulsion from East Africa in the 1960s and augmented by direct immigrants qualifying for professional and skilled entry to advanced economies. Since Pranab Mukherjee's 1982 budget, these 'non-resident Indians' (or NRIs) and their companies had been able to invest directly in Indian equities. The third class was the larger landowning farmers, who were prosperous after the huge crop-yield increases of the Green Revolution during the 1960s and 1970s, and who continued to enjoy tax exemption on their income.

The equity cult spread from nearly twenty major exchanges. The premier bourse was the century-old Bombay Stock Exchange located in Dalal Street, one of the teeming narrow streets of the city's old Fort district where brokers, businessmen, accountants and lawyers crammed into tiny offices in old stone buildings with the remnants of charming wooden and wrought-iron balconies. Although surmounted by a twenty-eight-storey office tower of cement, steel and glass, the trading floor in the podium operated until the mid-1990s much as it had done in the nineteenth century. Some computer monitors flickered on the periphery, but no one expected them to keep up with the frenetic trading done by brawling, shouting, gesticulating 'jobbers' in blue jackets – or with the thriving after-hours kerb market where shares were traded informally.

The paperwork was also miles behind the action. Share transactions were recorded on scraps of paper at brokers' offices, but transfers were not necessarily lodged with company registrars immediately. Settlements came every second Friday, causing a slowdown in trading and sometimes pandemonium when defaults were found. But brokers and traders need not settle even then, if they could afford the upfront margin payments and sometimes exorbitant interest rates on finance for a *badla* (carry-forward) deal.

Using this prototype futures system, settlement could be deferred for months – often amplifying speculative runs in prices. On occasion, a scrip would pass through fifty buy and sell transactions before being lodged for transfer of ownership. If the signature of the original seller did not pass muster, professional forgers operating in the side lanes of Dalal Street would guarantee an authentic-looking copy. It was an environment where 'research' was just another word for insider trading, where the key knowledge was finding out which stocks were going to be ramped upwards or driven down by cartels of moneybag brokers and operators.

Although it had thousands of listed companies and a nominal capitalisation similar to that of middle-sized stock markets like Hong Kong or Australia, the Indian sharemarket was not very liquid. Huge blocks of equity in the better companies were locked up by investment institutions or controlling families. Many of the smaller companies hardly traded at all. The 'floating' equity in the major companies forming the market indices amounted to a few billion US dollars. Even in the 1990s, a concerted move with a relatively small amount of funds, about $50 million, could make the market jump or crash.

Investors outside Bombay who could not hang around Dalal Street, browse the issue documents sold off barrows or pavements, or listen to the gossip while snacking on bhel puri from a nearby stall, had to rely on a network of subbrokers and agents reporting to the fully fledged stockbrokers in the big towns. They scanned a new crop of market tip-sheets with names like *Financial Wizard* and *Rupee Gains* for news of their stocks. In some small towns, investors impatient with their remoteness took trading into their own hands: teachers, shopkeepers and other local professionals would gather after work in public halls to conduct their own trading, settling on the basis of prices in newspapers from the city.

It was a situation made for a populist like Dhirubhai. His ebullience and punctilious nursing of relationships were transferred to a larger stage, using the mass communications techniques learned in marketing the Vimal brand name.

In those years, Dhirubhai and Reliance had a success story to tell. On the technical side, the polyester plant at Patalganga was put up in a fast eighteen months and put into regular production in November 1982. Construction and the debugging of production lines had been supervised by Mukesh Ambani, who had been pulled out of Stanford University while undertaking a Master of Business Administration degree and put in charge of the new project. Aged 24 at the outset and with a degree in chemical engineering, Mukesh Ambani won his spurs as an industrial manager at Patalganga. Reliance made sure that a comment by Du Pont's then international director, Richard Chinman, that such a plant would have taken twenty-six months to build in the United States, had wide publicity in India.

Dhirubhai still demonstrated his uncanny grip on government trade and industrial policy and their implementation. While the 'canalisation' of imports through the State Trading Corporation had been abandoned in April 1981 and polyester filament yarn (PFY) and partially oriented yarn (POY) placed on the 'open general list' of imports, the right to import the yarn was still confined to so-called actual users. The Customs House in Bombay took the line that these did not include large cotton textile mills – despite the growing demand for cotton–polyester blends – but only the small 'art silk' power-looms. Reliance had already organised power-looms as outsources, giving them polyester yarn and taking back their 'grey' cloth for finishing and dyeing at Naroda.

On 23 November 1982, three weeks after Patalganga went into production, the government put an additional Rs 15 000 a tonne duty on PFY and POY imports, allowing Reliance to raise its prices and still force India's small yarn crimpers and power-looms to buy its products. The policy switch had been telegraphed early in November by a submission made to New Delhi by the Association of Synthetic Fibre Industry that dumping of PFY and POY by foreign producers under the open general licence was causing a curtailment of local production and pile-up of inventories, leading to heavy losses.

The All-India Crimpers' Association, representing about 150 small processors who texturised PFY and POY into fibre ready for weaving and knitting, took out a series of anguished newspaper advertisements headlined: 'Should the country's texturising industry be allowed to die?' The crimpers said the case for anti-dumping duty was 'misleading, distorted and untruthful'. Domestic polyester output had risen 60 per cent in 1981 to 16 000 tonnes and still fell short of demand estimated at 50 000 tonnes a year. The rush into PFY production by new producers scarcely pointed to a glutted market.

Existing customs duties worked out to a total 650 per cent on landed costs for importers, topped by further excise duty and sales tax on the processed product. Texturised polyester yarn had become more lucrative for smugglers than the traditional gold, wristwatches and electronics – and huge consignments had recently been intercepted, usually misdeclared as some other low-duty goods. Instead a case existed for an immediate duty cut and freedom for anyone to import.

The pleas were ignored. 'The government has finally declared a deaf ear to our cry of anguish,' said the Crimpers' Association in an advertisement on 7 December. By its calculation, the effective duty on PFY and POY had risen to 750 per cent with the addition of the Rs 15 000 a tonne anti-dumping levy.

The Reliance plant at Patalganga immediately exceeded its licensed capacity and produced 17 600 tonnes of polyester yarn in 1983, its first full year, thereby doubling India's total output. The extra duty in effect added Rs 240 million to Reliance's revenue. In late 1984 Finance minister Pranab Mukherjee announced a new policy to 'endorse' higher than licensed capacity on the part of industry and consequently in late 1985 Reliance received an effective retrospective licensing of its capacity to 25 125 tonnes a year.

Along with the clearances for his capital issues, Dhirubhai also had an easy time from the revenue side of the Finance ministry. At no stage did Reliance ever pay corporate income tax on its profits, or even feel the need to make more than token provision for it. Constant expansion and heavy borrowing gave ever-increasing cost deductions to offset against profits. Reliance became the most famous of India's 'zero-tax' companies.

In his budget for 1983–84 Mukherjee made one of the government's periodic efforts to crack down on such companies, by amending the income tax law to require companies to pay 30 per cent of profits in tax after depreciation but before other deductions. Reliance avoided this by capitalising future interest payable on borrowings for its new projects, hugely increasing its asset value in one hit and allowing greatly increased depreciation claims to deduct from profits. Reliance remained a zero-tax company for nearly three decades after its listing. It was only in 1996–97, after the introduction of a 12 per cent 'minimum alternate tax' on company profits, that it made its first corporate income tax provision.

The collectors of indirect taxes were also friendly. While Reliance could not avoid the heavy domestic excise duties levied on manufactures at the factory gate, it was initially given considerable leeway in setting aside some production as 'wastage' not incurring excise. Bombay Customs accepted a 20 to 23 per cent 'bulk buyer's' discount given to Reliance by Japan's Asahi Chemicals up to 1982 and a 7 per cent discount on its purified terephthalic acid imports thereafter – whereas in other cases they might have inquired about under-invoicing.

Many officials in charge of customs and excise were drawn into the Reliance family rather than adopting the attitude of arm's-length enforcers. The journalist Kanti Bhatt recalled attending the marriage of Dhirubhai's daughter Dipti in 1983, when he joined the marriage procession, which in the Hindu tradition follows the groom to the venue, with the guests occasionally breaking into the twirling dance known as *dandiya raas*. 'I found myself in the street playing *dandiya raas* with the Finance ministry's chief enforcement officer,' Bhatt said.

For his investors, all this added up to greater profits at Reliance, which multiplied from Rs 82.1 million in 1979 to Rs 713.4 million in 1985 (8.69 times), on sales that rose from Rs 1.55 billion to Rs 7.11 billion (4.58 times) over the same years. The company was not India's most profitable, either in absolute terms or in terms of profit as a return on capital, net worth or turnover. But for the times, Dhirubhai was unusually generous with dividends, giving investors a return of at least 25 per cent on the face value of their shares from the time Reliance was listed.

But it was in the appreciation of their shares that the early investors in Reliance were rewarded most. In its first year of listing, 1978, Reliance had reached a high of Rs 50, five times the par value of the share, which was a high premium in those times. In 1980 it hit Rs 104 as Dhirubhai promoted the growth potential of the company's expansion plans at Naroda and Patalganga, and in 1982 it reached a high of Rs 186.

In that year Dhirubhai established his name among brokers and investors as a master of the stockmarket. From the middle of March 1982, a cartel of 'bear' operators reputed to be based in Calcutta started driving down his and other stocks in the Bombay market. The selling pressure was intense on 18 March, creating a half-hour of panic just before the close. The bears sold 350 000 Reliance shares, causing the price to fall quickly from Rs 131 to Rs 121, before Dhirubhai got his brokers to start buying any Reliance shares on offer. The more they sold – the number got to 1.1 million shares – the more Dhirubhai picked up, ostensibly on behalf of NRI investors 'based in West Asian countries'. Eventually the friendly brokers bought more than 800 000 of the shares sold by the bears.

It was an almighty poker game. The bears had sold short – in other words, they had sold shares they did not own in the expectation that the price would fall and let them pick up enough shares later at a lower price. Reliance itself could not legally buy its own shares. So who were the NRI investors who arrived so providently on the scene with more than Rs 100 million (then more than $10 million) to spend?

Six weeks later, after several further spells of bear hammering of Reliance shares, Dhirubhai called his opponents' cards. Every second Friday the Bombay Stock Exchange stopped new transactions while its members settled the previous fortnight's trades or arranged *badla* finance to carry them over. On Friday 30 April Dhirubhai's brokers used their right under the *badla* system to demand delivery of the shares they had bought for their offshore clients, failing which a *badla* charge of Rs 25 a share would be levied. The bear cartel baulked, throwing the exchange into a crisis that shut it down until the following Wednesday. In following days the price of Reliance shares rose to a peak of Rs 201 as the bear brokers desperately located shares to fulfil their sales, incurring massive losses.

By 10 May the Reliance price started easing, signifying that deliveries had been made. But Dhirubhai and his company had clearly arrived. Reliance was henceforth treated by major newspapers as a 'pivotal' stock in the market, and Dhirubhai himself began receiving panegyrics in magazine profiles as the 'messiah' of the small investor. Dhirubhai's brokers went on to pick up a further million Reliance shares by August 1982 for the mysterious NRIs, bringing the outlay since March to about Rs 260 million.

By late 1984 Dhirubhai had reached a new plateau of acclaim and thereafter frequently featured on the covers of Indian magazines. Over the next year he announced plans for a massive expansion of Reliance, by moving further back along the raw petrochemical chain to become India's first producer of purified terephthalic acid (PTA), to make the other main ingredient of polyester, monoethylene glycol (MEG), and to make the associated products linear alkyline benzene (LAB; for use in biodegradable detergents) and high-density polyethylene, a plastic. Patalganga would also be expanded via a 45 000-tonne-a-year plant to make polyester staple fibre (PSF) fibres of a set or staple length, which are spun together to produce a less shiny yarn than the long filaments in PFY.

Probably the pinnacle of Dhirubhai's popularity was reached on 20 May 1985, when Reliance hired Bombay's Cooperage Football Grounds as the venue for the annual general meeting to approve results for 1984. About 12 000 shareholders turned up to sit under canvas awnings stretched above the grass and to watch the directors via television monitors. It was reported as the first AGM ever held in the open and the largest ever meeting of shareholders – attracting note just for that fact the next day in London's *Financial Times*.

Dhirubhai arrived in a suit, but soon got down to shirtsleeves to report the previous year's 58.6 per cent jump in net profit and to list various new projects totalling Rs 6.72 billion in outlays. India had recently had its first taste of hostile takeover bids when the London-based expatriate Indian, Swraj Paul, had bought into the machinery manufacturers DCM and Escorts. If anyone tried that with Reliance, they would have to deal with 1.2 million loyal shareholders, said Dhirubhai to loud applause.

The shareholders enthusiastically approved a name change symbolising Dhirubhai's wider ambitions. The word 'Textile' was dropped from the company's name. After approval by company regulators in June, it was simply Reliance Industries Ltd.

But even the friendliest commentators felt compelled to mention that Dhirubhai had many critics and enemies who called him an arch-manipulator of politicians and bureaucrats. 'It is not for nothing that this dark horse from Gujarat has achieved the reputation in textile circles of being the best friend and the worst enemy one could have,' said *BusinessIndia*. In most cases, these criticisms were put in a way that gave Dhirubhai the chance for a free kick. Authors Margaret Herdeck and Gita Piramal quoted him as saying, 'Ideas are no one's monopoly': 'Those who criticise me and Reliance's growth are slaves to tradition.' If not to outright conservatism and complacency the criticisms were put down to jealousy.

But two of India's sharpest business journalists did get Dhirubhai to admit that stroking government was his biggest task. 'The most important external environment is the Government of India,' he told *India Today's* T.N. Ninan and Jagannath Dubashi. 'You have to sell your ideas to the government. Selling the idea is the most important thing and for that I'd meet anybody in the government. I am willing to salaam anyone. One thing you won't find in me and that is ego.'

The criticisms were brushed aside by most investors, however, as well as by many of the journalists. The 'dark' side of Dhirubhai was part of his attraction. It was a thumb in the nose at the bureaucrats, the corrupt politicians and an exploitative business elite seen as cornering the wealth of India and wasting it.

For the Gujaratis who formed much of the business and profes-sional class of Mumbai – but few of the big entrepreneurs – Dhirubhai was one of them. He had taken on and beaten the Parsis, the Marwaris and the Punjabis at their own game. Called 'Gujjus' and often sneered at by other Indian communities for their parsimonious, apparently money-obsessed ways, the Gujaratis had 'made it' through Dhirubhai.

If he had bent the rules, engineered loopholes, cleverly avoided tax or given bribes, Dhirubhai was only doing what any other industri-alist would do, given the opportunity or the ability to carry it out. How else would a complete newcomer with no capital or education get the breaks?

The only victims, it seemed, were the government, which did not get as much tax revenue out of Reliance as perhaps it should, and the bureaucrats, who could not get their vindictive pleasure out of blocking or crippling a private sector endeavour or rents from permitting it. After centuries of rule by alien governments, many Indians – especially the traders and farmers – had come to regard anything *sarkari* (govern-mental) as trouble. By the 1980s the government of independent India was similarly suspect in places like Bombay and Ahmedabad.

Dhirubhai worked in an office in Bombay's Nariman Point business district. He drove around town in a Cadillac (augmented by 1985 with a gold-coloured Mercedes). He took helicopters out to Patalganga and new sites in Gujarat (even using the Maharashtra state governor's helipad in Bombay for a while) and, as the years went on, was in touch with the highest in the land. But he still looked and felt like an outsider. 'Dhirubhai never moved around with the social crowd like the Wadias, the Godrejs, the Singhanias,' said one senior Bombay journalist. 'He was not considered in the same league – you know how snooty they can be. He would go to the Harbour Bar [in the Taj Mahal Hotel], have a drink, watch everybody, then leave.'

The sense of exclusion might have been what drove him onwards. It also lent an edge to his public image, turning him, like many of the newer movie characters, into a *khalnayak*, an anti-hero. Those who followed Dhirubhai in the stockmarket were not just part of the Reliance family but also members of an unspoken rebellion.

1

Friends in the right places

This was the public face of Dhirubhai Ambani. Known to a small circle of insiders was a different face. Shadowing the industrial and marketing activity, the published financial workings of Reliance, was a second operation: the systematic manipulation of share price, publicity and government policies in order to sustain the Reliance success story and keep the public money coming in. Every company attempts to some degree to improve these elements of its operating environment. Few have ever matched Reliance in its sustained efforts.

By being able to transform debt quickly into equity Dhirubhai seemed to have avoided the borrowing trap that eventually caught up with so many other stars of the global sharemarket boom in the

1980s. By expanding only into associated products, he created enormous internal economies for Reliance. But it was still a balancing act that required a lot of forward momentum and constant oiling of the machinery. It was generally agreed that Reliance's high share price was the single biggest factor in the ease it enjoyed in raising finance. Reliance shares were promoted relentlessly as a path to rapidly appreciating wealth. Dhirubhai was free with allocations to friends and clients from the directors' quotas of any issues, although these share parcels 'usually come with the stipulation not to sell for two years'.[1]

The business chronicler Gita Piramal also noted how central was the share price: 'Ambani realised that in order to seduce the public into investing in his schemes, he had to offer them something above and beyond what they were already used to getting. And this was the steady appreciation of their shareholding … At the time, Ambani didn't realise that he had mounted a treadmill from which he would never be able to step off.'[2] In theory that need not have been the case. Had the funds raised by Reliance been promptly deployed in productive investment, Reliance would have been able to rest on its laurels from time to time. But after the fast completion of the PFY plant in 1982 and the PSF plant in March 1986 at Patalganga, the company's investment targets constantly slipped. It faced political obstacles in front of new sources of funds.

And in any case Dhirubhai needed a constant, substantial stream of income to cover his political payments, top up the official salaries of his executives with cash (company law then placed limits on salaries) and keep various benefits flowing to his network of contacts. To some extent, this could be generated by market play in the management shareholding, spread between scores of investment and trading companies. This meant that Dhirubhai really was on a spiral he could not get off. Not that he wanted to. His daily activity was a constant adrenalin rush, in which he continually proved his mastery of India's markets in yarn, textiles, petrochemicals, shares and finally money itself. In the process, Reliance became a 'pure cash flow operation', according to a stockbroker who worked closely with Dhirubhai. 'They do not distinguish between revenue and capital,' the broker said. 'They only operate on a cash flow.'

Assisting Dhirubhai to juggle money between Reliance, associated private companies, banks and the markets was a close band of trusted staff. Some were family. Foremost was his nephew, Rasikbhai Meswani, who knew all the ins and outs of Dhirubhai's private accounts, including his contributions to politicians and parties, journalists and others. Others were old acquaintances from Aden or Saurashtra, like senior managers Indubhai Seth and brother Manubhai Seth, or Chandrawadan ('Mama') Choksi. The company secretary of Reliance, Vinod Ambani (no relation), was in most cases the common link to the growing number of shelf companies that often had their registered office, but not necessarily a nameplate, in the same address as one or other of the Reliance offices around Bombay or Ahmedabad and whose activities were put down as 'trading and investment'.

The story is told that Vinod Ambani or some other executive once came to Dhirubhai to get some guidance on what to name the host of new companies being spawned. Dhirubhai told him to get out an ancient Sanskrit scripture called *Vishnu Sahasra Nam* ('The 1000 Names of Lord Vishnu'). Many of the investment companies unearthed during later scandals did indeed bear the names of divine avatars.

If the nerve centre was the Reliance corporate headquarters in Maker Chambers IV at Nariman Point, or wherever else Dhirubhai happened to be, the essential plumbing was at the share registry and transfer agency for Reliance, which handled the ownership details and paperwork of the company's shareholders, some 1.2 million by the end of 1986. The registry was often described as 'in-house' but was in fact a separate company, Reliance Consultancy Services Ltd, which had several hundred staff of its own working in a large building in Bombay's distant industrial suburb of Andheri.

Dhirubhai met few objections to his accountancy from his auditors, in particular the firm of Chaturvedi & Shah, which cleared Reliance's books from the earliest days. One partner, D.N. Chaturvedi, spent a lot of his working time in the Reliance head office year round. The other name in the partnership was that of a son of a Reliance director until the early 1990s, Jayantilal R. Shah.

When Reliance went through difficult patches, one device to tide over poor profitability was to change the accounting year. Thus in 1978 when the removal of the High Unit Value Scheme forced a switch to the domestic market just as Reliance was going public, the company changed from an October–September year to a January–December year, even though it had moved from a July–June year only two years earlier. In a later time of troubles, 1987 and 1988, Reliance changed its accounting period in two successive years – making for four changes in fifteen years – before settling on the April–March year used by most Indian companies and the government.

One way to move the market is by weight of money. The best way, of course, is to use someone else's money. While Dhirubhai can rightly claim to be a father of India's equity cult, another guru was Manohar J. Pherwani who ran a government-sponsored share trust, Unit Trust of India, for nearly ten years until November 1989. Although it was set up by an act of parliament in 1964, UTI had been quiescent until Pherwani's arrival. Originally from Sindh, Pherwani was a desperately ambitious man, eager to make his mark and willing to step outside the orthodox to raise subscriptions to UTI funds, for example by sending mobile offices to middle-class neighbourhoods and prosperous rural areas to sign up new investors at their homes. During his chairmanship UTI's investible funds rose from Rs 4.6 billion (in 1979–80) to Rs 176.5 billion (in 1989–90). Nitish Sen Gupta quotes J.R.D. Tata as remarking at a seminar in Bombay, 'The capital market that N.K. Sen Gupta did so much to create has become a pocket borough of the UTI chairman, M.J. Pherwani.'[3]

Dhirubhai and Pherwani became close, and their success fed off each other's: Reliance's rising share price meant rising values of UTI units; UTI's heavy investment in Reliance helped Dhirubhai to keep the price going up.

Dhirubhai also had some funds of his own. Reliance's cash reserves could be lent to the associated investment companies to buy shares, or deposited in banks as informal additional security against loans to those investment companies to buy shares and debentures. But more often the market was moved by information or sentiment and these funds used to take a profit.

Until 1993, when the newly empowered Securities and Exchange Board of India applied new rules, India had no explicit law against insider trading, although companies were forbidden by company law from buying their own shares. It was accepted as normal, however, for companies to see that their share prices were boosted by friendly brokers and underwriters ahead of issues and often for sensitive information to reach some investors ahead of the public. Share market research was not so much concerned with intelligence about a company's performance as with which particular stock was being targeted for concerted price ramping and by whom. But Dhirubhai's year-round intervention in Reliance's share price, continued by his sons, was extraordinary.

To categorise Dhirubhai as an inside trader, however, does not do justice to the scope of his activities. His willingness to 'salaam' anyone and his cultivation of junior staff and newcomers had by the early 1980s created a huge network of friends in politics, government ministries and financial circles. Earlier, goodwill had been cemented by gifts of the famous 'suit-lengths' of material. After the float of Reliance in 1977 Dhirubhai was able to allocate parcels of shares or debentures from the 'promoter's quota' of any issue, with a profit virtually guaranteed by the gap between issue and market prices or by the prospect of conversion.

Again, Dhirubhai was not unique in cultivating officials. Many companies had their friends in the bureaucracy. Businessmen liked to get close to power, and the officials looked to post-retirement jobs or opportunities for their children. But, as always with Dhirubhai, it was the degree of cultivation that distinguished his approach to lobbying. His 'moles' were not just in the ministries of direct relevance to Reliance – Finance, Industries, Commerce, Textiles, Petroleum – but also in others like the Prime Minister's Office and Home Affairs where the general powers of the government were wielded. It meant that a signature was barely on a document or file in the Ministry of Finance, for example, before Dhirubhai was informed. The inside trading was not just in the affairs of Reliance Industries Ltd but also in the affairs of the Government of India.

His intervention went beyond information-gathering to the point of influencing or even controlling key bureaucratic appointments and thereby influencing policy or its interpretation. In many parts of India, government jobs have long been allocated by auction, the highest prices being fetched by those in revenue-raising and policing agencies where the opportunities for corruption are greater. In what was long regarded as the most debilitated state administration, that of Bihar, that auction was conducted more or less openly in a café in the main street of the capital, Patna. In New Delhi, police promotions and transfers were brokered for many years by a well-known city journalist.

In Bombay the competition was intense among the handful of senior bureaucrats with financial sector experience for the chairman-ships and chief executive positions of the government financial insti-tutions. Dhirubhai was active in the lobbying when the top posts fell vacant in the banks, insurance companies and statutory authorities. And as one old acquaintance noted, Dhirubhai would make a point of telephoning all candidates and assuring each one of his support. Even if it were not really decisive, the winner might be left thinking he owed his new job to Dhirubhai's backing.

Dhirubhai's most distinctive touch, however, was in his use of the press. Before him, G.D. Birla may have been equally master of the Licence Raj and keen to buy public and perhaps divine favour by the building of temples and colleges, but Birla disliked the press and never cared to mix with journalists – even though his family owned the *Hin-dustan Times*, one of India's strongest English-language newspapers.

Centuries of shielding their wealth from over-extended maharajas and nawabs, or from a hungry populace, had made India's merchants wary of ostentation and careful not to be seen to be overstepping their place in the social hierarchy. In more recent times, the Licence Raj had unleashed packs of inspectors against private wealth, and businessmen had become accustomed to being lectured by politicians and officials about the superiority of economic planning and directed investment.

Dhirubhai shared a certain contempt for the journalist. 'Throw some scraps to the street-dogs and crows before you feed yourself,' a family friend remembers him enjoining his sons Mukesh and Anil in the early days at Bhuleshwar. But he recognised how powerful the press could be in moulding the thinking of the public and the politicians.

The huge advertising expenditure of Reliance gave him an automatic hold over many of the less established newspapers and magazines. By the early 1980s the new technology of computerised composition and phototypesetting had led to an explosion of publishing in India, particularly in regional languages where it overcame the technical problems of complex scripts in an economical way. Gujarat was no exception to this. Advertising from Reliance was an important source of revenue for the Gujarati publications in Gujarat itself, Bombay and overseas.

Dhirubhai used his clout. The Gujarati columnist Kanti Bhatt remembered being called upon for help by a newspaper editor who had offended Reliance by printing a hostile paragraph, apparently fed by a rival Marwari-owned company. Reliance had immediately cancelled all advertisements. When he met Dhirubhai, Bhatt remembers him being furious, even throwing a telephone at one point. 'Mr Ambani called in his advertising manager and said: "Show me our advertising plans." Then he said to him: "Take out this particular newspaper." It meant a loss of Rs 600 000 a year for that newspaper.' After this charade, Bhatt went back to the editor and told him the message was that nothing could be written against Reliance if he wanted the ads. 'The next issue was damage control and a very long and favourable article was written,' Bhatt said. Advertising was restored. Later Bhatt was called in by Dhirubhai himself to find out why a Gujarati publication in Britain had suddenly begun printing a series of articles critical of Reliance. After talking to the publisher, Bhatt reported back: 'Sir, it is a plea for advertising.' The plea was answered and the articles stopped. 'You could multiply these examples by a million,' Bhatt said.

Dhirubhai could not wield the same power over the big metropolitan newspapers. But he could and did cultivate their journalists and editors. The Indian press tends to be like most of the other key institutions in the country: free, but in many parts corrupt except at the very top. Bombay's lowly paid financial journalists were used to receiving gifts from businessmen wanting publicity, and their proprietors are happy to have their salary bill subsidised in this way. Press conferences were followed by buffet meals and drinks and envelopes containing cash or gift vouchers handed around by public relations officers on the way out. The envelope system flourished most intensely during bull runs on the stock exchange when new company floats and issues have come thick and fast, and even a paragraph in a big English-language newspaper means recognition for a new company promoter. In Paris, waiters are known to pay the proprietors of certain fashionable restaurants for the privilege of being able to wait at the tables and collect tips. In Bombay some would-be business correspondents are willing to eschew salary altogether or even offer a monthly fee to the newspaper in return for being accredited as its reporter.

Reliance was a pioneer of envelope journalism. A senior commercial journalist in Bombay recalled that journalists would get vouchers worth up to Rs 2000 for goods at a Vimal shop called Laffans. Some in senior positions would get regular monthly payments, or issues of Reliance shares and debentures at par. 'Ambani's moles in the press were known as the "Dirty Dozen",' the journalist said. 'The point man was Rasikbhai Meswani. He was a thorough gentleman. His door was open twenty-four hours a day for journalists. People would go to collect on first of the month.'

Dhirubhai also realised that the reporter was not the final arbiter of what was published. He also cultivated desk editors and even editors. One who accepted Reliance debentures for himself, and help in arranging bank finance to pay for them, was Girilal Jain, editor of the *Times of India* for much of the 1980s.

The close journalists in the 'Dirty Dozen' would not only be used to get favourable news about Reliance printed prominently. They also became an extension of Dhirubhai's intelligence network, asking rival businessmen for their frank views 'off the record' about Reliance, then reporting them back. On the theory that rumour and gossip are more keenly heeded because they carry an aura of exclusivity, the pressmen would be used to plant opinions about the merits of Reliance activities and the failings of other companies. Occasionally the journalistic network would turn up details of illlegal or embarrassing activities by rivals that could be used to obtain peace or, failing that, turned over to authorities for punitive action or harassing investigation.

Many of the journalists regarded by their colleagues as being in the Reliance pocket would indignantly deny being bought. Indeed, some would have simply fallen for the perennial trap of getting too close to a source that had given them many good stories – then having too much friendship or ego involved to admit any negative news. And especially for the news magazines that were the liveliest and fastest-growing section of the Indian media in the 1980s – the last decade before privately owned television arrived with satellite broadcasts – Dhirubhai and Reliance were a colourful and fast-changing story. It was a highly effective image-making operation. But, perhaps inevitably, some accidental slips allowed the public glimpses of Dhirubhai's secret manoeuvres.

The opening developed in 1983 when Finance minister Pranab Mukherjee began giving some details in parliament to the response by non-resident Indians to the new sharemarket investment rules he had announced in his first budget, in February 1982. Previously NRIs had been allowed to make portfolio investments in Indian shares but were not allowed to repatriate their funds. The new system allowed NRIs, or companies and trusts owned at least 60 per cent by NRIs, to put money directly into Indian shares and to repatriate funds after selling their shares. It was implemented by the Reserve Bank of India in April that year – just as Dhirubhai was marshalling his response to the bear attack on his share price.

In a written answer, tabled on 10 May 1983, Mukherjee said that between April 1982 and April 1983, eleven overseas Indians had purchased shares and debentures worth a total Rs 225.2 million (then about $22.5 million) in two Indian companies. It was widely believed that the two companies were Escorts and DCM, targets of the raider Swraj Paul. On 16 May 1983, however, the *Business Standard* reported that in fact all the investments had been made in one company, Reliance, by investment companies overseas. 'It is believed that all these investment companies belong to Mr Dhirubhai Ambani himself, the promoter of Reliance Textiles.'

Answering questions from the left-wing opposition figure Professor Madhu Dandavate on 26 July, Mukherjee listed the eleven companies allowed to invest in Reliance, all of which he said were companies registered in the United Kingdom. Among the conventional names, two of the eleven stuck out for their cheekiness: Crocodile Investments and Fiasco Investments. The investments in Reliance accounted for 98 per cent of all investments made by NRIs under the new scheme – suggesting to critics that here was yet another policy tailor-made for Dhirubhai.

The tantalising dues were taken up by the Calcutta-based *Telegraph*, whose reporters found on 16 September that the companies named did not exist. Two months later, on 16 November, the *Telegraph* found that eight of the eleven named companies had appeared in the UK registry – but that the applications to register had not been lodged until 27 July 1983, the day after Mukherjee's reply in the Indian parliament. All were made through one channel, on the instructions of a single client.

On 22 November, just as parliament was about to rise for a week, Mukherjee tabled a correction to his 26 July reply: the companies were actually registered in the Isle of Man, the small island community in the Irish Sea. Mukherjee could have said he was technically right: the island is a British protectorate and part of the United Kingdom. But like the Channel Islands between Britain and France, it has its own tax laws and derives much of its income from providing tax shelters for foreigners.

Editorials asked how closely the central bank had scrutinised the eligibility of the eleven companies under the NRI scheme if the Finance minister could not even get their domicile right. 'Pranab Mukherjee: Minister of Finance or Reliance?' went the headline in the *Telegraph*'s editorial. On 14 December Mukherjee insisted that the different place of incorporation 'did not make any material difference' to eligibility and appealed to MPs not to 'kill the scheme'. The RBI had seen certified statements about the majority shareholders, but their identities could not be revealed on grounds of banker–client confidentiality. If 'black money' was being laundered through the NRI scheme, there were other laws to take care of it.

The press soon followed up the Isle of Man clue. In January 1984 it was revealed that company searches showed the eleven companies had been registered between 1979 and July 1982, initially with various English names as directors. In July 1982 the ownership and directors had changed: suddenly 60 to 80 per cent of the share capital in each company belonged to people with Indian names, mostly with the surname Shah. In ten of the eleven companies, common directors were two accountants domiciled in the Channel Island of Sark, Trevor Donnelly and his son John Donnelly, both well-known 'facilitators' believed to hold thousands of directorships in holding companies in various tax havens around the world.

In eight of the companies, the biggest shareholders were found to be one Krishna Shah, a resident of the English Midlands city of Leicester, and his family. In five companies, a couple called Praful and Nalini Shah, living in Flushing, New York, were directors. Four companies had one or other of two residents of Djibouti, Chimanlal and Jyoti Dhamani, on their board. Only in one company, Tricot Investments, were Indian names not on the board.

A mystified *India Today* reported that Krishna Shah was a former Leicester city councillor, born in Kenya, who had come to Britain in 1959 and had worked since as a railway guard and small businessman. Shah told the magazine's reporter he knew nothing about any companies in the Isle of Man.

> Someone in the companies was remarkably well informed on investment conditions in India, however. On 20 August 1982, the RBI had lifted a Rs 100 000 ceiling on share investments in any one company by non-resident Indians. Three days later, three of the Isle of Man companies applied to the central bank to invest Rs 20 million each in Reliance. Four other companies applied together on 24 September. Six companies made their share purchases on the same day, 15 October, at the same share price, which was a significant discount to the then market price.
>
> While each company had paid-up capital of only £200, three of them had managed to talk the European Asian Bank to lend identical sums of $1.65 million to each, through the bank's branch in Colombo, Sri Lanka, on 26 October 1982. All three bought Reliance shares at the same price, Rs 128.[4]

It was a sound piece of investigation, but no link with Dhirubhai had been found and many questions remained unanswered. Had the reporters spread their questions wider in the Gujarati diaspora, they might have discovered a very old connection. The leading name in Crocodile, Fiasco et al. was the same Krishna Kant Shah and fellow student activist whom Dhirubhai had helped spring from jail after the 1947 communal riot in Junagadh. After finishing his education, Shah had gone back to join the family business in Kenya. In 1959 he moved to Britain on his own, working for an engineering company for two years, then as a railway guard for eight years. In 1970 he quit British Rail and set up his own shop in Leicester's Hartingdon Road, selling hardware, saris, utensils and religious statues, and living in a flat upstairs.

His customer base was the fellow Gujaratis then congregating in Leicester after their expulsion from Uganda by Idi Amin at forty-eight hours notice in 1972 and the more gradual squeeze out of Kenya by Jomo Kenyatta's 'Africanisation' of commerce. By the mid-1990s about a quarter of the city's 400 000 population were immigrants, about 80 000 of them South Asian. Almost all the 65 000 Hindus were Gujarati. Shah was not very interested in making money from his fellow immigrants. Instead he sought their votes. In 1973 he got himself elected to the Leicester City Council, becoming the first South Asian on a city council in Britain, and served for ten years. 'He was not a great businessman,' recalls S.B. Khandelwal, proprietor of the Sari Mandir emporium in the city. 'He would often close up shop early to go on council business.'

Clearly Shah did not have millions of dollars to put into Reliance shares, or the financial knowledge to set up elaborate ownership arrangements through the Isle of Man, where he had never been, or to take out loans from a foreign bank in Sri Lanka to finance the purchase of shares in India through an Isle of Man company. He had, however, kept in touch with Dhirubhai, and his wife Induben had become a friend of Dhirubhai's wife Kokilaben. On trips to buy textile machinery in Britain, Dhirubhai would take Shah along, while Shah introduced Reliance's export manager Rathibhai Muchhala to many of the South Asian retailers in Leicester. In 1972 Dhirubhai brought his wife and children to Britain for a holiday, and the two families spent some time together. Later that year Shah's oldest son Sailash, who had just completed a diploma in textile manufacturing, went to a job at the Reliance factory in Naroda, where he stayed five years before returning to Leicester to help his father set up a new knitwear business. In 1977 Dhirubhai provided two cars for Sailash's wedding.

Krishna Kant Shah died in 1986, in the midst of a fresh controversy about the mysterious Isle of Man companies. At a meeting in 1995 Sailash Shah maintained that there had been no business connection between his father and Dhirubhai. Asked how it was that the Indian press and investigators had singled out his family as Dhirubhai's fronts, he would say only, 'I don't know how.'

That Dhirubhai did have a connection with the Isle of Man was indicated by the appearance in India during the mid-1990s of one Peter Henwood. An accountant running a company on the Isle of Man, Henwood had been instrumental during the 1980s in arranging layers of ownership for Dhirubhai's offshore holdings through several tax havens. Dhirubhai had become close to Henwood and his attractive wife, on whom he showered expensive gifts. Much later, Henwood tried to market his services to other Indian businessmen. Dhirubhai became alarmed and had Henwood followed on his visits to India. To protect his business interests, Henwood consulted a leading firm of lawyers in India.

Over the years 1982 to 1984 Dhirubhai also met problems within the 'Reliance family'. In 1982 junior office staff in Bombay petitioned the Reliance management about low salaries and being obliged to work long hours and on holidays without overtime pay. Then they attempted to join a trade union, the Mumbai Mazdoor Sabha run by R.J. Mehta. Some 350 were dismissed without notice, ostensibly on grounds of a 'reorganisalion', while others were transferred to Reliance offices in Gujarat. The dismissed workers said goondas (hired thugs) had beaten up one activist, and a deputy personnel manager had waved a pistol at a typist.

In December 1983 Dhirubhai had hosted a special lunch for all his 12 000 factory staff at Naroda to celebrate the wedding of his daughter Dipti to Dattaraj Salgaocar, the heir to a prosperous iron ore mine in Goa. It was a love match – Raj Salgaocar had been staying in the same apartment building in Bombay's Altamount Road as the Ambanis when he met Dipti – but a prestigious one for Dhirubhai, just as he had emerged as a tycoon himself.

The *bonhomie* at the wedding covered some mixed feelings on the factory floor. The Naroda workforce was seething. Within a few months, the textile hands were agitating for a wage increase, payment of overtime and removal of contract labour. Dhirubhai effectively nudged aside his elder brother Rainnikbhai from management of Naroda and put his younger son Anil in charge. In August 1984 the company suspended 160 of its workers and announced formation of a company union, the Reliance Parivar Pratinidhi Sabha (Reliance Family Representative Union), including 6700 workers and 1800 staff. 'The concept of unions has no place in our set-up,' the company's personnel manager told a newspaper. 'We believe in participative management.' Agitation continued within the plant. On the morning of 25 August the company announced suddenly that work was stopping and the plant was closed. Squads of Gujarat police waiting at the gate stormed in and charged the protestors with lathis (long wooden staves) and tear gas.[5]

Dhirubhai rode out this episode, but with regret. Not only had he lost the earlier affinity with his factory workforce but also arguments between Ramnikbhai Ambani and Anil had induced Dhirubhai's elder brother to distance himself from the company's operations.[6]

The blazing success as Dhirubhai proceeded to his triumphant general meeting in May 1985 carried some dark shadows. Many of those who opposed him had been crushed in ruthless displays of the state power he could manipulate: the police lathis and tear gas that fell on his own workers, the tariff changes and tax raids that hit his business rivals, or the ignominious transfers given to civil servants who held up his plans.

The opposition parties had been alerted to his connections with the ruling Congress Party and Indira Gandhi's office. The very resistance met by any query about Reliance only encouraged opposition politicians, including Janata's Madhu Dandavate and the Bharatiya Janata Party's Jaswant Singh, to press harder. Dhirubhai had a growing list of critics and enemies to feed them questions. It required only a sudden removal of his high-level protection for his complex fast-growth operation to be dangerously exposed.

8

The great
polyester war

On 23 November 1985 Bombay's sensation-seeking weekly tabloid *Blitz* came out with a cover story that soon had more than the usual crowds browsing at the newsstands. 'BIG 3 IN MAHAPOLY-ESTER WAR,' shouted the front-page headline. 'It's a Mahabharata War or rather, Mahapolyester War – in Indian big business style,' began a lengthy report that took up the whole of the front page and spilled into two full inside pages. 'There are only Kauravas, no Pandavas and no Lord Krishna. The reason is that none is without blemish. The fight is neither for inheriting the earth nor the heaven, but for one of the most lucrative industrial markets – that is, polyester filament yarn, where profits soar around Rs 80 to Rs 100 per kg.' Not only that, *Blitz* told readers in a front-page subheading: 'The Mahapolyester War goes beyond the industry to apocryphal stories involving serious political repercussions. According to New Delhi's grapevine, the old Pranab–Dhawan–Ambani axis responsible for Reliance's booming fortunes is currently reorganising its scattered forces with V.P. Singh, the Finance minister, as its principal target.'

Pictured as contestants in this dark war without heroes were Dhirubhai along with two competing textile magnates: Kapal Mehra of Orkay Silk Mills and Nusli Wadia of Bombay Dyeing. 'Among these Kauravas fighting each other, Reliance (Dhirubhai Ambani) and Orkay (Kapal Mehra) are the principal combatants, with Bombay Dyeing (Nusli Wadia) on the sidelines. Thanks to Reliance and its vast patronage and money power, Orkay got the wrong end of the sword, with the result that the patriarch of the family spent Diwali in jail after five attempts to bail him out had failed.'

Blitz's editor, Russy Karanjia, was right that a corporate war was about to spill over into politics. But his article was wrong about the main battle. Kapal Mehra had just spent fifteen days in jail over Diwali, the festival of lights that marks the new year in the Hindu calendar. He was facing massive penalties on charges of evading excise and customs duty. Earlier, his son had been abducted near Orkay's Patalganga factory, beaten up and dumped in a drainage ditch some miles away. Mehra was already knocked out of the combat.

In the bigger fight just warming up, Nusli Wadia was Dhirubhai's opposing gladiator. And while Wadia was bleeding, Dhirubhai was on the back foot. Things had started to go badly wrong for him in the second half of 1985. But *Blitz* was correct in painting this fight over a mundane textile and its chemical ingredients with the colours of an epic. It went on for years, reached to highest levels of politics, dragged in some of India's best talents, sullied some of them and made heroes of others and caused governments to fall. Far from being a tabloid beat-up, the Mahabharata Polyester War was central to Indian politics, for critical years in the 1980s – to the point where one former minister in the central government could state, with only a little exaggeration: 'The course of Indian politics is decided by the price of DMT [dimethyl terephthalate].'[1]

According to stories put out by Reliance sympathisers over the years, the war began with a snub. Back in the late 1960s and early 1970s, the social gap between Dhirubhai and Nusli Wadia could not have been much wider for two people in the same industry. Dhirubhai was a paan-chewing trader roaming from client to client in Pydhonie to sell his polyester and nylon yarns, flashy in personal tastes and with a small-town Gujarati social background.

In Bombay Nusli Wadia was Establishment. The Wadia family were Parsi, followers of the ancient Zoroastrian religion in Persia who had fled to the west coast of India in the tenth century AD to escape forcible conversion to Islam. In the eighteenth century, the Wadias had become shipbuilders to the East India Company in Surat. When British commerce shifted to Bombay the Wadias followed and joined India's first wave of modern industrialisation. In 1879 they set up Bombay Dyeing and Manufacturing Co., which moved from dyeing of cotton yarn into spinning the yarn, then into the weaving of cotton textiles. Under Nusli Wadia's father, Neville Wadia, chairman between 1952 and 1977, the company continued to modernise and became one of India's largest textile manufacturers and exporters.

Like many Parsi families, they adopted English ways in speech, dress and social behaviour. The Parsis have long been a cosmopolitan element in Bombay, and intermarriage with members of other Indian communities or foreigners was common. Neville Wadia had married the daughter of Mohammad Ali Jinnah, leader of the Muslim League in pre-independence India. Nusli Wadia had been born with all the advantages and had been educated at schools in Britain. Like his father, Nusli held British citizenship and travelled widely. As Dhirubhai was beginning his climb up from the yarn market, Nusli had just returned to join the family business. He was in his mid-twenties – some twelve years younger than Dhirubhai – handsome in an acquiline way, dressed in quiet but classic English fashion and always cuttingly direct in his impeccable English.

The Parsis, like many colonial elites, went through a crisis of self-esteem when the colonial power went home without them. Their own self-image became one of failure, eccentricity and emasculation. The younger Wadia was the great exception. He was anything but inclined to relax and live off inherited wealth. In 1971 his father wanted to sell the company and retire abroad. Nusli Wadia, then 26, enlisted the support of J.R.D. Tata to help in a shareholders' battle against the sale and rallied 700 employees in an offer of a staff buy-out of some shares. His father dropped the sale and, after handing the company over to Nusli in 1977, settled in Switzerland.

It was the first of many battles in which Nusli Wadia showed his remarkable fighting capacity when he felt his own vital interests, or those of friends who sought his help, to be under threat. Wadia was never inclined to take a public stage. He did not join business associations or appear constantly at conferences and seminars like many other big businessmen, or host lavish parties in hotels. He avoided the press. But he developed a wide circle of friends and contacts who came to appreciate his fearless advice. Among them were tycoons many years his senior, like Tata and later the press baron Ramnath Goenka of the *Indian Express*.

The Ambani version of the snub is that Wadia simply refused to buy C. Itoh & Co.'s yarn from Dhirubhai, for reasons that have not been explained. Another variation is that Wadia kept Dhirubhai cooling his heels in the corridors of Bombay Dyeing.

A more elaborate version is that Dhirubhai called on Wadia at Neville House during the early 1970s and made a presentation about the superior quality of his C. Itoh yarn. Wadia questioned the backing for this claim, whereupon Dhirubhai pulled out a copy of a test report made by Bombay Dyeing's own laboratory for internal company use. Wadia, according to this version, told Dhirubhai that next he would find Reliance telling his laboratory what to report and that he would not deal with him.[2]

Dhirubhai did not mention this incident, and Wadia has told inquirers he has no memory of it or any other such encounter with Dhirubhai, although he could not completely exclude it as a possibility. Whatever the case, Dhirubhai clearly felt put down and, according to many later articles by friendly writers, nursed the hope that one day he would have Wadia coming to him as a supplicant. The industrial rivalry developed after Wadia took over from his father at Bombay Dyeing and started moves to get the old cotton mill directly into the polyester production chain. In 1978 Bombay Dyeing applied to New Delhi for a licence to set up a DMT plant, and in December that year it received a 'letter of intent' (a preliminary approval) for a 60 000-tonne-a-year DMT plant to be located at Patalganga. It was a move that would have leapfrogged Bombay Dyeing past Reliance up the petrochemical chain. At the time, Dhirubhai was just moving towards applying for a licence to make polyester yarn, using DMT as his initial feedstock. Bombay Dyeing would have become one of only three domestic sources of the chemical. Wadia would have been in a position to apply Dhirubhai's own trick of calling down higher tariff protection and then squeezing a bigger profit out of dependent clients – who would include the new Reliance plant.

Although he was not close to the Prime Minister, Morarji Desai, Nusli Wadia had a good image with the Janata government. The Scindia family, one of the great Maratha ruling families and hereditary maharajas of Gwalior in central India, had had a business relationship with the Wadias through an investment company that gave them indirectly a minor shareholding in Bombay Dyeing. Madhavrao Scindia, the cricket-playing scion of the family, had entered parliament with the Jana Sangh before crossing to Congress, where he later flourished as a minister.

But as the months wore on in 1979, nothing happened with Bombay Dyeing's licence, which normally followed about six months after the letter of intent. Then the Janata government fell and new elections were called. Not long before the vote, Wadia received an invitation to come to New Delhi late in 1979 to meet Indira Gandhi and her son Sanjay He arrived in the capital with some presentation copies of Bombay Dyeing's new corporate history marking its centenary year, which he felt might be of interest particularly as Gandhi's late husband, Firoze Gandhi, had also been a Parsi.

Wadia was directed first to meet Sanjay Gandhi, who made a blunt demand for a political donation. Wadia demurred. 'Sorry, we just don't do that,' he said. 'None of us – the Tatas, the Mahindras, us – give money to political parties. We do not have black income. It's just not something we do.' On being shown in to Indira Gandhi and having presented the company history Wadia broke the subject directly. He knew the reason he had been summoned, but really it was not the way his company operated. He talked on, then noticed Indira was doodling on papers on her desk, looking away. Wadia took his leave and received a curt nod from Indira.

Two or three months after the Congress win in early January 1980, Wadia again received a call to New Delhi from Sanjay Gandhi. Having endured imprisonment and sustained invective for his Emergency excesses during the Janata period, Sanjay was now even more firmly ensconced as Indira's Crown Prince.

'From being a wielder of authority delegated to him by his mother, he had now become her partner in power,' wrote the commentator Inder Malhotra. 'At this time Sanjay's power was at its zenith and practically irresistible.'[3]

'You lied,' Sanjay greeted Wadia. 'Tata and Mahindra have paid.' This was almost certainly a bluff. Mahindra, well-established maker of Jeeps and other vehicles and machinery, and Tata were unlikely to risk their reputations by illicit payments, certainly from their central managements. But many years later sources close to the Congress Party insisted that some contributions had indeed gone to Indira Gandhi from the Tata group's flagship, the Tata Iron and Steel Co. It was clear that Wadia would get his licence only one way.

A few months later, however, Sanjay Gandhi was abruptly removed from the scene. He had been accustomed to venting his energy by taking up a light aircraft for aerobatics over New Delhi. On the morning of 23 June 1980, the plane crashed into a wooded area in New Delhi, killing Sanjay instantly.

The state funeral was marked by excesses of sycophancy, although expressions of relief were voiced in many quarters all over India. Indira allowed a posthumous personality cult to be constructed around her late son until she realised that Sanjay's widow Maneka, whom she detested, would benefit. Hence Indira speeded up the political induction of her eldest son Rajiv, who had been working as a pilot with Indian Airlines and keeping out of the public eye as much as he could. Rajiv had strong misgivings about entering politics, and his Italian-born wife

Sonia opposed it, although she and Indira got on well. But at the end of 1980 Rajiv left his airline job and adopted the uniform of politics, the Indian kurta pyjama suit, to become his mother's principal secretary. In June 1981 Rajiv was elected to parliament from his brother's constituency and made a general secretary of the Congress Party at the end of the year.

It was to Rajiv Gandhi that Wadia turned for help to 'unblock' his licence, some months after Sanjay's death. Rajiv was sympathetic to his complaint. 'If injustice has been done to you, I will see that justice is done,' he promised. Some time later, they met again, and Rajiv said he was meeting extraordinary resistance to his inquiries, in particular from Indira's private secretary, R.K. Dhawan, and from the Congress member of parliament (later Home minister) P.C. Sethi. But Rajiv's efforts eventually succeeded, and in June 1981 Bombay Dyeing received its licence for the DMT plant – two and a half years after the letter of intent.

Wadia still met obstacles. Bombay Dyeing bought a DMT plant second-hand from an American company and had it dismantled and shipped to India in two consignments at the end of 1981. When the shipments arrived in Bombay the company could not get them cleared by customs for nearly four weeks. Bombay's Collector of Customs, S. Srinivasan, then ordered a rare 100 per cent inspection of all contents. On leaving the customs service some years later, Srinivasan was retained as an adviser by Reliance.

Dhirubhai continued to enjoy beneficial policy changes throughout the rest of Indira's second prime ministership, thanks to the influence of friends like Pranab Mukherjee and R.K. Dhawan. After the raising of duty on polyester yarn just after his Patalganga plant became operational, licences for expansion came promptly after lodgement of applications. In three months, August to October 1984, Reliance was given letters of intent approving the biggest single investment India had yet seen in artificial fibres: a 75 000-tonne-a-year purified terephthalic acid (PTA) plant at Patalganga, plus a 45 000-tonne-a-year polyester staple fibre plant and a 40 000-tonne-a-year monoethylene glycol plant. In addition, the *fait accompli* of its 25 25-tonne polyester filament yarn plant was retrospectively 'endorsed' by raising the permitted capacity from 12 000 tonnes.

The Reliance move into PTA production gave a big clue to the source of Bombay Dyeing's problems, as it showed that Dhirubhai was also moving up the petrochemical stream to establish himself as a rival feedstock supplier to the fast-growing polyester industry. At that stage, no one else was making PTA.

According to background notes circulated in 1985 by Reliance, Dhirubhai had already begun switching his Patalganga yarn plant over to PTA feedstock and had completed the conversion during the first quarter of 1984. At that point, the Petroleum Ministry and the Industry Ministry had been notified and Reliance cleared to import its requirements of PTA. Out of the thirteen polyester units then in production, four others also began to use PTA for part of their feedstock requirements.

As we have noted, PTA was a substitute feedstock for DMT in the production of polyester. Both are usually made from the chemical para-xylene, which in turn is produced by 'cracking' the flammable liquid hydrocarbon naphtha, found in natural gas and petroleum liquids. Each feedstock had its advantages and disadvantages. DMT had been in use longer and needed less expensive containment vessels and piping in the plant, but in the polyester process it produced the toxic alcohol methanol as a by-product, for which a recovery system was needed. PTA required a more sophisticated purification process, corrosion-resistant equipment and more stringent control of catalyst mixing, but in polyester production gave a better yield to the paraxylene and MEG inputs. In practice, most polyester fibre plants were able to use either DMT or PTA with minor adjustments that could be made within a few months.

The licensing delays added to the cost of Bombay Dyeing's DMT plant, and it took Wadia more than three years to get it reconstructed and operational at Patalganga. But when it started production in April 1985 it was still a low-cost entry into a product that became the mainstay of Bombay Dyeing's sound profitability through to the late 1990s.

Until then, the only domestic supplier of DMT was government-owned Indian Petrochemicals, which made 30 000 tonnes a year against an estimated demand of 80 000 tonnes of DMT/PTA by Indian polyester producers in 1984. By the end of 1985 polyester output was expected to jump to about 150 000 tonnes, requiring 160 000 tonnes of either DMT or PTA. From April 1985 Bombay Dyeing would be well placed to capture this market, in competition with Indian Petrochemicals and with the other government-owned producer, Bongaigaon Refinery and Petrochemicals, which began its 45 000-tonne-a-year production in July 1985. But if Reliance started using PTA and managed to persuade many other polyester producers to do the same, the new DMT capacity risked redundancy.

As Wadia got his plant into operation in 1985, he encountered a sustained stream of press commentary describing his second-hand DMT plant as 'junk' and DMT itself as an 'obsolete' feedstock that would soon give way to the 'more modern' PTA. Many of these comments appeared under the bylines of those journalists who later became known as core members of the Reliance 'Dirty Dozen'.

Dhirubhai, as we have seen, was then in his most triumphant phase in the eyes of his investor public. But his political support had been drastically undercut, although it was not to become evident until later in 1985, when the struggle for supremacy in the polyester industry became a more evenly balanced, tooth-and-nail fight.

The cause was another violent death in the Gandhi family. At the beginning of June 1984 Indira Gandhi had ordered the Indian army into the Golden Temple in Amritsar, the holiest temple of the Sikh religion, to clear out the Sikh fundamentalist Bhindranwale. Eventually the army used tanks and artillery to subdue Bhindranwale's well-fortified rebels. The Golden Temple itself was damaged and important adjoining buildings destroyed. Sikhs felt their holiest shrine had been defiled by violence. On the morning of 31 October 1985 Indira walked into her garden and was shot at close range by two Sikhs in her bodyguard.

Rajiv was sworn in as Prime Minister later the same day by the President, Giani Zail Singh, and confirmed by the Congress Party soon after Indira's funeral. Elections were due early in 1985 on the expiry of Indira's five-year mandate in any case; Rajiv brought them forward to early December and received the benefit of a massive sympathy wave, lifting the Congress share of the vote to 49.1 per cent (from 42.3 per cent in December 1979) and winning an unpredented 401 seats (soon boosted to 415 in by-elections) out of the 545 in the Lok Sabha.

Despite his affection for his mother, Rajiv had been distant long enough from Congress circles to pick up the deep resentment on the part of many Indians at the pervasive corruption she had engendered. But for the sympathy vote, Congress might even have lost the elections, had its diverse opponents worked together. Rajiv was also aware of how new technology was helping to sweep aside regulatory regimes and empower individuals elsewhere in the world. He decided India and its politics needed to be opened up. But an element of hubris quickly crept in as well: Rajiv soon came to believe that the sympathy vote was actually enthusiasm for himself and his barely understood policies.

Among the first casualties were key friends of Dhirubhai. Rajiv sacked R.K. Dhawan from the Prime Minister's office within hours of his appointment. And in his first cabinet he replaced Pranab Mukherjee as Finance minister with V.P. Singh, a choice that was eventually to bring down the heavens both on Dhirubhai and on Rajiv himself.

Vishwanath Pratap Singh was to become one of India's most controversial politicians. He inspired enormous trust and hope in some sections of society, intense hatred as an opportunist and class traitor in others, and ultimately a lot of disappointment and disillusionment. The adopted son of a childless rajah in Uttar Pradesh, Singh had studied law and later physics with an eye to joining India's atomic energy research centre in Bombay, but settled on politics at the age of 38, when he won a Congress ticket to stand for the Uttar Pradesh state assembly. In the Emergency he stood by Indira and Sanjay and on Indira's return was installed as UP's chief minister. He was efficient and honest, but attracted most notice by giving police informal powers of summary justice to deal with the banditry sweeping the state. About 2000 alleged criminals died in 'encounters' with police. It was a sample of the ruthlessness Singh could show. But it was counterposed with a diffident streak to his character. A dabbler in painting and poetry, Singh often withdrew into himself. At critical moments, he would hesitate to commit. His most heroic roles were forced upon him.[4]

As Rajiv's Finance minister, Singh applied a carrot-and-stick approach to taxation. In his first budget, at the end of February 1985 for the year starting 1 April, Singh slashed income tax rates and wealth tax and abolished death duty. Industrial licensing laws were also relaxed and investment approvals streamlined. This new wave of reform sparked a stockmarket boom.

But business circles were less happy from mid-year when Singh began applying his second budget promise. The counterpart of lower tax rates, he had warned, would be stricter enforcement. The agencies under the Ministry of Finance that police the economic laws began raids on and inspections of some of India's best-known business houses for allegedly evading excise, concealing income or keeping funds off-shore. No one felt safe from Singh's inspectors.

Rajiv's new broom was also sweeping closer to Dhirubhai. As his DMT plant moved closer to production, Nusli Wadia had been lobbying hard for greater protection against imports of DMT and PTA. In particular, he argued that trade policy should support the big investment in domestic DMT capacity by Bombay Dyeing and the two state producers. Allowing a switch to PTA meant a loss of foreign exchange on imports that could be substituted domestically. The Petroleum Ministry was sympathetic to the argument that PTA imports should not be given any advantage, and recommended on 16 May 1985 that imports should be approved only after verification that domestic competitors were not damaged, as was already the case with DMT imports.

Thus, as Dhirubhai was holding his open-air shareholders' meeting in Bombay on 20 May 1985, the government was moving towards a decision that would have a drastic effect on Reliance's production and possibly force it to use DMT from Nusli Wadia's DMT plant. On 29 May the government announced that PTA was placed on the controlled import list with immediate effect.

Dhirubhai was not worried. For a ninety-day grace period from 29 May the government said it would allow those PTA imports for which irrevocable letters of credit had been opened against firm contracts by 29 May. It emerged that, by the time of the notification on that date,

Reliance had opened such letters of credit for 114 000 tonnes of PTA – more than enough to supply its existing and planned polyester capacity through to the opening of its own PTA plant expected at the end of 1986. Moreover, the letters of credit had been opened in a burst of frenetic activity with several banks over 27–29 May up to a few hours before the import policy change was announced. One revolving credit from Canara Bank for 2000 tonnes of PTA a month up to 30 June 1985 had been enhanced on 29 May itself to pay for 12 000 tonnes and the shipment date extended to 30 June 1986. Letters of credit were taken out also with three foreign banks on contracts signed some months earlier, for a further 42 000 tonnes.

On 27 May Reliance had got an entirely new contract for 50 000 tonnes of PTA registered with the Petroleum Ministry in New Delhi and covered the same day by letters of credit from three overseas banks at their Bombay offices. The Exchange Control Manual for banks in India required importers to submit original copies of registered contracts before letters of credit could be opened. Getting this all done during office hours in one day between New Delhi and Bombay seemed a miracle of logistics.

The government was unhappy to learn that its policy change to protect the domestic DMT industry had been so stunningly thwarted. It was even angrier as it learnt the details of the three-day Reliance rush to open letters of credit, suggesting the possibility that the pending policy change had been leaked to the company. Authorities told Reliance that the ninety-day grace period would be enforced: all the 114 000 tonnes of PTA would have to be landed by 30 September.

Fourteen thousand tonnes having arrived, Reliance took the government to court about the remaining 100 000 tonnes, arguing that the cut-off date was arbitrary and in violation of the implicit three-year guarantee of stability in import policies before 29 May. It also argued that it had 'switched over' to PTA and that to go back to DMT as a feed-stock would require 'crores of rupees' (one crore equals 10 million) plus new equipment and take 'several months'.

A single judge in the Bombay High Court awarded Reliance a 'stay' on the government's decision and authorised the company to import 5000 tonnes, which were already available for shipment. For the remaining 95 000 tonnes, the company should approach the government for a supplementary licence – on which the government should decide by 31 October, failing which Reliance could revert to the court for further interim relief.

The government appealed against this order to a more senior bench of two judges in the High Court. While waiting a hearing, the import duty on DMT and PTA was raised a further 50 percentage points to a total of 190 per cent. This did not deter Dhirubhai, as international market prices of the two feedstocks were falling rapidly. In court on 28 October the government argued against the clearance of the 5000 tonnes permitted by the lower court and for removal of the 31 October deadline for the remaining 95 000 tonnes. The bench dismissed the appeal, but agreed to stay clearance of the 5000 tonnes – the shipment was due in Bombay the next day – for seven days to allow the government to appeal to the Supreme Court.

This the government did. On 4 November the Supreme Court decided to allow Reliance to clear the 5000 tonnes of PTA but not to use it pending settlement. The government was given three weeks to make its case and Reliance a week after that to respond, with the High Court to make a final decision during December.

In the background of the litigation, Reliance kept feeding the press with accounts of the allegedly unacceptable quality of Bombay Dyeing's DMT, made at its 'second-hand plant'. A small polyester producer called Swadeshi Polytex had told the Industry Ministry's

Director-General of Technical Development about alleged defects in a 68-tonne DMT shipment from Bombay Dyeing: sacks supposed to contain DMT pellets were 20 to 80 per cent powder, black particles were found in the pellets, bits of thread, metal and wood were found in the bags and so on. The picture painted was of Bombay Dyeing pumping out filth from a wheezing, obsolete plant and angling for massive protection so it could jack up prices to struggling yarn-makers.

The lobbying and propaganda war became frenetic in early November. Reliance issued press notes that played up the cost and difficulty of switching polyester plants back from PTA to DMT: it was like modifying a diesel engine to run on petrol; the modification would involve 'huge expenditure' and take nine to twelve months. Another note put the investment at Rs 58.6 million (then about $4.6 million) and the time at twelve to fifteen months. If Reliance could not get its PTA, work would stop, with huge numbers of workers being laid off. On 2 November another polyester producer J.K. Synthetics actually announced it was suspending production at its plant in Kota because it was unable to get an import licence for PTA.

The private war got dirtier. According to the tabloid *Blitz*, two 'campaign briefs' were circulated by the Reliance office in New Delhi among MPs, officials and others. Orkay was accused of pledging the same stock with banks several times to get loans, issuing bogus bills, claiming tax rebates on non-existent production and under-invoicing imports of polyester chips to evade duty.

With his earlier excise evasion case still being heard, Orkay Silk Mills's Mehra was arrested on 1 November 1985 on another charge. He had allegedly evaded Rs 15 million in duty on polyester chip imports in 1982 and 1983, by under-invoicing the imports from C. Itoh & Co. in Japan, according to 'voluminous documentary evidence' collected by the Directorate of Revenue Intelligence 'from Japan' a few days earlier.

Mehra had bought the material 7.5 per cent below the regular price: evidence of 'under-invoicing' according to the policers, just a 'trade discount' according to Mehra.

Mehra's counsel, Ram Jethmalani, said a 'rival tycoon' had instigated the raids to sabotage a share issue financing Orkay's expansion. Later it was noted that Dhirubhai had been in Japan not long before, visiting among others C. Itoh & Co., which had been accustomed to giving Reliance a 20 per cent discount on polyester yarn sales. Whatever the case, Mehra spent fifteen days in jail before obtaining bail – missing the Diwali festivities – and for years was contesting claims for evaded excise and duty and personal fines.

The other target of the Reliance 'briefs' was Bombay Dyeing. It had been getting import policy on PTA and DMT changed to help it out of the 'total mess' created by its decision to buy a DMT plant originally built in 1953. The 1977 price of Rs 300 million had ballooned to nearly Rs 1 billion by the time it was reassembled. 'What else can be expected from a junk [sic]?' the Reliance note said.[5] Wadia also came under personal attack: a story put out by the newsagency United News of India quoted 'official sources' alleging Wadia and his wife were involved in a 'fraudulent' deal to sell land belonging to a Parsi trust of which they were trustees.[6]

But Dhirubhai was now fighting on two new fronts, as well as the legal battle for his PTA imports. On 26 October newspapers had begun reporting that the Central Bureau of Investigation – New Delhi's highest criminal investigation body, which deals principally with corruption cases – had begun inquiries into the possible leak of the decision to put PTA on the restricted import list in May. A few days later Finance minister V.P. Singh denied that he had ordered any inquiry, but newspapers reported moves at official level for an investigation in concerned ministries, including Finance.

For its part, Reliance said it was not aware of being under investigation and put out lengthy written explanations as to why its import contracts in May had coincidentally preceded the policy change. The 50 000-tonne PTA contract approved by the Petroleum Ministry on 27 May had been submitted to it on 14 May. The quantities it sought to import were not in excess of its own use over the eighteen months until its own PTA plant opened, nor could Reliance conceivably hope to evade the September duty hike. Reliance was a victim of 'mischievous propaganda' – the allegations were based on 'tailored facts and twisted information circulated by vested interests too obvious to name'.

On 29 October, however, Reliance took another blow which showed conclusively that the Finance Ministry was no longer a friend. On that day the Assistant Collector of Central Excise at Kalyan, covering Patalganga, presented the company with a 'show-cause' notice claiming that Reliance had evaded a total of Rs 272.34 million (then about $21.8 million) in excise on polyester production since October 1982 by under-reporting production and misdeclaring waste. Backed by nine pages of annexures giving the details of the polyester manufacturing process, the notice invited Reliance to argue why it should not be forced to pay the Rs 272.34 million, have its factory confiscated and pay an additional penalty for evasion. It was the biggest excise evasion charge in Indian corporate history and, even discounting the ambit nature of the Assistant Collector's proposed penalty, a big threat to the profit line in the Reliance results.

The company affected not to be worried. A press release on 15 November described the show-cause notice as 'routine' and noted that similar notices had been issued to other manufacturers in the Thane area. It was all part of a drive to raise revenue. The claim against Reliance was based on 'theoretical calculations and assumed technical information', the company said. 'The notice was issued in the normal course of business and the company would soon be filing a reply and expected no liability to arise out of the show-cause.'

But Dhirubhai was sweating. On 26 November it was revealed that a compromise on the PTA imports was being worked out. The government would allow actual users of PTA to import their own requirements for six months ahead, but would not allow existing users of DMT to switch over and import PTA. Meanwhile, the Bureau of Industrial Costs and Prices would commence a study of DMT costs, to help regulate prices so that domestic DMT had a cost advantage over imported PTA. The condition for Reliance getting import licences, it was suggested, was to drop its High Court action. It could hardly argue.

By this stage, too much corporate blood had been spilt for the dispute to be papered over and forgotten like so many controversies before. Kapal Mehra had been jailed and humiliated. Nusli Wadia, despite the tariff and quota protection given to domestic DMT producers, had been forced to close his new plant for months because of the feedstock glut that Dhirubhai had engineered by the PTA imports he had managed to get through and by the constant denigration of his product.

Dhirubhai had meanwhile lost his key lieutenant in charge of public relations and government contacts. On 30 August his nephew and Reliance director Rasikbhai Meswani had died suddenly. It took some years for other publicists and lobbyists to take his place. As 1985 drew to a close, Dhirubhai was being openly described as a monster threatening Indian democracy. *Blitz* observed: 'If the allegations against Dhirubhai Ambani and Reliance are proved, whether in the matter of evasion or in the alleged fraud of letters of credit opened with two foreign and three Indian banks for the import of PTA, then the conclusion becomes inescapable that, since 1969, a single industrialist had been literally dictating the government's textile and import policies and manoeuvring import rules to "kill" his rivals and maintain his lead in the market.'[7]

Although he had limited contact with V.P. Singh – confined to direct industrial concerns – Nusli Wadia had kept up his ties with Rajiv Gandhi and can be expected to have voiced similar concerns to those of *Blitz* about the impunity with which Reliance had operated.

At that point Rajiv was still fired with zeal to cleanse the Augean stables as well. When Congress Party delegates gathered in Bombay at the end of December to mark the centenary of the party's founding, Rajiv delivered a stinging attack on its corruption. On the backs of ordinary party workers rode the 'brokers of power and influence, who dispense patronage to convert a mass movement into a feudal oligarchy'. Rajiv attacked the legions of tax-dodgers in Indian companies and the 'government servants who do not uphold the law, who shield the guilty tax collectors who do not collect taxes but connive with those who cheat the state'. But industrial empires built on excessive protection, social irresponsibility, import orientation and corruption might not last long.[8]

The Mahabharata Polyester War had been lifted out of the factories of Patalganga and from the Pydhonie yarn market to the national arena.

9

The paper tiger

It was at this stage that the Polyester Mahabharata was joined by an entirely new set of combatants. It became a life-and-death struggle for Dhirubhai's company and the critical test of Rajiv Gandhi's efforts to clean up the Indian Government. Dhirubhai survived. Rajiv failed and lost power as a result.

The new element was 'Seth' (Master) Ramnath Goenka, the legendary Indian newspaper tycoon. From a Marwari trading background in Calcutta, Goenka had moved to the southern city of Madras in the 1920s – according to some accounts, at the instigation of his own family, as even they found him too hard to work with – and begun building up the chain of English-language newspapers put under a common *Indian Express* masthead in the 1950s. By 1985 the *Express* had India's biggest newspaper circulation, 670 000, from twelve regional editions.

Inclined to the Jana Sangh and critical of Congress, although never committed either way, Goenka was happiest in an opposition role, exposing cant and corruption. Like most Marwaris, Goenka was a strict vegetarian, but he did not shrink from drawing blood in print. In the 1950s he had employed Indira's husband Firoze Gandhi and encouraged his exposure of the Mundhra scandal. The *Express* had been one of the few newspapers to resist the censorship imposed by Indira during the Emergency and consequently had been put under all kinds of pressures, including a move to demolish its New Delhi buildings for alleged building code violations. Ultimately Indira had baulked at closing him down – some say because Goenka threatened to publish private papers of her late husband about their unhappy marriage.

In late 1985 Goenka was 81 and his health was starting to fail. But mentally he was still alert and combative. From his sparsely furnished penthouse on the twenty-fifth floor of Express Towers in Bombay Goenka intervened daily in editorial decisions on the *Express*, hiring and firing editors with great frequency He was far from reclusive, receiving a daily stream of visitors anxious to keep in his good books and flying frequently to New Delhi, where the *Express* had its own guesthouse.

Dhirubhai had been introduced to Goenka in the mid-1960s by Murli Deora, the yarn trader who was moving up in the city's Congress Party circles and later to become a member of parliament. Goenka had noted Dhirubhai as someone of promise, and thereafter the young Gujarati businessman made regular visits. Goenka was regarded as a family friend, addressed as 'Bappuji' (Grandfather) by the Ambani children. The *Express* frequently reported the controversies involving Reliance, but when protests were made Goenka seems to have placated Dhirubhai by explaining that his target was the Congress government.

Nusli Wadia also became a close friend and, as with the childless

J.R.D. Tata, became something of a son to the old Marwari. (Goenka's only son had died at an early age, depriving him of his only heir bearing the Goenka name.) Together with his wife, Wadia had got into a routine of having lunch or dinner at least once a month with Goenka. On one such occasion, around October 1985, Goenka asked Wadia how his business was going. Wadia made a noncommittal reply, but Maureen Wadia intervened and related the smear campaign against Bombay Dyeing in the press, including the *Express* group's own newspapers.

Goenka said little. But the next morning he arrived suddenly at Bombay Dyeing's head office, Neville House, across town in Ballard Estate and walked unannounced into Wadia's book-lined corner office. Goenka waved a file of press cuttings that were obviously planted information. The same morning his business newspaper, the *Financial Express*, had carried both an anti-Bombay Dyeing story and an editorial on the same subject. Goenka promised to crack down on the Reliance-sourced reports, both in the *Express* newspapers and in the national wire service run by the Press Trust of India (PTI), which he currently chaired.

But on 31 October the Press Trust put out a story based on a press statement by the Reliance public relations officer, Kirti Ambani, about the reports a few days earlier that Reliance was under CBI investigation over the PTA contracts in May. PTI quoted verbatim Kirti Ambani's statement: '… our enquiries reveal that there is no such CBI probe into the matter and that the whole issue is being motivated by a large private, textile company which also happens to be manufacturers of DMT. Our enquiries further reveal that this party is not in a position to dispose of its DMT and carry large stocks of about 5000 tonnes of DMT. The basic problem seems to be the quality of the said DMT.'

Goenka was outraged, especially when finding that Reliance had directly asked a PTI desk editor to run the press release against

Goenka's explicit orders. Goenka ordered a retraction and apology. On 1 November the PTI issued it: 'The Press Trust of India circulated yesterday a report based on a press release by Reliance Textile Industries Ltd, containing allegations against a reputable Bombay-based textile company. We did not verify the veracity of the allegations before issuing the report. We regret if the publication of the said report has caused any damage to the reputation of the party concerned.'

The old press baron took the issue up with Dhirubhai at their next meeting. According to two former confidants of Goenka, Dhirubhai admitted he used his influence to get a favourable press. 'I have one gold chappal [slipper] and one silver chappal,' he said, breezily. 'Depending who it is, I strike him with the gold chappal, or with the silver chappal.' (Another widely repeated version has Dhirubhai remarking: 'Everyone has his price.' He later denied saying this.)[1]

It was probably the most damaging blunder and misjudgement Dhirubhai made in his life. Goenka was outraged. He was already embarrassed enough by the ease with which Dhirubhai got his version of events into the *Express*. The inference he drew from the 'gold chappal, silver chappal' remark was that Dhirubhai saw no one, perhaps even Goenka himself, as being immune to his offers. It was just a matter of price. Goenka resolved to expose Dhirubhai, using all the resources and contacts at his disposal.

Alarmed at the unfavourable turn of government attitude and press coverage in November, Dhirubhai meanwhile made a desperate effort to restore himself to Goenka's favour and to head off Wadia's successful-looking campaign to have use of domestic DMT forced on the polyester manufacturers. One morning in December he telephoned Goenka and asked him to arrange an urgent meeting with Wadia in Goenka's presence so they could settle their disputes in an amicable way. Goenka called Wadia, who was reluctant. The old man persisted and called back in the afternoon to tell Wadia a meeting had been fixed in the *Express* penthouse for that evening. Left with little choice without causing offence, Wadia swallowed his misgivings and agreed to attend.

The three sat around a low table. According to one account, Dhirubhai did almost all the talking during the forty-five-minute meeting, proposing that Reliance and Bombay Dyeing carve up the polyester feedstock market between them or, alternatively, that Reliance help its rival to place its DMT. Goenka presided, taking off his sandals and resting his feet on the table. For long stretches of his monologue, Dhirubhai caressed the old man's feet.

At the close, Dhirubhai invited Wadia to the wedding of his second daughter Nina a few days later, then suddenly embraced the startled Bombay Dyeing chairman. 'So now we are friends?' he asked.

Wadia, highly embarrassed and still suspicious, mumbled a vague assent. Dhirubhai walked towards the elevator, then just as suddenly turned and prostrated himself on the floor facing Goenka. Then he left.

After the elevator door closed, Wadia turned to Goenka and said: 'I'll bet you that before the lift reaches the ground floor, he'll already be plotting where next to stick the knife into me.' Goenka reached over and gently slapped Wadia on the cheek: a tacit admonition not to be too cynical.

The next day, Dhirubhai telephoned Wadia at his Ballard Estate office and announced he was personally bringing an invitation to Nina's wedding. Wadia told him there was no need and after much persuasion Dhirubhai had the card brought over by an executive soon afterwards. On the day of the wedding, a Reliance manager arrived several hours ahead to 'escort' the guest. Wadia sent him away and went by himself. The reception was in the Cooperage Football Ground, scene of the Reliance shareholders meetings. Mukesh Ambani was waiting to escort Wadia in and offered to take him to the head of the line of guests waiting to greet the newly married couple and their parents on a podium. Wadia refused, and the two waited in the queue for about twenty minutes making awkward conversation. When he reached the stage, Wadia found a crowd of press photographers waiting to capture the two warring textile magnates together – the point of the exercise clearly being to dispel the atmosphere of dispute surrounding Reliance. Anil Ambani was deputised by Dhirubhai to escort Wadia out to his car, but Wadia sent him back at the gate.

Within a few days, hostilities had broken out again, and Goenka decided to press on with his investigation. The person he chose to find out the secrets of the Ambanis was not one of his famous editors, nor one of his reporters, nor even someone from the business milieu of Bombay but a young South Indian accountant from Madras whose name had not previously appeared in print except at the bottom of audited accounts.

Swaminathan Gurumurthy, then 36, was the product of a Brahmin family in a village 160 kilometres south of Madras. Blocked from university by Tamil Nadu's policies favouring lower-caste students, Gurumurthy turned to accountancy, and came to Goenka's attention while auditing the books of his Madras-registered companies. Like Goenka, he had also been drawn to Hindu nationalism in politics, joining the Rashtriya Swayamsevak Sangh (RSS or National Volunteers Order), a mass movement aimed at ridding the Hindu majority of a perceived defeatist attitude to other civilisations. The RSS had won a reputation for discipline and lack of corruption, making the political party it eventually sponsored, the Bharatiya Janata Party (BJP), seem the natural

126

successor by default to the failed Congress and communist alternatives – at least until new Hindu warriors themselves became tainted by power in the late 1990s.

In its economic ideas the RSS has been nationalist but suspicious of big capital, whatever its origins. The big company threatened the small shopkeeper and trader communities, a repository of traditional virtues. And, more recently, multinationals with their universal products and their marketing science seemed to be imposing a Western popular culture and lifestyle wherever they set up. 'I regard communism and capitalism as two sides of the same coin,' Gurumurthy told an interviewer some years afterwards. 'Both regard human beings as economic creatures. The only difference between them is whether ownership of wealth should be public or private and whether there should be profit or not. While communism will have a Chernobyl at any cost, capitalism will have it only if it demands high profit.'[2] In Dhirubhai's case, Gurumurthy was opposed to the monopoly power Reliance had developed. 'I would have rather had a hundred Ambanis than just one,' he put it.[3]

Still, it is ironic that Dhirubhai and Gurumurthy ended up on opposite sides. In the mid-1990s Gurumurthy was the leading light of the Swadeshi Jagran Manch, a BJP-affiliate that actively opposed the entry of multinational consumer brands like Coca-Cola and McDonald's. Dhirubhai was often projected as the new, fully Indian entrepreneur struggling against a business establishment left by the British, such as the Parsi companies, and later as a home-grown businessman fully in command of the latest technology and financial techniques: at last the authentic Indian corporate warrior.

Dhirubhai was of course closely identified with Congress by 1985, although he tried to maintain ties to opposition parties, too. What set both Goenka and Gurumurthy against Reliance was their sense of excessive power, of business drive exceeding its proper limits and of personal arrogance on the part of Dhirubhai himself. '... while other businessmen had some sense of guilt and shame about their wrongdoings, Ambani saw himself as an achiever against the law, the system,' Gurumurthy noted later.[4] Gurumurthy's background in the RSS also helped to immunise him against some of the 'cultural' defences of Dhirubhai's business practices. The Hindu revivalists were happy enough to work through the modern political and economic institutions left by the British. They were a movement of rule-followers, not rule-breakers. They wanted order, not anarchy. India was weak because its politicians could not make sensible laws and stick to them in the face of temptations put up by private interests. The rise of manipulators like Dhirubhai was not a result of Indians breaking out of their mental bonds but a symptom of their weakness.

Personally Gurumurthy had few chinks in his armour. He had got to work with important clients because of his own ability. Back in Madras he lived in a traditional extended family household, with everyone sitting on the floor at meals and eating with their hands. He dressed simply, usually with an open-necked shirt, and stayed in the *Express* guesthouse when in New Delhi or in a simply furnished room in the penthouse in Bombay. Periodically Gurumurthy would make pilgrimages to Hindu temples and holy sites around India, reappearing with saffron or vermilion *tilak* daubs on his forehead. He had both a strong sense of probity and a detailed knowledge of corporate accounting and law. He was an inspired choice for Goenka.

The question, in November 1985, was where to start. By that stage, the published information on Reliance made up a substantial file – much of it adulatory profiles repeating the same anecdotes. Gurumurthy decided to work from the two cases in which Reliance's secrets seemed to have come close to the surface: the High Court petition by Reliance to enforce the PTA import contacts financed just before 29 May that year, and the 1983 controversy over the purchase of Reliance shares by the Isle of Man companies.

In the *Indian Express* organisation, Gurumurthy had direct contact with the chairman and the newspaper's considerable resources within India itself. He found also that some of Dhirubhai's opponents in industrial and trade conflicts also kept information about Reliance. Notable among them was a Sindhi textile trader, Jamnadas Moorjani, who worked from a modest office in a back street of Bombay's Kalbadevi district but whose knowledge of markets and judgement was respected all over town. As president of the All-India Crimpers' Association from 1978 to 1982, Moorjani had led the campaign by the independent polyester texturisers against the duty hike on yarn in November 1982.

Although he found a pervading fearfulness about discussing Reliance, Gurumurthy also built up contacts with bureaucrats, bank officials and even Reliance employees who were uneasy about some of the company's transactions.

When it came to pursuing inquiries overseas, the little-travelled Gurumurthy relied initially on names suggested by Wadia, drawing on business contacts kept by Bombay Dyeing and associated companies. The initial contact was a firm of solicitors, Lee Lane Smith, in London's Lincoln's Inn Fields, who undertook a legal search of the mysterious shelf companies with names like Crocodile and Fiasco in the Isle of Man. In mid-December the solicitors engaged a private detective agency, King's Investigation Bureau, to help them trace the ultimate owners.

By then the atmosphere at Reliance was becoming one of a siege as the Finance Ministry's tax enforcement agencies and the Central Bureau of Investigation pursued their inquiries into the PTA letters of credit and the excise evasion charge. In February 1986 the years of living on adrenalin took their toll on Dhirubhai. He suffered a sudden stroke that left him partly paralysed down his right side and required immediate attention in an American hospital. For some weeks, the running of the company was left to his two sons, then aged 29 and 27 respectively.

Dhirubhai's critics were also shaken, by a sudden, still unexplained attack on Jamnadas Moorjani. Sensing a more sympathetic government in New Delhi, the crimpers had renewed their agitation for the anti-dumping duty of Rs 15 000 a tonne to be lifted. One evening in February, a gang of men attacked the unassuming Moorjani as he left his Kalbadevi office and walked to his car. He was slashed with long knives, one arm nearly being severed, but recovered quickly in hospital.[5]

In this vitiated atmosphere, the *Indian Express* launched its exposé of Reliance with a misleadingly theoretical-looking piece on the merits of allowing conversion of the unconvertible security carrying the modest byline 'By S. Gurumurthy': 'If the main rule prohibits something, get a sub-rule added which permits it. The main rule will no doubt exist in the book but the book alone. Business thrives on such rules. Touts make their fortunes, politicians enhance their power and bureaucrats their importance. Rule of law at once becomes sub-rule of law and sub-rule eventually becomes subversive rule. Let us get down to specifics …'[6] It was not the way a practised journalist would have opened, but Gurumurthy set out a powerful argument against the practice that had become a hallmark for Dhirubhai: raising debt by offering attractive interest rates, then converting it to cheap equity by the 'innovative' path of converting supposedly non-convertible debentures into shares.

This risked destroying the whole principle behind the distinction between convertibles and non-convertibles, reflected in the lower premium and higher interest rate on non-convertibles, Gurumurthy pointed out. No one would bother with convertible issues if it were allowed as a general practice. 'There is yet another mischief,' Gurumurthy noted. 'Those corporate managements which deal in their own securities can abuse this licence by buying these non-convertible debentures at a lower price and thereafter announcing conversion. There were allegations of this abuse in the only case of conversion of the non-convertible in recent stock market history.'

A week later, Gurumurthy returned to the attack. He began in the philosophical style that became his hallmark: 'Truth reveals itself, though often belatedly. This admirably suits the politician in power. The interregnum between truth and its revelation is generally a period of manipulation. In this interregnum alibis and half-truths rule. Finally unless someone is alert, truth gets confined to the archives. Result: alibis masquerade as truth.'

Gurumurthy recalled the grilling of the former Finance minister Pranab Mukherjee in 1983 over the non-resident Indian investment in Reliance and his defence that, while black money could be involved, this was not reason enough to kill a scheme bringing in much-needed foreign exchange. The figures, Gurumurthy wrote, showed that the NRI share investment scheme had brought in less than one per cent of the Rs 139 billion invested by NRIs in various deposit and investment schemes since 1981. The Rs 225 million invested by the eleven Isle of Man companies in 1982, augmented by a further Rs 6 million for a rights issue of debentures, had grown into a share portfolio worth Rs 1 billion. With bonus issues and conversions, it could grow into a holding worth Rs 8.58 billion or $650 million, a repatriable amount equal to 15 per cent of India's foreign exchange reserves at the time.

This form of investment was a dangerous game for India, Gurumurthy argued. With the sharemarket index doubling in the year past, it meant the country could have to return twice as much foreign exchange as it gained, when – if it had needed to – the government could have borrowed at a small margin over the London interbank rate. Nor was the scheme very honest: 'It appears to be tailor-made for motivated investment not altogether in the national interest.'

The arguments in these two articles were well made and stirred up a subject that smelled from the start. But the scenario of capital flight that Gurumurthy depicted was contradicted by one of the implicit assumptions made by the critics of Mukherjee. If Dhirubhai was the ultimate owner of the Isle of Man companies, how could he sell off their Reliance shares without depressing his own share price?

A week later, however, Gurumurthy moved into new allegations. 'Smuggling in Projects' was the headline on the first of a two-part story. In 1980–81 the Petroleum Ministry had been working on plans for a petrochemicals refinery at Mathura, which included a 150 000-tonne-a-year purified terephthalic acid plant. In March 1981 Reliance had submitted its licence application for a PTA plant the same size. To overcome the Petroleum Ministry's resistance, its Secretary was transferred in July 1983. In October 1984 Reliance got its preliminary approval for a 75 000-tonne plant. The proposed PTA plant at Mathura was cut back, to an output of 75 000 tonnes, and had been stalled in any case by lack of government funds.

Thanks to the help of Finance Minister Mukherjee, Reliance looked like having 100 per cent of India's PTA production and 34 per cent of the country's combined DMT and PTA output. Its control of other feedstocks, by-products and end-products in the polyester chain ranged from 38.6 per cent up to 62.5 per cent, according to Gurumurthy. India's anti-monopoly law defined a dominant undertaking as one with more than 24 per cent of national installed capacity, but none of Reliance's applications had been referred to the Monopolies and Restrictive Trade Practices Commission.

132

Gurumurthy had been working until then from published knowledge. On 15 May 1986 he began reporting from the results of his own investigations, in a three-part series entitled 'Reliance Loan Mela' – *mela* meaning a fair or bazaar and 'loan mela' referring to the notorious practice of Congress politicians handing out loans from government banks to their constituents in carnival-like ceremonies. The Reliance loan mela was not a case of giving a few hundred rupees to a poor family to buy a buffalo or irrigation pump, said Gurumurthy. 'It has to do with crores of rupees smuggled from banks in an ingenious and brazen scheme to divert public funds to private ends.'

Two very large issues of partially 'non-convertible' debentures by Reliance during 1984 and 1985 had been jumped on by a swarm of small companies, whose registered addresses were often those of Reliance companies and employees. Each had raised finance from the big Indian banks by pledging Reliance shares and debentures as security, or with guarantees from Dhirubhai's younger brother Nathubhai, often in identical, simultaneous transactions that breached central bank rules on loans for speculative sharemarket purchases.

Gurumurthy asked what point there could be in, say, Mac Investments (an Ambani investment company) borrowing Rs 1.5 million from Canara Bank at 18 per cent interest to buy debentures carrying 13.5 per cent interest. The borrower must have known that the capital appreciation of the Reliance shares, obtained from conversion of the non-convertible portion of the debentures, would yield a profit of 400 per cent. The Ambani management would also have consolidated its hold on Reliance by borrowing to buy its own company's shares – which was expressly forbidden by the Reserve Bank. Reliance had already started talks with the Ministry of Finance to have the two series of debentures fully converted. The company's shares had already started booming in expectation. 'If this is not speculation then what is?' asked Gurumurthy.

Gurumurthy had not done so well in his overseas inquiries. The lawyers and private eyes engaged in London were laboriously searching company records in tax havens to trace ownership of the NRI investors in Reliance, but results were slow in coming. A letter from the London contacts on 16 April enclosed a fresh report from King's Investigation Bureau with the comment that it was 'very feeble'.

King's had been asked to look into nearly 120 companies, ostensibly owned by non-resident Indians, which had invested either directly in Reliance shares, as in the 1982 case, or by subscription to the Reliance B and F series debentures. Possibly with the help of concerned banking officials, Gurumurthy had also obtained lists of NRI companies that had borrowed from the Bank of Oman and certain other banks to buy into the Reliance issues.

The nationalised Bank of Baroda had played a big role in financing the issue. Mostly from its London office, the government bank had advanced a total US$33.5 million to NRI companies and individuals, apparently nominated by Reliance, to help them to subscribe to the F series debentures. This was about 40 per cent of the Rs 1.08 billion investment made by NRI sources. The loans had similar terms: two percentage points over the London interbank rate, or 10 per cent a year, while the return from interest was 11 per cent after tax. The investors were clearly after the capital gain from eventual conversion to equity.

The detectives had exhaustive searches made on the names in the Channel Islands as well as the Isle of Man, but most turned up negative. In the Isle of Man they found that ten of the eleven controversial companies from 1982 had undergone a sudden change of ownership and directors in August 1985. The two most provocative names had also been changed to something more innocuous: Crocodile Investments had become Asian Multi-Growth Investments, and Fiasco Investments had become Asian Investments.

With the ten companies, the various Shahs and Damanis of Leicester, Berlin, Djibouti and New York had suddenly transferred their 55 to 80 per cent shareholdings in August 1985 to newly formed holding companies in the British Virgin Islands with names matching those of the Isle of Man companies they now owned. Inquiries in Leicester found that the Shahs had not received any noticeable jump in their wealth from the sale of control over equity by then worth more than Rs 1 billion or US$80 million. Indeed, family members professed the same degree of ignorance as they had in 1983. By then, Krishna Kant Shah – Dhirubhai's old Junagadh schoolmate – was too ill to meet anyone (and died in May 1986).

The New York investors, Praful and Nalini Shah, turned out to be a middle-class young couple mostly living off Praful's average-size salary as clerk in a city law firm. They had bought their modest home in the suburbs for $49 000 with a $34 000 mortgage and drove an eleven-year-old Dodge. They had not apparently come into any recent wealth either, but any connection they had with Dhirubhai was not discovered.

As of August 1984 the British Virgin Islands had had a company code designed for the discreet investor. Called the International Business Companies Ordinance, it allowed companies to issue shares to an unnamed bearer who was allowed to vote at company meetings. Companies could issue non-voting shares, so that technically an NRI could own 60 per cent of the capital to comply with the Indian rules but have no voting rights at all. And it could have faceless shareholders through trusts, corporate bodies and the like. Directors and shareholders could even participate in meetings by telephone.

Including these companies, Gurumurthy's inquiries found that a total of thirty-two companies registered in the Isle of Man or the Channel Islands had subscribed a total Rs 141 million to the F series debentures. The ten British Virgin Islands companies had subscribed

Rs 50 million. And forty-one companies in the United Arab Emirates had been lent an average of Rs 1 million each by the Bank of Baroda to subscribe.

Out of the new names in the British tax havens, the searches found that new directors had been appointed in August and September 1985, just after the F series issue. Many had an Indian resident of Dubai, Homi Ratan Colah, as their new director wielding majority control. Others had people of Indian names listed as residents of Nigeria.

The Dubai companies had some fanciful names taken from various ancient Sanskrit scriptures: ten from the *Vigneshwara Ashtotra* and twelve from the *Sandhya Mantra*. Several others took names from the avatars of Lord Shiva and other divinities. Reliance's Middle East 'coordinator' and Dhirubhai's old colleague from Besse & Co. in Aden, Bharat Kumar Shah, subscribed Rs 35 million in the names of himself and his family. In the first week of September 1985 he had sent a list of borrowers including himself to the Bank of Oman.

Through a firm of Panamanian lawyers with an office in London, the investigators had also done a search in Panama on more than a hundred company names matching those on the list of Reliance investors. They found some of the names, all registered on the same day in July 1985. Listed among company officers were two members of an Indian firm of chartered accountants in Dubai that had done work for Reliance. But the London investigators reported back to Bombay that their local agents had not been able to get information out of the Panama lawyers who had incorporated the companies. 'Our agents have been advised that this is a most delicate matter and should not be pursued further,' they said.

It was unsatisfactory – and tantalising, given that the trail seemed to lead through the tax havens and corporate hideouts of the globe back towards India. The leads in Panama and Dubai were not enough to build a story on. But it was enough for Gurumurthy to resume the chase abandoned by the Indian press in January 1984 – when, he claimed, the Ananda Bazar Patrika group had been warned off by the withdrawal of all Reliance advertising.

In a four-part article published over 11–14 June – under the heading 'Reliance, crocodiles & fiascos' – he went through the story of the Isle of Man companies once again, emphasising the series of coincidences that pointed to a single manipulator close to the action in Bombay. Given the secrecy rules applying in the British Virgin Islands, how was the Reserve Bank of India to verify that the companies had 60 per cent control by non-resident Indians, as required by the Indian rules? Had the central bank even been informed of the changed control in 1985? Gurumurthy also highlighted the way in which changes in the investment rules had been timely for the investments by the Isle of Man companies. Between late March and August 1982, during two bear attacks against Reliance, some 1.872 million shares in the company – nearly 10 per cent of the then issued capital – had been bought by brokers on behalf of unnamed NRI investors.

The investment rules had been relaxed first on 14 April 1982, just after the first bear attack, to give repatriation rights to NRIs and extend investment freedom to companies, partnerships and trusts with 60 per cent NRI ownership. Then on 20 August, just after the second attack, the rules were further relaxed to remove the Rs 100 000 (face value) ceiling for any one NRI investor. Instead, each NRI investor could hold up to 1 per cent of the paid-up capital of the company. Instead of having to distribute the 1.872 million Rs 10 shares among 187 owners, the requirement was now just ten separate shareholders. Only on 9 August 1982, Gurumurthy pointed out, had the various Shahs and Damanis acquired their 60 per cent-plus control of the ten Isle of Man companies. The amendments to the investment rules had clearly been 'tailor-made'.

So far, it had been just words – wounding as they were to Dhirubhai and Reliance. But within three months the *Indian Express* campaign led to action. Late on the night of 10 June 1986 the government announced a ban on the conversion of non-convertible debentures into shares. The board of Reliance had been called to meet the next day, 11 June, specifically to decide to recommend conversion of the E and F series debentures at the annual shareholders meeting two weeks later. Only on 4 June a meeting of finance officials had given 'in principle' approval for conversion, and the Reliance share price had jumped to a high of Rs 392. The government's decision meant that the company had lost a chance to extinguish Rs 3.23 billion in debt and make a corresponding boost to its reserves and net worth, while cutting about Rs 480 million in annual interest. The debenture holders had lost the chance of a quick 200 per cent gain on their original investment. Even before trading opened in the Bombay Stock Exchange on 11 June, Dalal Street was crowded with investors offloading their Reliance debentures in 'kerb' transactions.

More bad news was coming in. On 17 June Finance Minister V.P. Singh presided over an 'open house' hearing of claims and counterclaims about the Rs 15000-a-tonne 'anti-dumping' duty that had been applied on polyester yarn back in November 1982. Anil Ambani represented Reliance. Jamnadas Moorjani attended for the All-India Crimpers' Association to oppose the levy. The next day, Singh abolished the duty, and yarn prices dropped 20 per cent immediately. The same month, the authorities placed an extra duty of Rs 3000 a tonne on imports of PTA to help the domestic manufacturers of the alternative feedstock DMT.

Dhirubhai was also embattled on several other fronts. The Central Bureau of Investigation was looking into the alleged leak of the May

1985 policy change on PTA imports, the Reserve Bank of India into the 'Reliance loan mela'. In addition, both Reliance and Bombay Dyeing were being drawn into complicated litigation launched by small share-holders who seemed to have ample legal resources at their disposal. The same complaints were also being taken to ministers, the Company Law Board and the heads of financial institutions by backbench MPs sud-denly seized with the urgency of the accounting intricacies involved.

Dhirubhai's response to the crisis was typically flamboyant and combative. On 26 June he held his meeting with shareholders as scheduled. The Cooperage Football Ground had been replaced as too small a venue. Instead, 30000 investors flocked to the Cross Maidan, a large central park in Bombay, and sat under canvas awnings. The small investors were anxious for their annual theatre. They wanted to see how Dhirubhai was shaping up after his stroke in February and the onslaught by the *Indian Express.* They expected Dhirubhai to come up, once again, with the unexpected and get around the conversion ban.

Dhirubhai did not disappoint, although delivering his speech was obviously a physical strain for him. Reliance would soon come out with a new, fully convertible debenture issue on a rights basis to existing share and debenture holders and would convene an extraordinary gen-eral meeting to approve it. The company would try again to win per-mission to convert the E and F Series. The company was drawing up plans for a further Rs 20 billion investment in new and existing prod-ucts, including plastics at the proposed petrochemical plant at Hazira in Gujarat.

But the news continued to get worse for Dhirubhai. Pleas to Goenka by Mukesh and then Dhirubhai himself had brought a temporary truce in the *Express* campaign. But other publications were taking up the attack on Reliance. On 5 July the tabloid *Blitz* published letters and tel-exes which suggested that a Bombay branch of the state-owned Canara

Bank had doctored a letter of credit for PTA imports by Reliance to get a larger amount booked before the import policy changed.

The Reserve Bank of India meanwhile gave its preliminary findings on the loan mela. It found that nine banks had given advances totalling Rs 592.8 million in India during 1985 to sixty-three companies apparently associated with Reliance, against security of Reliance shares and debentures. Reliance had placed money with all the nine banks, totalling Rs 919 million, as deposits, not collateral. Several of the borrowing companies had been established very recently and, in some cases, with a capital of only Rs 1000 or Rs 10000, although they had borrowed amounts as great as Rs 9.5 million. The purpose of the loans was generally stated as 'working capital' or 'purchase of shares'. In all cases, the security offered was shares or debentures of Reliance, held either in the name of the borrowing company or that of another company connected with Reliance. The banks had not worried about repayment capacity of the companies, or looked into the end use of the funds.

The loans had not broken every rule. RBI directives required that shares pledged against loans of more than Rs 50000 be transferred to the lending bank's name. This had been complied with, generally. The loans had been repayable within thirty months, in some cases twelve months, and thus were not long-term loans (five years and more) that required RBI approval. But by granting large advances to Reliance-linked companies, possibly to help strengthen the controlling interest, the banks had not adhered to the 'spirit' of the RBI guidelines: that loans be given to assist productive activity.

The Bombay Stock Exchange had earlier doubled the margin – the up-front payment ahead of settlement – on buyers of Reliance shares, from Rs 40 to Rs 80 because it was aware of heavy buying by the company's own network to support the tumbling share price. This limited Dhirubhai's ability to stem the rout. But things went so badly, with

Reliance dragging down the whole market, that the exchange also put a similar margin on sales, putting shackles on the bears as well.

Gurumurthy then weighed in with yet another sensational allegation that kept the share price falling: Reliance had smuggled in an industrial plant worth Rs 1 billion.[7] In late 1985 and early 1986, Gurumurthy said, Reliance had imported the components of its new 45 000-tonne-a-year polyester staple fibre plant in consignments by sea through Bombay and by air through the Bombay air cargo terminal. Dispersed among the same containers were the components of a second plant, able to make 25 000 tonnes a year of polyester filament yarn.

This had been the third case of smuggling in yarn-making capacity by Reliance, he said. In its original yarn operation set up in 1982, Reliance had actually imported a 25 000-tonne-a-year plant under the guise of its licensed 10 000-tonne plant. The 're-endorsement' scheme of Pranab Mukherjee had allowed Reliance to legitimise this in 1984. At the same time it had been allowed to import 'balancing equipment' to match the capacities of the polycondensation units (which make the polyester) and the spinning lines (which extrude it into yarn). The Rs 183.8 million worth of 'balancing equipment' the company had been licensed to import in early 1985 was actually an additional yarn plant capable of making 20 000 tonnes a year. Together with the newly smuggled third plant, Reliance now had a yarn capacity of 70 000 tonnes at Patalganga, as against its licence for 25 125 tonnes.

Each of the second and third plants consisted of a polycondensation unit and four spinning lines. Bought new, each would cost about Rs 2 billion and second-hand, about half that. 'Doesn't the enforcement branch want to know where Reliance got the foreign exchange to pay for these?' asked Gurumurthy.

In a follow-up article, the *Express* connected the 'smuggled' yarn capacity with a change in policy announced on 3 July 1986 by the

Minister of Industry Narain Dutt Tiwari, whom the newspaper had described as an 'unabashed Reliance admirer'. Tiwari said polyester producers were now free to switch production between staple fibre (spun from cut lengths of yarn) and filament yarn. Reliance would now be able to churn out more of the high-priced filament yarn without attracting notice. The policy applied to manufacturers with a poly-condensation capacity of 30 000 tonnes and a filament yarn capacity of 15 000 tonnes – another apparently 'tailor-made' criterion that only Reliance then fitted.

On 20 August a team of six officials and engineers from relevant ministries arrived at the Reliance factory to see exactly what machinery was installed. According to a report on the mission by its leader, M.S. Grover, to the Ministry of Industry on 10 September, 'Messrs Reliance either did not give the information timely or the information given was inadequate.'

The officials met Reliance representatives a second time at the Customs House in Bombay on 22 August. The answers were still not satisfactory, and several other follow-up meetings were held in New Delhi, leading to a presentation by Reliance on 1 September. The offi-cials were still unsatisfied: Reliance refused to give precise specifica-tions of equipment because it was 'proprietary knowledge'.

The committee asked Reliance at least to explain how the capacity of the PTA unit's air compressor – a component that gave a clue to the overall plant capacity – was nearly 50 per cent greater than needed for the licensed plant and how the polyester filament yarn plant came to have twelve spinning lines instead of the eight cleared for import. On the first point, the officials appeared to have been left uncertain. On the second, Reliance said the four extra spinning units were made from disassembled parts shipped with the four second-hand spinning lines brought in as part of the 'balancing equipment' in 1984. Reliance executives were disputing that any precise tonnage could be assigned to a given plant. With constant meterage (length of fibre produced) almost any tonnage could be produced by varying the denierage (thickness) of the filament, it maintained. In its applications for licences, Reliance had made certain denierage specifications. At no stage had the government told it of any policy decision that the controlling factor was the tonnage.

In their conclusions, the officials knocked down the denierage arguments about capacity and homed in on the one fact that was obvious to the eye. Instead of the eight spinning lines that Reliance was cleared to import, its factory was operating twelve lines. Nowhere in any of the documentation produced by Reliance could any reference be found to this additional capacity. As for the complete filament yarn plant, the inspectors rated its capacity at between 55000 and 63000 tonnes a year – more than double the licensed output of 25 125 tonnes.

The report, crammed with numbers and dry engineering detail, was passed to the Customs Service, which then looked back through the records of equipment imports by Reliance. It was to lead four months later to Bombay Customs, so often sympathetic to Dhirubhai in the past, handling Reliance a show-cause notice alleging that the company had smuggled in spinning machines and undeclared industrial capacity worth Rs 1145 billion. The Customs valued the duty evaded at Rs 1196 billion and invited Reliance to ask why this should not be levied. In addition, the company faced the possibility of fines up to five times that amount and confiscation of the smuggled goods, while individual executives could be prosecuted for smuggling.

Meanwhile, Dhirubhai's friends in the government and Congress Party were ducking for cover. Pranab Mukherjee had been miserably sidelined by Rajiv Gandhi. At the party's December 1985 centenary conference, Rajiv had snubbed him by calling a lunch break during

Mukherjee's speech defending Indira's economic policies. Then, in April 1986, Rajiv had summarily expelled Mukherjee from the party after newspapers began reporting a revolt by Indira loyalists against his leadership.

In Gurumurthy's articles, the *Indian Express* had fired a devastating broadside at some of Dhirubhai's weakest defences. It had been an expensive lesson for having got on the wrong side of the old Marwari newspaper baron sitting at the top of Express Towers.

10

Sleuths

To see Bhure Lal on his evening walk around New Delhi's Lodhi Gardens was to know at once a man not easily diverted from his objective. Military-style moustache always neat, eyes narrowed on some distant point ahead, arms swinging, Bhure Lal attacked his exercise routine with the intensity of a soldier on a desperate forced march to lift a siege. Friends among the senior bureaucrats who favoured the Lodhi circuit struggled to keep up with his blistering pace.

The military bearing was no affectation. Bhure Lal had joined the Indian Army on a short-term officer's commission soon after the Chinese attack along the eastern borders in 1962 and saw action against Pakistan in the 1965 war. He retired from military service with the rank of captain in 1970, when he won a place through examination in the elite Indian Administrative Service. After several district posts in Uttar

Pradesh, he became a secretary to V.P. Singh when he was the state's Chief Minister. At the end of March 1985, just after Singh as Rajiv's Finance minister had declared his war on the black economy, Bhure Lal was made Director of Enforcement in the Ministry of Finance, responsible for finding transgressions of India's highly detailed and restrictive exchange control laws. By early 1986 he too had joined the attack on Dhirubhai.

The Director of Enforcement enjoyed wide discretionary powers about whom he investigated and was allowed to operate with minimal circulation of reports outside his own office to avoid compromising arrests and search raids. In addition, Bhure Lal had the confidence of his immediate superior, the Revenue Secretary in the Ministry of Finance, Vinod Pande, who in turn was a confidant of V.P. Singh himself. It was a closed circle that frustrated Dhirubhai's network of sympathetic officials within the Finance Ministry among whom many fellow bureaucrats and politicians placed the able and ambitious head of the ministry, the Finance Secretary S. Venkitaramanan.[1]

Bhure Lal made his first foray overseas to pick up Dhirubhai's hidden financial trails in May 1986. He went to London to look into the ownership of the Isle of Man companies, but found a baffling wall of secrecy in the tax havens. He travelled to Leicester in an attempt to persuade the Shahs to talk, but arrived a few days after the family head, Krishna Kant Shah, had died. His attempt to prosecute the Kirloskar group over its alleged front company in Germany had also failed because the suspect company's financial statements could not be sequestered.

The Enforcement Directorate also raided the Bank of Credit and Commerce International (BCCI) in Bombay and brought charges against its local general manager and five other staff under a special law against smuggling of currency, which went by the acronym

COFEPOSA. Bhure Lal met the head of the BCCI's Asian operations, Swaleh Naqvi, and offered to go soft on the bank's staff provided it supplied all details of Dhirubhai's suspected transactions to fund the purchase of Reliance shares by the offshore companies. Naqvi agreed, but reneged once back in London and asserted that as a Luxembourg-domiciled bank, the BCCI was not bound by Indian law. The BCCI was closed by the Bank of England and other Western central banks in 1991 amid allegations that it was a major money-laundering operation for drug traffickers.

To clinch a prosecution under the Foreign Exchange Regulation Act, the enforcers needed to produce evidence of the overseas 'leg' of a *havala* transfer. Bhure Lal became convinced that his intelligence agency would have to tap non-official sources to obtain the breaks it needed to build a case. But the private investigation agencies he found in London were too expensive for his office to hire out of its discretionary funds. Requesting a special budget would have blown the cover completely on his inquiries.

India's own embassies in foreign capitals were worse than useless. In a later note on his 1986 inquiries, Bhure Lal complained that any information given to Indian missions was usually passed on to the suspect. When the Enforcement Directorate had sought information from the Indian Embassy in Washington about suspected secret commissions paid by the American grain-trading giant Louis Dreyfus Corporation to the New Delhi industrialist Lalit Thapar's Ballarpur Industries, the embassy had telexed a vigorous complaint back to the Ministry of External Affairs.

The enforcer discussed his dilemma in September with his superior, Revenue Secretary Vinod Pande, who in turn raised the problems during his frequent meetings with V.P. Singh. The Finance minister gave his clearance to the proposal to use foreign investigating agents, on condition that any payments be made after receipt of evidence. The choice of the agents and other operational matters were left to the Director of Enforcement.

It was left to Gurumurthy to point Bhure Lal towards the help he needed. The two had met first in July, in the coffee shop of New Delhi's Janpath Hotel. Thereafter through the second half of 1986 they had had informal meetings when Gurumurthy was in the capital, in the Taj Mahal Hotel's coffee shop, in Nehru Park, then at the *Indian Express* guesthouse.

Gurumurthy had also been in London in May on a separate visit. With Goenka's resources behind him, he had not been deterred by the expense of British sleuths. But the inquiries by King's had come to an impenetrable wall of secrecy in Panama and Dubai. His attention was turning to the United States where initial inquiries had not unearthed much evidence. Parallel with his published articles, Gurumurthy had circulated a stream of detailed position papers to concerned officials and politicians about the various allegations against Reliance. In some cases, these papers made recommendations for corrective action – some of which were taken up, as with the banning of conversion of non-convertible debentures – or for further investigation.

Nusli Wadia had also kept up his contact with Rajiv Gandhi about Reliance. The two got on well: they were of similar age, each had a Parsi parent and both were considerably more cosmopolitan than their everyday cohorts. Early in 1986 the Prime Minister agreed that Reliance should be targeted. As a fuller picture of Dhirubhai's operations emerged, Rajiv also agreed that the case of the smuggled factories, and the disguised payments that must have been made for them through illegal *havala* channels, were the most vulnerable points on which Dhirubhai could be nailed. Rajiv wanted to hear the full story first-hand from Gurumurthy. Accordingly arrangements were made through

Wadia for a series of meetings over a week around the end of August, but in the event the veteran Congress politician and Gandhi family loyalist Mohammed Yunus spoke to Gurumurthy instead.[2]

In late September Nusli Wadia was also making inquiries while on a visit to New York. The American-based Praful Shah, who had been listed as a shareholder in some of the Isle of Man companies, remained a mystery. Seeking a way of pressuring Shah to talk, Wadia consulted a New York accountancy firm called Kronish, Lieb, Weiner & Hellman to see whether Shah had been breaking any American laws. A partner advised that an American resident such as Shah would have had to declare any income derived from the investment in his name, whether or not it was distributed to him, and that the sale of his shares would be a 'taxable event'.

In October, Gurumurthy was given the name of a private investigation agency based on the outskirts of Washington, the Fairfax Group. The agency had been founded in 1983 by a former government anti-fraud investigator named Michael Hershman, then 41. The Madras accountant went on to Washington and spoke to Fairfax on behalf of Goenka.

By then, Gurumurthy had published his articles on the 'smuggled' filament yarn capacity, and it had become clear that the counter-parties to any secret payments by Reliance would have been either the suppliers of the equipment, principally Du Pont, or the American engineering firm that arranged the purchase and shipment of second-hand plant, Chemtex Fibers Inc. Hershman pointed out that he would need an authority from the Indian Government to get the companies to divulge material they would otherwise classify as commercial in confidence.

At Gurumurthy 's request Hershman visited India, arriving in New Delhi early on 15 November 1988 and checking into the Oberoi Hotel. Over the three days of his stay Hershman was introduced by

Gurumurthy to Bhure Lal and reached agreement to work for the Government of India in return for a contingency payment of 20 per cent of any moneys recovered – a reward in line with standard payments to informers by the Enforcement Directorate, although the amounts involved were potentially huge in the Reliance case. The three targets for investigation were Du Pont and Chemtex, regarding the supposedly smuggled yarn plant, and BCCI about the financing of the non-resident investments in Reliance. Hershman started making inquiries about BCCI in London during a stopover on his way back to Washington and soon realised that he was on dangerous ground. A tough-looking young Sikh knocked on the door of his hotel room and warned him against asking questions about BCCI.

It was not until 21 December that Bhure Lal arrived in New York to get down to work with Hershman, who came to his hotel along with his Fairfax colleague Gordon McKay. On 22 December they went in to see Joseph D. Bruno, head of the Criminal Investigation Department in the Internal Revenue Service. Bhure Lal sought from Bruno whatever help could be provided to trap certain well-known operators of the Indian *havala* trade providing dollars in the United States in return for rupee payments in India – which Bruno agreed would be illegal in the United States if they exceeded US$10 000 and had not been cleared under American foreign exchange laws. Bhure Lal asked for help on the Dreyfus case, involving the alleged $3 million commissions on supplies of cooking oil to India's State Trading Corporation over 1982–86. And he pursued the same lines as Gurumurthy and Wadia in the Reliance puzzles.

Bhure Lal detailed the involvement of the New York legal clerk Praful Shah in the Isle of Man companies, supplying the company names and the amount of dividends and interest on debentures that should have accrued to him from Reliance. This income had not been declared to US tax authorities, Bhure Lal said. Praful Shah did not have the resources for the investments placed in his name and had claimed to be the nominee of Krishna Kant Shah in Britain. But nor was K.K. Shah rich enough, and he had not declared his investments to the UK Inland Revenue. The real investor was suspected to be an Indian who siphoned off funds in a clandestine manner and got them recycled through the Shahs, thereby evading payment of taxes in India. Praful Shah refused to disclose his source of funds, and Bruno was urged to investigate.

The Indian official then mentioned the role of BCCI, through its London operations, in the Isle of Man investments, citing the names of senior BCCI executives, including Swaleh Naqvi and a Mr Abidi (probably referring to the BCCI's founder, Agha Hasan Abedi). BCCI had provided much of the funding to ten of the Isle of Man companies over 1982–83, along with the European Asian Bank in three cases, channelling the loans through the company facilitators in the island tax haven. The loans had been repaid in New York on 14 June 1985 by credits to the two banks. Who had made the payments and how? Who had stood guarantee against the loans by the two banks?

Along with Gordon McKay from Fairfax and a lawyer from a Delaware law firm named J.E. Liguori, Bhure Lal went on to the Du Pont headquarters at Wilmington to tackle the chemicals giant. The trio were met by a director, E.D. Oyler, and a legal adviser, Geoffrey Gamble, and handed over a sheet of fifteen questions about payments for the purchase of plants and technology by Reliance and a list of twenty-five offshore companies, including many registered in the Isle of Man to see whether these had been party to any transactions.

A week later, on 30 December, Gamble called Bhure Lal and handed over Du Pont's reply to the questionnaire. Bhure Lal was deeply disappointed in the answers, which he felt had flicked the ball to Chemtex and given Du Pont itself some escape clauses. 'To the best of our information and belief at this time, the capacities of the plants are as indicated in the contracts which were approved by the Indian Govt,' the document said. 'To the best of our information and belief, no second-hand equipment has been sold directly by Du Pont to Reliance from Canada, the United States or anywhere else.'

Was any other equipment procured by Chemtex? 'To the best of our information and belief, no.' Did Reliance pay amounts to Du Pont before approval from the Government of India other than from India, and were those payments adjusted by Du Pont after receiving money from India after approval? 'No.' Did Du Pont have any business relations in India with [twenty-five names of Isle of Man and other investment companies]? No reply was attached.

Bhure Lal had found most of the people he wanted to meet in Chemtex to be out of town over the Christmas–New Year period. He got through to an assistant legal counsel, who suggested he call the company offices on 2 January, Bhure Lal's last day in his authorised tour, already extended once. He rang and found the office closed.

After returning to New Delhi on 3 January 1987, Bhure Lal continued to correspond with Du Pont by telex and letter, with Fairfax acting as his agents in Washington. He reported verbally to Revenue Secretary Vinod Pande, who was busy with budget preparations and did not want to hear details. On 29 January the Du Pont lawyer Gamble gave five more documents to McKay. Bhure Lal was again disappointed: the papers concerned agreements made in 1981 for the original polyester yarn plant at Patalganga, not the additions made over the following five years. On 11 February he wrote again to Gamble with eight further questions.

The enforcer had meanwhile met an executive vice-president of Chemtex, Julio J. Martinez, who had come out to India around 21

January – to avoid dealing with the Fairfax agents, Bhure Lal suspected. Martinez promised full cooperation, but his reply sent on 2 February failed to satisfy Bhure Lal, who wrote back: 'As I told to you over phone, I was disappointed with your inadequate response and cannot help feeling that your letter conceals a distinct unwillingness to come out with correct facts, your assurance of cooperation notwithstanding.'

Bhure Lal enclosed a six-page list of queries about the equipment supplied by Chemtex to Reliance from Du Pont's Hamm Uentrop Plant in West Germany. He wanted details of payment, copies of documents such as invoices, certificates about the condition of the machinery and a detailed list of items. How was it, he asked, that the three spinning units originally supplied by Chemtex (for a nominated 10 000 tonnes a year of polyester filament yarn) had resulted in actual production of 18 000 tonnes when the additional nine units gave only a further 15 000 tonnes in installed capacity and 6000 tonnes in actual capacity?

By that stage, government engineers had confirmed the presence at Patalganga of machinery imported without licence. The Ministry of Industry had accepted the Reliance explanation that four of its spinning units had been 'split' into eight units 'to suit layout requirements', but the Finance Ministry had not been convinced. After further inspections at Patalganga in December, the Customs Directorate issued its show-cause notice on 10 February 1987 charging Reliance with smuggling, under-invoicing plant worth Rs 1.14 billion and evading duty of some Rs 1.2 billion. Who had paid for the smuggled machinery and how, Bhure Lal wondered. In addition, who had paid Du Pont the royalties due for extra polycondensation capacity and spinning lines, which amounted to something between $6 million and $12 million?

Du Pont and Chemtex could not be forced to answer, unless Fairfax found some breach of American law in the transactions. But they might find themselves blacklisted in the world's second most populous country where levels of textiles and chemicals consumption were extremely low. Indians were quick to take offence at any implied disparagement of their sovereignty by foreign multinationals, and the disaster at the Union Carbide plant in Bhopal, where thousands of Indian residents had been killed or maimed by a toxic gas leak in 1984, had hardly helped the image of American chemical companies.

While the law enforcers were closing in on his foreign transactions, Dhirubhai was under increasing pressure on the home front. The successive accusations in the press and the mounting load of show-cause notices against Reliance had allowed the bear operators in the Bombay sharemarket to get the upper hand for the first time in several years. The bears pushed down the Reliance share price from its peak of nearly Rs 400 towards Rs 200 at several moments during the year.

In spite of the defiant message given in June by Dhirubhai before his assembled shareholders at the Cross Maidan, the company was undergoing its first profit squeeze since it went public in 1977. The ban on conversion of its E and F Series of debentures had swollen its interest bill, and the removal of the anti-dumping duty on polyester yarn and additional duty on PTA imports had sharply cut the profit margins on its products.

Dhirubhai desperately needed more cash in the company. An attempt to float a new finance and leasing affiliate, Reliance Capital and Finance Trust Co., at a substantial premium had been rejected by the Controller of Capital Issues. The answer was the Reliance G Series of fully convertible debentures opening on 29 November 1986. In June, the directors had proposed an issue of 20 million debentures of Rs 200 each to existing share and debenture holders. This would bring in Rs 4 billion and, with a 25 per cent retention of any excess subscriptions, a total of Rs 5 billion – making it India's biggest ever issue at that time. Each debenture would be convertible into one Reliance share on 30 June 1987, earning 13.5 per cent interest until then. Within a little more than six months from a successful issue, Reliance would once again transform debt into massive new capital.

By the time the extraordinary general meeting needed to approve the issue convened on 28 August, the premium on conversion had been pared down in the light of the less favourable market. The company now proposed an issue of 32 million debentures at Rs 125 each. Reliance would raise the same total but would have to dilute its share base a lot more. The shareholders accepted Dhirubhai's forecast of increased profits for 1986.[3]

Dhirubhai could still run a good meeting. But the question was: did the Ambani magic still work in New Delhi and in the market?

The answer to the first part was 'no'. On 27 October the Controller of Capital Issues eventually cleared the issue, but only on condition that each debenture would convert to two shares. In other words, the premium on the basic Rs 10 share had been brought down from Rs 190 to Rs 62.5. Even then, it was going to be a tricky issue to market. Income tax authorities raided sharebrokers in mid-November, causing a brief shutdown at the Bombay exchange and locking up large volumes of share certificates for inspection. Several other big issues were also planned for December, in a market where the bears were dominant.

Dhirubhai decided to go in quickly and boldly. Directed by Dhirubhai and executed by a dozen leading stockbrokers, Reliance had 15 000 of its retail outlets, wholesalers and suppliers set up as collection centres for subscription forms, some of them formally appointed as subbrokers. Scooter-rickshaws fitted with loud speakers cruised the streets of Bombay and other cities, spruiking the issue. In Ahmedabad, Reliance had subscription forms scattered from a helicopter over the

suburbs. The big American stockbrokers Merrill Lynch were engaged
to market the debentures to non-resident Indians worldwide.

The share price was still shaky. Knowing that the flow of funds for
Reliance's price support had been cut, stockbrokers close to Reliance
had begun to borrow *badla* (carry-over) funds even at interest rates of
36 per cent in order to postpone deliveries. The company had tried to
give the impression that it was back in favour – by virtue of the approval
of the G Series and a meeting between Dhirubhai and Rajiv Gandhi
in October – but these were formalities. The issue was always going to
be cleared, to fund the new projects licensed over 1984–85. The price
was the real issue.

The Reliance share price continued to fall, as word spread of the
seriousness of the customs and excise evasion inquiries, touching a low
point of Rs 179 on 25 December. On 5 December the Customs, Excise
and Gold (Control) Appellate Tribunal dismissed an appeal by Reliance against the show-cause of October 1985 alleging evasion of Rs 273
million in excise. The case could go on to adjudication.

But the share price then began to climb upwards, partly as a result of
a bold plan executed by a young recruit to the Reliance finance section.
Anand Jain, then 29, had been a schoolmate of Mukesh Ambani before
qualifying as an accountant. He joined Reliance at the beginning of
December 1986, when Dhirubhai was persuaded to let him take over
management of the share market operations from his old colleague
Chandrawadan ('Mama') Choksi. Jain managed to get hold of confidential Bombay Stock Exchange records giving the reported positions
of Bombay's big stockbrokers in Reliance shares. In many cases, these
were at wide variance with the positions Reliance knew to be the case
from its own registry. Jain threatened to expose the brokers, bringing
down heavy penalties on their heads, unless they immediately squared
their positions by taking delivery of Reliance shares. The rout ended,

and many of the bears suffered ruinous losses. Jain, who later went on to head the Reliance Capital and Finance Trust arm of the group, had won his spurs. He soon became a replacement for Dhirubhai's late nephew Rasikbhai Meswani as the company's chief troubleshooter and dealmaker, the inside track to getting transactions and orders from Reliance. By the mid-1990s he was being referred to around Bombay as the 'third son' in the Ambani circle.

By early February 1987 the G Series issue could also be claimed a dazzling success. The block of debentures reserved for the public, worth Rs 1.32 billion, won subscription applications of Rs 4.94 billion in total. The Rs 880 million reserved for non-resident Indians had Rs 1.5 billion offered. Together with the Rs 1.6 billion subscribed by shareholders and Rs 200 million by staff, the total money subscribed came to Rs 8.24 billion. Dhirubhai thus had Rs 3.24 billion more than the Rs 5 billion he could keep. Even with a 'rapid refund' scheme for unsuccessful applications, he could keep the money to play with for at least two months.

In addition, to ease the pressure on the Reliance share price, the company's share registry, Reliance Consultancy Services, sat on the rush of share transfer applications lodged just before the 29 November cut-off date for the G Series rights attached to shares. According to stock exchange rules, ownership transfers were to be made within a month of delivery, but by late February 1987 investors and brokers were screaming that some 3 million shares were still in limbo. By keeping these out of the market, the company created a scarcity of floating shares that helped keep the price rising from the late-December nadir.

The financial pressure was off, temporarily. Reliance had the funds to complete its PTA and LAB plants, which were way behind schedule (the polyester staple fibre plant had opened six months late, in July 1986) and to refurbish its image of technological prowess. And

157

Dhirubhai could still claim that the small investors believed in him, in their millions. Reliance now claimed the largest shareholder base of any company in the world: 2.8 million.

But the fight against the bears in the stockmarket during 1986 to stop a freefall of his share price had drained his personal reserves, the parallel fund that had sustained the Ambani magic. Huge amounts had been spent on counter-publicity to the *Indian Express* and efforts to block his political critics. One senior broker close to Dhirubhai at that time estimated that Dhirubhai had lost about Rs 5 billion by early 1987, not including the fall in value of his shareholding.

Dhirubhai would also have known by then of a drastic profit decline for Reliance, its first since listing. In fact his forecast of a profit rise for 1986, made less than two months before the financial year closed, in retrospect looked puzzling. The annual results for 1986 published in April 1986 showed that net profit had dropped to a mere Rs 141.7 million, lower even than the first half profit the G Series prospectus had reported and an 80 per cent fall from the 1985 profit.

And then there was the unshakeable enforcer Bhure Lal, eyes fixed ahead, who had quickly dismissed an attempt at a conciliation by Mukesh Ambani at a meeting granted during the year. By January 1987 Dhirubhai would have been hearing back from his contacts in Du Pont and Chemtex and the dilemma his deals had put them in. The Customs Service was about to issue its show-cause notice on the allegedly smuggled yarn plant in February.

Dhirubhai had some more financial breathing space, but he was still in a closing trap.

11

Letting loose a scorpion

Dhirubhai Ambani needed something more. He needed to unlock the doors in New Delhi that had suddenly become closed to him in 1985. The master key was obviously Rajiv Gandhi – but how to win over a young man who clearly regarded Dhirubhai as the epitome of everything that had been wrong with the Licence Raj and the Congress Party?

Although he had grown up in the household of prime ministers, Rajiv had been born without the ruthlessness that distinguished Indira and her other son Sanjay. Rajiv seemed to lack the mental drive to push himself to higher achievement. He had failed to complete his degree at Cambridge. And until he was drafted into the party by Indira after Sanjay's death, he had been supremely happy flying in the Indian Airlines domestic fleet. Even after five years in the prime ministership, he left some acquaintances with the feeling of a personality not fully matured, not hardened into adulthood. Capable of great affection and enthusiasm, he tended to let emotion push his judgements – as in the quickly reached 'settlements' of deep-rooted ethnic and communal disputes in Punjab and Assam, which soon became meaningless in the absence of the follow-up measures only a skilled politician could deliver, or in sometimes grandiose and adventurist foreign policy initiatives.

Not too deep down, Rajiv was also prone to panic. When his initiatives went awry, as they tended to do among the deeply cynical and entrenched vested interests of his complex country, he would sometimes overcorrect his well-meant impulses by shabby manoeuvres or hurtful shows of a petulant temper. Rajiv had expelled the more egregious members of his mother's inner circle, but only to install his own favourites. Later known as the 'coterie', they formed a barrier between the Prime Minister and his party, between Rajiv and reality.

Within a few months of his Bombay speech in December 1985 about the Congress powerbrokers and corrupting business links, Rajiv was starting to have second thoughts. The speech had been mocked within the party as the thoughts of a greenhorn. The tax and foreign exchange raids launched by V.P. Singh from April 1985 had brought constant complaints from big business. Few had resulted in completed prosecutions, but the arrests, searches and seizures – all immediately publicised – were humiliating punishment enough for moneybags used to getting nosy officials called off with a quick call to New Delhi.[1]

By April 1986 the press was reporting an imminent revolt by Indira Gandhi loyalists. Pranab Mukherjee gave an interview defending his record and was promptly expelled on 27 April. Around mid-year, Arun Nehru – Rajiv's first cousin and Internal Security minister – who was also regarded as close to Dhirubhai, became estranged from the Prime Minister. He was dropped from his ministry in October. In June the commentator M.V. Kamath was writing that Rajiv's honeymoon was over, because of the Bombay speech and raids on industrialists.[2] The editor of the *Times of India*, Girilal Jain, was quoted as saying that big businessmen could no longer meet the Prime Minister. On 6 August Rajiv was bailed up about the raids at a meeting with the Calcutta Chambers of Commerce and admitted within hearing of journalists that they might have gone too far.

In late August or early September, Rajiv opted out of the meetings arranged with Gurumurthy. In October he met Dhirubhai for their first direct and private meeting since becoming Prime Minister. But it is still not clear at what stage Rajiv might have begun to perceive Dhirubhai as an ally After all, the nascent revolt in the Congress Party had featured politicians identified with the Ambanis.

There remains the wonderful story, widely told in Bombay and New Delhi, that in their first meeting Dhirubhai bluntly told Rajiv that he was holding a huge amount of funds on behalf of Rajiv's late mother and wanted to know what to do with the money. Apocryphal or not, it became part of India's political folklore because it fitted with Dhirubhai's reputation for both brazenness and keen judgement of character (and was much later used in *Guru*, the posthumous film version of Dhirubhai's life that was promoted by his son Anil).

Undoubtedly Dhirubhai used the meeting to outline his big plans for industrial expansion and how these would fit into Rajiv's vision of a high-tech India. The rapprochement seems to have been assisted meanwhile by Dhirubhai's implanting the perception that his enemies were traitors to Rajiv as well. In particular Dhirubhai would have picked on the suspicion felt by V.P. Singh towards Amitabh Bachchan, megastar of the Bombay cinema, who had been drafted into Rajiv's winning Congress slate at the end of 1984. The Bachchan family had been close to the Nehrus back in their common home town of Allahabad. Amitabh and Rajiv had grown up together. Elected from Allahabad, Bachchan was seen by Singh as a potential threat to his own power base in the surrounding state of Uttar Pradesh. In late 1986 Singh's staff were said to be alleging privately, without ever producing the slightest evidence to support it, that Bachchan and his businessman brother, Ajitabh who had taken up residence in Switzerland, had huge wealth hidden in Swiss bank accounts.[3] According to a later report, it had been through Amitabh Bachchan that the October 1986 meeting between Dhirubhai and Rajiv had been arranged.[4]

On 2 December 1986, during a debate in parliament, a minister disclosed that the Central Bureau of Investigation – which comes under the Prime Minister's control, through a junior minister – had started an inquiry into whether Gurumurthy was being given unauthorised access to secret government papers. A leak from the Industry Ministry's Directorate-General of Technical Development (DGTD), the apparent basis for Gurumurthy's articles in August about the 'smuggled' Reliance plants, was indicated as the specific focus. The DGTD was encouraged to make a formal complaint, which it did on 11 December – adding, either bravely or for the record, that the 'favours purported to have been shown to Messrs Reliance Industries Ltd by the officials of this office may also be investigated into'. On 21 December the CBI raided Gurumurthy's office in Madras and took away a number of documents.

The Enforcement Director Bhure Lal, who set off on his visit to the United States later in December, is understood to have suspected that he was being shadowed from India by an agent of Reliance. Within days of Bhure Lal's visit, a person who identified himself as an inquiry agent retained by Bhure Lal appeared in Bern, Switzerland, and began making inquiries about Ajitabh Bachchan. The Indian Embassy and possibly Bachchan himself became aware of this. The embassy queried New Delhi, and Bachchan might have contacted his brother.

Rajiv Gandhi was taking a New Year holiday with his family in the Andaman and Nicobar Islands. Amitabh Bachchan joined the Gandhis for part of the holiday, something that was publicised accidentally when the Indian airliner carrying Bachchan was diverted to Rangoon because of technical problems.

The Gandhis returned to New Delhi in mid-January 1987. New Delhi was in one of its periodic military flaps about Pakistan. Earlier in the winter, India itself had conducted army manoeuvres on its western border, but these had now concluded. Yet Pakistan had just moved tank formations to forward areas. Rajiv called his cabinet together to assess the threat. On the evening of 23 January he abruptly asked V.P. Singh to leave the Finance portfolio and take charge of Defence. Rajiv had been holding the portfolio himself, but the situation now required a senior cabinet minister overseeing Defence full-time. Singh could hardly refuse, and the transfer was made and announced the next day.

Bhure Lal had reported on his American visit to his immediate superiors in the Finance Ministry and was to file a written 'Tour Report' later in February, which included the results of his follow-up correspondence with Du Pont and Chemtex. Soon after Singh was transferred, the Prime Minister's office asked to see all the Enforcement Directorate's records regarding the Fairfax inquiry, and Bhure Lal briefed the Cabinet Secretary, B.G. Deshmukh, about it on 28 January.

Around that time, his departmental head, the Finance Secretary S. Venkitaramanan, also pressed the Enforcement Director two or three times to reveal the subjects of his inquiries, explaining that if the ministry was going to be put in 'hot water' he should be forewarned. Bhure Lal demurred. The word was already out in the press that Bhure Lal had engaged an American private eye and that his targets included several big Indian companies and 'a superstar politician'.[5] Later, rumours in New Delhi suggested that a private eye had found evidence of Rs 6.5 billion in a Swiss bank account in the name of a company called Macny Adol Brothers (perhaps a Lewis Carroll-like distortion of 'Matinee Idol Brothers'), allegedly owned by the Bachchans and unnamed 'Italians' with Indian links. No evidence of any such company or bank deposit was ever produced but, combined with the appearance of the self-proclaimed investigator in Switzerland, the rumours added to the heat under the Prime Minister's friends.

The government's legal machinery was meanwhile working against Reliance on the customs and excise evasion questions. Dhirubhai was not yet out of the soup. But V.P. Singh was uneasy. On 9 March he asked for Bhure Lal's file on Fairfax to be sent across to him at Defence in South Block and annotated in a margin that he had approved the engagement of a foreign detective.

Around 10 or 11 March copies of two sensational letters were shown to Rajiv, most likely through one of the senior bureaucrats in his office, Gopi Arora. The letters were to have dire consequences for Rajiv Gandhi. How they reached the Prime Minister's office has never been revealed. Both were apparently written on the letterhead of the Fairfax Group. The first, dated 20 November 1986, said:

> Dear Mr Gurumurthy
> Dr Harris apprised me of his useful meeting in New Delhi last week with Mr R. Goenka, Mr N. Wadia, Mr V. Pande, Mr B. Lal and yourself. Now that the group has been retained to assist the Government of India we hope to expedite end result.
>
> We received only US$300 000 arranged by Mr N. Wadia. As considerable efforts have already been made and expenditure incurred, it is advisable Mr Goenka arranges during his forthcoming visit to Geneva an additional US$200 000. We shall refund both amounts on receipt from the Government of India to

E. Briner, Attorney, 31, Cheminchapeau-Rogue, 1231, Conches, Geneva.

We shall apprise Mr Goenka in Geneva about the progress made on source of funds for purchase of Swiss properties of Mr Bachchan. We shall contact Mr Goenka at Casa Trola, CH-6922 Morcote (Ticini), during his visit.

Yours sincerely

(sd) G.A. McKay

The second letter carried no date:

Dear Mr Gurumurthy

Please send me the following details to continue our investigations:

(i) The details of rice exports by the Government of India to the Soviet Union;

(ii) Documents relating to the non-resident status of Mr Ajitabh Bachchan from the records of the Reserve Bank of India.

When Mr Bhure Lal visits here next time, we will make his stay pleasant.

Yours sincerely

(sd) G.A. McKay

The treachery of V.P. Singh and other friends like Nusli Wadlia seemed confirmed. Financed by Wadia and his mother's old foe Goenka, the conspiracy was aimed at striking down Rajiv through his old friend, Bachchan. The details seemed to corroborate the plot: the Swiss attorney Briner was an old friend of Goenka who had visited him in Bombay a year or so before. Casa Trola, the address where Goenka was to be contacted, was meant to be that of Nusli Wadia's retired father. (But the composer of the letter had got it wrong: the name of the house, Casa Fiola, was actually misspelled, and it was not close to Geneva but on the Italian–Swiss border.)

A panic-seized Rajiv handed the letters to the Central Bureau of Investigation, who immediately assigned the case to the team already investigating the apparent leak of the DGTD report to Gurumurthy. According to the complaint filed by the DGTD, the relevant file on Reliance had indeed disappeared for two weeks in July 1986, reappearing on a certain desk on 25 July, and Gurumurthy had appeared to have drawn upon it for his August articles on the 'smuggled' plant.

But the CBI's two investigating officers, Yashvant Malhotra and Radhakrishna Nair, were reluctant to prosecute under the Official Secrets Act, originally passed by the British in 1923 to protect the Raj against embarrassment by nationalists and only slightly modified in 1949. How could it be used against an Indian journalist who had exposed in a newspaper the activities of a commercial enterprise? It was hardly the kind of offence listed in the Act: 'passing surreptitiously information or official code or pass-word or any sketch, plan, model, article, note or document which is likely to assist, directly or indirectly an enemy'. If Gurumurthy was to be penalised for his methods, they argued, Reliance should also be investigated for the apparent offences he had revealed.

The 'Fairfax letters' seemed to give the CBI's director, Mohan Katre, the national security grounds that were so far lacking for a prosecution under the Official Secrets Act. The bureau's full resources were thrown into the job. All files on the Reliance investigation were collected from the Enforcement Directorate. At 10.30pm on 11 March Bhure Lal was called at his home: he was being transferred to run the Finance Ministry section handling currency and coinage, one of the ministry's most routine tasks, and was to hand over charge of the directorate the following morning. At the same time, the Enforcement Directorate itself was removed from the responsibility of the Revenue Secretary, Vinod Pande, and was placed under the Finance Ministry's

Department of Economic Affairs, which came directly under the Finance Secretary, S. Venkitaramanan.

On 12 March arrest and search warrants were sent by air to Madras and Bombay. At 1.30am that night, a team from the CBI arrived at Gurumurthy's house, put him under arrest on charges of criminal conspiracy and breaches of the Official Secrets Act and seized carloads of documents. In Bombay the agency arrested a partner in Gurumurthy's accountancy firm.

Later on 13 March the CBI turned up and ransacked the *Indian Express* guesthouse, where Goenka happened to be staying. Wadia and the controversial Hindu 'god man' Chandraswami were calling, separately, on Goenka. Both were allowed to leave after being searched. As the CBI detectives went through his papers, Goenka had a telephone call. It was Dhirubhai, offering to help out in any way he could. Goenka slammed down the receiver.

At this point, the letters and their existence were not public knowledge. The waters were muddied even further by the splash in the *Indian Express* on the morning of 13 March of a highly critical letter written to the Prime Minister by the President of India, Giani Zail Singh. The elderly Sikh president, who regarded himself as India's senior statesman, had been trying to assert himself over the young Gandhi heir. Zail Singh had refused his assent to one government bill on postal services earlier in 1987; he accused Rajiv of not consulting him on the Punjab, where insurgency was getting worse. He now rebuked Rajiv for undermining the President's high office and warned he would not just be a 'spectator' to this process. That the *Express* should get hold of his letter was not surprising: Gurumurthy had drafted it and Goenka's close adviser, S. Mulgoakar, had improved the English. In their search of the newspaper's New Delhi guesthouse, the CBI found a copy of the draft, with the corrections.

Brought to New Delhi, Gurumurthy was put through nearly forty-eight hours of straight questioning, most of it about the supposed targeting of the Bachchans. Meanwhile, the CBI issued a press notice that 'reliable information' had been received on 11 March that Gurumurthy and others had been in contact with certain foreign detective agencies and had passed on sensitive information from government files. Incriminating evidence had been seized during the searches. Through friends who brought in food and clothes, Gurumurthy was able to pass out the word to Goenka that the government had possession of certain letters. The bureau produced Gurumurthy before Delhi's chief magistrate on 17 March, listed four charges under the Official Secrets Act and sought an extension of custody. The CBI mentioned for the first time that it possessed a letter stating that Gurumurthy had made payments to Fairfax.

Represented by advocates Ram Jethmalani and Arun Jaitley, Gurumurthy admitted contact with Fairfax but pointed out that the investigators had been hired by Bhure Lal. In his bail application, the *Express* writer said that as a journalist he was not bound to disclose how he gained access to the contents of government files and that a lot of relevant information had been obtained by persons working for Reliance itself: 'a company powerful enough to have in its possession extracts from government files relevant to its pending demands and conduct of industry'. For its part, the CBI was 'not carrying on either an intelligent or an honest investigation' and was allowing itself to be used as an instrument of blackmail and harassment. In the course of his address, Jethmalani repeated the rumour about the Bachchans being involved with well-connected Italians in the Swiss company 'Macny Adol', thus getting the rumour into print under court privilege for the first time.

When, on 20 March, the Calcutta newspaper the *Statesman* published the first of the controversial 'Fairfax letters', Gurumurthy's allies and the public were able to see what was happening. Goenka was able to point out that he was out of the country at an international press meeting when the alleged meeting of conspirators took place in New Delhi. Nuances of the English used in the letter – in particular the erratic use of the definite article – showed an Indian rather than American hand. Michael Hershman, and his deputy McKay said the letter was a forgery using a transferred letterhead from his company. It would have been stupid and unprofessional to put such material on paper, they said.

The evidence backing the CBI case was looking shaky, and Gurumurthy was released on bail on 23 March after ten days confinement. Somewhat prematurely as it turned out, he declared that the press could trust the judiciary to help when the executive arm of government ran amok.

On 31 March a parliamentary debate broke out on the affair. The junior minister helping Rajiv run the Finance Ministry since V.P. Singh's exit, Brahm Dutt, had returned from a mysterious week-long trip to Italy in February, denying speculation that he had crossed by land into Switzerland. Dutt told parliament that Fairfax had merely been 'informers' for the Indian Government, provoking Singh to stand up and 'share responsibility' for hiring the agency. Hershman told reporters that he had been engaged by Bhure Lal and had a letter to show it. Dutt also revealed what seemed to be new evidence of the conspiracy. A computer print-out from the register of the Oberoi Hotel in New Delhi showed that Hershman had been booked into the hotel under the name Harris in November 1986 by Bombay Dyeing and that Nusli Wadia had been staying in the same hotel during his visit.

A claque of ministers and MPs from the Congress Party then began a concerted attack on V.P. Singh in parliament. The former Finance minister had endangered the national security of India by encouraging a foreign agency, one probably linked to the US Central Intelligence Agency, to obtain damaging material on prominent Indians. Sensitive material had been passed to Fairfax that could be used by CIA operatives to blackmail and embarrass India.

The clamour, which went on for five days, was led by the former Foreign minister and reputed beau of Indira Gandhi, Dinesh Singh, who went to sit by Amitabh Bachchan when he finished his own speech. The choice of Dinesh Singh, another member of India's minor royalty, seemed designed to counter any backlash from V.P. Singh's own Thakur caste. The beleaguered Defence minister walked up to Dinesh Singh. 'You've thrust a knife into my body,' he said to him in Hindi.

'What else could I have done?' replied Dinesh Singh, with a shrug.[6]

That Rajiv Gandhi had countenanced, possibly encouraged, the attack was obvious to V.P. Singh – a suspicion not allayed when Rajiv asked his colleagues to stop a proposed commission of inquiry under two Supreme Court judges to look into all aspects of the Fairfax affair. (V.P. Singh was correct: Dinesh Singh later confirmed that he had been instructed by Rajiv.)[7]

The terms of the commission given to the panel – Justices M.P. Thakkar and S. Natarajan – on 6 April also confirmed that Rajiv was interested in only one side of the case. The two judges were ordered to report within three months on the circumstances under which Fairfax had been engaged, for what purpose, under whose authority, on what terms and conditions, whether the agency was competent for the task, whether any payment had been authorised or made, what information had been received by the government from Fairfax, what information the government had made available to Fairfax and whether the security of India had been prejudiced.

The appointment came under strong attack as a diversion from a parliamentary inquiry in which all political aspects could have been investigated and from the CBI's failing attempt to prosecute Gurumurthy under the Official Secrets Act. 'The decision is as muddled as the original fiasco which the probe intends to resolve,' wrote the advocate Ram Jethmalani in the *Indian Express* the next day. 'The decision is lacking in political honesty, is clearly calculated to subvert the due process of justice and intended only to make the judiciary a sharer in the government's amazing follies.' In an observation that was later to get him into trouble, Ram Jethmalani also wrote that the CBI's counsel had admitted in Gurumurthy's bail hearing that the two Fairfax letters had been shown to Gurumurthy during his interrogation.

But Rajiv's move was given credence from a weighty analyst. The *Times of India* editorialised that the commission's appointment was an 'impeccable move'. In several signed articles over April and May the grand old newspaper's editor, Girilal Jain, urged readers to keep an open mind about the possibility of the CIA or other sinister interests being involved in the Fairfax affair, possibly to collect material for later use against India, and he asked whether the Fairfax Group was not 'semi-political in character'. Jain had not been an admirer of Rajiv before, but he had invested heavily in Reliance debentures in 1985, with the help of a BCCI loan.

V.P. Singh decided to test Rajiv's support. The material employed was a coded telegram to the Defence Ministry from the Indian Ambassador in West Germany sent around the beginning of March. In 1983 the Indian Navy had ordered two submarines from the German builder Howaldswerke Deutsche Werft (HDW). These were delivered in 1985, and negotiations were under way for a second pair to be built under licence in Bombay's naval dockyard. The Germans had agreed to a 10 per cent price cut, but the ambassador informed New Delhi they were unwilling to give a further cut because they were still bound by contract to pay a 7.5 per cent commission to the Indian agent who had originally clinched the order.

Rajiv's government had loudly banned use of agents in all defence deals in October 1985, so it was a good test case. Singh had already asked the Finance Ministry's two economic intelligence arms to report on the involvement of agents in the arms trade. On 9 April Singh asked his ministry's Secretary, S.K. Bhatnagar, to investigate the HDW case, then issued a press release about it. He sent the case file through normal channels around to Rajiv's office at the other end of the North Block of the Secretariat Building, annotating the names of the London-based Hinduja brothers, whom Bhatnagar understood to be the agents – although they later denied involvement. The file arrived on Rajiv's desk after newspapers published Singh's disclosure on 10 April.

Predictably enough, his move created a renewed furore against Singh within Congress, where the vested interests saw him as letting the side down, betraying his own team. To those in the know it was also an embarrassment to the Gandhi family: negotiations had begun with HDW in 1980 when Sanjay Gandhi was ascendant. The reaction from Rajiv's office was cool. Singh went to see the Prime Minister on 12 April and did not get the support he was angling to draw out. Later that day he resigned from the cabinet.

Events pushed Rajiv and Singh further apart. Four days after Singh resigned, a reporter named Magnus Nilsson reported on Swedish Radio that the Swedish armaments firm Bofors had paid a large commission to agents in a US$1.2 billion purchase of artillery by the Indian Army. The Bofors deal had been signed in March 1986, six months after the ban on the use of middlemen.

Rajiv fumbled his response, giving contradictory statements in parliament. He issued a scornful denial on 17 April and on 20 April said the Swedish Prime Minister, Olaf Palme, had confirmed that no middlemen had been used. His claque of Congress supporters stepped up their campaign against V.P. Singh, who spoke out in his own defence. Within a couple of weeks, Singh was touring the country explaining that his efforts to attack the black economy had been subverted by the very people he was targeting. Rajiv refused his suggestion to call a Congress parliamentary meeting to discuss the Fairfax, HDW and Bofors issues. On 2 June the Swedish Government's Audit Bureau confirmed that an even bigger amount of money than that reported by Swedish Radio had been paid to agents.

The atmosphere became even more feverish. Since March, there had been speculation that the disgruntled president, Giani Zail Singh, was thinking of dismissing Rajiv and appointing another prime minister, under hitherto untested reserve powers of his office. The Swedish audit report, contradicting Rajiv's assurances to parliament, could be a ground for his dismissal. On 17 June a state election in Haryana, adjacent to New Delhi, saw Congress almost wiped out there by a farmer-caste politician, Devi Lal, who had derided the Bofors deal in his campaign speeches.

Zail Singh backed down when he was bluntly informed by Arun Shourie, recently restored as editor of the *Indian Express*, that he would get no support from Ranmath Goenka. The old press baron had realised that Rajiv's replacement as Congress leader could just as easily be Arun Nehru – perceived as Dhirubhai Ambani's man – as V.P. Singh. The President then scouted for support from Congress dissidents and opposition parties for him to nominate for a second term as President, running against the official Congress candidate, when his term ended in July. The President is elected by MPs from the central parliament and state assemblies by secret ballot, so this provided a risk-free path for Congress to ditch Rajiv, who would have been obliged to resign if his candidate were defeated.

But the support promised was patchy and equivocal: the old Sikh backed down and retired quietly in July. Rajiv was beleaguered by further evidence of the trail of payments from Bofors pointing closer to his own circle, but he was firmly in charge of Congress. The party would sink or survive with him. In July it expelled V.P. Singh. The dumped politician was wryly stoic in a verse penned around this time: 'I have been cut into pieces/But my value remains the same;/I was a solid coin/ Now I have become small change.'[8] Singh's wan mood did not last long. In September, he launched the Jan Morcha (People's Movement) against the government, in which group, ironically enough, he was joined by Arun Nehru.

The Thakkar–Natarajan inquiry into the engagement of Fairfax meanwhile ground on, showing a wooden adherence to its narrow terms of reference and firmly closing off avenues that might allow the erstwhile investigators of Reliance to open up the substance of their charges. The original three-month term was extended twice, first to October and then to December. The first four months of hearings were held in secret, and it was only when open hearings began on 14 August that some of the evidence produced by the government began to emerge and the bent of the CBI as the commission's investigating agency became apparent.

Only Nusli Wadia was declared, under the law governing commissions of inquiry, a person likely to be 'prejudicially affected by the inquiry'. In theory this protected him against self-incrimination and enabled him to call and cross-examine witnesses; in practice the right was refused by the judges. Throughout the inquiry the two judges came under attack in the press for refusing to state what the rules of evidence were: whether 'beyond all reasonable doubt', as in criminal cases, or 'weight of probability', as in civil suits. Wadia was refused access to all papers put before the commission. In one instance, a judge took evidence without notice at his own residence.

Evidence and questions were swapped between the commission and the CBI. Wadia's declared status before the commission gave him no protection against action by the CBI on evidence that was presented to the two judges. On 31 July a senior CBI officer flew to Bombay and organised the arrest of Wadia for checking into a hotel as an Indian national. In India, foreigners are required by law to pay their hotel bills in foreign exchange, often at a higher effective tariff than Indian guests. As a British citizen, Wadia would have been obliged to do this on his travels within India. He maintained he always did so but that a hotel clerk might have assumed he was Indian when completing a register. Wadia was detained seven hours before being granted bail, close to midnight.

Two things were clear: the CBI was using evidence collected in the course of its Fairfax investigation, and no case was too petty for the senior echelons of India's premier anti-corruption agency when a political enemy of the government (as Wadia had rapidly become) was involved. On a complaint by Wadia's counsel, Ram Jethmalani, Justice Thakkar said the commission had not asked the CBI to harass Wadia. They were acting on their own.

Jethmalani himself faced a contempt of court complaint in a New Delhi magistrate's court, brought in May by the CBI, which insisted it had not shown the two 'Fairfax letters' to Gurumurthy during his interrogation. The existence even of the letters was now in question. The commission refused a request by Wadia for them to be produced. 'We do not know whether they exist or not,' Thakkar said, arguing that they were no longer relevant.

On 1 September, the day after the Indian parliament rose from its monsoon sitting, 400 officials under the Finance Ministry's Director of

Revenue Intelligence, B.V. Kumar, raided the eleven printing centres of the *Indian Express* around India. They seized documents, inspected printing machinery and took away several employees for questioning. Later, the agency charged the *Express* with evading Rs 3.3 million in customs duty by misdeclaring the speed of a printing press it had imported, of owing Rs 27.5 million in back taxes and of violating foreign exchange laws by making payments abroad in cash. Many of the tax offences alleged against the *Express* were already under dispute. It was noted that the leader of the raids, B.V. Kumar, had been in the customs office in Ahmedabad previously. No one in the Indian press saw the raids as anything but a blunt warning by Rajiv to the *Express*, by then leading the criticism over the Bofors scandal.

From the Fairfax office outside Washington, Hershman had given interviews to Indian journalists, contradicting several claims made by the government. He insisted he had been engaged by Bhure Lal, had been promised payment on a contingency basis and had not taken any money from either Gurumurthy or Wadia. The government formally ended his engagement on 27 May after V.P. Singh had mischievously asked whether India's national security was still being compromised.

To a questionnaire from the Thakkar–Natarajan Commission, Hershman asked to be satisfied first what the purpose of the commission was, given that all the facts about his engagement were known to the government; what action had been taken about the forgery on Fairfax stationery; and what action had been taken on information provided by Fairfax in the course of its inquiries. The two judges replied that these questions were beyond their scope. 'The commission hopes that you will be good enough to realise that instead of cooperating with the commission and furnishing the information, you are virtually reversing the roles,' they complained. Hershman refused to cooperate and became a critic thereafter of a 'cover-up' implicit in the commission's role.

The former Enforcement chief, Bhure Lal, had been called in for extended and gruelling interrogation by the CBI on two occasions in late March, then was called to give evidence by the commission. The Revenue Secretary, Vinod Pande, was also called. He had met Wadia several times, always in his office, first around the end of 1985 to discuss duty revision on PTA and DMT, then to discuss an excise raid on Wadia's company, Formica India, in November 1986. But he had also met Dhirubhai and Mukesh Ambani four or five times over 1986.

Pande himself had also been moved in mid-May. In the bureaucratic equivalent of being put out to grass, he was put in charge of the Department of Rural Development. His replacement as Revenue Secretary was Nitish Sen Gupta, the former Controller of Capital Issues in the early 1980s during Dhirubhai's golden run in the share markets.

Evidence given by all the suspected conspirators was mutually corroborating, although Bhure Lal was left quite isolated in his decision to hire Fairfax. Clearance to hire a foreign detective on contingency had been given only in general terms by his superiors. The CBI wanted to prove that Wadia and possibly Goenka had been funding Fairfax secretly and allowing Bhure Lal to think he had hired it on contingency. But it could not rely now on the discredited 'Fairfax letters'. The CBI needed some other clinching evidence.

The CBI and the counsel assisting the commission, the Additional Solicitor-General, G. Ramaswamy, concentrated on the hotel arrangements for Hershman in New Delhi. But these seemed to point only to the possibility of a second forgery. A computer print-out from the Oberoi Hotel showed that Hershman had been booked in by Bombay Dyeing. But this computer entry had been created the day after Hershman's arrival: the hotel's management admitted that the detail could have been given by someone telephoning in. From Washington, Hershman said he had not met Wadia at any time and had paid his own hotel bill with his credit card and had the sheet to prove it. Ramaswamy went into a detailed study of Wadia's bill, including his laundry account and food charges, in an effort to show that he was paying for more than one person. Wadia, it turned out, had his wife with him and his father was visiting from Switzerland. The hunt for treason had turned into a farce.

At the end of August, just before the raids on the *Indian Express*, Ramaswamy was angrily urging the judges 'not to take it lying down' when a magazine questioned whether, rather than getting at the truth of the Fairfax affair, the end result of the Commission of Inquiry would be a 'frame-up' of Nusli Wadia.

In the outcome, when the Thakkar–Natarajan report was handed to the government on 30 November and published on 9 December 1987, it did what Rajiv had obviously wanted it to do. It censured V.P. Singh for exposing India to security risks by allowing Bhure Lal to engage a US detective agency that employed some former CIA officers. The report concluded that Wadia had played an active role in the engagement of Hershman by Bhure Lal and had sponsored Hershman's stay at the Oberoi Hotel where he himself was also staying. Bhure Lal and the Government of India had been used as 'instruments' to serve the purposes of Wadia, who had an 'animus' against Reliance through business rivalry. But there was no evidence that Bhure Lal knew about Wadia's interest and role. It was inconceivable that Fairfax would ever have agreed to work on the system of rewards for information.

V.P. Singh declared the report 'a monument of injustice'. Rajiv Gandhi said it completely exonerated his government and had identified those who had joined hands with foreign agents in a conspiracy to weaken the country.

The origins of the forged Fairfax letters were never investigated, nor was the identity of the 'detective' who had appeared in Switzerland and started inquiries about the Bachchans. Together they showed the workings of a bold and unconventional mind, the existence of an impressive intelligence network and an uncanny grasp of human weakness.

The furore the letters set off caused a fatal split in Rajiv Gandhi's government, which just over two years earlier had won a record majority in parliament and seemed able to achieve a transformation of India's economy. By the end of 1987 Rajiv Gandhi was a discredited leader heading for electoral defeat. Possibly his government's decay would have happened anyway after the revelations in Sweden about Bofors. The trail of commissions was eventually shown to lead through Swiss bank accounts to at least one family friend, an Italian company representative in New Delhi. But perhaps Rajiv might have faced up to this scandal if he had kept his head about the alleged Bachchan aspect and continued to ally himself with those trying to nail down Reliance, thus possibly keeping their support.

The Bofors scandal made unbridgeable a rift that had already occurred. On top of corruption later came all the other issues of Indian politics: religion, caste, region, language, control of water resources, wealth disparities and so on. It has been overlooked that the split that eventually brought Rajiv Gandhi down can be traced back to the commercial rivalry between Reliance Industries and Bombay Dyeing over control of the Indian market for polyester feedstocks. The remark of the former minister that 'the course of Indian politics is decided by the price of DMT' seems all too true, at least for this tumultuous period.

The end result of the Thakkar–Natarajan Commission was, predictably, worthless. Even if Wadia had made secret payments to Fairfax, possibly breaking the foreign exchange law (although as a foreign citizen he was entitled personally to keep funds overseas), only by a long stretch of the imagination could India's security have been considered at risk. The exercise was called a 'cover-up' and a giant 'red herring'. Beyond the end benefit, there was nothing to connect Dhirubhai to the 'Fairfax letters'. But old friends who knew him from the early days might have thought perhaps of a different phrase: *Bichu chordiya* – Letting loose a scorpion.

12

Business as usual

The clouds were parting above Dhirubhai. His enemies and critics had been exiled from their positions of economic control. If the Prime Minister did not regard Dhirubhai as a friend and ally, at least he perceived Dhirubhai's enemies as his own enemies. And as the Bofors scandal became more and more embarrassing, with Ram Jethmalani and Gurumurthy trumpeting each new revelation, Rajiv Gandhi was suddenly feeling very threatened.

But Dhirubhai was in a tight position financially. At the end of April 1987, two weeks after V.P. Singh's resignation, he announced Reliance's poor results for the calendar year 1986. The profit was barely enough to cover a dividend of 25 per cent on the Rs 10 par value of the share, cut in half from the 50 per cent declared in 1985, and even that was denounced as a product of accounting jugglery. The polyester staple fibre plant had been completed six months behind schedule, and the PTA plant was a year overdue. Diminished cash flow was the reason for the delays, but the company's reputation for mastery of technology was deflated. The customs and excise evasion cases and the CBI's criminal investigations were still alive.

After the 1986 results, the collapse in the Reliance share price brought down the whole market, until the government nudged the Unit Trust of India and other institutions into a market support operation. The share market boom set off by Rajiv's 1985 initiative in economic liberalisation had ended. This was particularly grim news for Dhirubhai. As well as trying to restore high profits to Reliance, he also faced the task of rebuilding the estimated Rs 5 billion of his private funds lost in defending his empire in 1986.

Rajiv's government did all it could do to help, with Narain Dutt Tiwari a sympathetic listener as Minister of Commerce and for some months also Finance minister. On 7 May 1987, just after the Reliance results, it announced a string of changes in the import regime for polyester and its ingredients, ostensibly to help the whole domestic industry cope with what was portrayed as a weakening market. Polyester staple fibre, of which Reliance was about to become the biggest Indian manufacturer, was taken off the 'open general list' for imports – meaning any textile weaver could import it – and 'canalised' through the State Trading Corporation, a government agency that usually kept the import tap closed. The 'specific duty' of Rs 3000 a tonne put on imports of PTA and DMT in 1986 after lobbying by Wadia's Bombay Dyeing was removed. As DMT imports were also canalised and effectively stopped, this benefited PTA users – chiefly Reliance, which was still a few months off getting its own PTA plant into production. Extra allocations of foreign exchange were cleared for the PTA plant and the catalysts it used. Patalganga's PSF capacity, larger than the licensed 45 000 tonnes, was legitimised by a 're-endorsement'. The duty on N-paraffins, the petroleum feedstock used to make the detergent ingredient LAB, was cut by 75 per cent. Reliance was the only LAB manufacturer in India that needed to import this ingredient, as the others were all integrated into local refineries that made it. A new scheme of export incentives on polyester yarn and fibre exports handed out some cash rebates, excise concessions and 'replenishment' rights for imports.

The Finance Ministry also gave prompt clearances for steps to improve the company's cash balance. Within ten days of an application by Reliance, the Controller of Capital Issues cleared a rights issue of new shares to existing shareholders that raised Rs 1.98 billion. The government-run insurance companies, banks and investment funds became more interested in working capital loans, subscription to debentures and sale-leaseback arrangements on equipment.

The Controller of Capital Issues also cleared a proposal to 'pre-pone' (bring forward) the conversion of the G Series debentures by six months, to 31 July 1987, taking Rs 5 billion off the company's debt. This was barely five months after the debentures had been allocated among the subscribers. Many had not even received their certificates. Now they were being hurried into conversion.

Reliance issued a notice on 6 July calling an extraordinary general meeting of shareholders on 8 August to approve the early conversion. On 1 August it sent a circular letter to the debenture holders stating that if they opted for early conversion they need not send any communication. If they had not sent an attached form by 25 August, they would be deemed to have opted for conversion. According to litigants, who managed to delay but not stop the conversion later in the year, the 1 August circular reached many debenture holders only on 20 August – too late to be sure of sending their objection to conversion.

The litigants, who included some trade unionists representing

Reliance workers at Naroda, claimed that many investors might have wanted to hold on to their debentures for the full year and earn their 13.5 per cent interest. Big financial institutions had been already informed in mid-year by Reliance that profits and dividends for 1987 would stay low and that easing of the company's interest burden was vital. With the connivance of the government and its public financial arms, the litigants were saying, the small investor was being exploited so that Reliance could save some Rs 330 million in interest.

Debenture holders were also to discover that their bonds had been issued in units of ten, which meant the two-for-one shares they received on conversion were in lots of twenty – not regarded as 'marketable lots' in the stockmarket where the normal basic parcel was fifty shares. This meant delays while Reliance Consultancy Services, the group's share registry carried out the splitting and consolidation of share certificates into lots of fifty. The newly created shares were not, in any case, listed in the various stock exchanges until February 1988, meaning that for some six months after conversion the shares were not tradeable and could not add to any selling pressure on the price.

Despite all the help the government provided, Reliance was indeed still facing a dismal year. To stave off announcing a loss, it resorted to a desperate accounting move. The period of its accounts was to be shifted from the calendar year to the April–March fiscal year used by the government, meaning that the 1987 year would actually have fifteen months and end in March 1988. But by March, according to later analysis, Reliance was still showing a profit of only some Rs 130 million, even less than the 1986 result.

On 28 April 1988 Reliance announced that it would extend its year by another three months, not of course because of its lack of profits so far, but on the novel ground of 'synchronising' the commissioning of the PTA and LAB plants with the accounting year. By that stage, more favourable breaks had been given by the government in its budget for the year starting April 1988. The excise on yarn and fabrics was lowered: Reliance had been among several producers that had raised prices ahead of the budget speech, then announced that they were cutting prices to 'pass on' the benefits of the excise cut to consumers. A week after the budget speech, as an afterthought, the import duty on the polyester ingredient MEG was cut sharply.

When the figures for the eighteen-month-long 'year' were announced in November, Reliance announced another 'record' result, of Rs 807.7 million net profit on Rs 17.7 billion in sales. It was certainly the company's largest profit yet, but when annualised it was still down on the Rs 713.4 million profit declared in 1985. It had been helped by more creative accountancy, notably the capitalising of the entire interest cost of the PTA and LAB plants and a new basis of provision for depreciation, which had added Rs 245.4 million to the bottom line. By the financial ratios such as return on capital, which investment analysts used to gauge a company's efficiency and relative profitability, Reliance had shown less than spectacular results.

The justification for Reliance's hunger for money was the industry vision Dhirubhai could conjure up for his shareholders. At his annual general meeting in June the venue was an enclosed suburban hall rather than under the blue sky of the Cooperage Football Ground or the Cross Maidan. But Dhirubhai still looked up from the financial mires to a future of massive silver cracking towers, distilling columns and chemical containment spheres on the barren coastline of his childhood.

The company had been allocated 280 hectares of land at a new industrial zone called Hazira, on the banks of the Tapti River, across from the ancient textile trading port of Surat where the East India Company had set up its first trading 'factory'. Reliance planned to move into petrochemicals, making high-density polyethelene, polyvinyl chloride and caustic soda – the ingredients for the plastics revolution that had reached households in South-East Asia but not yet India, where sugar or cement was still shipped in jute sacks, women hauled water from their pumps or tanks in brass or steel urns, shopkeepers expected customers to bring their own containers for milk or rice and farmers lugged steel irrigation pipes across their fields or just gouged crude channels in the earth.

All the plants listed for construction at Hazira had been cited as proposed activities by Reliance when it garnered subscriptions to its G Series debentures in November 1986, and the acquisition of land at Hazira had been reported to Reliance shareholders in June 1987, along with the dismal 1986 results.

The site remained a swamp, as Dhirubhai tried to muster more cash and credit to start building his dream. At the end of May 1988 Reliance had applied to the Controller of Capital Issues for permission to make yet another massive debenture issue to finance its Hazira project, this time though a newly created subsidiary called Reliance Petrochemicals Ltd. The fully convertible debentures would be priced at Rs 200 each and bring one Rs 10 share in the new company immediately on issue, with the remainder being converted to more shares in two stages over the next three to seven years. The issue would raise Rs 5.934 billion towards an investment estimated at Rs 25 billion by the time it was completed in 1994.

The issue was cleared early in July 1988 and opened for subscription at the end of August, even though, as the *Indian Express* pointed out, Reliance Petrochemicals did not appear to have yet obtained the industrial licences it needed for the project. It was also the first case of a new company with no assets against its name being allowed to issue fully convertible debentures, which was against the policy laid down by the Finance Ministry controllers until then. The *Express* also questioned whether Reliance was raising money a second time, through the subsidiary, for the same projects the G Series debentures were supposed to fund. Reliance persuaded the Supreme Court to bar the *Express* from publishing anything on the validity or legality of the approvals obtained by Reliance Petrochemicals in connection with the issue. The order was lifted on 23 September after the issue closed. By then Dhirubhai had 2.3 million new investors in his empire, among them many of the existing 1.8 million shareholders in the parent company.

The petrochemicals plant would make Reliance only the second producer of high-density polyethylene in India and its biggest producer of PVC. But Dhirubhai's ambitions were racing even further ahead. In October that year the economic affairs committee of Rajiv's cabinet approved his proposal to build a gas cracker – a plant that breaks down the components of natural gas into different petroleum gases – alongside the petrochemicals plant at Hazira. It would produce 320 000 tonnes a year of ethylene, 160 000 tonnes of propene and 50 000 tonnes of butadiene. The feedstock would come from the nearby South Bassein natural gas field being developed by the government's Oil and Natural Gas Commission.

This was another big project, using proprietary technology of the world's petroleum and engineering giants. How was Dhirubhai to finance this when the big petrochemicals plant had just been put off the parent company's own rather stretched accounts?

Dhirubhai already had his eye on one of the jewels in the Indian corporate world, which he felt a friendly government had put in reach. The Bombay engineering firm of Larsen & Toubro, founded by two Danish engineers in 1938, had become one of India's biggest listed companies by 1987, with assets of Rs 9 billion, annual sales of Rs 5.8 million and gross profit of Rs 820 million. It was building all kinds of factories, making offshore platforms for the new oil and gas discoveries in the Bombay High field and fabricating high-performance equipment for India's nuclear power, space and defence programs. It was something of a strategic national asset.

As far as ownership went, the Danes had retired from the scene. The firm's shares were widely dispersed, but the government's financial institutions held a combined 42 per cent that decided the fate of its management. It had made some ill-timed diversifications into shipping and cement, but was a conservatively run company with an impressive range of technical expertise. While regarded widely as 'sleepy' and not giving its potential performance, it was still making a return on net worth that was twice that of Reliance in the bad days of 1986–87. It was immensely rich in internal cash reserves and borrowing power – a tempting takeover target, and the Dubai-based Chhabria brothers had already started nibbling in the market in 1987. But without the support of the institutions, no raid could succeed.

In May 1988 the Bank of Baroda, one of the score of nationalised commercial banks, decided to get into investment banking and to set up a subsidiary called Bank of Baroda Fiscal Services, soon abbreviated to BoB Fiscal. Two months later it asked the Unit Trust of India (UTI) and the Life Insurance Corporation (LIC), two of the biggest institutional investors in the share market, to help it start a portfolio by selling it baskets of shares. Oddly, 63 per cent of the basket from LIC and 46 per cent of the basket from UTI (by value) were Larsen & Toubro shares, bought for a total Rs 270 million on 3 August. BoB Fiscal sold these shares two days later for Rs 300 million to V.B. Desai & Co., a firm of share-brokers who did a lot of work for Reliance. Later in August, BoB Fiscal repeated the same exercise with the General Insurance Corporation (GIC), taking delivery of Larsen & Toubro shares for some Rs 141 million, about 55 per cent of the basket from GIC. These were also sold to V.B. Desai & Co. two months later. The brokers then transferred the two lots of shares, amounting to 8 per cent of Larsen & Toubro's equity to the Reliance offshoot Trishna Investments. Reliance suddenly emerged in October as the biggest non-institutional shareholder in the blue-chip firm.

Meanwhile, the Company Law Board, not until then the most vigorous regulator of corporate misdemeanours, had been activated by a minor scandal in the Larsen & Toubro management over the use of a company-owned apartment. The financial institutions agreed that it was time for a new broom. On 11 October 1988 Mukesh Ambani and the Reliance director M.L. Bhakta joined the Larsen & Toubro board by invitation. Dhirubhai proclaimed the new alliance 'a merger of the professional skills of Larsen & Toubro and the entrepreneurial skills of Reliance'. It meant greater risk-taking ability for Larsen & Toubro, he told journalists.

Reliance continued to buy Larsen & Toubro shares in the market, helped by a share price that had fallen on news of their effective takeover. It had built up a stake of about 20 per cent by early in 1989, when Dhirubhai was invited in as chairman and Anil Ambani also appointed to the board.

Just what Dhirubhai had in mind about greater 'risk-taking' came soon afterwards. In March 1989 Larsen & Toubro raised Rs 800 million for 'working capital' in a convertible debenture issue, then put Rs 760 million into Reliance shares to cement the relationship. It was paying over 12 per cent interest to the debenture holders and earning about 2.5 per cent in dividends on the shares.

In September 1989 Dhirubhai announced some other measures to tighten the alliance. Larsen & Toubro's shipping division would acquire two new ethylene carriers, which could be used to deliver feedstocks to the Reliance Petrochemicals plants at Hazira. And Larsen & Toubro would be given the job of building the new Rs 5.1 billion natural gas cracker that would eventually give an in-house supply of ethylene and other feedstocks.

The downside was that Larsen & Toubro itself would be financing the order it had just won. It would raise Rs 8.2 billion (Rs 9.43 billion with retained oversubscriptions) through a 'mega issue' of debentures. Out of this, Rs 6.35 billion would be given to Reliance as 'supplier's credit' for the natural gas cracker that Larsen & Toubro would build for Dhirubhai's company at Hazira.

Dhirubhai explained that the deal with Reliance would give the engineering firm access to gas-cracking technology that it could apply to projects all round the world. Around this time, Dbirubhai was also talking up some grand infrastructure projects in which Larsen & Toubro could take a lead: an undersea tunnel linking crowded inner Bombay with the open land across its wide harbour; a long dam across the Gulf of Cambay gradually collecting fresh water behind it; a super-highway linking Bombay, Delhi and Agra. It was time for Larsen & Toubro to think big.

As he was with Reliance. In December 1988 Dhirubhai announced he was applying for permission to build an oil refinery with a capacity to produce 6 million tonnes a year at Bharuch in Gujarat. Until then, oil refining had been reserved for government-owned or -controlled companies. His chances of approval were slim (and his application was turned down six months later), but Dhirubhai declared that, sooner or later, New Delhi would realise that it could not finance all of India's burgeoning refining needs. Other diversifying projects put up around this time included sponge-iron, power generation, television tubes and pharmaceuticals, none of which made much progress.

But bankers and accountants looked at the potential downside. The supplier's credit would be given to Reliance at 15 per cent interest, a margin of 2.5 percentage points above the rate Larsen & Toubro would be paying investors. But this was a puny return on funds that could be used to expand Larsen & Toubro itself. And the amount of supplier's credit, to one company and one project, was equivalent to some 55 per cent of Larsen & Toubro's total assets. It was a massive exposure for the company to a single risk.

Gurumurthy cried 'plunder' in the *Indian Express*, as the Ambani takeover progressed. The helpfulness of Dhirubhai's friends in the financial institutions, notably the chairman of the Unit Trust of India, Manohar Pherwani, was noted. Gurumurthy recalled that the chairman of the Bank of Baroda, Premjit Singh, had also helped Reliance out in the past by providing $25 million in loans for overseas Indians to subscribe to its F Series debentures in 1985. An enterprising and evidently plausible reporter on the *Express*, Maneck Davar, made a trip to southern Gujarat, where he found the sons and daughter-in-law of the bank chairman running a polyester yarn texturising company set up in October 1986. It took partially oriented yarn from the Reliance plant at Patalganga, then sent the crimped yarn back to Reliance, earning an estimated profit of Rs 5.5 million a year. Davar inquired whether he too could send yarn for texturising: he was told the firm worked only for Reliance. No one in the government wanted to know.

Dhirubhai had meanwhile moved further up in his scale of living. In November 1988 the entire Ambani clan had moved away from Usha Kiran, the Altamount Road building where he and his brothers owned flats. The new family home was a seventeen-storey apartment building named 'Sea Wind' off Cuffe Parade in Colaba, close to the business heart of Bombay. An Ambani company had bought the building in its entirety, and the family spread out through its upper floors. The first five floors were devoted to car parking, the sixth and seventh to a gymnasium and swimming pool, and several other floors to guest rooms.

Dhirubhai was also on the way to satisfying an urge to counter the *Indian Express* in print and perhaps to attain the indefinable status of the media baron. He had talked for some years of getting into the media business and already had a successful advertising agency, Mudra Communications, which was ranked fifth in India by annual advertising billings. This helped to pressure editors, as we have seen, but Dhirubhai wanted an editorial voice of his own.

He had looked at several newspapers that came on the market and had earlier bought a controlling interest in the pro-Congress newspaper, the *Patriot*, which had made vitriolic attacks on Nusli Wadia in response to the *Express* campaigns. At the end of 1988 his son-in-law Raj Salgaocar bought the Bombay weekly newspaper *Commerce*. Financially ailing, it had passed through five owners in recent years, including Kapal Mehra of Orkay Silk Mills, but had a useful business and economic research bureau. Prompted by Salgaocar and Anil Ambani, Dhirubhai agreed to transform *Commerce* into a mainstream daily business newspaper, to be modelled on London's *Financial Times*. As editor he hired Prem Shankar Jha, a former editor of *The Hindu*, son of a former foreign secretary and government economist and himself a noted writer in the academic world on India's political economy. Jha hired nearly sixty of India's best journalists, paying salaries that set a new benchmark for Indian newspapers. But partly due to a foul-up in ordering printing equipment, the new *Observer of Business and Politics* was not to launch until December 1989 when, as we shall see, it was already too late to turn the political tide, even if Dhirubhai's hired pens had been able.

His problems with the law were being pushed aside. The director of the CBI, Mohan Katre, had not been keen on investigating the allegations raised by the *Indian Express*. Early in 1987 the anti-corruption agency's additional director, Radhakrishna Nair, had recommended prosecution over the backdating of the letters of credit for the PTA imports in May 1985, but Katre had effectively sent the file on a bureaucratic wild goose chase by referring it to the Finance Secretary S. Venkitaramanan, who in turn referred it to the Ministry of Law and Justice. On 25 November 1988 the junior Finance minister, Eduardo Faleiro, told parliament that the CBI's report had been examined 'in consultation with the RBI and no further action is contemplated for the matter'.

In 1987 Katre had been a prominent guest in the VIP box at the World Series cricket tournament, sponsored that year by Reliance. The venue for the New Delhi games was a stadium at a convenient walking distance from the office complex housing India's security and intelligence agencies.

Nair volunteered for early retirement in 1988.

By launching a High Court action, Reliance had stalled the 1985 show-cause action started by the Assistant Collector at Kalyan for alleged evasion of Rs 270 million in excise on its polyester yarn production. There was still the show-cause notice issued in February 1987 over the alleged smuggling of its Rs 1.14 billion worth of yarn equipment and evasion of Rs 1.2 billion in duty. Reliance had tried to get the Bombay High Court and the Customs, Excise and Gold (Control) Appellate Tribunal to quash this notice also, but without success. It was due for hearing in April 1988 before the Bombay Collector of Customs, Sukumar Mukhopadyay, who was regarded as an upright official immune to political and other pressures. The scheduled hearing on 25 April had to be called off when Mukhopadyay was summoned to New Delhi for a meeting of western India collectors of customs, convened with little notice by the junior Finance minister in charge of revenue,

Ajit Panja. The hearing was relisted for 5 May. On 4 May Mukhopadyay was transferred to a new position and the case postponed again.

The new Bombay Collector, K. Viswanathan, took his time to familiarise himself with the case. Nearly eight months later, on 31 January 1989, he announced his decision to drop the smuggling charges against Reliance. 'There is no direct evidence, documentary or otherwise, of undervaluation,' he ruled. '... the charge of undervaluation is based on a capacity which is founded purely on theoretical calculations and calculating them by misreading the relevant data of the documents of contract ... Reliance Industries Ltd had not exceeded their licensed or the designed capacity and the capacity of the plant imported by them is neither in excess of the contract nor is the import contrary to the import licence.'

The battle with Nusli Wadia's Bombay Dyeing had moved upstream in the petroleum product chain from PTA and DMT to their common ingredient, paraxylene. Once again with funds to spare, Reliance was getting its long-delayed PTA plant into operation during 1988 and achieved commercial production late in the year. The PTA plant, as we have seen, included its own paraxylene-producing unit, which used napththa as feed stock. Bombay Dyeing's DMT plant continued to use paraxylene, which it needed to import for lack of domestic supply.

In March 1988 the government raised the customs duty on paraxylene from 85 per cent to 120 per cent, even though world market price for the feedstock had recently moved up from around $400 a tonne to $685. At this stage, Reliance was still using imported PTA on which duty had been cut ten months earlier. Bombay Dyeing was the only Indian importer of paraxylene and now received a double hit from the world price and the duty hike.

Reliance also received another benefit for its Patalganga paraxylene plant. In July 1988 the Finance Ministry granted it the status of a refinery, ahead of some twenty other napththa-based industries also seeking the same ruling, including National Peroxide, associated with Bombay Dyeing. The status meant that Reliance could get its napththa from domestic refineries at the concessional price of Rs 30 000 a tonne instead of Rs 100 000. The decision had been opposed by two members of the Central Board of Excise and Customs, B.R. Reddy and Jyotirmoy Datta, who pointed to the massive subsidy it implied through loss of excise, but they were overruled.

On 1 March 1989 the government cut the duty back to 90 per cent, but transferred paraxylene imports from the open general list to the 'canalised' category with the government-owned Indian Petrochemicals Ltd as the importing agency. In effect, this meant that Bombay Dyeing's independent sourcing of the vital feedstock was throttled back. The official in charge of petrochemicals called a meeting of paraxylene users, including Bombay Dyeing and Reliance, to ask whether there were any surplus supplies. A week or so later Reliance notified the government that it had about 40 000 tonnes to spare and that there was no need for imports.

If this indicated that Reliance indeed had greater capacity at Patalganga than authorised, the excess was quickly legitimised: in March the 'minimum economic size' for PTA plants under the industrial licensing system was raised from 100 000 tonnes a year to 150 000 tonnes and in June to 200 000 tonnes. The minimum size for DMT units remained at 60 000 tonnes.

Wadia remonstrated with the government over the next three months, taking his complaint to the Cabinet Secretary, B.D. Deshmukh. Reliance had effectively taken over the profitable paraxylene business from the government's own Bharat Refineries, using its napththa. Meanwhile Indian Petrochemicals was keeping Bombay Dyeing on a hand-to-mouth supply line for its paraxylene; the company ran out of the vital feedstock twice in this period. Reliance was asking the equivalent of the landed cost of imports, about Rs 28 000 a tonne, for its surplus. Bombay Dyeing estimated that its cost of manufacture was between Rs 10 000 and 11 000 a tonne. With domestic excise and sales tax a combined 19 per cent, this suggested a profit of Rs 11 400 to 12 400 a tonne. Wadia argued that paraxylene should be made available to all DMT and PTA producers at the same price, as set by the Bureau of Industrial Costs and Prices. This would be about Rs 7000 a tonne lower than the Reliance price.

Over this period, street protests and court actions against the government's treatment of Reliance made little progress, although they kept the allegations against the company alive. In October 1988 the Shetkari Sanghatana (Farmers' Organisation), which had been campaigning for three years against artificial textiles on behalf of cotton growers, announced that it would blockade the Reliance factory at Patalganga. But the movement's leader, Sharad Joshi, was persuaded to drop his plan. In December 1988 two activists employed Mahesh Jethmalani and a colleague to sue the government and others over the CBI's failure to prosecute on the evidence it was alleged to have assembled against Reliance. By contrast, the CBI had shown 'extraordinary zeal' in prosecuting trivial offences by those who had exposed alleged illegalities by Reliance.

Bombay Dyeing's lobbying got it nowhere. Dhirubhai was counted as a major backer of Congress for the general elections due at the end of 1989. Rajiv was turning back the clock in an effort to recapture the dynastic magic. In early March his mother's former political manager,

R.K. Dhawan, returned to the Prime Minister's office as an officer on special duty. Rajiv had set aside his 'preppy disdain' for the 'oily haired Punjabi *babu* [clerk]' and returned to Indira's style of functioning.[1] Dhirubhai had his own contact back in court.

By November 1989 Indian Petrochemicals cut off the supply of imported paraxylene altogether, while the government dropped excise on domestic supplies. Nusli Wadia was compelled to buy 4000 tonnes from Reliance, paying Rs 22000 a tonne, which still left Dhirubhai a fat profit margin on his sale. By that time Dhirubhai had many other worries, but he must have savoured this humiliation for Wadia at the end of this second phase of the Polyester Mahabharata.

13

Murder medley

S ince March 1987 the tables had been turned against Nusli Wadia and the *Indian Express*, both beleaguered on many fronts.

Ramnath Goenka's health was failing, and the old Marwari newspaper baron was spending long spells in hospital. But he was continuing the fight, even though the *Indian Express* was facing its worst period since Indira's Emergency. By the end of 1988 more than 230 prosecutions had been launched against the group by agencies in charge of company law, customs, income tax, foreign exchange and import quotas. Government advertising was withdrawn and banks directed to refuse credit. In Bangalore, the *Express* had continual trouble with its communications lines. Staff were harassed by goondas. A previous ally in exposing Reliance, the tabloid *Blitz*, had switched sides by mid-1987 when it captioned a picture of Express Towers as the 'House of Forgers' and called its editor, Arun Shourie, the 'Ace of Liars'. By late 1989 the *Express* group was on the brink of collapse, Shourie later revealed.[1]

From how high up the pressure started is indicated in the memoirs of the senior civil servant, Madhav Godbole. As Finance Secretary for the state of Maharashtra during 1986–89, Godbole was instrumental in denying requests by Reliance for additional concessions in state sales tax on production at Patalganga – one request being for sales tax breaks on production in excess of licensed capacity. Godbole recounts direct requests in person by Dhirubhai and Mukesh Ambani, lobbying on Reliance's behalf by the Marathi-language writer Bal Samant and by Congress MP Murli Deora, a string of invitations to concerts at Dhirubhai's home and a call from the Reliance public relations department asking whether Godbole and his wife would be interested in some shares from the directors' allotment in a current Reliance issue. Godbole refused all requests and offers. In April 1989 anonymous telephone threats to his home late at night caused Godhole to obtain police protection. Finally, the state's Chief Minister, Sharad Pawar, called Godbole in and told him of 'a lot of pressure from 7 Race Course Road' – the prime minister's official residence in New Delhi.[2]

After his arrest by the CBI in August 1987 for a wrong entry in a hotel ledger, Nusli Wadia encountered many other challenges apart from his intense battle over paraxylene. He and his companies were scrutinised for any possible violations of the Companies Act, the foreign exchange regulations and customs and excise regimes. Income tax inspectors revisited his tax returns for the previous thirteen years.

In the early hours of 12 July 1989 Wadia returned to Bombay's Santa Cruz airport from an overseas trip. Immigration officials served him with a deportation order, which said the Government of India had declared him an undesirable alien. Wadia had just over twenty-four hours to leave the country of his birth, where he had spent most of his life and where his family had a continuous record of business for more than 300 years.

He began an urgent legal appeal and got a court to stay the expulsion order. But the message was clear: if Wadia did not buckle under to Ambani's industrial supremacy and pay his prices, all mechanisms of the state could be manipulated to make his position in India untenable. His former friend Rajiv Gandhi had completely switched sides.

But just as the opposing forces seemed to have backed Wadia into a tight corner, the most bizarre episode in Bombay's textile Mahabharata began – one that was soon to cover the Ambanis and Reliance with great embarrassment and bring a collection of characters from Bombay's violent underworld briefly on to the centre stage of Indian commerce.

A week after his return to Bombay, Wadia was told that his life was in danger in his home city. Chief Minister Sharad Pawar telephoned Wadia at his home fronting the Arabian Sea at Prabhadevi waterfront. Without giving details, he warned the textile tycoon of a conspiracy to assassinate him. A squad of police commandos arrived soon after to mount a twenty-four-hour guard on Wadia's home. Two cars packed with armed police were assigned to escort Wadia's limousine around the city.

Pawar was an old friend of Wadia and no friend to Dhirubhai. He had parted company with Ambani's principal political investment, Indira Gandhi, in the late 1970s and had run a rebel Congress Party in his own state. Brought back into the mainstream Congress only recently by Rajiv Gandhi and installed as Chief Minister, he remained an ambitious and independent-minded satrap whom Gandhi's loyalists regarded with great suspicion. Prominent among these loyalists in

Maharashtra was the former city mayor and the Congress MP for South Bombay, Murli Deora, the old yarn market colleague of Dhirubhai. By then Pawar was feeling some heat himself from Reliance for failure to overrule Godbole on sales tax and for other hold-ups in state government clearances. Pawar believed Reliance was stirring up certain land scandals being levelled against him by party dissidents.

Even so, Wadia suspected that the security scare was a ruse to keep him under guard and keep his activities closely monitored. The next day, he gave the guards the slip and vanished for several hours. On his return, Pawar was again on the telephone and rebuked Wadia, warning him the threat was serious.

Wadia continued to be tied up with his appeal against the deportation order. On 26 July he applied to the Bombay High Court to be recognised as an Indian citizen. On 28 July he faced no less than the Additional Solicitor-General of India, G. Ramaswamy, who spent an entire day in court opposing his application. In addition the CBI Director, Mohan Katre, came down from New Delhi and spent the day watching the proceedings, a highly unusual level of interest given that the case was not one involving his agency. As the CBI is the only agency that can investigate judges, his presence might have been intended to intimidate the bench. Ramaswamy argued that Wadia had never been an Indian citizen and that, even if he had, his application for British passports in 1964 and 1984 had automatically extinguished any claim to Indian nationality.

But on the evening of 1 August a sensational development suddenly put Reliance in the dock. Detectives of Bombay's Criminal Investigation Department arrested Kirti Vrijlal Ambani, a general manager of Reliance in charge of public relations and customs and excise matters, and charged him before a magistrate with conspiracy to murder Nusli Wadia.

Also arrested and charged as chief co-conspirator was a strange companion for the Reliance executive: one Arjun Waghji Babaria, already widely known around Bombay as a small-time popular music band leader playing under the name 'Prince Babaria and His Orchestra'. Then aged 40, Babaria had frequently organised entertainment evenings that brought Bombay's milieux of business, cinema and crime together. Favouring black sequinned suits, see-through black shirts and a gold medallion as stage costume, Prince played the drums in his band while 'playback' singers and dancers pumped out hits from Hindi movies. Such figures as the actor Sayeed Jaffrey, Haji Mastaan, who was during his life the reputed kingpin of gold and electronics smuggling in Bombay, and several senior businessmen are among those figured in Babaria's photo-album of musical parties. Two years earlier Babaria had taken his musical troupe to Dubai to provide the night's entertainment at the birthday party of Dawood Ibrahim, the pre-eminent don of the Bombay underworld, later to be accused as mastermind of the bombings that rocked the city in March 1993, killing nearly 300 people.

Among Babaria's circle of acquantainces was Kirti Ambani, then 47. A long-time Reliance employee, he was originally named Kirti Shah but became so devoted to the Reliance founder that he had changed his own name to Ambani. Babaria had called occasionally at Kirti Ambani's office. At a party for Babaria's young son in 1987 Kirti had been a chief guest, his presence being recorded on video and camera.

The character of each of the two accused immediately threw a degree of implausibility over the alleged assassination plot: Kirti Ambani, a middle-management company man with an engineering degree, fond of playing chess, who had wife and children in the suburbs; Prince Babaria, a sentimental and pudgy figure of middling talent, desperately proud of his pretty wife Hema and their two children and living, as it turned out, in a police barracks at Bhendi Bazar – where his forebears had made a living for six generations as police informers.

Bombay business circles were incredulous enough that a Reliance employee would even think of taking out Wadia. Life was and is cheap in the city: right through the 1980s and 1990s leading businessmen in the construction and transport industries were victims of contract killings carried out for amounts of less than two thousand dollars. But the Ambanis' constantly expanding ambitions seemed to place them on a level of corporate behaviour well above this vicious jungle. Their chosen weapons were the robust publicity offensive, the judicious stimulus to bureaucrats and politicians, and an unfailing ability to interest big and small investors in their schemes.

In compiling evidence on the alleged conspiracy against Wadia, the police also revisited earlier cases – such as the bashings and attacks met in the past by the son of Orkay Silk Mills chairman, Kapal Mehra, Jamnadas Moorjani of the Crimpers' Association and embroidery exporter Bipin Kapadia. Statements were taken from Moorjani and Kapadia. Wadia also recalled a threat from 'terrorists' that had forced him to withdraw his two sons from their boarding school in the Himalayas at Kasauli in 1987. Nothing but the coincidence that all had at some time or other been in commercial rivalry to Reliance was established.

The police case, as eventually presented to court in October 1990, was that Kirti Ambani was deeply involved in the Reliance fight with Wadia's Bombay Dyeing Ltd for monopoly control of paraxylene. By limiting access to cheap imports, Reliance was trying to force Bombay Dyeing to buy Reliance's surplus paraxylene, on which the price was 280 per cent above the production cost. The two companies were in a 'hectic campaign' during July–September 1988.

After his job as Reliance press spokesman had been largely taken over by Anil Ambani and hired journalists in 1987, Kirti Ambani's duties continued to be 'liaison' with customs and excise officials. The police presented one example of such a contact, a former customs inspector named Umedsingh Sarraiya, who in 1974 had handled the customs bond placed by Reliance. Sarraiya had frequently visited the old Reliance offices at Court House and had been introduced to Kirti Ambani by Dhirubhai's nephew Rasikbhai Meswani, who was then in charge of customs matters. Sarraiya had continued social meetings with Kirti until 1989, at each other's home, or at small hotels and restaurants around Bombay, with Kirti usually picking up the tab. Other customs officers sometimes joined them. Sarraiya also admitted to police that he had been demoted for graft in the early 1980s, having been caught taking money from a passenger while on duty at Santa Cruz airport.

The police alleged that, in November 1988, the bandmaster Babaria had contacted a criminal called Ivan Leo Sequeira, alias Shanoo, whom he had known for a year or so through a mutual friend who played the Hawaiian guitar. Sequeira, then 29, had been convicted of a murder ten years earlier but acquitted on appeal in 1984. In 1988 he was again facing charges of shooting someone and was on bail.

Babaria had a proposition. A big industrialist was to be attacked and killed. 'He told me that we would be getting much money in that case,' Sequeira later confessed in a sworn statement before a magistrate. Babaria later revealed the target was Nusli Wadia, but did not immediately reveal who was paying, saying only that he was a 'big man'.

On 13 December 1988 Babaria and Sequeira went to the Ritz Hotel in Bombay's Churchgate area to meet Kirti. The Ritz is a small hotel close to the Nariman Point business district and was frequently used by Reliance and many other companies for middle-level meetings. Kirti had booked a room on the Reliance account and was generous with company hospitality at the lunchtime meeting, as the three consumed ten bottles of beer and various snacks.

Sequeira, introduced as 'Shakil', said Kirti had then discussed the plan to attack Wadia. Kirti gave him newspaper cuttings with photographs of Wadia, as well as Wadia's address and telephone numbers. Sequeira left the meeting and waited downstairs. Babaria came down, and Sequeira said he was interested in the job but wanted an advance. Babaria said Kirti had agreed to pay '50 lakhs' (Rs 5 million, then worth about $300 000) for a successful job.

The next day Sequeira rang Babaria and was told Kirti had agreed to pay Rs 500 000 in advance. The two met the same afternoon at a restaurant near Babaria's home. Babaria went outside to a lane and came back with a plastic bag containing Rs 150 000 in cash, which he gave to Sequeira. The police collected evidence of substantial cash withdrawals from Reliance bank accounts around this period, advances made to company employees, adjustment of bad debts and internal cash transfers. 'All these tend to suggest of [sic] possible manoeuvring of accounts for dubious expenditure,' the indictment said.

Thereafter, Sequeira dodged Babaria's increasingly anxious phone calls inquiring about plans for an attack. After several weeks, Babaria went to Sequeira's house and told him Kirti was inquiring about progress. At a second meeting, on 21 February 1989, the three sat drinking by a hotel swimming pool on Kirti's Reliance expense account and again discussed plans for the killing. Sequeira pressed for more of the promised advance and was duly passed another Rs 150 000 via Babaria at the Shalimar restaurant the next day

As more weeks went by without action, Babaria came under more pressure from Kirti Ambani. Sequeira said he was evading Babaria's calls to a neighbour's telephone and instructing his family to tell callers he was not at home. In April Babaria engaged another criminal named Ramesh Dhanji Jagothia to help carry out the attack. Jagothia was later to surrender to police two pistols made in local workshops, along with ammunition. Babaria also contracted a mechanic named Salim Mustaq Ahmed to steal a car and drive it in an ambush of Wadia's limousine, at an agreed price of Rs 50 000.

Together with Jagothia, Babaria went to Sequeira's home later in April and managed to find him. Babaria pressed Sequeira to get in touch with Kirti, and the next day Sequeira telephoned the Reliance general manager at his office. 'He was very upset,' Sequeira said in his sworn statement. 'He told me he was taken to task by his boss. I told him that I would return the advance money. But he told me that he was not interested in getting back the money. He was interested in getting the job done.'

In May Babaria and Sequeira met a very unhappy Kirti Ambani at another hotel. 'He told me that he was suspecting our intention,' said Sequeira. 'He was upset. He was about to cry. He was saying he was unable to face his bosses. I assured him that the nature of the work was serious and if anything goes wrong each one would come in trouble. He was not very happy by hearing all this.'

After this meeting, Babaria pressed Sequeira once or twice, but – according to Sequeira – came to realise that he was not really interested in the job, which Sequeira admitted himself. 'When Babaria approached me with the offer I thought that it was a good opportunity to me to make good money,' he said. 'But when I came to know that the person involved is an industrialist and a prominent figure I realised that it was too dangerous and I decided to back out. However, I was knowing that the persons who wanted us to do the job were also connected with industries and it was possible for me to knock out as much money as I can by dodging them. With this idea I knocked from them the sum of three lakh rupees.'

In a later interview, Babaria freely admitted to his role in organising the murder conspiracy and said that his assembled hit squad had actually tracked Wadia at three locations with a view to carrying out an attack. On one occasion, he claimed, they followed Wadia to a bungalow in the Western Ghats. 'We wanted to kill him but were two hours late so the operation failed,' Babaria said. On the other attempts, the gang tried to catch Wadia outside his home and again outside a hospital where Wadia had gone to visit the ailing Ramnath Goenka.

Babaria claimed that the advance actually paid to him by Kirti Ambani totalled Rs 1.3 million, suggesting that if Sequeira had played his cards better he could have squeezed even more money than his Rs 300 000. This accords with the sudden flush of money enjoyed by Babaria at the end of 1988 and early 1989, when he lavished gold jewellery from Bombay's top jewellers on his wife Hema, bought two old cars and a new sound system for his band, and had a priority telephone installation at his small house in the Bhendi Bazar Police Lines.

The plot came unstuck in mid-July, however, when one of the gang talked about it while drinking in a bar and was overheard by a police informant. The gang member was taken in for questioning and revealed the details. As the gang was rounded up, the sensational identity of the alleged target and client of the gang received attention from the city's most senior detective, the Joint Police Commissioner (Crime), Arvin Inamdar.

Babaria's new telephone line allowed the police to collect more evidence against Kirti Ambani by tapping calls between the alleged conspirators. On 22 July they recorded Babaria calling Kirti and mentioning details of the murder plan. Babaria asked Kirti if he knew whether Wadia was in town. Kirti replied that Wadia was in Mumbai because his appeal against the visa decision was fixed for 24 July. Kirti asked about the execution of the plan. According to the police court papers, Kirti said he was 'fed up with only assurances, dates and no results'. The people chosen for the job were not capable and his account should be settled – that is, the advance returned. Two days later, Kirti is quoted saying that 'neither he nor his boss were interested in the work any longer'. Babaria had been dodging him for nine months, and Kirti had found out from his own sources that nothing had been done to execute the plan. Babaria pressed to be allowed to continue, but Kirti again asked for the money back and told Babaria to get Sequeira to ring him.

Soon after, Sequeira agreed to turn approver, or state witness, and cooperated in an attempted telephone entrapment of Kirti Ambani. Sequeira rang to ask Kirti whether he wanted his Rs 300 000 back. Kirti evaded a clear rely, but the police said it was clearly established that Kirti knew Sequeira (under an alias) and that the money had been paid to him.

When the full implications of the plot became apparent, the chief detective Inamdar briefed Bombay's Police Commissioner, Vasant Saraf. In turn, Saraf took Inamdar and his case file up to Chief Minister Sharad Pawar, who carefully read through all the evidence. Having ordered the special protection for Wadia, he told the police to examine every finding with extreme care. On 31 July Pawar rang the office of Prime Minister Rajiv Gandhi in New Delhi and briefed the Cabinet Secretary, B.G. Deshmukh. Pawar said arrests were imminent. Kirti Ambani and Prince Babaria were picked up the following evening and charged.

Pawar's message had rung the alarm bells in Gandhi's office. As it was clear that the Bombay police were too far advanced for their investigations to be called off, Gandhi's advisers turned their efforts to damage control by getting the highly politicised Central Bureau of Investigation (CBI) on to the case.

Later reports said that Pawar himself had suggested to Deshmukh then that, in view of the 'political sensitivity' and interstate aspects of the case, it should be taken over by the central government. Other reports said that Pawar had succumbed to strong pressure from Gandhi's office to make the request. Pawar later insisted it was his own suggestion. Even before the arrests, the Director of the CBI, Mohan Katre, had suddenly arrived in Bombay on 1 August and started pressing the local detectives for details of the case. On 4 August the central government issued a notification transferring the case to the CBI. To the league of Ambani critics, this meant the murder case was destined for the same process of suppression by partisan investigation as the Gurumurthy allegations two years earlier. An action was mounted in the Bombay High Court, in the name of one Professor Ramdas Kishoredas Amin, opposing the transfer to the CBI and asking for measures to prevent vital evidence being interfered with or deliberately 'lost'. The High Court gave an interim stay order and placed all the records and cassette-tapes of telephone intercepts under the court's own custody.

The central government appealed to the Supreme Court of India, fielding the most senior members of its Attorney-General's office, backed by hired senior advocates. The bench of three judges decided on 16 August to modify the High Court order, allowing the CBI access to the sequestered records and tapes, provided that true copies were kept under seal. The case was left with the CBI, but the chief investigating officer of the Bombay Police was to be associated with further investigation.

Around the same time, the enterprising reporter Maneck Davar of the *Indian Express* found evidence that tended to confirm suspicions that Mohan Katre was indeed one of 'Dhirubhai's people'. Davar had heard that Katre's only son Umesh Katre had a business relationship with Reliance through a company called Saras Chemicals and Detergents Ltd. Posing as a small industrialist, Davar placed an order for three tonnes of the detergent ingredient LAB. The transcripts of Davar's telephone conversations with Katre junior make it clear that he and Saras were commission agents for Reliance chemical products, so closely related to Reliance that they were able to promise gate passes and receipts directly from Reliance to avoid extra sales tax for the purchasers. Davar found that the younger Katre was earning Rs 5.4 million a year from his Reliance connection, enough to buy an apartment in Bombay at which the CBI director himself stayed when visiting the city, as well as a Mercedes-Benz, which was then a rare luxury in India.

The CBI director's response was that he had no knowledge of his son's business activities. Arun Shourie commented in the *Indian Express*: 'Is it possible – and that in an Indian household – that you, the only son, should suddenly start making Rs 5.4 million a year and your father should not know? Specially if, as is the case in this instance, you have no particular qualifications other than being the son of the Director of the CBI to bag such a lucrative agency?' Shourie recalled a famous court judgement against a state Chief Minister, which made it the duty of senior public officials to investigate rumours or signs that their children were extracting benefits or being given benefits by virtue of their parent's position. The law against corruption fitted Katre to the dot, Shourie said.

As well as recalling Katre's intervention to have the *Express* critic Gurumurthy arrested under the Official Secrets Act in 1987, Shourie listed five investigations that had been 'buried' by the CBI under Katre's direction: the alleged gift of a Rs 250 million power plant by a foreign supplier; over-invoicing of raw material imports for PTA production; the surreptitious addition of a paraxylene plant to the Reliance complex at Patalganga without an industrial licence; clandestine royalty payments for chemical processes; and the antedating of letters of credit in 1985 to obtain foreign exchange worth Rs 1 billion.

Katre had not only been assisting Reliance directly, he had also been hounding Wadia as well. 'When was the last time you heard of the Director of the CBI sitting at the hearings of a case – even a case as important as say the assassination of Mrs Gandhi or the trials of the worst terrorists?' wrote Shourie. 'But Katre has spent hours and hours personally sitting through and in a most conspicuous place where the judge could see him, the day-to-day hearings on the case about Nusli Wadia's passport, a case in which the CBI is not even a party!'

Wadia himself gave no sign of knowing anything about the conspiracy until after the arrests on 1 August. When a reporter rang him for comment about 'the case', Wadia initially started talking about his visa case. But when interviewed by the police soon after, he certainly gave credence to the plot. 'In the last eight to ten years there have been certain incidents in the course of our business and that of Reliance Industries,' he said. 'I feel that these incidents could have motivated Kirti Ambani, an employee of Reliance Industries, to consider me an enemy.'

In a later amplification to a CBI superintendent in December 1989, Wadia admitted that he had been involved with the *Indian Express* as a friend of Ramnath Goenka, its owner: 'Mr Goenka and I both shared the same perception that the Ambanis and RIL, their company, had subverted and manipulated the government to such an extent that they were able to have their way in virtually every field through assistance from the government being directed entirely in their favour. This was possible as they had a large number of powerful supporters both among the bureaucrats and politicians in power. The *Indian Express* in a series of articles exposed many of the wrong doings of RIL and the favours that were granted out of turn to it. I through my association with the *Indian Express* helped and was indirectly involved in some aspects of the publication of these articles. I was also associated with Mr Gurumurthy who was the author of the said articles.'

Mukesh Ambani, when interviewed by the CBI on 1 June 1990, was at pains to play down the 'rivalry' with Wadia and the effect of the 'misinformation' conveyed by the *Express*. He did not blame the *Express* articles for his father's paralytic attack in 1986, which he said was a hereditary illness. Kirti Ambani had come directly under Mukesh Ambani, but had no authority to spend large sums of money. 'About Kirti Ambani's alleged involvement in a case of this type, we came to know through his arrest,' Mukesh said. 'In fact it is hard to believe that we needed or need any retrogative [*sic*] step for our survival, as a few times back, we were supposed to be close to power.'

In the immediate aftermath of the arrests, the response of Reliance had been to cast suspicion on a counter-conspiracy against the Ambanis themselves and to play up the rivalry angle. 'As the case is *sub judice*, we have been advised not to comment on the charges levelled against [Kirti Ambani],' a company press release said on 1 August. 'But [we] would like to state that this appears to be a deliberate frame-up aimed at embarrassing and maligning our organisation at a point of time when one of the group companies is going in for the largest public issue in corporate history. It is a matter of great regret that an innocent employee of the company is being dragged into such an unseemly controversy resulting from business rivalry.'

Reliance executives had spread the idea that the conspiracy had been cooked up by Wadia, Pawar and the *Indian Express* group with the simultaneous objectives of nobbling the debenture issues for the Reliance Petrochemicals plant at Hazira, getting Wadia out of his difficulties with visas and raw material supplies and (for Chief Minister Pawar) striking a damaging blow at Rajiv Gandhi.

They pointed out that Pawar's state government had appointed as prosecuting counsel the senior advocate Phiroz Vakil, who had earlier represented Wadia and Gurumurthy in the Thakkar–Natarajan inquiry

Dhirubhai Ambani's home town, Chorwad, in 1996. (H. McDonald)

The former house of Ambani's parents, on the outskirts of Chorwad. (H. McDonald)

Junagadh street scene. (H. McDonald)

The former Bahadur Kanji School (now Vivekananda High School) in Junagadh where Dhirubhai studied, and the city where he and his friends plotted against the dog-loving Nawab. (H. McDonald)

Tony Besse, chairman of Besse & Co. (Navin Thakkar)

Aden's British establishment on parade, 1963. (Navin Thakkar)

Guru of the 'equity cult': Dhirubhai Ambani inspires his shareholders at an AGM held in a Mumbai football ground. (*India Today*)

The textile market area of Mumbai, scene of Ambani's early business career after returning from Aden. (H. McDonald)

Ambani and Sons: Anil (left) and Mukesh with Dhirubhai at Maker Chambers IV, Mumbai, soon after they returned from studies in the United States. (*India Today*)

Ramnath Goenka, owner of the *Indian Express*, studies a work of Hindu philosophy. (*Indian Express*)

Dhirubhai Ambani plots his next move at a shareholders' meeting. (*India Today*)

Nusli Wadia, the Parsi textile tycoon who took on Dhirubhai Ambani. (*India Today*)

Indian Express investigator S. Gurumurthy is produced in court flanked by two Central Bureau of Investigation officers after his arrest in March 1987. (*India Today*)

Some bad PR: Kirti Ambani is released on bail after his arrest for conspiracy to murder Nusli Wadia. (*India Today*)

Under siege: Dhirubhai confers during the crises of the late 1980s. (*India Today*)

Bad vibes: bandmaster 'Prince' Babaria was arrested in 1989 for conspiracy to murder Dhirubhai Ambani's rival in the polyester business, Nusli Wadia.

V. Narasimha Rao, India's prime minister 1991–96, presided over an era of liberalising reforms and was a more conditional friend of Dhirubhai than his Congress predecessors. (Dieter Ludwig)

Combined talents: Mukesh and Anil at the Hazira petrochemical plant, November 1997. (*BusinessWorld*, New Delhi)

Prescient pose: Mukesh and Anil in a photo-shoot, November 1998.
(*BusinessWorld*, New Delhi)

The patriarch and the mother who presided over the split of the empire: Kokilaben and Dhirubhai not long before his death in 2002. (*BusinessWorld*, New Delhi)

Generational change: an ailing Dhirubhai is helped by Anil and Mukesh. (*BusinessWorld*, New Delhi)

Mukesh and Anil help carry Dhirubhai's body from Sea Wind to the cremation ground. (*BusinessWorld*, New Delhi)

Showdown at Maker Chambers: Anil walks into the 27 December 2004 meeting of the Reliance board. (*BusinessWorld*, New Delhi)

Public rupture: Anil talks to reporters after his vain confrontation of Mukesh at the 27 December 2004 board meeting. (*BusinessWorld*, New Delhi)

into the Fairfax case. (It was not mentioned that Vakil had also appeared against Pawar in another case.) Had they researched the background of Babaria, they might also have pointed out his descent from a long line of police narks. An anonymous note was circulated among press people in Ahmedabad, alleging a history of mental illness in Kirti Ambani's family.

Against a general scepticism that murder was part of the Ambani repertoire – and a belief that, if it had been, the plotting would have been more competent – this frame-up theory found plenty of takers.

The CBI continued to give every appearance of an active investigation, but a fatal flaw had been introduced by the CBI into the prosecution case. The body of evidence amassed by the police against Kirti Ambani and Babaria was highly circumstantial, drawing on hotel records and bank transactions that backed the alleged sequence of meetings between the conspirators and the transfer of money to the proposed hit team and on the telephone taps made at a late stage when Kirti Ambani was highly reluctant to take the plot further. Was Kirti the instigator of the plot, or had Babaria trapped him into it?

The crucial additional evidence was the confession of Sequeira, the hit man who had turned government witness. Without his testimony, the plot looked highly improbable and amateurish, Babaria hardly being convincing as a hard man of the underworld. Under Katre, the CBI arrested and charged Sequeira as Plotter No. 3 – a step that invalidated his earlier testimony to the Bombay police and completely destroyed any prospect of his testifying in court to implicate the others.

After the initial appearance of Kirti and Babaria in August 1989, the case disappeared from public view. Soon after the CBI took over, both the accused were allowed bail. Babaria said Kirti Ambani arranged half of the Rs 50 000 he posted. The other characters like Sequeira also got bail and sank back into the Bombay underworld.

The conspiracy case has been neither withdrawn nor proceeded with, but remains in judicial limbo. The backlog of many thousands of cases in the Indian court system is a convenient place to bury politicised scandals. Whether the Kirti Ambani episode was a murder conspiracy or a frame-up remains waiting its judicial test more than two decades later.

14

A political deluge

In the second quarter of the year India is limp with heat, waiting for the monsoon rains to arrive. For Dhirubhai, the monsoon of 1989 was less a relief than a forerunner of the political deluges to come.

On 24 July it brought cloudbursts to the Western Ghats and coastal hinterland of Bombay. The valleys around Patalganga became channels for the immense run-off; the new industrial zone built right by a river bank was soon under two metres of water. The Reliance factory had no protective flood walls nor any flood insurance. Its much-inspected machinery was immersed in mud and water for days. It was a disaster that threatened the very solvency of Dhirubhai's company, which had just struggled back to real profitability after three years of financial jugglery.

It was a crisis that brought back some of the old Ambani magic, recalling the fast assembly of the original polyester yarn plant. Mukesh Ambani once again assumed direct charge on the spot. Under the direction of its engineers, Reliance brought in an army of contract workers to disassemble the machinery, clean and oil each part, then put the whole thing together again. The plant was back in operation after a month, a triumph of Indian labour intensity under expert direction.

But even this brought its controversy: the *Indian Express* reported that Reliance was seeking Rs 2.25 billion in concessional loans from the government financial institutions, to finance yet another covert expansion under the guise of rehabilitation. By September, the Syndicate Bank was organising an emergency consortium loan of a more modest Rs 850 million.

Another flood was undercutting the Congress government. V.P. Singh's decision not to form a new party but to try to unify existing parties was paying off. In October 1988 splinters of the old Janata coalition began moving back together, with the merger of the Janata Party and the Lok Dal into the Janata Dal.

A month later, the Janata Dal formed an affiance with regional parties from Assam, Andhra Pradesh and Tamil Nadu, called the National Front. As Rajiv neared the end of his five-year term, the National Front formed working relationships with the Left parties and, less trustingly, with the other main force opposing Congress, the Bharatiya Janata Party (BJP) – the Hindu nationalist party that had taken the old Jana Sangh elements back out of Janata. The elections on 22 and 24 November 1989 saw Rajiv's Congress crash from its 415 seats of 1984 to only 192 seats in the 545-member Lok Sabha.

It was still the largest party as the National Front had gained only 144 seats. But with support from the BJP's eighty-six members and the Left's fifty-two and with Rajiv relinquishing any claim to try to form a government, the National Front was invited to do so. After five days in which a leadership challenge from the veteran Janata leader Chandrashekhar was diffused, V.P. Singh was sworn in as Prime Minister.

Although he could not avert the storm, Dhirubhai had taken some steps to protect himself. In July 1989 the Indian share markets saw massive selling of Reliance shares by investment companies controlled by non-resident Indians. They were moving their funds into foreign currency non-resident accounts, a necessary step towards repatriation and a protection against both a share market fall and a currency collapse. If these were the Reliance-owned companies, it did not necessarily mean that Dhirubhai was selling out his own stock. Reports at the time said two sets of brokers appeared to be working on behalf of Reliance, one set to sell and the other to take delivery.

It was a sound precaution: during the two months to the election, the Reliance share price lost a third of its value, against a slight rise in the overall share market. All other Ambani-related stocks (Reliance Petrochemicals, Larsen & Toubro and various debentures) also fell. The institutions that had once rushed to help prop up his share prices now held back, anticipating a change of government. The investors who had converted their G Series debentures at Rs 72.5 now had a stock worth Rs 70. With some glee, the *Indian Express* reported that Reliance, 'who straddled the industrial arena like a colossus during the Congress (I) regime [i.e. Indira Gandhi's prime ministership], is now facing a winter of despair'.[1]

The new government saw all of Dhirubhai's old opponents back in power. Singh brought back the former Revenue Secretary Vinod Pande from Rural Affairs to be his new Cabinet Secretary. The former Enforcement Director, Bhure Lal, was put on the Prime Minister's staff as a special officer. The new Finance minister was a proponent of public sector investment, Madhu Dandavate, who had also been a leading critic of the Ambani style.

Those seen as friends of Dhirubhai were now on the outer. The new government soon transferred the officials it saw as Dhirubhai's protectors in the Finance Ministry, including the Finance Secretary, S. Venkitaramanan, the Revenue Secretary, Nitish Sen Gupta, and the chairman of the Central Board of Direct Taxes, A.S. Thind. The CBI director, Mohan Katre, was retired and the agency set to work on tracking the Bofors and other scandals that had surfaced under the previous government. The Unit Trust of India's chairman, Manohar Pherwani, and the Bank of Baroda's chairman, Premjit Singh, were shifted early in 1990.

The various cases against Reliance were revived. On 12 December the Central Board of Excise and Customs, through its member, K.P. Anand, issued a fresh order accusing the Bombay Collector of Customs, K. Viswanathan, of 'inconsistent reasoning' and 'grave' errors of judgement in his decision to drop the charge of smuggling in the extra polyester yarn plant. Reliance had illicitly imported four spinning lines and deserved 'severe penal action'. Viswanathan was transferred on 2 January 1990. The new Collector in Bombay, A.M. Sinha, took the case up again before the Customs, Excise and Gold (Control) Appellate Tribunal early in February. This time the former Additional Solicitor-General, G. Ramaswamy, who had tried to nail Wadia in the Thakkar–Natarajan inquiry, was back in private practice (while a lawyer who had appeared for the *Indian Express*, Arun Jaitley, was now in Ramaswamy's old role). Ramaswamy now pleaded for Reliance.

Another minor customs scandal was later unearthed. Investigators in the Central Customs and Excise Board found that in November 1982, when Reliance was assessed as owing Rs 312.8 million in duty and a court action had failed, the then Collector of Customs in Bombay, B.V. Kumar, had allowed the company to pay in 138 instalments over the next two years, resulting in an implicit interest cost to the government of Rs 30.3 million.[2] Kumar was shifted in January 1990 from the Central Board of Customs and Excise.

In May 1990 the Bombay customs revisited the Reliance plant at Patalganga at less than a day's notice and took detailed notes on machinery in the new purified terephthalic acid plant. On 11 May it issued a new show-cause notice of some 170 pages, alleging that Reliance had imported a PTA plant with a capacity of 190 000 tonnes, against its licensed capacity of 75 000 tonnes a year. The captive paraxylene plant, declared to have a capacity of 51 000 tonnes, could actually turn out about 400 000 tonnes a year, according to the customs evaluation. The under-declaration at the time of import was put at Rs 1.74 billion and the duty evaded at more than Rs 2 billion. The response from Reliance spokesmen was that the charges were part of the same vendetta, promoted by Nusli Wadia; the machinery was all covered by licences; and the excess capacity was authorised under the government's 're-endorsement' scheme.[3]

From January 1990 the new government had also been scrutinising the tariff protection given to Reliance. Officials from the Ministries of Finance, Textiles and Petrochemicals had been studying the import duties on polyester fibres and their ingredients, with a view to sharp cuts. According to the press reports, the government saw lower tariffs as the simplest way to cut Reliance down to size: it could be carried out almost instantly with few avenues of legal appeal and would be politically saleable as a move to cut cloth prices.[4] On 25 February the government enforced a 25 per cent cut in the price of PTA.

But it was in the new corporate alliance with Larsen & Toubro that the Singh government managed to hit Dhirubhai the hardest. The financial institutions, which still had a combined 37 per cent holding as against the Ambanis' 20 per cent, were instructed to remove Dhirubhai from the firm's chairmanship. In early April 1990 the Life

Insurance Corporation took the first steps towards calling an extraordinary general meeting of shareholders to have all the Reliance nominees
removed from the board. On 19 April Dhirubhai bowed to the pressure
and resigned, on condition that the three other Reliance men stayed
on the board. A career manager with various public-sector enterprises
and banks, D.N. Ghosh, replaced him as chairman. Ghosh's first action
was to get Larsen & Toubro to sell off the Reliance shares on which
the firm had spent Rs 760 million a year earlier. The sale, at an oppor-
tune moment later in the year, actually made the firm a Rs 170 million
profit. The second action was to reduce the limit on suppliers' credit to
Reliance to Rs 2 billion – and that only to cover work being done by
Larsen & Toubro itself. The proceeds of the Rs 8.2 billion debenture
issue, successfully floated in October 1989, were diverted to Larsen &
Toubro's own expansion in cement and machinery manufacturing.

The prize had been snatched away. Dhirubhai was left with a huge
gap in his financing for his gas cracker at Hazira, for which costs had
escalated from the original Rs 7.2 billion to about Rs 8.46 billion. The
Indian financial institutions were talking about bridging finance, but
insisting that Dhirubhai first tie up his technical agreements for the
plant and get the land transferred from the Gujarat state government.
They were also humming and hawing about the special funding for
the flood clean-up and repairs at Patalganga. The Reliance share price
sank even lower, to levels not seen since the company's early days, hitting a low of Rs 50 in March.

Dhirubhai's new newspaper, launched as the *Observer of Business
and Politics* in December 1989, was not the influential voice that his
son Anil and son-in-law Raj Salgaocar had expected. Dhirubhai had
taken more direct control himself, as it became clear that the new government was going on to the attack against Reliance. He began to have
suspicions about the paper's editor, Prem Shankar Jha, who had been

keeping company with Rani Jethmalani, daughter of Dhirubhai's old legal and political foe Ram Jethmalani. Two trusted journalists, R.K. Mishra and B.S. Unniyal, were appointed as deputies. Jha himself had been approached by V.P. Singh in February 1990 about becoming the Prime Minister's media adviser, but had asked for six months to make a decision. He returned from a trip to Kashmir late in March to find that two senior writers had resigned over Unniyal's policies.

Jha warned Dhirubhai that fifty of the original fifty-eight journalists were also close to quitting. But within two weeks Jha himself had decided to quit and told Dhirubhai he was joining Singh's office. 'It was the only time I have ever seen him silenced,' Jha remembered.[5]

The mood at Reliance became ever more defensive. For the public record, Dhirubhai and other figures put a brave face on things. But the tone of the company's anonymous briefings to journalists became one of hurt pride, of a wrongly persecuted victim. Dhirubhai and his boys had recognised that the names Reliance and Ambani required some image work. Kirti Ambani had been hustled out of his public relations role after the murder conspiracy scandal the previous year. The 'corporate affairs' side of the company was greatly expanded, with the recruitment of skilled publicity managers in both Bombay and New Delhi.

In the capital, the vice-president handling government relations, V. Balusubramanian, was now working overtime cultivating politicians in the ruling coalition and the parties backing it from the outside. As in 1979, when Dhirubhai helped Indira Gandhi bring down the Janata government, he was now probing for weaknesses and susceptibilities. Both Dhirubhai and key figures in the V.P. Singh government saw it as a desperate fight to the death. 'There was hardly a day when we did not spend several hours pondering how we might bring down V.P. Singh,' recalled one senior Reliance executive, about 1990. 'And I suppose that in his office there were people who spent as much time plotting how to do the same to us.'[6]

The government was soon falling apart by itself, in any case. Singh's deputy Prime Minister, Devi Lal, had unilaterally announced a write-off by the nationalised banks of their small loans to farmers, a step that eroded the capital base of many banks to zero. Lal's son, put in charge of Haryana, was proving a thuggish embarrassment. Thus compromised by his own deputy, the Prime Minister had tried to pick up the economic liberalisation he had begun under Rajiv Gandhi in 1985, through a drastic shift in the government's investment priorities in the new five-year plan starting in April 1990. The weighting would shift from public-sector industry to agriculture and rural development, where the growth and employment response was greatest. Controls on private investment, domestic and foreign, would be relaxed. The tax system would be simplified and the tax rates eased to win greater compliance.

To help win support for reforms from the many defenders of state-directed industrial investment in the government, the economic adviser in the Prime Minister's office, Montek Singh Ahluwalia, circulated a paper at Singh's request in June which pointed out that India's rising domestic fiscal deficits and increased dependence on foreign borrowings were taking it towards an external payments crisis. India needed sharp remedial measures – including cuts in public-sector spending, a rupee devaluation and recourse to restructuring loans from the International Monetary Fund and the World Bank.

The debate was a political free-kick for the 'bull elephant who had been pushed out of the herd, Chandrashekhar',[7] who still thought he was the rightful leader of Janata Dal. A former Young Turk of the Congress Party who had made his exit many years before Singh, Chandrashekhar was the ultimate Indian politico. From a similar upper-caste background to Singh's, but from the gangster-ridden coal-mining district of Dhanbad in Bihar, Chandrashekhar was a man of deals and electoral trade-offs behind a conventional mantle of Nehruvian socialism. With gusto, he attacked the proposals of Singh and Ahluwalia as a sell-out of Nehru's heritage and the enslavement of India to foreign capital. Singh backed down, and the resulting statement of policy did nothing to slow India's drift closer to insolvency.

In early August the Prime Minister finally steeled himself to sack his deputy, Devi Lal. Then, in the pivotal decision of his prime ministership, Singh abruptly announced that, with immediate effect, 27 per cent of jobs and places in the central government, public-sector enterprises and colleges would be reserved for candidates from the 'backward classes' (comprising mostly members of the Hindu lower castes). This fulfilled an election promise by the Janata Dal to implement a report commissioned by the previous Janata government in 1979 from a former Chief Minister of Bihar, B.P. Mandal. It was potentially good electoral politics, as the lower castes comprised 51 per cent of the Hindu population. The other parties kept silent, knowing that Singh had beaten them to the biggest of all 'vote banks'.

But the children of the upper castes and the well-off had no such inhibitions. The Mandal policy intensified their nightmare of finding jobs after graduating, as 22 per cent of places were already reserved for the former Untouchables and the 'tribal' population. Students staged anguished protests in New Delhi streets, provoking a brutal police reaction that saw several shot by volleys of rifle fire. Agitation and confrontations spread across northern India (southern India already had even greater lower-caste reservation policies at state level). In September students began immolating themselves. Over two months, 260 people died, either in protest suicides or from police gunfire.

By then, also, the BJP had resumed its own appeal to the hearts of

Hindu Indians, through a cult built around the warrior divinity Ram of the *Ramayana* epic that was designed to cut across caste barriers. It targeted a small mosque built by a general of the Muslim emperor Babar in 1532 in the northern town of Ayodhya as having displaced a temple marking Ram's actual birthplace. It began a countrywide mass 'pilgrimage' on Ayodhya to press for the mosque's replacement with a new Ram temple. Murderous violence broke out between Hindus and Muslims through the next two months.

Singh had not prepared India for his new Mandal policy and failed to justify it afterwards. He looked remote and indifferent to the blood-shed in the streets. His timing looked opportunistic, designed to steal Devi Lal's thunder. Many New Delhi journalists were themselves of upper-caste, privileged backgrounds and took strongly partisan atti-tudes against V.P. Singh. The Mandal reservations and the widening gulf with the BJP put Singh on opposing sides to key figures in his earlier attack on Reliance. Gurumurthy had become a close adviser to the BJP leader, Lal Krishan Advani, while Arun Shourie, editor of the *Indian Express*, was vehemently opposed to the new reservations.

As the Singh government was weakened, Dhirubhai's fortunes revived. The turn could even be plotted on a graph of the Reliance share price, which began rising steadily from July 1990. The government was dis-tracted by its numerous splits and battles. The customs cases had been successfully bogged down by petitions seeking a stay of proceedings in the Delhi High Court. It was clear that further legal appeals could delay a final judgement for a decade or more. Aides like Vinod Pande, who pressed V.P. Singh to make a concerted effort to expose and tame Reliance while he had the chance, found the Prime Minister abstracted and diffident. Dhirubhai had also won over a crucial supporter of the government, the Marxist Chief Minister of West Bengal, Jyoti Basu, by announcing plans for a big new polyester factory in his state under a newly created subsidiary called Reliance Bengal, although it was never built.

Although it was obliged to report mounting contingent liabilities over its customs and excise cases, Reliance was climbing back shakily from its setbacks of 1986 and 1987 as the Indian economy raced into high growth under pressure of big government deficit spending and raised imports financed by borrowing. After the eighteen-month 'year' of 1987–88, Reliance had had a nine-month year for 1988–89 (July–March) in which net profit of Rs 793.7 million was reported. In September 1990 Dhirubhai convened shareholders at a Bombay auditorium for his annual meeting. The profit for the twelve months of 1989–90 (April–March) was Rs 905 million, a drop of nearly 15 per cent in annualised terms, but due to the provision of Rs 440 million for the flood damage at Patalganga.

The meeting saw Dhirubhai paint his big pictures again. But for the first time, he faced hostile interjectors and heckling. Shareholders complaining about the recent lack of bonus share issues and shouting charges of financial wrongdoing by the management pressed towards the podium, which was soon full of security guards ringing the directors. The pandemonium forced an adjournment.

In September, as it became more obvious that Singh was losing support, Chandrashekhar began mustering support for a revolt within Janata Dal and making overtures to Rajiv Gandhi's Congress Party. By early October nearly thirty of the party's MPs were listed in newspaper reports as disaffected. On 23 October the Janata Dal state government in Bihar stopped the BJP leader Advani's own march on Ayodhya, and the BJP immediately withdrew support from V.P. Singh's government. The BJP continued to send thousands of devotees into Ayodhya, culminating between 30 October and 2 November in a suicidal assault against Uttar Pradesh armed police ordered to defend the mosque by the state's Janata Dal Chief Minister, Mulayam Singh Yadav.

While all this was happening, Chandrashekhar and Rajiv Gandhi continued their efforts to split Janata Dal away from Singh. Dhirubhai was among four leading industrialists who financed their campaign, in which the going rate for a defection was said to be Rs 4.5 million. On 7 November fifty-five of the party's MPs, or about a third of its parliamentary membership, voted against the government. After a day of stormy debate, Singh resigned, and three days later Chandrashekhar was sworn in as head of a minority government supported from the outside by Congress. Reliance shares leapt to their highest point in more than two years.

When Dhirubhai reconvened his adjourned shareholders meeting on 13 November, this time at the Wankhede Stadium where international cricket tests are held in Bombay, the more friendly political environment seemed to be reflected in his less defensive mood. The critics were still there, asking for a bonus, but Dhirubhai said their rights to debenture issues had been a kind of bonus. To questions about use of corporate funds in toppling the V.P. Singh government, Dhirubhai said such reports were 'conjecture'. The new political set-up had emerged without the Ambani hand, he said.

First half results showed that Reliance was on the way to displacing Tata Iron and Steel as India's most profitable company in 1990–91. To help build its new gas cracker, which would continue the growth, Reliance was now proposing two new bond issues, raising Rs 4.56 billion in convertibles and a further Rs 1.14 billion in non-convertibles. This would replace the lost supplier's credit from Larsen & Toubro.

The new Prime Minister, Chandrashekhar, had gained a poisoned chalice. By allowing the Ram devotees to undertake token work on their new temple at Ayodhya, he put off the final confrontation (which was to take place in December 1992, when massed zealots demolished the mosque), and the communal violence gradually tapered off. But the postponement of the economic reforms he had so opportunistically engineered in mid-year now rebounded against him. The New York credit-rating agencies had lowered their rating of Indian sovereign debt in August. Iraq's invasion of Kuwait sharply pushed up India's oil import bill, while some three million Indian workers had to be evacuated from the Gulf at government expense, and their remittance income was then lost. Singh had approached the IMF for an emergency loan in October. In December Chandrashekhar took up the request and gained $1.8 billion in emergency credit, on condition that New Delhi took steps to cut its deficit and deregulate the economy. Always the pragmatist, Chandrashekhar swallowed the medicine that he had said would enslave India. His Finance minister, Yashwant Sinha, began drawing up a budget for 1991–92 (April–March), which had to include cuts in consumer subsidies and reduced public-sector investment.

Rajiv by then was alarmed, both at the appearance of competence Chandrashekhar was showing and at being seen to support unpopular measures. He feared that Chandrashekhar would take any political credit that was going and palm off the blame on to Congress. He decided it was time to make his own move for power. At the end of February 1991 Rajiv forced Chandrashekhar to postpone the budget for three months and to introduce a temporary finance bill, which made only minor fiscal adjustments. On 6 March Rajiv forced Chandrashekhar to resign. The President appointed Chandrashekhar as caretaker Prime Minister and set fresh national elections for late May.

The deferment of the budget caused the IMF to stall any further external financing until after the elections. Non-resident Indians began withdrawing their government-guaranteed foreign currency deposits with the Indian banks, a capital flight that was to take out a billion dollars by June. With foreign reserves below $1 billion, less than two weeks' import cover, the caretaker government authorised the Reserve Bank of India to apply emergency measures, which it did in March by virtually halting imports and sharply raising interest rates to around 20 per cent. The economy shuddered into recession.

Meanwhile, the initial optimism about Reliance's prospects under the Chandrashekhar government had been dissipating as Chandrashekhar showed little urgency in reversing the policy changes made by V.P. Singh.

Dhirubhai's friends had begun to move back into positions of economic and financial control. The former Finance Secretary, S. Venkitaramanan, was made Governor of the Reserve Bank of India, replacing R.N. Malhotra, as a matter of priority. Several accounts say that Dhirubhai's lobbying was decisive. In November 1990, even before Chandrashekhar was sworn in, Dhirubhai had told one diplomatic visitor: 'Mr Malhotra will be replaced shortly and the new RBI governor will be Mr S. Venkitaramanan.' Dhirubhai indicated that it was his recommendation.[8]

In March 1991 Venkitaramanan had in turn appointed the former Unit Trust of India chairman, Manohar Pherwani, as chairman and managing director of the central bank's housing refinance subsidiary, the National Housing Bank.

But Larsen & Toubro had remained outside Dhirubhai's control, even though in January a junior minister assisting Chandrashekhar, Kamal Murarka, had observed that Larsen & Toubro was 'Ambani's company'. Reliance was holding back its new debenture issues because it saw a weak reception in the market, although ostensibly delays in approvals were cited. With cost overruns in the Reliance Petrochemicals plant at Hazira, let alone the future gas cracker, it still badly needed the supplier's credit. To rub in the loss, Larsen & Toubro's chairman, D.N. Ghosh, had started the new year by writing to Dhirubhai pointing out that Reliance was late in paying Rs 1 billion on bills for work done by Larsen & Toubro. Mukesh Ambani lamely replied nearly a month later, claiming that Larsen & Toubro itself was behind schedule in some work.

On 15 February Ghosh had resigned at the request of the government. But the resulting uproar in the newspapers – Gurumurthy wrote under the headline 'L & T under hijack again' – had caused the financial institutions to delay a board meeting to appoint a successor. Before Reliance could overcome this hesitation, the government had fallen and the appointment had come under the rules banning a caretaker administration from making major appointments. The plum had stayed just out of reach.

Chandrashekhar and his ministers had been proving unruly clients in any case. The Reliance political lobbyists in New Delhi faced constant demands for cash to keep the government's small band of MPs from defecting again. As the minority government became shakier in February the scramble for funds became even more desperate. Eventually, the Reliance political team were getting almost daily demands for large bundles of cash from Chandrashekhar's office and his key political managers such as the Law minister, Subramaniam Swamy. The dependence on one capitalist was a particular irony in the case of Chandrashekhar: as one of the 'socialist' Young Turks in the Congress Party of the late 1960s, he had led the attacks on the industrial licences awarded to the Birlas that had caused the 1969 Hazare inquiry.

While the economy slowed down, the politicians fanned out for an election held, unusually, in the hottest months of the year. The results from the first of three days of voting on 20 May showed that Rajiv Gandhi would not have achieved the same comeback as his mother had done in 1980. Congress would have slid back even further from the 1989 result of 192 seats, to perhaps 160 seats out of 544 in parliament's lower house. It would still have been the biggest party, and Rajiv would have tried to govern with the support of smaller parties while an enhanced BJP waited to topple him.

But that was not to be. On 21 May 1991, as Rajiv campaigned in Tamil Nadu for the next round of voting, he was killed by a suicide bomber sent by the Tamil Tiger separatists in Sri Lanka. His assassination created a sympathy wave in the later stages that gave Congress an increased tally of 226 seats. Rajiv left a well-planned strategy for economic reform that applied the measures advocated since 1990.

Whether Rajiv might also have changed his business friends yet again is something that will never be known. The Bofors scandal was still very much alive, and he would have spent his second term keeping a lid on it. But a tantalising indication that he might have changed his view of Dhirubhai comes from an account of a meeting between Rajiv and Nusli Wadia in early May 1991, about three weeks before Rajiv's death.

Wadia had a call from Rajiv early in the week, asking for a meeting. Wadia was busy preparing for an important business trip overseas the following Saturday, but Rajiv insisted. So, after completing his work, Wadia flew up to Delhi on the Friday evening, arriving at Rajiv's heavily guarded bungalow on Janpath about 11pm. It was their first meeting since the Fairfax affair, and both men were edgy.

Rajiv opened up by complaining about the *Indian Express* sniping, which continued against him. Wadia exploded. This was nothing compared to what Gurumurthy and he had suffered: arrest, harassment by the bureaucracy, constant inspections, his passport and visa problems, and finally the murder conspiracy. Wadia asked Rajiv why he had refused to see him when the forged Fairfax letters were announced. Rajiv said he was not aware of any approach. Wadia said he must have known. It was general knowledge that Rajiv's secretary, V. George, to whom he had spoken, always took in requests for meetings for Rajiv to tick or cross off.

Rajiv explained that once the Thakkar–Natarajan inquiry was appointed he was committed to a course of action. He also reminded Wadia about the 'detective' asking questions in Switzerland. Wadia pointed out that this was part of the whole forgery plan. Did Rajiv appreciate, he asked, that his panicky decision based on the forgeries – this one avoidable thing – had started the whole confrontation that ultimately brought the downfall of his government?

The conversation went on past midnight. Refreshments, coffee, soft drinks and sweets were sent in as the two men talked on into the small hours. Wadia must have abandoned plans to find a hotel room. Finally the napping aides in the hallway heard a flurry of voices. It was about 5.30am, and the first light was coming through the tall neem trees and bougainvillea vines in the garden. Rajiv and Wadia came out into the portico and stood waiting while Wadia's driver was roused. Before Wadia turned to get into his car, he and Rajiv shook hands. It was evident that they parted as friends once again.

Wadia went straight to the airport and took an early morning flight back to Bombay. That evening he flew out of Bombay to Europe. He was still abroad three weeks later when he heard that Rajiv had been assassinated.

15

Under the reforms

After the shock of Rajiv Gandhi's murder, the Congress Party chose an elder as its new leader. P.V. Narasimha Rao had been in the top circles of power for much of a long career in politics. He had handled the Ministries of Home Affairs and External Affairs with great skill under Indira and Rajiv, and his intelligence and erudition (in nine Asian and European languages) were undoubted. But after an undistinguished stint as Chief Minister in his home state of Andhra Pradesh, he had been judged lacking in the charisma needed for the prime ministership. In 1991 he was already 70 and was preparing to retire from parliament when the party installed him as a stopgap chief.

But those who expected an early leadership fight within Congress or an early return to the polls had reckoned without Narasimha Rao's rejuvenated taste for power or his gift for intrigue, which was Kautilya (the third-century BC Indian 'Machiavelli') applied in a modern setting. From his minority starting point in parliament, Narasimha Rao steadily built up a Congress majority by attracting defectors from opposition parties and managed to serve out his full five-year term.

For the first two years at least, Narasimha Rao provided the political umbrella under which the long-delayed economic reforms could be introduced. India in 1991 and 1992 illustrated perfectly the adage that 'bad times make good policies'. To carry them out, Narasimha Rao installed as Finance minister the career government economist Manmohan Singh, who had reached the bureaucratic pinnacles of the ministry as Finance Secretary and then central bank Governor in the 1980s. The Cambridge-educated Singh had spent much of his earlier career helping to construct the edifice of government-planned investment. But then a spell making a comparative study of the world's less-developed economies for the South Commission, a body representing many developing nations, had crystallised doubts and begun a Pauline conversion in him towards market-based allocation of resources. Singh was soon backed by the elevation of Montek Singh Ahluwalia (the economist who wrote the 1990 reform paper) as Finance Secretary. The two Sikhs, almost invariably in austere grey-blue turbans, became the public face of reform.

Within a few days of the government taking office at the end of June 1991, Singh devalued the rupee by 20 per cent to encourage prompt repatriation of export earnings. In the deferred budget for 1991–92 (April–March), delivered at the end of July, he abolished licensing in most industries, raised fertiliser prices to cut subsidies, warned that loss-making government enterprises would not be supported indefinitely and relaxed controls on foreign investment. The second budget, at the end of February 1992 for the 1992–93 year, carried forward the same policies and pointed towards an Indian economy opened to global trade and investment flows by the end of the decade or even sooner. The rupee was made largely convertible on the current account, meaning that its exchange rate was to be set increasingly by the market, and more import items were transferred to the open list. Import tariffs, which had once ranged higher than 300 per cent, were to be no more than 110 per cent and much lower for capital goods. Foreign companies were welcomed into the petroleum sector from the wellhead to the petrol pump. The policing and pricing of new share and debenture issues by the Controller of Capital Issues was abolished, with vetting for fraud taken up by the new Securities and Exchange Board of India (SEBI). Indian companies were permitted to issue convertible securities over-seas, such as Eurobonds, and foreign portfolio funds were to be allowed to buy and sell shares directly in Indian markets. 'We must not remain permanent captives of a fear of the East India Company, as if nothing has changed in the last 300 years,' Singh declared in his 1992 Budget speech. 'India as a nation is capable of dealing with foreign investors on its own terms. Indian industry has also come of age and is now ready to enter a phase where it can both compete with foreign investment and also cooperate with it.'

The first test of how helpful the new government would be to Reliance came less than a month later. On 26 July 1991 the company's subsidiary Trishna Investments had used its substantial shareholding in Larsen & Toubro – then about 18 per cent even after it had returned the 7 per cent stake acquired through Bank of Baroda Fiscal to quell criticism in 1989 – to requisition an extraordinary general meeting of shareholders a month later. The meeting was to vote on two motions: that Mukesh Ambani be made the company's managing director and that Dhirubhai be reinducted to the board.

The prize was another shot at the blue-chip's cash. The funds from Larsen & Toubro's 1989 debenture issue had not yet been deployed,

234

because of a court action, then a need to get government clearance for a change from the originally proposed use. Dhirubhai was still desperately short of funding to complete the petrochemical complex at Hazira and move on to the new gas cracker. The financial institutions were frowning on a revival of the supplier's credit plans, and in May 1991 Dhirubhai had let it be known that he was expanding Reliance's own new debenture issue from Rs 5.7 billion to Rs 9 billion. But he had still not gone to market with it. Larsen & Toubro was still dangling for the taking.

'With friends in the government,' commented one newspaper writer, 'they [the Ambanis] are unlikely to have problems.'[1] Others were not so sure. 'Times are such that no bureaucrat will openly come out or do something which is perceived to be blatantly pro-Ambani,' noted *BusinessIndia*.[2] Dhirubhai indeed had many friends in the government or in the Congress leader ship, including old Indira or Rajiv loyalists such as R.K. Dhawan and Satish Sharma. But Narasimha Rao was too cautious and in too precarious a political position to give direct favours, and the Finance Ministry now had the strict Manmohan Singh in charge.

In a drive reminiscent of his old debenture placement campaigns, Dhirubhai began canvassing Larsen & Toubro shareholders to give Trishna their proxies to vote at the meeting. The takeover in 1988 had given Reliance two vital footholds, which the V.P. Singh government had not dislodged. A former assistant company secretary at Reliance had been installed as Larsen & Toubro's secretary, and Reliance Consultancy Services had been made the company's share registry in place of a Tata Group firm. It meant that Reliance had no trouble in getting all details of the shareholders. Over the month before the 10.30am meeting on Monday 26 August, about 200 agents for Reliance collected 107 000 proxies. By the weekend before the meeting, Dhirubhai and his team were convinced they had Larsen & Toubro in the bag and were already celebrating. Mukesh had resigned as executive director of Reliance and was ready to take over as vice-chairman and managing director of Larsen & Toubro.

But the renewed takeover attempt was a trumpet call to the Ambani critics of five years earlier. The *Indian Express*, Nusli Wadia, influential publisher R.V. Pandit and Ram Jethmalani all made frantic attempts to persuade ministers and officials that it would be improper to let this corporate jewel fall to the Ambanis.

A new press war broke out, with each side going to the extent of questioning the other's patriotism. In the *Express*, R.V. Pandit pointed out that Larsen & Toubro carried out vital defence work, seeming to suggest that the Ambanis could not be trusted with national secrets. Dhirubhai's *Observer of Business and Politics* recalled that Wadia was the grandson of Jinnah, founder of Pakistan.

Until the last minute, the government was disinclined to give any particular instruction to the financial institutions on how to vote their huge shareholdings. Jethmalani had failed to get a court injunction halting the meeting and was to fail again at an application to a judge at his residence on the Sunday morning.

However, the Ambani critics had been collecting testimony from some Larsen & Toubro shareholders that their names had been taken as proxies by Trishna without their consent. By the end of the last week, they were alleging forgery of proxies on a massive scale. Wadia contacted the then Janata Dal MP George Fernandes on the Saturday afternoon and got him to table a faxed message about the alleged forgeries in parliament just before it adjourned.

The opponents of the takeover managed to get through several messages to Narasimha Rao's senior staff, who appeared startled by the warnings that the government could be seen as party to a forgery in a case that might be heading to court. The pressure worked. The Cabinet Secretary came back with the response that the institutions would maintain the status quo at Larsen & Toubro.

It was then a matter of seeing that the instruction got through to the institutions in time. On Sunday morning calls to the chairman of the Life Insurance Corporation found he knew nothing about the decision. The cabinet office was then prompted, and it assigned an officer to the job in a special 'control room' to circulate the decision to the chairmen of the institutions. At 8.30 on the Monday morning, two hours before the meeting, the LIC chairman spoke to Mukesh Ambani and told him as gently as possible that unless the motions were withdrawn the institutions would vote against them.

Shareholders were already packing into the Birla Matashri Auditorium, close to Churchgate railway station. It was too late to call off the meeting. The Larsen & Toubro directors, including Mukesh and Anil Ambani, appeared on the podium and pandemonium erupted. Unaware of the government's decision, agitated shareholders rushed the microphones set up in the aisles and fired off volleys of questions and accusations. There was cheering and jeering by rival factions. The directors were shouted down as they tried to speak. Eventually they gave up and retreated behind the back curtain to exit the auditorium through a stage door. A swarm of shareholders surged on to the surrendered stage.

The shouting continued for half an hour, but it was all over. Dhirubhai had suffered what he later told close confidants was his greatest defeat. The government institutions went on to appoint a seasoned Larsen & Toubro executive as the new chairman. A Supreme Court ruling in May 1992 cleared the way for conversion of the 1989 debentures, diluting the Reliance stake down to about 8 per cent, the company's original entry level. The alleged forgery of proxies was never fully investigated. Police prepared to raid the godown where Reliance had stored the proxy forms, but were called off by the Maharashtra Chief Minister's office half an hour before they moved in.

Within Reliance, the failure was a sobering lesson that times were changing for Indian business. The government could no longer so obviously play favourites if it wanted to entice foreign investment. The value of licences had gone. Tariffs and excise duties were still high, but the trend would be to lower and uniform rates. Financial markets and institutions would have their transactions and performance scrutinised in public. The 'level playing field' was the motto of the times. The transformation had just begun, but this was the way it would be, sooner or later.

The implications for industries like Reliance was that their production would have to attain world-competitive cost levels by the time the economy was fully opened. His expansionary vision had put Dhirubhai in a good position. Whether by 'smuggling' capacity or not, his polyester and petrochemical plants were the largest in the private sector and had the best economies of scale. By getting in early with his petroleum projects, he could keep his capital costs down and be ready for the time when the sector was deregulated and prices were brought down to world market levels.

Dhirubhai and his sons astutely portrayed themselves as part of the new India, raw-spirited capitalists champing to have the bridles of failed Nehruvian socialism removed. The investment fund managers who flocked to Bombay from Hong Kong, Singapore and London from the end of 1991 were also inclined to overlook the 'colourful' past. 'Someone who can smuggle in a whole factory clearly has something going for him,' one Kleinwort Benson researcher remarked at the time.[3]

Imbued with the notion of 'emerging markets' – forgetting that Bombay's stock exchange, set up in 1875, was among the world's oldest – the fund managers had reached India after selling their clients on the business ventures of Thai and Indonesian generals, Chinese People's Liberation Army units and East Asian dynasties newly listed on new stock exchanges. India was a cinch by comparison. Soon research reports were piling up, pointing to India's large middle class and its hidden savings, the basic soundness of its British-style legal and corporate institutions, the skill of its top administrators and managers, and the political safety valves in its complex but democratic political system.

Dhirubhai had actually fared rather better under V.P. Singh's prime ministership and its aftermath than he had under Singh's earlier tenure in the Finance portfolio. Reliance's results for 1990–91 (April–March) showed a tough year, but sales had grown 13 per cent to Rs 21.05 billion and net profit 39 per cent to Rs 1.25 billion. The new year, 1991–92, had started out with little growth in sales or profit, given the brakes on the economy. But Dhirubhai asked his shareholders, at their annual meeting in October 1991, to look at Reliance's massive projected expansion now that licensing had been removed on nearly all the company's products.

This meant that the existing Patalganga plant would be further expanded to 'international size', and its supplies of naphtha and kerosene would soon come by pipeline from the Bharat Petrochemicals refinery at Chembur, whose own plans for downstream expansion had been virtually pre-empted by Reliance. The new petrochemicals complex was rising by the Tapti River at Hazira, on the former tidal flat reclaimed by use of a massive Dutch dredger and extensive piling. Its monoethylene glycol plant came into production late in 1991, and its polyvinyl chloride and high-density polyethylene plants were expected on stream during 1992. But the cost had blown out 70 per cent from the original Rs 10 billion because of the rupee's devaluation and the failure of government authorities to chip in their share of the power plant and jetties. Financially the subsidiary Reliance Petrochemicals was struggling.

At this point, Dhirubhai decided to merge the petrochemicals arm back into the parent company. The shareholders of Reliance Petrochemicals approved the move at a meeting in August 1991, held at Hazira where not too many of the 2.4 million stock-holders could have turned up. The meeting also allowed the early conversion of the remaining portions of the company's big debenture issue and the issue of fresh shares to the Reliance parent company at par in payment of a loan from it. The merger was announced as a decision by both boards on 28 February 1992 and made effective from 1 March.

Three of Bombay's leading chartered accountancy firms recommended a swap of ten Reliance Petrochemicals shares for one Reliance share. It meant that Reliance acquired the massive assets of the subsidiary at a discounted price and from 1992–93 was able to add its growing production stream to its own sales or keep them in-house at cost for use at Patalganga. The depreciation benefits of the subsidiary's investment were transferred to Reliance, where they were a shield against corporate income tax for several years. Reliance's profits indeed showed a strong leap the next year. Reliance shares had risen high again, so few of the subsidiary's old shareholders were complaining.

Even before the first foreign portfolio funds were authorised to invest from mid-1992, the Indian sharemarkets had enjoyed a spectacular boom on the euphoria generated by the reforms. The 1991–92 boom helped Dhirubhai quickly overcome his Larsen & Toubro disappointment. A new debenture issue in December 1991 raked in Rs 9.87 billion, a new record for corporate issues in India, and four months later it rolled over one of its big debenture issues from 1985 for another seven years.

The source of the subscription money puzzled Finance minister Singh and many of his officials, given that the central bank was still applying a tight liquidity squeeze, with interest rates around 20 per cent, as part of its attack on the external payments crisis. Then it was discovered that bank reserves were being turned into speculative cash. To help finance the huge government deficit, commercial banks were obliged at that time to keep a total 54.5 per cent of their deposits in government securities and cash. To make more profit from this compulsory investment, the banks traded and swapped their holdings of bonds issued by the treasury or government corporations in search of higher yields. Changes in interest rates would raise or lower the market value of bonds carrying rates fixed at earlier times. The deregulation of interest rates on bonds early in 1991 allowed public-sector enterprises to offer much higher rates on new issues, so the market value of their existing bonds fell sharply.

At the end of 1991 banks were more keenly trading their securities in search of higher yields. Banks were the only parties authorised by the Reserve Bank of India (RBI) to trade in 'gilts' (government securities), but several brokers had established themselves as trusted middlemen for particular bank treasury departments. The RBI was ill-equipped to control this growing market. Its register of who owned which gilts at any time was through handwritten entries in Dickensian ledger books at its old building in Bombay, and new ownership notes were sent by post out to banks. To speed up their transactions, the banks and brokers developed their own informal system outside the central bank's aegis, through the use of chits called 'banker's receipts' or BRs, which were simply certificates issued by the banks themselves indicating that they owned the securities being sold.

According to brokers and bankers involved, the practice began in 1984–85 when the bond portfolios of several public-sector banks were churned over on behalf of Congress Party fund-raisers for Rajiv Gandhi's election, raising Rs 4 billion.[4] The Reserve Bank was aware that bankers' receipts were being issued without the backing of actual securities, but did little about it. For ten years until 1992, the RBI's deputy Governor supervising banking operations was Amitava Ghosh, later criticised in a Joint Parliamentary Committee report on the scam as having taken a 'casual' approach to his role. Dhirubhai is widely credited with having swung Ghosh's unusual second term as deputy Governor.

The entry of public-sector enterprises (PSEs) in the late 1980s stepped up the unofficial market's tempo with a new 'portfolio management scheme', whereby the enterprises (and private-sector companies) would lend their spare cash to the banks, which would make high-yield investments on their behalf. The transfer was not a deposit (in which case the banks would have had to put 54.5 per cent into their reserves) and no return could be guaranteed. The risk would be on the enterprise, not the bank.

That was the theory anyway. In practice, the banks competed for PSE funds by giving an 'indicative' return. The PSEs wrote the placement down as a 'deposit' in their own books. If the banks made more than the indicated return, they kept it. The risk stayed with the owner of the money. In practice, the banks were not equipped to make high-return speculative investments, usually in the share markets and developed informal relationships with brokers. But because the banks were not allowed to lend money to brokers, a subterfuge was needed. The cover was a fake securities transaction, whereby the broker obtained an unbacked BR from a compliant bank to give in return for the funds.

The transaction would usually take the form of a 'ready-forward' or 'repurchase option (repo)' deal, whereby there would be an agreement to sell back the security after a certain time.

Dhirubhai, according to the brokers, became interested in the money market in the late 1980s and played it to recover some of the funds lost in the desperate 1986–87 defence of the Reliance share price. He had built Reliance's fund-raising operations to such a level that one analyst likened them to a virtual banking business parallel to and almost as important as the polyester business.[5]

The best known figures in the 1992 repo boom, broker Harshad Mehta and his brothers, had been caught in the crushing of bear brokers engineered by Dhirubhai's 'third son' Anand Jain at the end of 1986. They had escaped lightly after pulling a family connection: one of the brothers was married to a daughter of the vice-chairman of the Industrial Credit and Investment Corporation of India, a major lender to Reliance. The father-in-law had interceded with Reliance auditor D.N. Chaturvedi. Chastened, the Mehtas stayed clear of Reliance and turned to the money market.

Around November 1991 the Mehtas put in a call to Anil Ambani to break the ice. Their first meeting discussed the 1986 affair; it was agreed to let bygones be bygones. They started meeting frequently. The Ambanis were concerned about their share price, which was languishing despite the efforts of their brokers. They wanted to be first in India with a Euro-issue (i.e. securities priced in foreign currencies and issued in markets such as London) and to sell it at a high price.

The Mehtas found that Reliance was still seen in the market as a seller of its own shares. Every time the price rose Rs 20 or so, its brokers would start booking profits. The Mehtas agreed to start pushing up the share price, on condition that Reliance itself stopped selling. The intervention worked. It was against a background of wild bullishness in the market, but the ramping of Reliance was a substantial cause in itself.

Harshad Mehta became 'the Big Bull' – a title once given to Manohar Pherwani in his days heading the Unit Trust of India. Mehta's fellow Gujaratis came to regard him as a second Dhirubhai. It caused some pique at Reliance that a mere broker was achieving such glory and even presuming to correct Dhirubhai on his investment strategy. The Mehtas were buying up debentures that Reliance was selling, particularly those of the struggling Reliance Petrochemicals and Larsen & Toubro.

A small incident might have helped to persuade the Ambanis that Harshad Mehta was getting too big for his boots. Harshad and Anil Ambani had descended together in the elevator at Maker Chambers IV, the building housing Reliance's head office in Nariman Point, and stood together on the steps while their cars were hailed. Harshad's arrived first, a gleaming new Toyota Lexus, at that time the only one in India. Anil looked at it in admiration and made some complimentary remark. Harshad promptly handed over the keys and told Anil: 'Take it, it's yours.' Anil refused, but the gesture might have left him feeling patronised.

A net was closing in on the Mehtas in any case. The central bank's Governor, S. Venkitaramanan, had been trying again to goad his deputy Governor, Ghosh, into cracking down on the BR trading between banks. He was also intrigued by Harshad Mehta's apparently inexhaustible source of funds. An income tax raid on Mehta in February 1992 had failed to crack the secret because the Mehtas kept their data on encoded computer disks. Venkitaramanan had not quite put his suspicions together and made the mental link, but he was getting closer. In March he asked the State Bank of India to look at Harshad Mehta's account. The bank reported huge inward and outward flows of money. During April the State Bank began pressing Mehta to reconcile the huge shortage, Rs 6.2 billion, in his business with it. He sought to roll over the obligation and on 24 April brought in cheques to settle his dues.

But by then the scam was out. On 23 April a young business reporter, Sucheta Dalal, on the *Times of India* had reported a Rs 5 billion shortfall in the State Bank's treasury on account of transactions with a broker called 'the Big Bull'. The music stopped, and ten leading banks were left with a Rs 40 billion gap in their books.

It soon emerged that Harshad Mehta had paid his dues with funds provided by a fully owned subsidiary of the central bank itself, the National Housing Bank. Venkitaramanan, after his own appointment by the Chandrashekhar government, had brought back the former Unit Trust of India chairman Pherwani as the Housing Bank's chairman and managing director. Still wildly ambitious, Pherwani had thrown the bank into the thick of the repo-based securities trades. When Harshad Mehta was squeezed by the State Bank, the Housing Bank had obliged him with cheques made out to ANZ Grindlays Bank. Mehta had deposited these into his own account with ANZ Grindlays, then paid the State Bank of India.

According to sources close to the Mehtas, Dhirubhai had been the first person Harshad Mehta had contacted when put on the spot by the State Bank. Dhirubhai had told him: 'Don't call anybody. I'll look after the matter.' According to an account by the financial journalist R.C. Murthy, at a meeting with Harshad Mehta and 'an industrial tycoon', Pherwani had agreed to bail out Mehta.[6] One acquaintance confirms that Pherwani said Dhirubhai had been the person who interceded for Mehta. 'I was forced to do,' Pherwani told this person. However, the Mehta-linked sources deny that a joint meeting took place between Pherwani, Dhirubhai and Mehta.

Pherwani had been the fall guy for Dhirubhai once before, losing his Unit Trust of India job over the Larsen & Toubro affair. Now he faced complete disgrace. Harshad was unable to pull off the big securities deal he promised Pherwani, whereby a government corporation would have parked the funds through him with the Housing Bank. Pherwani resigned on 9 May. In the early hours of 21 May family members found him dead at his Bombay home. The journalist Murthy got a phone call and rushed to the house about 8am. Pherwani's body looked 'blue', he remembers. It was cremated at 11.30am the same day with the face covered instead of left open in the normal Hindu way. The death was ascribed vaguely to a 'heart attack'. Murthy and many others believe Pherwani committed suicide.

The opening up of the securities scam led to investigations by the Reserve Bank of India, the Central Bureau of Investigation and finally a Joint Parliamentary Committee. Senior bankers were sacked; several brokers and bankers arrested (including Harshad Mehta) and a special court set up to try those charged. Three ministers ultimately lost their posts for improper financial dealings. The blame was widely spread among financial system regulators, including the Reserve Bank Governor, Venkitaramanan.

The links between Reliance and Harshad Mehta or other brokers were never made explicit throughout the entire investigation, although the favours shown to Reliance by several banks were criticised in the parliamentary committee's report. It noted how funds placed by the Oil and Natural Gas Corporation (ONGC) in portfolio management schemes with two banks had been channelled through brokers into Reliance shares; how Reliance had recruited the ONGC chairman immediately on his retirement; and how some banks had given large amounts of credit to Reliance and its associated 'front companies' through bill discounting. In a general note on the overall scam, it said: 'There is some evidence of collusion of big industrial houses playing an important role.'

The Congress majority in the committee, who included Dhirubhai's old friend Murli Deora, prevented the probe going any further than that. A note by the opposition minority pointed out that there were still gaps in the investigation and that the CBI had made many lapses (its chief investigator, K. Madhavan, had resigned in protest during the inquiries). A second note by three Left MPs pointed out that the Reliance name had surfaced more often that those of other industrial houses, but this must still be only 'the tip of the iceberg'. One MP who was on the committee recalls: 'There was always a lurking suspicion that big interests were behind the scam, but there was no trace. It was one reason why we put all the evidence in the parliamentary library instead of having it destroyed, which is the usual practice. There was some resistance to this.'[7]

Many of the committee members also had their doubts about the central bank Governor, Venkitaramanan. In the 1980s, as head of the Ministry of Finance, he had been openly accused in the press of belonging to a pro-Reliance clique of officials and was distrusted because of this by his then minister, V.P. Singh. His appointment as Reserve Bank Governor was generally seen in Bombay as a favour called by Dhirubhai during Chandrashekhar's brief prime ministership. It emerged also that Venkitaramanan's son was linked in a business venture in Madras with Dhirubhai's son-in-law, Shyam Kothari.

This sorry linkage took some years to emerge, however, and the Reliance issue of global depositary receipts was successfully put to the market in Europe from 11 to 18 May despite the financial mayhem breaking out back in Bombay. Fortunately for Reliance, the CBI did not move in to arrest Harshad Mehta and his brother Ashwin until well after the issue closed, on 4 June. By late 1993 the market bounced back as international investors discovered the 'India story' *en masse* and prices climbed to a new record .Dhirubhai's connections with the scam had been buried and, as he might have said to his old friends in the yarn market, a first-class fountain had been built on top. Or so it seemed.

In December 1993 Dhirubhai announced that a duplicate of Patalganga would be added to Hazira in a second polyester–PTA complex. In September 1993 he had also entered a joint venture with ICI, Terene Fibres India, to take over ICI's polyester fibre plant, with a capacity of 30 000 tonnes a year, at Thane, outside Bombay. The three polyester works would make Reliance the fourth biggest producer in the world (after Germany's Hoechst, America's Du Pont and Taiwan's Nanya) and the only one with production integrated from napththa down to fabrics.

The integration was to move even further back upstream. In February 1994 Narasimha Rao's cabinet decided to award three oil and gas discoveries in the Arabian Sea to a consortium involving Reliance with the Houston-based Enron Oil and Gas Corporation and the government's own Oil and Natural Gas Corporation, which had discovered and delineated the fields but did not have the funds to develop them. Two of the fields, Mukta and Panna, were then estimated to contain 265 million barrels of oil and the third, Mid- and South-Tapti, 67 billion cubic metres of gas, although much later it was alleged that Reliance knew the reserves were likely to be much larger. Cost of development was put at Rs 38 billion (then about $1.25 billion) of which Reliance was responsible for 30 per cent. Enron would be the operator initially but after five years would transfer the role to Reliance.

The results for 1993–94 showed that Reliance had edged past the

Tata Iron and Steel Co., founded in the first decade of the century, to become India's largest private-sector company measured by annual sales, operating profit, net profit, net worth and assets. Its 2.4 million shareholders were the most widely spread equity base of any industrial company in the world.

But even as it was coming back into a single image, Reliance was creating new windows on the screen. In the main picture was the gas cracker at Hazira, consuming much of the parent company's financial resources. It was running years behind schedule (it eventually came on stream in the 1996–97 year, some three years late), but this had been due to eighteen months of delays in getting the final licence issued after the November 1988 letter of intent from the government. Then it had been decided in 1992 to expand its capacity to 750 000 tonnes a year of ethylene (from 400 000 tonnes).

Because of this burden, any other new projects would have to be started off the Reliance books. In 1992 Reliance came out with two new subsidiaries. Two of its associated investment companies had been transformed into Reliance Polypropylene Ltd and Reliance Polyethylene Ltd to build new plants making those products within the Hazira complex. The need for separate companies was explained by the equity involvement of the Japanese trading house Itochu (the former C. Itoh & Co.), which was to contribute $50 million for a 15 per cent stake in each firm, making it the biggest investment planned by a Japanese firm in India at that point. The issue of equity shares and optionally fully convertible debentures in November 1992 was wildly oversubscribed: the share issues by around a hundred times in each case and the debentures by three to four times. All in all, about 10.5 million investors offered Rs 34.43 billion. Dhirubhai was able to keep Rs 3.25 billion for each company, and the rest was a loan at 15 per cent interest until it was refunded by mid-March 1993.

Even before they were born, the Reliance 'twins' – as the two new companies were dubbed – were the cause of controversy. SEBI had noted that their shares were being ramped on the Mumbai Stock Exchange and insisted that the prospectuses carried the warning: 'The current market price of the shares is not a true indication of the actual worth of the shares as the current market price is only as a result of circular and thin trading among a smaller number of interested parties.' But SEBI found that this had occurred before it issued its new stockmarket regulations. The problem was shuffled over to the Bombay exchange, which identified the brokers involved but did not press penalties. The 'twins' later became problem children.

The secret was revealed – but then only to a few Mumbai insiders – in a leaked investigation by the Deputy Commissioner of Income Tax in Bombay, G.S. Singh, in 1994. In his report *Piercing the Corporate Veil*, the tax official found that during the 1992–93 financial year, thirty-seven small investment companies controlled by Reliance had received nearly Rs 600 million from Reliance via Reliance Capital to buy rights attached to partially paid shares the affiliates owned in the twins. Each of the original shares in the twins had rights to no fewer than forty new shares attached. The group companies had acquired the shares in the twins mostly in May 1992, at Rs 17.50 a share, soon after they were renamed on 19 May 1992. The rights could be exercised in the public issue at the end of 1992. The cut-off date for owning the rights, announced in the issue documents later in the year, was 6 June. It was a nicely timed investment by the thirty-seven group companies. Reliance had later paid the companies Rs 39 for each right; that is, for a Rs 17.50 investment, the companies had received Rs 1560. An investment of Rs 644.6 million in the twins' partly paid shares shows up in the Reliance accounts on 31 March 1993, accounting for the rights purchase plus fees to Reliance Capital. Those looking for insider trading before the twins' merger two years later had missed this earlier example of funds being taken out of Reliance.

Dhirubhai had also begun setting up a new company to carry out his biggest dream, building a full-scale oil refinery. In 1992 he had gained clearance from the Foreign Investment Promotion Board attached to the Prime Minister's office for Itochu to take 26 per cent of the refinery's output of 9 million tonnes a year. In August 1993 he announced that Reliance Petroleum would make its inaugural capital raising through an even more complex issue called a triple option partially convertible debenture. Subscribers were offered debentures with a face value of Rs 60. Of this, Rs 20 was to be converted into equity shares at par, one on allotment and one after eighteen months. The Rs 40 balance, non-convertible, would be paid back, doubled, in three annual instalments from the sixth year (equivalent to an effective 14.35 per cent annual interest). Two attached warrants for shares could be sold on the market, or exercised for Ps 20 each. Alternatively, investors could get their money back on the Rs 40 non-convertible portion after forty-six to forty-eight months and receive two shares from the warrants at Rs 20 each.

If Dhirubhai had previously made the non-convertible convertible, the new issue was surpassing. Investors would get equity shares immediately in a business that did not yet exist and which was years away from earnings and would have non-convertible debentures that would not earn any returns until the sixth year. It was extremely cheap money until then, almost free.

But when put to the market in November 1993, it raised the targeted Rs 21.72 billion from institutional investors and the public, and was oversubscribed three times. Reliance itself put in Rs 5.773 billion, taking the total proceeds to Rs 27.493 billion, or close to $1 billion at that time. Itochu was no longer in the picture and not mentioned in the prospectus. The absence was not really explained. Together with another partly convertible debenture issue to Indian institutions along with overseas suppliers' credits, lease finance and some overseas borrowings, the issue was to fund the refinery's cost of Rs 51.42 billion by its planned completion in three years time; that is, late 1996. Dhirubhai now had 2.6 million shareholders in Reliance Petroleum as members of his 'family'.

Almost immediately, the project met delays on the ground, as disputes were reported with landowners on the site at Moti Khadvi, about 25 kilometres outside Jamnagar on the west side of the Saurashtra peninsula. Court actions were to continue until May 1996 when the company established its hold over 2240 acres. But by the time Dhirubhai arrived on 23 January 1995 for the *bhumi puja*, or ritual ground-breaking prayers, which involved the breaking of a coconut and the chanting of Vedic scriptures by a Hindu pundit, the size of the refinery had expanded in his plans to 15 million tonnes a year. There would also be another petrochemicals complex alongside it, making 1.4 million tonnes a year of paraxylene and other downstream products, and a third PTA plant of 350 000 tonnes.

The cost of the refinery was now put at Rs 86.94 billion and the petrochemicals works were another Rs 45 billion. However, the completion date had slipped two years, to late 1998 or 1999, which would be just before the returns on the non-convertible part of the debentures were due. Would Reliance Petroleum then disappear back into the parent company, many investors wondered, in another many-for-one share swap? Would there be more delays and more expansions?

The new investors, especially the foreign portfolio funds, had by then learnt that Dhirubhai was capable of constant surprises. Reliance was moving in so many directions simultaneously that it was hard to put the whole sum together. Probably only Dhirubhai, his two sons and a few others had the whole equation in their heads.

The cachet with the new foreign investment funds had been turned into cheap finance raised in London, Luxembourg and New York. Despite the mayhem in the Bombay capital markets in May 1992, Reliance had then been the first Indian company to float Global Depository Receipts (GDRs), a convertible bond priced in US dollars but initially priced in a linkage with the Reliance share price in India. It had been a Herculean effort of share price support against the background of the securities scam and, once the issue closed on 18 May, Reliance had to offload the shares it had bought on the market on to the books of friendly Indian institutions, mutual funds and merchant banks which had been persuaded that helping India's first GDR issue was a patriotic duty. Within two months the GDRs were trading at a 25 per cent discount to the issue price.

When India's financial image recovered the next year Reliance was back with a $140 million Euro-convertible bond issue in November 1993 managed by Morgan Stanley, whose investment guru Barton Biggs rated Reliance scrip one of the best buys in Asia. Many other investment advisers then saw Reliance, the most liquid security in the sharemarket, as a 'surrogate' for the entire Indian market.

Anil Ambani, the more outgoing of the two sons, became the public face of Reliance in the numerous 'roadshows' held in world investment centres from then on. In February 1994 the company made the biggest GDR issue yet, of $300 million, after some delays in permission from the Ministry of Finance, which had noted that the proceeds of the previous Euro-issues had not yet been completely used for the designated purpose and that Reliance seemed to have money to play the share market.

The foreign enthusiasm was dashed considerably at the end of 1994, however, when Reliance carried out two manoeuvres that many investors felt had broken important assurances. On 22 October Reliance announced it was placing 24.5 million shares with Indian financial institutions to raise a total Rs 9.43 billion to fund its oilfield developments. It emerged that the Unit Trust of India had put in Rs 7.73 billion, the rest coming from the Life Insurance Corporation and the General Insurance Corporation A five-year 'lock-in' applied, meaning that the institutions could not sell the stock for that time.

Just over two weeks later, Reliance announced that it was merging the 'twins' Reliance Polypropylene and Reliance Polyethylene into itself, in a share swap set by two accountancy firms that seemed quite generous to the shareholders of the two subsidiaries, which were still a year away from production. Foreign investment fund managers were livid. Early in October Reliance had presented its first-half results to market analysts in Hong Kong. The Reliance financial manager, Alok Agarwal, had been repeatedly asked whether the company had any plans to raise equity capital in the near future. Agarwal and other company executives had left everyone with the impression that there were no plans to do so. Now within a month, Reliance had made two moves that involved the issue of about 99 million new Reliance shares, expanding the share base by more than 30 per cent.

The foreign funds had by then lifted their combined shareholdings to 13 per cent of previous total equity on the expectation of very strong growth in earnings per share, a widely used yardstick of the profitability of a share. Their analysis was now way out of touch. Profits would be spread over a much greater number of shares, so earnings per share would be much lower. To complaints that Reliance had given no hint of such a 'dilution' of equity the company rather lamely said it had not specifically ruled it out.

Some fund managers in Bombay threatened a revolt, telling Reliance they would vote their shares against the merger at the extraordinary general meeting called to approve it on 6 December 1994. They produced evidence of heavy buying of shares in the twins before the announcement. For those in the know about the swap ratio, it would have been either a cheap entry into Reliance itself or a chance for some insider-trading profits.

One investor that was not complaining, oddly enough, was the Unit Trust of India. It was not clear whether its top officials had been told of the twins' impending merger, even though it was announced only two weeks after the private placement and had an immediate and unfavourable impact on the Reliance share price. If the merger plan had not been foreshadowed, UTI might have been able to argue that a material event had not been disclosed and to seek redress for its unit-holders. If it had been told, the performance of its managers was open to question.

No one was arguing with the logic of consolidating the twins into the parent company at some stage. It added sales, assets and profits while eliminating the sales tax that would apply to transactions between separate companies. But this should have happened closer to the time the twins' plants came on stream.

The investment bankers did not ostracise Reliance for very long. The angry fund managers in Bombay were called by their head offices in Hong Kong and London and told not to make a fuss at the 6 December shareholders meeting. There were still some fat fees to be earned from managing new capital issues and borrowings. Reliance had burnt bridges with many equity investors in Europe. But there was still the debt market and the whole new world of the American debt and equity markets to tap into, which it proceeded to do.

The retreat of the Indian Government from its monopolising of

255

many infrastructure sectors had also opened up numerous opportunities. Dhirubhai had often used the old-fashioned adage 'Stick to your knitting' to keep his executives looking at associated activity (his first industrial activity had actually been the knitting machines at Naroda). The sons were keen to try something new. If tenders were won, that's where Reliance would go.

Many projects were proposed by the mid-1990s, including a software technology park near Hyderabad, a small transport aircraft with Hindustan Aeronautics Ltd in Bangalore, diamond mining with South Africa's De Beers Corporation in Madhya Pradesh, and a tollway from Mumbai to Pune. The firmest steps, however, were in power and telecommunications. Reliance gained approvals for three mid-size power plants in Patalganga, Jamnagar and Delhi. It also won the licence to operate a basic telephone service in Gujarat, in partnership with the American utility Nynex, called Reliance Telecom, for a licence fee of Rs 33.96 billion payable over fifteen years. The only competitor would be the cash-strapped and trade union-bound government telephone service and two private cellular services. In addition, Reliance Telecom won licences to run cellular services in the states of Madhya Pradesh, Orissa, Bihar, West Bengal, Assam and Himachal Pradesh and in the north-eastern hill states for modest total licence fees of Rs 3.37 billion over ten years. The telephone licences covered nearly a third of India's population but (aside from Gujarat) were in some of its poorest regions.

In addition, Dhirubhai also appeared to be gearing up for more corporate power-play. Over the course of 1995–96 (to March), the Reliance shareholding in Larsen & Toubro jumped from 5.96 per cent to 8.73 per cent, while its holding in the cash-cow Bombay and Suburban Electric Supply Co. moved up slightly to above 6 per cent. The neglected subsidiary Reliance Capital and Finance Trust was also charged up with sizeable capital through rights issues and private placements and renamed simply Reliance Capital, under Anand Jain.

Around the end of 1993 most of Dhirubhai's old Aden colleagues remaining in service were eased into retirement. Mukesh and Anil felt these men no longer had the drive necessary to push Reliance's huge expansion forward. Some were a little bitter that they could not stay on. The Gujarati flavour of the company was further diluted by the recruitment of more managers and technical staff from other parts of India. The family also formalised a split of assets that saw Dhirubhai's two brothers Ramnikbhai and Nathubhai give up their remaining executive roles in Reliance and concentrate on their own personal businesses outside. Although both remained on the board, it was made clear that their children were not in the line of succession to run the company – although the two sons of Dhirubhai's nephew and close associate, Rasikbhai Meswani, who had died in 1985, were taken on as executive directors once they finished their education.

The reorganisation was an effort to prevent two of the failings that had hit many other Indian companies once they passed from the control of the founding entrepreneur who typically ran them as personal fiefdoms: mixing personal and corporate finances, and delegating little authority to managers. When such empires passed to two or more pampered sons, frictions are almost inevitable, and usually the only solution is a split of assets and businesses. In some cases this was relatively amicable, as with the children and grandchildren of G.D. Birla. In others it was bitter, as with the Modi brothers and cousins, and required intervention by banks and financial institutions that had investments or loans with the group. The result has been a plethora of groups holding the same family name, distinguished by the initials of the particular owner, who tends to continue the pattern of person-alised leadership.

In a diverse conglomerate like the original Birla or Modi groups, a split can be beneficial. In a highly integrated company like Reliance it was potentially disastrous. To all appearances, as Dhirubhai aged, his succession planning looked free of immediate trouble. The two sons had never shown any sign of dispute or dissatisfaction with their posi-tions at Reliance. The older son Mukesh's elevation to vice-chairman, after Ramnikbhai Ambani, Dhirubhai's older brother, stepped down as joint managing director, seemed to indicate general acceptance that he would take charge eventually. As Dhirubhai slowed down in his sixties and attended the office for a shorter working day, Mukesh assumed more and more of the major decisions, although Dhirubhai retained the ultimate say.

Reserved and deceptively mild in appearance, Mukesh was regarded as highly determined and even ruthless by acquaintances, as well as being a talented engineer and manager. Anil appeared content as the public image-maker of Reliance, talking to the press and investors.

The question mark was whether between them the two sons would show all the attributes of Dhirubhai, especially his genius for forging personal relationships at all levels and, perhaps, his boldness of vision. This concern was addressed by an attempt to showcase the widening range of professional skills in the company's expanding workforce.

But the Ambanis seemed caught in a dilemma. Formalising the company's process of deciding new policies and strategies or taking run-ning decisions could rob it of its ability to move fast and grab opportu-nities. Reliance could end up like the slow-moving, committee-driven corporate bureaucracies it often derided.[8]

As Dhirubhai moved closer to realising his dream of an integrated petroleum empire and of handing on a modern corporation, however, events took a turn that made Bombay wonder whether the Ambanis and Reliance had changed at all in essence from the buccaneering days of the early 1980s. Suppressed scandals came to the surface, including a dispute that seemed to question Dhirubhai's most often professed loyalty: to the millions of shareholders in his 'Reliance family' who had put their savings into the security of Reliance shares.

16

$\mathcal{H}$ousekeeping secrets

On 29 November 1995 Mumbai's Bombay Stock Exchange faced perhaps the biggest challenge to its existence in its scandal- and crisis-ridden 120 years. A letter arrived that day from Reliance Industries, signed by a junior executive on behalf of its board. Recalling that Reliance had been first listed on the Exchange in November 1977, the letter said: 'We regret to state that we are constrained to terminate the said listing.' The six-page letter went on to blast the Exchange for singling out Reliance for 'biased and prejudiced action' and accused some of its board members of being part of a cartel of 'bears' that had been hammering down the company's share price, to the detriment of its millions of investors. It was now moving to the new National Stock Exchange (NSE), a computerised rival set up by the government as an alternative to the score of unruly, often casino-like city exchanges.

Reliance at that time had a weighting of about 10 per cent in the Bombay Exchange's most commonly used index of price movements, the thirty-share Sensitive Index or Sensex. The most liquid of the 6500 listed stocks, it typically accounted for almost 30 per cent of the daily trading volumes. Dealing in Reliance shares was bread and butter for Bombay's brokers. The company and its founder Dhirubhai had been credited for much of the explosion in share ownership among the Indian public since the 1970s. Now Dhirubhai was taking his bat and ball and moving to another pitch. If Reliance were allowed to move, Mumbai's exchange suddenly faced obsolescence.

But whatever the jitters among its broker members, Dhirubhai was wrong if he thought the Exchange's executive board would be quickly cowed. Its president, Kamal Kabra, immediately likened Reliance to a 'fugitive from justice' fleeing to another jurisdiction.

At issue was whether Reliance had knowingly issued more than one copy of each share and deliberately mixed up records of share ownership. If such suspicions were true, it meant that Reliance had been giving worthless paper to investors, or giving them shares owned by someone else. It could be fraud. It would threaten the most basic trust underpinning India's capital markets.

The controversy exposed the secret workings of Dhirubhai's system for retaining control of Reliance and at the same time generating massive cash flows. Devised and operated by market professionals, it was exposed accidentally by market amateurs.

Since his stroke in February 1986 Dhirubhai had been careful to keep up his exercise and worked hard to bring back full dexterity to his right side. He employed a well-qualified young physiotherapist, Rajul Vasa, who soon became a regular visitor to the Ambani household first at

Usha Kiran, then Sea Wind. As well as paying her normal fees, Dhi-rubhai rewarded Vasa with allocations of Reliance shares.

In January 1994 Rajul and her husband decided to cash some of their paper wealth and and sold 26 650 Reliance shares through a broker. Then, in April, the Vasas wrote to the Reliance share registry, Reliance Consultancy Services (RCS), notifying the loss of certificates for 33 809 shares – including the ones they had earlier sold. They got new certificates and sold these shares to Merrill Lynch.

The broker in the original sale found his transfer rejected by RCS and filed a complaint with the exchange. In September 1995 the exchange began recovery of the money. Reliance was represented by Anand Jain: strangely, he offered to settle the outstanding claim imme-diately, putting down a pay order for Rs 10.8 million, on condition that the investigation and penalty action be halted. The Exchange's board met and considered the action. On the face of it the persons at fault were Rajul Vasa and her husband. So why should Reliance step in?

The board decided that money was not enough. On 16 October the Exchange sent a show-cause notice to Reliance. Neither Reliance nor RCS had raised any queries with the Vasas or told the buyer, a com-pany called Opera Investments, about the issue of duplicates for the shares it had presented. It had not filed any complaint with the police, or told the Exchange of any steps to enforce an indemnity given by the Vasas when they applied for the duplicates or, 'despite the obvious fraud', started any legal proceedings. Reliance was thus guilty of gross negligence, if not an accomplice.

Almost at the same time, another time-bomb blew up. One of the financial houses deeply involved in the 1992 securities trading scandal had been a fast-growing and politically well-connected firm called

Fairgrowth Financial Services Ltd. It was caught up in a mass of claims before the special court set up to handle the scam cases, presided over by Justice S.N. Variava. It had bought 1.5 million Reliance shares in February 1992. When they were presented to RCS the registry asked Fairgrowth to withdraw the transfer and promised to sell the shares in the market for Fairgrowth. It was the last Fairgrowth saw of the shares or its money.

In October 1995 Fairgrowth asked Justice Variava to compel Reliance and RCS to tell it where the shares went. News of the two cases, Fairgrowth and Rajul Vasa, became the talk of the markets. Rumours that duplicate shares were in circulation caused a sharp fall in the price of Reliance shares in Mumbai and of its GDRs in London.

Reliance read a plot into the cast of characters ranged against it. Two of the most vocally critical Bombay Stock Exchange directors were M.G. Damani and Rajendra Bhantia. Damani was an old Exchange bear. Bhantia was a friend of Nusli Wadia and had been connected to Fairgrowth previously. The Fairgrowth lawyer, Mahesh Jethmalani, son and legal partner of Ram Jethmalani, had defended Wadia in the Fairfax affair and appeared against Reliance in the court battles of the 1980s. The old fighting instincts were roused. It wrote to SEBI chairman D.R. Mehta, claiming that the Vasa case was being blown up by an old bear cartel.

The Bombay Exchange continued to hold firm. After another combative meeting with Reliance representatives on 14 November, its board decided on a three-day suspension of trading in its shares, starting on 16 November. The news was in the next morning's paper before the formal notice arrived at Reliance late in the afternoon, too late to take out a High Court restraining order before the suspension came into effect. Dhirubhai had to endure the humiliation.

On the day the suspension started, the special scam court dealt a second blow. Justice Variava froze the transfer of the shares sought by Fairgrowth and demanded that Reliance tell him where they now were 'even if you have to place thirty people on the job for twenty-four hours'. The exchange declared the 1.5 million shares bad delivery.

Then the Unit Trust of India announced that it had bought a lot of 2.4 million Reliance shares in December 1991 and sent them for transfer to RCS. They had discovered in early 1995, after queries by tax inspectors, that the share certificates sent back by RCS in their name covered shares with different distinctive numbers. Out of them, they now found that 870 000 came from the batch of 1.5 million sold to Fairgrowth and declared frozen by the court.

Reliance quickly explained that 'certain investors' had delivered the original lot of shares to UTI, then taken them back and replaced them with different shares. As the sellers were the same and the shares equal in all respects, RCS had processed the transfer and given UTI the second batch of shares. It was a highly unsatisfactory explanation. UTI had not been consulted and was left with 870 000 shares – perhaps more – on which Fairgrowth was asserting a lien. Had RCS been as casual about ownership in other cases? Who were these operators who could withdraw shares from the registry after selling them?

The market was reeling under the shocks to its confidence. Then Reliance upped the stakes by listing on the NSE and applying to delist from the Mumbai Exchange.

Once the Mumbai Exchange made it clear that it would refuse permission to delist, on the grounds that Reliance was hardly a defunct or bankrupted company with no remaining activity in its shares, the ball was in the court of the government, which could overrule the Exchange. After initially welcoming Reliance's interest in its new baby, the NSE, the Ministry of Finance had woken up to the implications of exchange president Kamal Kabra's 'fugitive from justice' remark. SEBI chairman D.R. Mehta was called in by the Finance Secretary, Montek Singh Ahluwalia, and asked to seek a compromise.

Over the following days, delegations of venerable stockmarket leaders called on the warring parties, pouring wise words on the aggravated feelings of the Ambanis on one hand and the Exchange's young bloods on the other. Both sides were looking for a way for Reliance to back off. It was found in a letter from the Exchange on 4 December, rejecting the request to delist and asking Reliance to withdraw it. The company did so, claiming it had made its point.

It was a climbdown. Reliance was soon back on the defensive. The UTI angle to the Fairgrowth affair had opened up a whole new avenue of investigation for regulators, the press and members of parliament. UTI said it had learnt that the sellers of the 2.4 million shares had been Reliance group companies, and press inquiries found that some of the switched shares were still with small investment companies run by the Reliance company secretary Vinod Ambani; Amitabh Jhunjhunwala, the chief executive of Reliance Capital, also being involved.

The switched shares had now been replaced by a third lot sent over to UTI by RCS. Why? Was it an attempt to get the scam-tainted shares out of circulation? Could they be duplicates also? Could the 1.5 million shares sold to Fairgrowth be the same lot of 1.5 million that, according to the reports on the 1992 scam, were bought and sold in a repo deal worth Rs 600 million that involved Citibank, ANZ Grindlays and the brokers Hiten Dalal and Harshad Mehta in mid-April 1992?

Then there was the mysterious Raju Vasa case. The original buyer of her shares, Opera Investments, turned out to be another Reliance front company. Its broker, V.K. Jain, was a brother of Reliance Capital's Anand Jain and had been active in the Larsen & Toubro proxy battle. What was behind this strange affair in which all parties to the transactions seemed to be linked?

Mukesh Ambani had been in New Delhi meeting MPs and assuring them that share-switching was common practice. He explained that liquidity and tax minimisation were the reasons behind the switch. Reliance had two groups of satellite companies. One group was investment companies with large lots of shares who never sold. If they did sell, the capital gains tax would be huge. But they lent them to share-trading companies in the second group who used them for initial liquidity in deals. Later the trading firms would replace them with newly acquired shares on which the capital gains would be slight.

The Ministry of Finance had asked UTI to check its experiences with twenty other big companies. It had found the share-switching practice not to be common at all. The Bharatiya Janata Party finance spokesman Jaswant Singh also produced two examples of Reliance shares, sold in 1989 by the Syndicate Bank, where shares of the same distinctive numbers appeared in two certificates. Mukesh's explanation was not wholly convincing.

On 20 December the Finance minister, Manmohan Singh, ordered a joint inquiry by the Securities and Exchange Board and the Department of Company Affairs, which had overlapping jurisdiction in applying company law. Singh asked all financial institutions to verify that their share portfolios did not contain switched or fake shares. The Income Tax Department would also continue inquiries it had started in 1992 into the tax evasion aspects of the scam.

SEBI had already started inquiries on its own initiative and gave an interim report in mid-January 1996. According to this report, the seven custodians of shares for India's investment institutions held between them 138.9 million Reliance shares, about 30 per cent of the company's paid-up capital. Out of these, 6.73 million had been switched; that is, the share certificates received back from RCS after transfers bore different distinctive numbers or transferor's names from those lodged.

RCS itself found some more shares held directly, taking the total of switched shares to 7.03 million (4.7 million with UTI). Except for a very few shares, all the switches had taken place between March and October 1992. None had been detected by the custodians. Those of the original shares not transferred remained with the original owners, who were 'trade associates' of Reliance.

The Securities Board investigators had found RCS less than helpful. According to their letter sent to the RCS chief executive in March 1996, the registry had given two differing versions of the UTI share switch to the board in December and hence neither could be trusted. RCS had reported corruption of its database and a loss of audit trail because of a conversion of computer systems, but 'the fact that corruption of data is predominant in select folios of the parties involved in switching makes the explanation of RCS untenable', the Securities Board letter said. The records were a shambles, in effect, and much of them in the switching cases seemed to have been faked.

But perhaps the best insight into the Reliance back-shop operations came from the report *Piercing the Corporate Veil*, by G.S. Singh, whose officials had been looking at the Reliance front companies since June 1994. The taxmen had found 206 companies run by the Reliance company secretary Vinod Ambani from a Reliance office in Nariman Point. During 1991–92 Reliance had paid Rs 313 million to these companies in various fees, enabling Reliance to reduce its tax liability and the companies to settle their own losses or to make investments in Reliance shares and debentures in order to maintain management control.

The tax officers focused on one of the 206 front companies, Avshesh Mercantile Ltd, to give a detailed picture of share market activities. Their account supported the explanation given by Mukesh Ambani to the MPs. They traced a sale of Reliance shares to UTI, this time a lot of 3 million sold on 22 May 1992 – four days after the first GDR issue closed – by thirteen group companies known as Group A. On that day none of the thirteen firms owned any Reliance shares. The shares delivered to UTI had been 'borrowed' from fourteen other group companies, known as Group B. When UTI sent them for transfer, the shares were switched for shares bought from Dhyan Investment and Trading, then a wholly owned subsidiary of Reliance Capital, and the originals returned to Group B.

Mahendra Doshi, the broker in the sale, said he had dealt with Anand Jain and Manoj Modi of Reliance Capital for the delivery of the shares. He knew nothing about the sellers; Jain had told him the company names to which contract notes and bills were to be issued. The shares had been handed over by another Reliance Capital executive, Tushar Sarda, and the proceeds handed to him. Six months earlier, Doshi had carried out a similar sale to UTI of 2.2 million shares. Jain had initially denied knowledge of the thirteen Group A companies, then admitted to being involved in the sale.

According to correspondence produced by RCS, the fourteen Group B companies had requested the registry to inform them of any transfers lodged by third parties for their shares, because the shares were placed from time to time as collateral, on condition that they not be transferred in the name of the creditor unless approved by them. The tax inspectors said this was not supported by evidence, and the letters were found to be fabricated. The sales were real and the income from them should be taxed. The swapping of shares was a systematic evasion of capital gains tax, by substituting the newly bought shares of Group A for the older and more cheaply acquired holdings of Group B. Not a single case of switching for sellers outside the group was found.

The tax-reduction explanation made some sense, but did not fit with everything that Reliance was saying. It had pointed out that the switching had been confined to the period March–October 1992, yet

Mukesh Ambani had said it was a common practice. If it had made good tax sense in 1992 and had been legal, why not continue it?

Some business analysts tended to believe that the share-switching occurred as a part of the cover-up of Dhirubhai's close involvement with brokers in the 1992 scam. They speculated that shares handled by such brokers as Harshad Mehta and Hiten Dalal were hurriedly dumped on friendly institutions such as UTI and the Canara Bank funds as the scam broke in April 1992. Others veered to an explanation put up by twenty-seven MPs in parliament, alleging systematic pledging of duplicates of shares owned by the Ambanis and other management investors, which would be switched if they were ever sent for ownership transfer in the company-controlled registry and would never be in marketable lots. One former fund manager, admittedly no friend of Reliance, recalled a case in 1989 where a bank sold him shares pledged by Reliance. The company raised hell with the bank to get the shares taken back and exchanged for others.[1]

As the bedraggled Narasimha Rao government, hit by scandals over *havala* trades and telephone licences, neared the end of its five-year term, some other controversies came back to haunt Dhirubhai and Reliance.

In January 1996, the government filed an appeal in the Supreme Court against the ruling by the Customs, Excise and Gold (Control) Appellate Tribunal that had upheld the controversial 1989 decision of the former Mumbai Collector of Customs, K. Viswanathan, to drop the charges of evading duty on the 'smuggled' polyester yarn plant at Patalganga. Later that month, a team of CBI officials flew to Bombay and suddenly revived the case against Dhirubhai and others of back-dating the letters of credit for the PTA imports in May 1985.

It seemed to be a warning shot by Narasimha Rao. Reliance had been falling behind in the campaign funding it had promised the Congress Party, apparently seeing no point in pouring further money into a lost cause. The company was also suspected within Congress of stirring up the telephone licence scandal in order to distract attention from its own problems.

In 1995 a young police officer with the Central Bureau of Investigation in Mumbai, Y.P. Singh, had begun digging into the private placement with the Unit Trust of India and the two government insurance giants in 1994. His request to see the papers on the placement caused panic at UTI. The highly unfavourable placement had been forced on the institutions by senior figures in the Narasimha Rao government, he concluded. He listed some twenty illegalities, including conspiracy and fraud, and recommended charges against a string of senior officials.

After picking up signs of discontent among Oil and Natural Gas Commission engineers during a visit to a Bombay High oil platform, Singh also began looking into the award of the Arabian Sea oil and gas fields to the Reliance–Enron–ONGC consortium in 1994. The bidding had been extremely bitter, with rival groups accusing Reliance of inside knowledge of tender evaluation criteria that were kept unclear for others. Singh found that the new owners had come into the fields with little compensation to ONGC for its past costs of exploration and preliminary development. The new operators had also been given a highly unusual bonus on the oil price guaranteed by the government.

Singh asked his superiors at the CBI for permission to start a preliminary inquiry. Instead, in March 1996, he was abruptly transferred back to the Maharashtra State Police, after being accused of mishandling another case. Singh lodged an appeal with an administrative tribunal. However, two other authorities – the Planning Commission member G.V. Ramakrishna (a former Petroleum Secretary and SEBI chairman) and the Comptroller and Auditor-General's office – took up similar criticism of the oilfield contracts. In October 1996 the private secretary of Satish Sharma, the Petroleum minister at the time the contracts were awarded, told the CBI that Reliance had paid Sharma Rs 40 million between June 1993 and February 1994 (and that two other companies involved in bidding had also made payments). Reliance denied the allegation.[2]

If Dhirubhai had rubbed Narasimha Rao the wrong way, his relationships with the opposition parties were also ambivalent. Sections of the Janata Dal and Left continued to regard him as anathema, yet he had successfully cultivated many of their leaders at state level. In the Hindu nationalist camp, he paid court to senior BJP leaders, but some party MPs such as Jaswant Singh had been Ambani critics for more than a decade, and his old nemesis, S. Gurumurthy of the *Indian Express* campaigns, had become a close adviser to senior figure L.K. Advani. Their hostility was often neutralised in party forums by a claque of Ambani supporters, such as the BJP secretary-general Pramod Mahajan, who once defended Dhirubhai as 'not someone who sleeps with you then refuses to recognise you in the morning'. The metaphor would not have been to the taste of the RSS-trained cadres of the party.

Within the BJP leadership, Dhirubhai became distrusted for the split he helped engineer in the party's Gujarat branch soon after it took power in the March 1995 state elections. Dhirubhai backed a lower-caste BJP leader called Shankersinh Waghela in disputes with the newly elected Chief Minister, Keshubhai Patel. In September 1995 the two openly split, and Dhirubhai flew Waghela's faction of state MPs to the central Indian village of Khajuraho, famed for its erotic temple carvings, to keep them together. Around this time, national BJP leader Atul Bihari Vajpayee was appalled to find Dhirubhai on the telephone, putting forward a 'solution' to the Gujarat crisis: Waghela should be made deputy Chief Minister. Highly embarrassed, Vajpayee refused. A year later, Waghela ousted Patel's faction and formed a government with Congress backing. It is not clear whether Dhirubhai had any intention to destabilise the BJP nationally or just install a cooperative state government to help his industrial plans.

Having gathered damning material on the share-switching cases and little on the supposed 'bear conspiracy' against Reliance, the SEBI and the Department of Company Affairs shuffled responsibility for prosecution between them and eventually the decision fell into the limbo caused by the calling of elections for early May 1996. The elections produced a three-way hung verdict, with the BJP having narrowly the largest number of seats. It decided to form a government, knowing it was unlikely to pick up support. Vajpayee was sworn in as Prime Minister, with Jaswant Singh as Finance minister and Ram Jethmalani as Law minister – a combination unpromising for Dhirubhai.

India's first BJP government lasted only two weeks – but long enough for Jaswant Singh to order a show-cause notice to be issued to Reliance for breaches of the Companies Act. Jethmalani excused himself on endorsement of Singh's order, saying he had made too many appearances for and against Reliance, and it passed to the next government to implement. Jaswant Singh's decision resulted in twenty-nine charges being laid against Dhirubhai, other executives and his companies in a Mumbai magistrate's court, including a serious one mentioning 'intent to defraud'.

But Dhirubhai had plenty of friends in the thirteen-party Janata Dal-based coalition that took over, including the new Prime Minister, H.D. Deve Gowda, who flew back to Bangalore to resign his job as Karnataka state Chief Minister in Dhirubhai's executive jet. In October the entire duplicate share and switching issue was wrapped up by a government decision to allow Reliance to 'compound' the charges – a process whereby a company simply pays a set fine for technical breaches and avoids a prosecution in court. Reliance had argued that the offences had been inadvertent, due to pressure of work on the registry. No loss had been caused to shareholders, no gain to the company. The magistrate, A.M. Thipsay, agreed that intent to defraud had not been substantiated. The total penalty came to Rs 6.396 million, while RCS was suspended from operations for six months from April 1997.

The issue had ended with a whimper, commented the *Business Standard*. 'The case called for a lifting of the corporate veil and judging whether the entire episode was more than a result of clerical error.' Instead, it had ended with 'a tap on the wrist'. It had been a close call, a crisis almost ranking with the 1980s Polyester Mahabharata. Once again Dhirubhai had scraped through.

17

Dhirubhai's dream

The twentieth century drew to its close with many clouds hanging over Reliance and Dhirubhai – and over India itself. The company had escaped narrowly from the sharemarket scandals of the decade, and its political and financial environment looked less favourable. Because of its capital controls and better regulated, more mature financial sector, India escaped 'contagion' by the financial crisis that swept out of Thailand through South-East and East Asia from mid-1997. But it suffered from a general suspicion of emerging markets, and its economy went into a stagnant phase.

The collapse of Congress rule in New Delhi had been followed by two years of unstable coalition government headed by the populist, lower-caste-oriented Janata Dal, first under Deve Gowda, then under Inder Kumar Gujral. When this regime too fell apart, mid-term elections in February–March 1998 brought the Hindu nationalists of the Bharatiya Janata Party back into power under Atal Behari Vajpayee. One of the Vajpayee government's first acts, in May that year, was to conduct a new round of nuclear weapons tests in the Rajasthan desert and declare India an overt nuclear weapons state, with Pakistan following suit two weeks later. One result was imposition of economic sanctions by the United States and several of its allies, including Japan. These did not directly hit trade or borrowings by private sector companies like Reliance, but threatened inflows of general economic development aid from both the foreign governments involved and the World Bank and placed advanced technology transfers under tighter scrutiny. The bomb tests created a wave of nationalist euphoria among Indians, but they added to the economic gloom.

More to the point for Dhirubhai, the BJP's return reinstated in positions of power many figures who had gone after Reliance with a vengeance while in opposition or private practice – notably Jaswant Singh, Swaminathan Gurumurthy, Arun Shourie, Ram Jethmalani and Arun Jaitley. As we have seen, Jaswant Singh had used his brief two weeks as Finance minister in Vajpayee's first short-lived government in 1996 to launch company law prosecutions against Reliance over the share duplication scandal. Was nemesis about to descend on Dhirubhai?

The question was tested before the year ended, with one of those intermittent moments when India's different worlds collide – in this case big business, government and organised crime, associating one of Dhirubhai's key Reliance fixers with breaches of official secrecy and a mafia outfit implicated in the 1993 terrorist bombings in Mumbai. It made for delicious reading by India's newspaper- and magazine-consuming public, but could hardly have been more embarrassing with Hindu nationalists in power and a border dispute with Pakistan six months later.

Enter one Romesh Sharma, a former peddler of coat hangers who by the late 1990s had found a profitable niche as a 'land-grabber' in New Delhi. His *modus operandi* was to rent a large property, refuse to pay any rent, then produce forged documents of completed sale when the owner sought to evict him. A demonstrated propensity to kidnap, beat and blackmail – along with links to the shadier side of the Congress Party in Delhi and to Dawood Ibrahim, the Dubai-based crime boss of Mumbai said by Indian police to have organised the 1993 bombings at the behest of Pakistan's Inter-Services Intelligence – usually produced silence in Sharma's victims.

Under surveillance by Delhi police, Sharma overreached himself by applying his land-grabbing techniques to a helicopter. He had chartered the aircraft from Mumbai's Pushpak Aviation to help his run for election in March 1996 in a Uttar Pradesh seat. Sharma lost his deposit but kept the helicopter, having persuaded its naïve owners to enter a dummy sale deal, allegedly to avoid exceeding the limit on electioneering expenditure. In October 1998, to help ensnare Sharma, police got a Pushpak executive to attempt to repossess the machine from Sharma's sprawling 'farmhouse' residence on the outskirts of the capital. The executive was beaten up, bound and carted off to an office run by Sharma in the centre of Delhi before police sprung the trap and rescued him. Sharma was investigated for kidnapping, forgery, illegal firearms and tax evasion and held under a national security act that cut off the usual escape route for the well connected: the tolerant and much-abused Indian system of bail. In what was obviously going to be a prolonged detention, he began to brag of his connections.

One was V. Balasubramaniam, chief of the Reliance government relations and corporate affairs office in New Delhi. Known widely as 'Balu', the Reliance lobbyist was one of Dhirubhai's oldest lieutenants, with a relationship said to go back to 1974 when Dhirubhai recruited the talkative, impish-faced Tamil former clerk at Burmah-Shell. Some said Balu, then 61, was the most trusted confidant of the Ambani family. The magazine *India Today* reported:

> He was their eyes and ears in Delhi, the person who knew
> everyone who mattered and was reputed to have instant
> information of the passage of every important file. This mattered
> in the heyday of the licence-permit raj when success depended
> on what Dhirubhai described as 'managing the environment'.
> In RIL's phenomenal growth during the 80s, not least when
> Pranab Mukherjee was Finance minister, Balu's role was seminal.
> He complemented the entrepreneurial genius of Dhirubhai …
> Indeed, so deep is Balu's political influence that it is being said
> that 'the draft budget papers were not leaked to Balu. Balu leaked
> the budget to the ministry'.[1]

Immediately after his arrest, Sharma told the police that the ownership transfer papers for the helicopter were held by Balu. Far from being intimidated, Delhi's joint police commissioner Amod Kanth went to collect the papers, which Balu handed over with a demand for a receipt. Sharma then went on to reveal that he and Balu were partners in two unlisted real estate companies, both using the name Reliance. He also claimed that, back in the 1980s, Balu had asked him to help with threats being made against Dhirubhai's son-in-law Raj Salgaonkar by the Dawood Ibrahim gang – which he had called off immediately with a phone call to Dawood's lieutenant, in Balu's presence. Reliance denied any dealings with Sharma and said that Balu's contacts 'if any, were in his personal capacity'. But the connection intrigued the police, who went on to raid Balu's home and office.

There they found material that took the investigation in entirely new directions. In the office, the police alleged, they found a copy of a secret cabinet minute about the problems of the post–nuclear test economic sanctions against India, the record of a meeting between key departmental heads about plans to privatise public sector enterprises and an internal Petroleum Ministry recommendation to its minister for changes to customs and excise duties on oil and oil products. Some of the documents had been faxed to numbers in Mumbai, with the addressees including Dhirubhai, Mukesh and Anil Ambani and the Reliance director (and Ambani cousin) Nikhil Meswani.

Rather more lurid suggestions were made by the perennial scandal-mongering MP of the opposition Janata Dal, Subramanian Swamy, who alleged that the police had found in Balu's residence forty-two computer disks containing a huge volume of secret and highly sensitive data emailed from the Finance Ministry. Swamy implied that this included the complete list of people who had made voluntary disclosures of previously unreported income, under a tax amnesty that had netted the government great amounts of revenue. This list had been forwarded via Sharma to Dawood Ibrahim's gang 'for use in extortion'. As *India Today* noted, it was a case of the footnote overshadowing the main text, even a story as lurid as that of Romesh Sharma.

Vajpayee's Home minister and the BJP's most senior Hindu militant, Lal Krishna Advani, had declared the Sharma prosecution a 'test case' for national resolve, saying it showed how the 'Indian state has become so porous, frail and soft' – but now it was veering on to a very different target from criminal gangs and Pakistani agents. At his direction, the case was taken over by the Central Bureau of Investigation, the same agency that had pulled so many earlier punches with Reliance but which in this case appeared determined to press the attack. On 19 November teams from the CBI raided Balu's house and office again in Delhi, and in Mumbai they stormed into both the headquarters of Reliance at Nariman Point and the Ambani family's home, Sea

Wind. Balu and two of his senior staff, along with Reliance as a corporation, were charged with offences under the Official Secrets Act and the Indian Penal Code for a conspiracy to receive and possess classified documents. All were vigorously denied by a Reliance spokesman.[2]

But, unusually for an official secrets case (and in contrast to the CBI's handling of Gurumurthy in 1987), the CBI did not place Balu or the other Reliance accused under arrest, and the prosecution virtually disappeared from public view for more than three years. In April 2002 lawyers for the three accused obtained rulings that overturned warrants issued by a lower court in Delhi, which would have obliged them to attend hearings of the charges. During May–July 2003 lawyers for Mukesh and Anil Ambani also obtained a stay on summonses requiring them to appear as defendants representing Reliance. There the affair seems to have disappeared into the Indian judicial limbo of pending cases. (In 2003 Sharma received a two-year jail term for the helicopter theft, but walked free as he'd already spent more than that time on remand. He then faced a succession of other charges.)

While it lasted, though, the scandal was an uncomfortable reminder of a past that Dhirubhai and Reliance were trying to forget. And the attacks on the probity of Reliance and the Ambani family kept coming.

In December 2000 a member of the Indian parliament named Raashid Alvi, belonging to the Bahujan Samaj Party based on the former Hindu outcaste populations of India's northern states, handed Vajpayee, the Prime Minister, a 1600-page dossier raking over many of the previous decade's contentious share-dealings around Reliance. When Alvi gained no response from the Prime Minister, he went public with his dossier in April 2001, forcing the Department of Company Affairs to take up his allegations.[3]

At the end of 2001 another old Ambani assailant re-emerged. Swaminathan Gurumurthy, the young chartered accountant who had produced the devastating series of exposés in the *Indian Express* in 1986, had become leader of a group called the Swadeshi Jagran Manch, which opposed the entry of foreign companies and brands into India. Although not occupying any government position or seat in parliament, Gurumurthy remained highly influential with sections of the ruling BJP, and his corporate expertise was much drawn upon to reconcile the periodic splits in the families and caste communities controlling some of India's big companies, banks and other institutions. From his office in Chennai (formerly Madras), Gurumurthy became incensed again at what he saw as blatant and gigantic 'fraud and breach of trust' by the Ambani directors of Reliance.

In a thirty-eight-page formal letter of complaint to the Securities and Exchange Board of India (SEBI), he alleged that an annual general meeting of Reliance Industries in December 1992 had authorised the issue of non-convertible debentures with or without detachable warrants (which could be transferred separately and give a right to shares) worth Rs 3 billion. Reliance directors or any entities associated with them were barred from buying into such an issue. During 1993 the Reliance board had authorised a directors' subcommittee comprised entirely of Ambani family members to apply the resolution. But instead of one issue, the Ambanis made two – under the same resolution by the shareholders' meeting. One was an issue of debentures worth Rs 3 billion with non-detachable warrants to UTI, entitling them to 7.48 million equity shares, which worked out at a price of Rs 401 a share, a hefty premium on the then market price of around Rs 300 but offset by the interest that would be payable on the debentures. The other issue was also for Rs 3 billion, but this one was taken up by thirty-four private companies in the network of Ambani ownership entities exposed in the share-switching scandal. These debentures, with detachable warrants, entitled the thirty-four companies to no less than 60 million shares, at an effective price of Rs 60 a share. When the debentures were converted and the rights under the warrants were exercised in January 2000, the Ambanis through their investment companies gained an extra 11.38 per cent of Reliance. The issue to UTI had been overpriced, Gurumurthy said, and the second issue to the thirty-four Ambani-linked companies was 'unauthorised and fraudulent' and should be cancelled.

Gurumurthy sent copies of his complaint to the Prime Minister and other ministers concerned with law enforcement and corporate affairs. But more than a year later he was still writing letters trying to stir action. As he said in a poignant note to a letter sent to the Finance minister, Jaswant Singh, in January 2003: 'I would never have got into investigating Reliance Group but for the fact that there is today not a single newspaper or magazine, which would publish anything against this group. Not a single political party or leader who would expose their misdeeds. Not a single official who would conduct a fair and fearless investigation against them.'[4]

Alvi's charges had met a spirited response from Reliance, in a sixteen-page letter to the Finance minister (then Yashwant Sinha) dated 27 July 2001, under the name of Yogesh Desai, the chief corporate publicist.[5] But Reliance didn't have to try too hard to defend itself. Gurumurthy's despondent note was accurate enough: no one had the energy, trust or resources to take on the company. Reliance was too big, too much part of the 'India story' that was once again seizing imaginations in the world's financial centres and India's own middle class.

The sniping and criticism continued, but Dhirubhai was above it all. In June 2000 he was able to tell shareholders at his annual general meeting that the huge new oil refinery at Jamnagar, with a capacity expanded to 27 million tonnes a year, had been completed in just three years of construction and within three months had been ramped up beyond full capacity. (After its first full year of operation, Dhirubhai reported in June 2001 that output had been 107 per cent of rated capacity.) Covering the arid Saurashtra landscape with a sculpture of silver piping, tanks, retorts and towers, ablaze with powerful lights through the night, it was India's biggest single private industrial investment, having cost Rs 250 billion or $6 billion. Even the vast mango plantation around it was aimed at the record book. Visiting the project, Dhirubhai had asked the Reliance executive handling agriculture, I.M. Thimaiah, whether the 66 000 trees made it the biggest mango grove in the world. Thimaiah searched the internet and found a reference to the Mughal emperor Akbar having had the biggest-ever plantation, with 100 000 trees. Thimaiah immediately ordered 36 800 more trees, thinking, 'We'll make Dhirubhai the new emperor.'[6]

Immediately Jamnagar accounted for 25 per cent of India's entirely oil refining capacity. It was now one of the biggest in Asia, with capital costs for each tonne of output put at 30 to 40 per cent below those of its regional competitors.

Speaking in what turned out to be his last address to shareholders, a meeting called in April 2002 to approve the long-expected plan to merge the petroleum subsidiary back into Reliance Industries, Dhirubhai recalled the Reliance legend, that all this had been achieved in one lifetime ('We are still a first generation enterprise') and that owning an oil company had been his plan all along. 'In my youth, I had left India, to work as a sales attendant at the retail outlet of a multinational energy company in Aden. At that time, far away from my native shores in Gujarat, I had a dream of coming back to my country and creating India's own global energy giant.'[7]

It's unlikely that many people had been using words like 'global' and 'energy' in the 1950s, least of all in Aden. Reliance was still a small player alongside the multinational petroleum majors, and its exports, although growing fast, were still only a small part of the group's sales, while the group was largely dependent on imports of crude oil from other producers. But Dhirubhai certainly now had his own oil company, positioned to grow with India's oil energy and petrochemicals demand as it caught up with world consumption levels, and the group had bought twenty-five oil and gas exploration blocks around the shores of India.

As well as pumping out diesel and petrol, the Jamnagar complex included huge production lines for many of the petrochemical ingredients needed by Reliance factories, like paraxylene, naphtha and polypropylene. This enabled Reliance to cut its dependence on imports and outsourcing and once again reap great cost-savings from vertical integration, 25 to 30 per cent of Jamnagar's output being consumed within the group.

The scale of its refineries and crackers at Jamnagar and Hazira in fact put Reliance in a position of market dominance in most of its petrochemical products. By mid-2001 Dhirubhai was able to report that the company had more than 51 per cent of India's polyester market and more than 80 per cent of the markets for the polyester intermediates PX, PTA and MEG. It produced 52 per cent of the polymers (plastics) consumed in India.

While Reliance was starting to shift out of cheap textiles and lay off 4600 workers in this area, it was not about to lose its interest in polyester. Dhirubhai foreshadowed an expansion of polyester capacity by a third over the following two to three years, to 1.2 million tonnes a year, by 'de-bottlenecking' and expanding existing plants and acquiring other producers. Dhirubhai noted that India's consumption of polyester had grown from 50 000 tonnes a year when he opened his first plant at Patalganga in the 1980s to about 1.3 million tonnes. But this was only a third of the consumption levels in China.

With Jamnagar in production, the Reliance group accounted for more than 3 per cent of India's gross domestic product and contributed about 10 per cent of the central government's indirect taxation revenues. Reliance Industries and Reliance Petroleum had been India's No. 1 and No. 2 private sector companies. The combined market capitalisation was Rs 450 billion or $9.3 billion, making it by far the country's biggest non-government business group and the first to make the *Fortune* 500 list of the world's biggest companies.

The group was also starting to pour investment into two of India's crucial but underdeveloped infrastructure sectors: telephony and electric power. In 2001 India still had only 30 million telephone connections for its one billion people, and even its biggest cities were subject to frequent blackouts.

Reliance had outlaid heavily to acquire mobile telephone licences covering a third of the country's area and population in the mid-1990s rush, but hardly the best bit of the Indian market. The fifteen states covered by 26 per cent-owned Reliance Telecom included the impoverished West Bengal, Bihar and Orissa and by mid-2001 had provided only 380 000 subscribers. There was also a fixed-line operator's licence for Gujarat. But Dhirubhai was able to sketch plans to escape this regulatory net, with a separate venture called Reliance Infocomm, which was to spend some $5 billion on a nationwide fibre-optic network to provide broadband data services and, according to a preliminary approval, 'basic' telephone services across most of the country, about which we will read more startling developments in a later chapter.

Reliance had also begun a move into power generation, making a limited offer for shares in Bombay and Suburban Electric Supply Co.

(BSES), the country's biggest surviving electricity supplier and distributor in the private sector and, largely because of that, India's most efficient utility. By mid-2001 Reliance had become the biggest shareholder in BSES, owning 30 per cent of the company.

After the petroleum subsidiary's merger, Reliance had 3.5 million individual shareholders, meaning that one in four Indian share investors had a stake in Reliance. They had seen its net profits grow by 29 per cent a year on average during the 1990s. By March 2001 it yielded 30 per cent of the total profits of the Indian private sector and 10 per cent of profits if government-controlled corporations were included. Accounting for about 12 per cent of total Indian share market capitalisation, it had weightings of 22 to 25 per cent in the main market indices.

It was not a company for anyone, even the highest authorities in India, to take on lightly. And while foreign investors owned 23 per cent of the company in 2001 and, to further its overseas capital raising, the company was putting itself under international audits, the foreign investment custodians remained passive – if often sceptical or bewildered – participants in the Reliance story.

In the early 2000s there was less and less interest in curbing Dhirubhai's methods and a growing sentiment that India needed more like him. The BJP and its coalition remained in power under Vajpayee for six years. As the government settled in, it became more focused on economic growth, the consumerist dreams of the middle classes and the reassertion of India's place in the world economy.

America's quick forgiveness of the nuclear test was signified by President Bill Clinton's visit in 2000. Pakistan's sneak invasion of Kashmir at Kargill, an attack by Islamic militants on India's parliament in December 2001 and Vajpayee's logistical help for the American interventions in Afghanistan and Central Asia after the 11 September 2001 attacks by al-Qaeda all encouraged a benign view of India as a strategic pillar in Asia, counterbalancing both anti-Western sentiment in the Islamic world and the rising economic and military weight of China.

A strong thread of the BJP's ideology was rejection of the statist economic legacy of the Nehru era, epitomised in the large and, in many cases, moribund state-owned enterprises that dominated the formal sector of the economy and consumed an inordinate share of government revenue. To reinvigorate the sell-offs and shut-downs started under Narasimha Rao, Vajpayee chose Arun Shourie, who had been Goenka's editor of the *Indian Express* from 1987 to 1990, covering the aftershocks of the Gurumurthy series and the Bofors scandal. With a doctorate in economics from Syracuse University in the United States, Shourie had been an economist at the World Bank early in his career. He had become a prolific independent columnist and polemicist after leaving the *Express*. Always ready to cultivate potentially valuable contacts in their up-and-coming phase, Dhirubhai had made sure his own newspaper, the *Observer of Business and Politics*, carried Shourie's column. The BJP drafted him into the Rajya Sabha, and in July 2000 Vaypayee made him India's first Minister for Disinvestment (later adding information technology and communications to his role).

Pointing out that previous governments has wasted some $8 billion propping up thirty public sector enterprises over the previous decade, Shourie set about an ambitious program to raise more than $2 billion by selling down government stakes in a score of enterprises, including food processors, metallurgical firms and the suddenly demonopolised telecom carriers.

Reliance had one spectacular loss in this program. It was keen on acquiring a controlling stake in the long-distance telecommunications agency Videsh Sanchar Nigam Ltd, a highly profitable carrier. Thanks to its network of informants, it was confident its bid was three rupees per share higher than that of its main rival, Tata. However, at the last minute before the tender closed, Ratan Tata decided to raise his firm's bid sharply, from Rs 175 to Rs 203 a share.

From Dhirubhai's point of view, the most interesting were the two smaller players in the oil refining sector, Hindustan and Bharat, and the state-owned Indian Petrochemicals Ltd (IPCL). The largest refiner, Indian Oil Corporation, was vastly bigger than Reliance (at 60 million tonnes annual refining capacity) and not for sale, except in small portions cautiously parcelled out to institutions and other investors with the government retaining 82 per cent. Indian Oil had outbid Reliance for the smallest of the state refiners, the nationalised Indo-Burmah Petroleum. Hindustan or Bharat would have been attractive to Reliance. As well as some small and elderly refineries and, in Bharat's case, operating production platforms in the Bombay High offshore field, each had some 4500 petrol stations across the country, which would have given the new producer an instant retail network. But political jitters stalled any immediate sell-down of the refiners. Out of the corporate *navratna* (nine jewels) of the public sector, it was a near-controlling 26 per cent stake in the listed petrochemicals giant IPCL that was put up for tender in early 2002.

When bidding closed in mid-April that year, Reliance emerged far ahead of the field, offering Rs 231 a share at a time when the IPCL share price was hovering around Rs 93. The next closest bids came from Indian Oil at Rs 128 a share and the detergent producer Nirma at Rs 110, while the government's reserve price was later disclosed as Rs 131. For Rs 14.91 billion, Reliance had captured the jewel, Shourie announced on 17 April 2002.

More than a year later, Shourie was to give a revealing account of the process. He talked of 'unbelievable pressures' to have Reliance disqualified. 'The pressures brought not just this transaction but almost the whole disinvestment program to a halt,' Shourie said. But the government had decided to stick with its rules. 'If Reliance fell foul of those guidelines, then it must be disqualified, no matter what, if it did not, it must be allowed to bid, no matter what.' Shourie said that 'throughout the period, Dhirubhai never contacted me as he was getting to know what was going on – for he had sources in places where mere journalists like me do not even know there are places'. But following the results, Dhirubhai had rung Shourie and in a voice 'choked with emotion' had said: 'I know what you have been put through – anyone else would have given up. I will never forget … I do not care about business. I care about relationships. No one in my family will ever forget.'[8]

Dhirubhai did not live long enough to savour these triumphs. The merger of the oil-refining subsidiary, to create the integrated giant that was now Reliance and the capture of the state 'jewel' IPCL turned out to be the culmination of his remarkable career. Within weeks, on 24 June 2002, Dhirubhai was felled by his second massive stroke. He lingered in a coma on life support for twelve days, while India's business circles also went into a kind of suspended animation; then he died on 6 July.

The next day's funeral rites brought an outpouring of public mourning that was unusual in its sweep for a business figure, more akin to the orgies of grief at the passing of major political or cinematic stars. Indeed, these Indian worlds also joined in paying their respects, helping draw in crowds of ordinary citizens to throng Dhirubhai's last journey through the streets of the great city on the Arabian Sea.

After the long days of their bedside vigil, Mukesh and Anil were with Dhirubhai when he expired without regaining consciousness. Anil later recalled that Dhirubhai's personal physician, a Dr Pandey, had predicted the morning of that Saturday that his patient would choose such a day to die. '*Sir planning mein chaltey hain na?*' Pandey said. '*Sir jayenge to Saturday raat ko hi jayenge.*' ('Sir is going according to plan, isn't he? If Sir goes then he will go on Saturday night itself.') As he explained: 'Sir is a person who will not inconvenience anybody. If he goes on Saturday night, it will be after a day's work. The funeral will be on Sunday. As that's a holiday, there will be no office, people can attend, there will be no traffic for the funeral site. It will be over by evening and on Monday morning, everyone can get back to work.' Dhirubhai indeed died later that day, shortly before midnight. Anil recalled getting home at 2.30am, grabbing some sleep, then going to tell Koki-laben around 5am:

> She saw my face, folded her hands and asked: 'When did it happen?' I told her and she said, 'Did he go peacefully?' I said, 'Yes, he had a big smile on his face.' I said I would bring Papa back home at 8am. My mother said, 'I will be ready to receive him.' She was very composed. And seeing my grief, she said to me: 'Your father has gone to heaven – that is his permanent home. God sent him to earth on a mission. He chose India and he chose this family. Now there are others to carry on his mission here, so God needs him back in heaven to do His work.' It was a mother's way of comforting her son. She also did it to convey the message that her husband would want life to go on.[9]

Dhirubhai's body was laid out in the lobby of Sea Wind amid cloth hangings in white, the Hindu colour of mourning, huge photographs of his smiling face in earlier times and garlands of roses. Sticks of incense wafted sweet smoke through the heavy mid-monsoon air, and speakers carried the holy songs 'Shri Krishna Sharnam Mamah' and 'Om Bhur

Bhuvasva'. From 9am that Sunday, the great and the humble of India began filing past the body in the customary ceremony of *darshan*, the imagined communication with the spirit of the dead person. Dressed in white traditional clothes, Dhirubhai's four children – Mukesh, Anil, Nina and Dipti – and daughters-in-law Nita and Tina stood in a receiving line, thanking visitors with folded hands.

The mourners included chiefs of establishment business like Ratan Tata, Adi Godrej and Anand Mahindra, as well as some fallen business heroes like the former Unit Trust of India chairman P.S. Subramanhyam and stockmarket ramper Ketan Parekh. From the world of national politics came the deputy Prime Minister, L.K. Advani, the former Prime Minister, H.D. Deve Gowda, and the opposition Samajwadi party leaders Mulayam Singh Yadav and Amar Singh, along with a procession of political heavyweights in Maharashtra state and old political cronies like Murli Deora and, representing the Congress matriarch Sonia Gandhi, her old family lieutenant R.K. Dhawan. From the film world came Amitabh Bachchan along with his wife Jaya and son Abhishek (who was later to play a thinly disguised Dhirubhai in the bio-pic *Guru*)among other Bollywood leading lights.

There were many ordinary people, too: thousands of Reliance employees, dozens of former colleagues in Mumbai's textile yarn markets and even a few from Chorwad village like Chandrakant Pathak, a childhood playmate of the Ambani brothers. 'Dhirubhai was a visionary in the true sense,' Pathak told one reporter. 'He was destined for greatness. He managed to achieve what most people cannot even dream about. But he never lost his humility. He was a very humble man who never forgot his roots.'

Thobanbhai Lodhia, a trader in dried coconut and ginger in the southern city of Calicut, who had been on a business visit to Mumbai and stayed on for the funeral, was one of the numerous small investors in Reliance shares. He had put Rs 5000 into the company a decade earlier and watched it grow. 'Whenever I attended the annual general meetings of Reliance, Dhirubhai used to tell me: "It is not my company. It is your company." That is the kind of commitment he had towards small investors like me,' Lodhia told a succession of reporters, amid frequent bursts of tears. Even the merely curious were not turned away; like a ragged band of 'gypsies' whose only knowledge of Dhirubhai was that he was the father-in-law of a Bollywood starlet.

Late in the afternoon, the iron gates of Sea Wind were closed to the public and Dhirubhai's body was placed on the open tray of a truck and heaped with flowers. The gates opened and the cortège set off along the sweep of sea front where Dhirubhai had once gone on his early morning exercise walks, chatting to a retinue of colleagues and contacts. Mukesh and Anil paced alongside the body, followed by many of the celebrity mourners, along a route strewn with petals and arched by cloth banners praising Dhirubhai. It was reported that 'many a tear-eyed investor present at the funeral hailed their beloved business wizard, saying: *Dhirubhai amar rahe* (Long live Dhirubhai).'

After taking an hour to cover two kilometres, the procession stopped in a park where Dhirubhai's body was transferred to a bamboo stretcher and carried on the shoulders of Mukesh, Anil and other male relatives to the Chandanwadi cremation ground, where it was placed on a pyre of sandalwood and ghee that was set alight by the two sons, as two Hindu priests chanted Vedic funeral rites. The next day Mumbai's Mulji Jetha, the world's biggest textile market, was closed in respect, but in line with Dr Pandey's prediction, it was back to work at Reliance.

The initial evaluation of Dhirubhai came in a succession of tributes. Advani said Dhirubhai had embodied initiative, enterprise and determination. 'He was one of the greatest achievers in the country and would remain an inspiration for others,' the deputy Prime Minister told reporters on leaving Sea Wind. Prime Minister Vajpayee said, 'The country has lost iconic proof of what an ordinary Indian fired by the spirit of enterprise and driven by determination can achieve in his own lifetime.'

Some portrayed Dhirubhai in a saintly light, which might have amused him. The state governor of Maharashtra, P.C. Alexander, said, 'The nation had lost one of the doyens of the modern Indian corporate community, a philanthropist and above all a great human being endowed with great compassion and concern for the underprivileged sections of the society.' Indu Jain, chairman of the *Times of India* parent company Bennett Coleman, described Dhirubhai as a 'model father and business genius, whose futuristic vision and spirit of entrepreneurship made him one of the world's leading wealth emperors. We salute him equally for ensuring that his legacy as a master builder with a social conscience will be carried forward by his wife Kokilaben and sons Mukesh and Anil, who have already proved to be exemplary corporate citizens.'

It was left to President K.R. Narayanan to sound a more quizzical note, appropriately enough for one who had been a student of Harold Laski at the London School of Economics, then a protégé of Jawarharlal Nehru in the early post-independence years: '[Ambani's] emergence as a leading figure in the corporate world has been cited as a remarkable example, which needs to be studied in depth to highlight his important role in our country's quest for economic growth and regeneration.'

One of the first to take up this challenge was the economist C.P. Chandrasekhar of Nehru University in New Delhi. Gingerly running over the legends of Dhirubhai breaking both regulations and governments ('Fables such as these, built often on a modicum of truth and sometimes from thin air, were testimony to the success of Dhirajlal Hirachand Ambani'), Chandrasekhar positioned Dhirubhai as a pioneer of capitalist renewal inside India. When he started out, the industrial licensing system was decaying. Intended to allocate investment evenly and prevent monopoly, licences had actually been cornered by existing oligopolists, whose position was further reinforced by import barriers. 'This made the licensing system completely *ad hoc* and arbitrary, enabling new entrants to manoeuvre the system in their favour. It was here that Dhirubhai exercised his acumen to win favour with, manipulate and benefit from the power of the bureaucracy and the political class.'[10]

By choosing the underappreciated sector of artificial fibres, Dhirubhai had been able to drive a wedge into a manufacturing sector protected against new entrants and had build up plants with greater economies of scale than existing producers, helped by his early grasp of the capital-raising potential of the sharemarket. The attack on domestic oligopoly produced a globally competitive group.'[11]

A business journalist, Harish Nambiar, contrasted the huge public display of mourning for Dhirubhai with the more circumspect funerals for the representatives of earlier corporate achievement like J.R.D. Tata and Aditya Birla, when there had been no 'weepy scenes' in the streets. This seemed to signal a decisive shift in India's thinking: 'I think in the death of Ambani, Indian sensibility might have finally changed course irreversibly from being primarily a socialist country to become an unabashedly capitalist one.' As Nambiar wrote, the 'umbilical chords' of Nehru's socialism had been cut:

> He also did one thing that only a post-Nehru entrepreneur could
> conceive of: sharing his wealth with individual investors who
> bankrolled his dreams on the strength of Reliance dividends
> … In doing so, Ambani made a huge base of small investors

partake of his profits. In that respect he was a Robin Hood to Indian investors; he may not be the most moral or even legitimate businessman, but he was generous to his hordes … Ambani may have broken all the laws of the land, manipulated all its politicians and priced each and every influential man in power to reach where he did. But much like Maradona's hand of God goal, eventually … Indians will remember him and his company as the eventual winner and Reliance shareholders will revere him as their deliverer.[12]

Much less ambivalent encomiums continued through to Dhirubhai's seventieth birth anniversary on 28 December that year, when under the Communications minister Pramod Mahajan, an old ally of Reliance, the Indian post office issued a commemorative five-rupee stamp with Dhirubhai's portrait. At a ceremony attended by the minister, Anil portrayed his late father as a humble *karmayogi*, someone who works devoutly at his lot in life. Soon afterwards, a new President of India, A.P.J. Abdul Kalam, awarded Dhirubhai posthumously the Bharat Ratna (Jewel of India), the country's highest civilian honour.

On the first anniversary of Dhirubhai's death, in July 2003, Abdul Kalam also gave the inaugural speech at a memorial lecture. But an ancillary speech by Arun Shourie, the Disinvestment minister who had supervised the sale of the Indian Petrochemicals stake to Reliance, gained the most notice and sparked off a critical assessment of Dhirubhai's career. Recalling the IPCL tender, Shourie declared that his attitude towards Dhirubhai had gone through an almost '180 degree turn' over the years:

> I first learnt about him through the articles of my colleague S. Gurumurthy. The point in most of the articles was that Reliance had done something in excess of what it had been permitted

to do: that it had set up capacities in excess of what had been licenced, that it was producing in excess of those capacities. Most would say today that those restrictions and conditions should not have been there in the first place, that they are what held the country back. And that the Dhirubhais are to be thanked, not once but twice over: they set up world class companies and facilities in spite of those regulations and thus laid the foundations for the growth all of us claim credit for today.

Shourie then paraphrased the Austrian economist Friedrich von Hayek, a proponent of free enterprise capitalism, in saying: 'By exceeding the limits in which those restrictions sought to impound them, they helped create the case for scrapping those regulations.[13]

The minister was roundly castigated for his remarks. Paranjay Guha Thakurta, a business journalist and college lecturer, pointed out that while the Reliance bid might have given the government far more cash than it had expected, IPCL had cash resources of Rs 27 billion, far in excess of what Reliance had paid, and assets with a replacement value of Rs 100 billion (although it must be remembered that a 26 per cent stake would not give Reliance a free hand to plunder these). 'The minister … is perhaps being a bit too naive. Surely he knew that there would not have been "unbelievable" pressures on him – from various quarters including from with the Union Cabinet – if so much had not been at stake for the Reliance group?' Thakurta wrote. Reliance had been eyeing IPCL for at least four years. 'Why? The reason is disarmingly simple. By being at the helm of affairs at IPCL, the Ambanis are now able to control at least two-thirds of the total Indian market for all kinds of petrochemical products.'[14] The veteran Indian journalist T.J.S. George also disagreed with Shourie's ideas, which 'seemed to hold up as virtue precisely what he and his world had earlier exposed as vice':

... those who had even a vague memory of [Gurumurthy's] 1986
articles would have marvelled at the classic example of *suppressio
veri, suggestio falsi* [by suppression of the truth, suggestion of
the false] that the Minister provided. He misled his audience
about the contents of the articles and the intent of their author.
S. Gurumurthy's articles did not even remotely see Dhirubhai's
activities as a patriotic move to prepare the ground for Reform.
On the contrary, he used an array of facts and figures to prove
that Reliance was habitually breaking the laws of the land at the
expense of the country.[15]

In the *Economic Times,* senior journalist M.K. Venu noted some
'serious problems' with Shourie's effort to fit Dhirubhai into the
'Hayekian framework' of entrepreneurialism:

The way the regulatory framework is evolving in our country
would make Hayek turn in his grave! In his seminal work, *The
Road to Serfdom*, Hayek drew a clear distinction between the
Rule of Law and Arbitrary Government ... It will hardly be
an exaggeration to say that in India the regulatory framework,
whether in the telecom or energy sector, has failed to pass
this fine Hayekian test. So there is also a flip side to allowing
entrepreneurial spirit to test the limits of law. The key question
is: how do you protect the Rule of Law and 'known rules of the
game' from being subverted by big business?[16]

Venu gave as a prime example the 'inverted import tariff structure'
allowing big business able to enter raw material sectors to squeeze their
smaller downstream customers while remaining protected by high
tariffs against foreign competitors. Indeed, through to the end of the
BJP-led government in 2004, downstream users of plastics and other
petrochemicals were complaining of the Reliance–IPCL dominance
of local supply and New Delhi's slowness in reducing tariffs on the
imported alternative. It was not until a new Congress-led coalition

introduced its first budget in early 2005 that tariffs on basic chemicals and intermediates went below 10 per cent.

If Shourie had handed Dhirubhai a bonanza and turned Hayek into a charter for breaking inconvenient regulations, he also gave a telling vignette of Dhirubhai's attitude to political power and the rules. Some time in the 1990s Rupert Murdoch had called on Dhirubhai during a visit to explore opportunities for satellite and cable broadcasting in India. Dhirubhai asked whom he had seen in New Delhi before flying down to Mumbai. Murdoch replied that he had seen the Prime Minister, the Finance minister and a number of other ministers and officials. Dhirubhai then delivered what Shourie described as a *guru mantra*, or wise man's precept: 'Ah, you've met all the right people,' he said. 'But if you want to get anywhere in India you must meet all the wrong people.'[17] Dhirubhai himself never quite became one of the 'right people' and was probably proud of it.

18

The polyester princes

The polyester king was dead. What now for the polyester princes? At the height of the 1980s battle over the polyester market, the tabloid newspaper *Blitz* had used the *Mahabharata* analogy. That had lacked one crucial element, however: fratricide. That was about to be supplied.

Mukesh and Anil had got an early warning about their father's mortality with his first cerebral stroke in 1986. Barely returned from their graduate schools in the United States, they had been thrown into the leadership of Reliance in their twenties. Now, there seemed little debate or hesitation about the transition. Mukesh, as the older brother, moved to replace his father as chairman and Anil became deputy chairman. They shared the job of chief executive. It seemed a good mix. Things quickly became business as usual at Reliance.

Even before Dhirubhai's passing, the two sons were taking Reliance away from its long-standing doctrine of tight integration. Suddenly polyester, petrochemicals and even oil were looking like not the exciting new face of modern technology but 'old industry'.

Instead of making tangible products, the buzz was the information economy. The hottest stocks on the Indian sharemarket were the leading information technology houses, Infosys and Wipro, and a host of competitors in the southern Indian cities of Bangalore, Chennai and Hyderabad. Connected by overnight satellite data downloads from their customers in the United States, they worked on an entirely different plane from Reliance and its like. Set up in the 1980s, these software houses had flourished outside the jungle of industrial licensing in which Reliance and its rivals had to stalk official favours. They attracted India's elite logical minds to university-like parks that were actually called 'campuses' rather than workshops or offices. These centres soon became the focus of an Americanised lifestyle for young professionals mostly living away from their parents and who wouldn't be seen dead in polyester.

Although annual revenues were only a fraction of Reliance's sales, at around $3 billion for both Infosys and Wipro in the year to March 2007, their market capitalisations often exceeded that of Reliance. Founded by N.R. Narayana Murthy in 1981, Infosys by then had 75 000 employees worldwide, including many in China, and was dealing with hundreds of thousands of job applicants worldwide. Wipro had been a small producer of cooking oil and soap (the letters of its name taken from Western India Vegetable Products) until its owner, Azim Premji, took it into computer assembly and software in 1980. By 2007 it had 68 000 employees serving customers like Boeing, BP and Sony. In the new century, it was Infosys and Wipro that headed lists of the 'best' or 'most admired' companies in the business magazines. It was Premji and Naranaya Murthy who were turning up at global business conventions as the faces of the new India rather than the Ambanis, and their successes were being cited as reasons why the Indian economic tortoise might one day catch up with the Chinese hare.

It must have rankled more than a bit with the intensely competitive Ambani brothers. The group was already dominant in many products and waiting on government divestments and oil exploration results to expand its upstream oil business. Jamnagar's completion freed up massive internal cash flows. Dhirubhai's old motto of 'Stick to your knitting', or vertical integration, had lost its appeal. Instead, the cash was poured into diverse new businesses only loosely related to the long-standing core activities of Reliance – assuming these are reckoned as being textiles, petrochemicals and petroleum. But an alternative view of Reliance's 'core competencies' is abstracted from its record: time- and cost-effective completion of highly complex and advanced technology projects and unmatchable ability to manage relations with government. Both were called into play when, led by the sons, Reliance launched itself into telecommunications, electric power, financial services and biotechnology.

As explained later by Mukesh Ambani, the company's leadership had been acutely aware of the IT opportunity being seized by Infosys and Wipro. Mukesh had lived close to Silicon Valley in his year at Stanford University and had mentioned the 'arbitrage opportunity' for Indian software houses – the huge gap between wages of American and Indian software engineers – in a speech in 1995. Reliance had signed a joint venture agreement with Microsoft, but had decided to let the opportunity pass. 'I was very focused on building various competencies in Reliance and we were not ready to do two things at the same time,' Mukesh recalled. 'It was a big risk for us to get into IT, especially because it was hugely effort-intensive. In my language, I said we have too much soap on our body and we need to take a bath in the chemicals business.' A few years later, with Jamnagar and Hazira nearly completed, the Ambanis felt able to think more boldly about new ventures. Mukesh recalled a meeting with his father at Maker Chambers.

> We had three thoughts. One was the fundamental belief that
> we will invest in businesses of the future and we will invest in
> talent. We clearly saw that from oil to fabric was a value chain
> of opportunity and it will remain so for many future decades.
> We executed that well and created enough disruptions in the
> polyester, plastics, refinery and the upstream business of oil
> and gas. We had very good cash flows. In late '90s, we had two
> options. One was to make the current business more global,
> bigger and better. The other option was to use our cash flows to
> do something else. We were sitting right in this room and my
> father said, 'Now it is your call. What you would like to do?' I
> said, 'We must use the competencies and cash flows to make a
> difference to millions of Indians.' He said, 'That's exactly what
> I had mind. Let's do it.' The strategy was: while we strengthen
> our current business, we will use our cash flows to invest in the
> businesses of the future. That's how Infocomm was born.[1]

The group had already made some forays away from its patch. It had bought into India's biggest reported petroleum find in decades, a gas deposit estimated at two trillion cubic feet in the Krishna–Godavari basin of the Bay of Bengal coast. For its earlier oil developments, in the Arabian Sea, Reliance had partnered the American natural gas developer and trader Enron, which also built a very large and controversial power plant in Dabhol, Maharashtra, south of Mumbai. As well as feedstock for petrochemicals, gas offered the chance for Reliance to follow another path of vertical integration, to electricity generation. By 2002 the group had gained a controlling interest in the main Mumbai electricity supplier BSES and had renamed it Reliance Energy when ownership reached 41 per cent. With it, Reliance acquired three power projects in Maharashtra.

In 1996–97 Reliance became worried when Dow Chemicals announced they were looking at making plastics from the bio-organism *E. coli*. 'It looked like our business would be ruined because we would buy naphtha and these guys would make plastics from salt and water,' Mukesh recalled. The Ambanis hurriedly set up a study group to watch industrial biotechnology, which developed into a long-term research activity covering human and plant biotech that kept the group positioned in the sector without incurring huge costs. The biotech effort involved some plantations in Gujarat and laboratories around Mumbai working on stem cell treatments. Mukesh told one interviewer in early 2004 that the aim was to be a biotech 'Microsoft', supplying the software or techniques for various applications.

Much of this effort was located in a 56-hectare estate on the outskirts of Mumbai named Dhirubhai Ambani Knowledge City. It was designed to match the campuses of the new IT star companies in southern India and help attract the same kind of talent. And the hottest new venture was the one mentioned by Mukesh.

The company had joined the mid-1990s frenzy for telephony licences, as we have seen. But pure communication would not deliver a 'sustainable value' unless it converged with information services. Driven by Mukesh, the group set up an entirely new subsidiary, Reliance Infocomm. The productive core of this enterprise was its own network of optical-fibre cable, designed to carry a massive volume of cellular and fixed telephony and broadband internet-based services (which had been completely liberalised in 1998 when the Vajpayee government ended the monopoly on internet service provision held by the government telecom carrier Videsh Sanchar Nigam Ltd). In mid-2001 Mukesh was talking of a $5 billion investment program, with $2 billion for 60000 kilometres of cabling, to link 115 cities across India. By the time he took over the Reliance leadership after Dhirubhai's death the next year, the network was occupying an army of labourers, while Infocomm had 3500 staff and was planning to double their numbers within a year, many recruited from companies attuned to marketing goods direct to consumers like Hindustan Lever and Cadbury-Schweppes. Mukesh was racing to grab what he called a 'once in a lifetime opportunity' to lay down and own the knowledge economy's equivalent of the railway and thus become the 'carrier's carrier' for India's IT industry.

The venture also showed Reliance's characteristic quick grasp of the possibilities of combining technical alternatives and regulatory loopholes to outflank its rivals – which once again brought on it an intense controversy. In March 1999 the Vajpayee government had rescued the private telephone operators from the consequences of their reckless bidding for licences just a few years earlier. Many had no hope of paying what they had promised, risking collapse of the effort to lift India out of its backward telephone coverage. Private-sector basic or landline services were operating in only two states, and cellular services had only a million subscribers between them. The whole sector was caught up in litigation, involving operators and two arms of government, the latter in some cases fighting each other in court.

Under a new telecom policy, the licence fees were forgiven, replaced by a percentage of revenue, in return for operators agreeing to loss of their previous duopolies in each regional 'circle' and to drop all litigation. The two state telephone companies were cleared to start cellular services in each of the twenty circles, and preparations were made for a tender to add a fourth operator in each. In August 2000 the government opened up domestic long-distance calls to unlimited competition; Reliance was one of two private groups given immediate clearance. The industry moved ahead and consolidated into fewer operators.

But Reliance quickly swooped on an entirely new opportunity offered by New Delhi's green light for fixed-line telephone operators to offer 'wireless-in-local-loop' services, in which the 'last mile' of the telephone connection was by radio wave passing from a fairly compact base transmission unit (attached to a pole or rooftop) to a handset that could be carried around within range of that tower's signal. Known as 'the poor man's cell phone', it cut the cost of connecting a household to a quarter of the cost incurred in using copper wires. Developed in India, it has been used in such countries as Madagascar and Fiji. The technology allowed countries like India to expand their telephone subscriber base much more quickly and cheaply than wiring up individual households to a local exchange. With India's 'teledensity' (households with telephones) having risen from 0.8 per cent to only 3 per cent between 1994 and 2001, the basic telephony sector was not exactly jumping and clearly was not on track to meet the Vajpayee government's target of 7 per cent density by 2005.

But local-loop telephones also potentially eroded the value of cell phone licences, for which the operators had by early 2001 paid Rs 70 billion in spectrum and other charges. As the authorities pushed the idea, the cell phone operators expressed alarm, with the Tata group's head Ratan Tata writing to Vajpayee calling it a 'significant deviation' from the 1999 policy. Nonetheless, the Communications ministry (held by Vajpayee, with junior minister Ram Vilas Paswan assisting him), accepted recommendations that local-loop was just a minor add-on service to basic telephony and that the population should not be deprived of its benefits. In January 2001 his officials announced guidelines for local-loop services with a maximum roaming range of 10 kilometres and said that spectrum would be offered free on a 'first come first served basis'. A rush of 132 groups applied for licences, including some of the cellular operators opposing the policy, and in March 2001 Paswan's ministry announced that out of forty approved local-loop licences, Reliance was cleared to operate in eighteen of India's twenty telecom circles, Tata Teleservices in fifteen circles and the controversial Himachal Futuristic Communications in seven. The cell phone operators immediately declared it suspicious, with a former head of the telecommunications regulator declaring that 'the government knowingly took a decision contrary to its own policy'.

Vajpayee referred the issue to the government's Group on Telecom and IT Convergence, which included ministers Pramod Mahajan, Arun Jaitley and Sushma Swaraj. The terms of reference showed the outcome the government sought: the group was asked to find whether the 1999 new telecom policy permitted 'limited mobility' by fixed-telephone companies. If it did, then how best should the service be introduced? If it did not, how could the policy be modified to introduce limited mobility? The panel duly concluded that the 1999 new telecom policy did allow basic operators to offer local-loop, but adjusted the split of revenue from long-distance calls to match that applied to cell phone operators.[2]

The replacement of Paswan with Mahajan as Communications minister in August 2001 handed the responsibility to a politician far more notorious for his affinity with the Ambanis. Mahajan promptly overruled advice from his own regulators for a technical safeguard – a particular interface standard to a public switching architecture – to make sure local-loop services remained just local. This was not necessary, the ministry decided. The cell phone operators pursued a legal case against the decision all the way to the Supreme Court, which in December 2002 ruled against them. By that stage Mukesh was all but ready to start the Reliance Infocomm service, which had now mutated into a fully cellular service, with subscribers given multiple registrations to allow roaming service throughout the eighteen circles. Even its name, IndiaMobile, flaunted what was going on.[3]

Mukesh had adopted a different cellular technology from that in general use in India. Instead of the global system for mobile communications (GSM), adopted by the first wave of operators, Infocomm had decided on the code-division multiple access (CDMA) standard used notably in the United States and in South Korea. In shades of the old propaganda about chemical pathways to making polyester, Reliance projected its cellular technology as more advanced than the other form. There was not actually much between them, but the CDMA pattern gave it a ready supplier of systems from American companies and mass supply of cheap handsets from South Korean electronics groups.

Together with the absence of heavy licence fees, this enabled Mukesh to launch a service that severely undercut existing cellular services on price. Swarms of would-be tycoons were signed up as 'Dhirubhai Ambani Entrepreneurs', paying a deposit for the opportunity to market *Dhirubhai ka Sapna* (Dhirubhai's Dream) schemes to consumers, which involved low deposits for a handset to be paid over three years and a base of free local outgoing calls.

On 27 December 2002, the eve of what would have been Dhirubhai's seventieth birthday, Mahajan was guest of honour at Reliance Infocomm's big launch event in Mumbai, having also persuaded Vajpayee to contribute one of his Hindi poems – read live by the Prime Minister by videolink. Mahajan, who was to unveil the postage stamp in Dhirubhai's honour the next day, was effusive in his praise of the Reliance Infocomm's network control centre at the New Mumbai 'campus' where rows of young professionals sat at computer work stations facing two enormous video walls. It was 'better than NASA', he said.

But after what was described as a 'high-voltage' launch, the service started running on low power. The competing cellular services responded by slashing their prices and refusing connectivity to their networks from basic service providers. The private basic operators then tried routing their calls through the public sector telephone networks to mask their origin, but these calls were detected and blocked. The government networks retaliated by blocking calls from the cell phone operators. This tit-for-tat squabble brought chaos over the following month, until regulators set new rules for connections and tariffs.

Mahajan's interest in Reliance led to the first big reverse in a career that seemed to be taking the former journalist and lifelong RSS activist towards the 'second-generation' leadership of the Hindu nationalists. Mahajan's tongue had run away from him in his enthusiasm at the Infocomm launch. He had said Dhirubhai's contributions had not been sufficiently appreciated by those in authority. If *naachnewali aur gaanewali* (singers and dancers) could be given the Bharat Ratna, the country's highest civilian award, why not Dhirubhai? The late tycoon was a man who had made several people ministers, Mahajan said, and now he was being denied his due. The implied criticism of Vajpayee was too much, on top of the tarnishing allegations of favouritism and, perhaps worse, that Mahajan had already brought on a ruling party still not quite used to being friendly towards Reliance.

In a cabinet reshuffle on 29 January 2003 Mahajan was dropped from the government and sent back to run the BJP as its general secretary, while his Communications ministry was transferred to Disinvestment minister Arun Shourie. While Mahajan's transfer was partly aimed at boosting the BJP organisation with his communication skills and 'realpolitik' approach, it was also to silence criticism within Hindu groups about his 'nexus with some big industrialists and "others"'.[4]

The drive for subscribers also faltered. Many marketing connections used by new 'entrepreneurs' were local *paanwallahs* and small shopkeepers who had little understanding of the schemes they were selling, in either technical or financial terms. A lot of customers signed up to get their handsets with little intention or ability to meet their monthly payment obligations. It was discovered that the use of Dhirubhai's name was not a great selling point, and the entire marketing effort had to be revamped.

Still, Mukesh did turn the potentially dire situation around. Shourie came in with a stern warning to all telephone players to stick to their permits but, as months went by, showed himself not anxious to thwart the local-loop operators and their customers. In April he had decided against complying with a regulator's order to show cell phone appellants seven documents relating to the original decision to allow limited mobility – according to one report because it might embarrass Mahajan and the BJP. By mid-year, as we have seen, Shourie was praising Dhirubhai as someone who had helped hasten reform by proving the absurdity of the licensing rules. In October 2003 Shourie announced that Reliance Infocomm had been exceeding its licences, but its situation could be legalised by a new 'unified' telecom licence covering all services. Reliance bought one of the licences for $340 million, including a $116 million penalty for its past violations. Gurumurthy, the long-time critic, wrote that the authorities were 'condoning a deliberate illegality. And it is happening because Reliance is in a position to control the levers of power.'

It was something Reliance could shrug off. 'When you're successful, your competitors will try to find alibis for your success,' it said in a statement responding to Gurumurthy.

The fact was that the old critics of Reliance within the Hindu nationalist camp were in disarray. Jaswant Singh did object, but didn't pursue it far, out of loyalty to the Prime Minister, Vajpayee. Arun Jaitley put up a sustained fight but not to the point of resignation, which might have made a difference. Ram Jethmalani was too burdened in his law portfolio to give it much attention. Advani, the Home minister, was deeply troubled by the ethics of what was being done in the telecom field but, with his reputation for stirring up communal violence with Muslims, was not on a strong political footing.

Most importantly, Vajpayee was in favour. Mukesh was said to be one of the few individuals in India allowed to ride in his own car into the prime-ministerial compound on Delhi's Racecourse Road and drive up to the front door. For security reasons, nearly everyone else, including ministers, had to alight at the gate and use a shuttle car up the driveway. The key figure on Vajpayee's staff – the official, some said, who was 'effectively the Prime Minister' – was the National Security Adviser, Brajesh Mishra. He was another of the circle of influential figures cultivated by Dhirubhai through his think-tank, the Observer Research Foundation, chaired by Rishi Kumar Mishra, a former Congress upper house member and former editor-in-chief of Dhirubhai's newspaper, the *Business and Political Observer*. Friendly with many senior figures in the major political parties, R.K. Mishra had been active in 'Track Two' diplomacy with Pakistan undertaken to further Vajpayee's bold play for peace over Kashmir. Author of three books on the Vedas, this Mishra was often described as 'the intellectual face of the Reliance group' and the centre of a 'brahmin network' in Delhi that had transferred its services from Dhirubhai to Mukesh. As Vajpayee's chief gatekeeper, Brajesh Mishra clashed heatedly with those like Nusli Wadia who came to Racecourse Road to persuade the ageing Prime Minister against the tilt of policy towards Reliance. After the BJP election defeat in 2004, Brajesh Mishra joined the board of the Reliance-sponsored foundation.

Legalised by his new 'unified' licence, Mukesh was claiming to have six million subscribers by the end of 2003, a million more than the previous cell phone leader, Bharti Telecom, had built up in nine years. India's total cell phone base had leapt from 11 million to 25 million. By the end of 2004 total cellular connections had exceeded 44 million and surpassed fixed-line connections for the first time. Infocomm had made its first move outside India, paying $211 million for the London-based Flag Telecom and its undersea cables connecting Asia, Europe, the Middle East and the United States. Mukesh was talking of the services he hoped to deliver via his customers' cell phones, including railway and other transport bookings, purchases using personal identity codes instead of credit cards, and medical monitoring.[5]

Within two years of Dhirubhai's death, the company was firmly back in the favourable coverage of the international business press, with *Time Asia* reporting an upbeat mood after the 'doubt that swirled around the conglomerate' after the patriarch's death and the *New York Times* headlining a corporate profile 'A giant so big it's a proxy for India's economy'. Some questioned whether the two sons could fill their father's shoes or whether such different characters work together, *Time Asia* reported. 'The flashy Anil, who is married to a former film actress, likes designer clothes and jogs every morning, his chauffeur driving slowly behind. Mukesh is sedate and prefers spending time with his children or catching up on technical journals.'

The newspaper took a more benign view: 'The Ambani brothers now overseeing the vast Reliance empire seem to be good foils for each other. Anil, 44, Reliance Industries' vice-chairman, is an outgoing man, a financial whiz married to a former Bollywood movie star. Mukesh, 47, the company's chairman, is a quiet man, an engineer who is a stickler for detail ... They inherited their father's tenacity, his intuition in consolidating businesses, even his ability to work India's convoluted bureaucratic system to their advantage.'[6]

Each article said there were no evident signs of 'friction' between the two brothers – but added the words 'right now' or 'for now'. It was a wise qualification.

19

Corporate Kurukshetra

B ut actually there were signs of friction – and within months of Dhirubhai's death. The journalist who had broken the Harshad Mehta scam, Sucheta Dalal, reported the 'conspicuous absence' of Anil at the big launch of Reliance Infocomm on 27 December 2002, saying that the younger brother had 'stolen the show' by not turning up, on flimsy excuses of feeling ill or attending business in New Delhi. 'For many months now, the corporate grapevine has been rife with reports that all is not well between the two brothers,' Dalal wrote.[1]

The event had featured Mukesh and his wife Nita, pursuing the projection of Mukesh as the face of Reliance. Anil, who had been the group's spokesman to the media and financial institutions for several years, was spending more time at business seminars and on media panels. Reliance Infocomm was billed as the work of Mukesh in bringing to life his father's dream. In a long television advertisement, Dalal noted: 'Anil has been carefully edited out, even from an annual general meeting clip, where the two sons had invariably flanked the father on two sides.'[2]

The two brothers were mixing in different worlds. Mukesh was trying to project Reliance as a modern corporation run by professional managers. He surrounded himself with his senior executives, only a couple from within the family (the cousins Nikhil and Hetal Meswani), the rest old and trusted recruits like his former schoolmates Anand Jain and Manoj Modi and outsiders Satish Sheth and Amitabh Jhunjhunwala.

Anil projected a more emotional view of Dhirubhai, frequently harking back to the early childhood memories of the crowded Bhuleshwar *chawl* and putting his father in an almost saintly light. His friends were mostly outside the company, including some older Mumbai business leaders like the Godrej family, Amitabh Bachchan and the omnipresent political wheeler-dealer Amar Singh. Anil stayed away from the Infocomm launch, but was in Mumbai for the introduction of the Dhirubhai Ambani postage stamp by Mahajan the next day.

The younger son had previously backed away from what was expected of him. Instead of letting his parents find him a wife, he had insisted on marrying the film actor Tina Munim against their great opposition. In his early forties, he had pulled himself out of the slide into sedate middle age. An American at an investment roadshow in New York had given him some blunt, personal advice: 'Well, Mr Ambani, the company looks in great shape and we have great confidence in its future. But have you looked at yourself recently in the mirror? … If you are not in good shape, I don't think your company can be in good shape.' Anil took the advice to heart and threw himself into a strict diet and early morning jogging regime that saw him lose

35 kilograms in weight. By 2001 he was running a half marathon once a week, swimming and learning the upper-class game of polo. He was as frequently photographed in his running vest and shorts as in a business suit, showing off his new lean form.[3]

The younger son had also evidently taken to heart his father's *guru mantra* that, to get ahead in India, you had to know the wrong people. Among all the 'wrong people' in the eyes of genteel society in India, few would have figured more prominently than Amar Singh, the portly *bon vivant* MP. Born in 1956 in the ancient Uttar Pradesh city of Aligarh, but raised in Calcutta where his grandfather had gone for work, Singh was scion of a modestly well-off family of Thakurs, a subdivision of the land-owning Rajput caste. He had made his way through a Catholic college, set up some small businesses, then found his vocation as a maker of connections that brought him close to senior political and media figures. In 1996 the rising lower-caste leader Mulayam Singh Yadav was Chief Minister in Uttar Pradesh. He persuaded Singh to join his Samajwadi (Socialist) Party as general secretary and take an upper house seat in New Delhi. They formed an alliance with the Lucknow-based tycoon Subroto Roy, a Bengali who had made a fortune in chit funds, a form of money-lending, and put it into a major Hindi-language newspaper group, a large printing press and a domestic airline under his brand, Sahara. The combination was a powerful one, raising the Samajwadi role in the coalition politics that had become the Indian norm. Singh's official bungalow of Lutyens design, although protected by heritage laws, was transformed with white marble bas-reliefs of naked cherubs and angels, a large Jacuzzi with gold taps, massive plasma-screen video systems in many rooms and a remote-control opening ceiling in the dining room that displayed a roof garden through a miniature replica of the glass pyramid at the Louvre. Thronged with aspiring film starlets and sundry characters, the bungalow became party central for Delhi's political influence peddlers.[4]

Anil became drawn into this heady milieu and, as one of India's wealthiest people and vice-chairman of its largest private industrial combine, was instantly welcomed with all of its flattery. It is said to have alarmed his mother, especially when tabloid newspapers and trashy magazines began linking him with female Bollywood stars and openly speculated on the prospects of a second stellar marriage (without, it must be noted, any evidence of more than passing acquaintanceships; later, there were allegations these rumours were spread to undermine Anil). Kokilaben had opposed the marriage to Tina in 1991, but by now had accepted her as the mother of two grandchildren.

Mukesh was also concerned. For some time, according to the *Out-look* magazine's business editor, Alam Srinivas, who later revealed himself as a conduit of leaks by Anil, he had thought of his younger brother as a potential 'squanderer' and had already taken steps to protect the family ownership of Reliance. 'For a long time, Mukesh had been uneasy about Anil. He had misgivings about the younger brother's professionalism, business acumen and sense of corporate strategy. Mukesh thought Anil went a bit overboard, both in his personal and professional life. And a number of Anil's decisions could – and did – end up hurting the interests of RIL, its board and its shareholders.'[5]

Dhirubhai had realised that the share-switching scandal of 1996 had blown the cover of the network of private investment companies through which the Ambani family churned its 34 per cent joint stake in Reliance (individual members of the family owned a further 5 per cent and the Meswani relatives a further 7 per cent, bringing the total extended family holding to a little over 46 per cent). The opposition MP Raashid Alvi had given further details in the dossier he published in 2001, listing 251 investment companies with names like Yangtse

Trading, Madhuban Merchandise and Ornate Traders, whose directors included various accountants, employees, sales agents and other contacts of the Ambanis.

Dhirubhai had asked Mukesh to reconfigure the entire network, which he began to do with the help of Anand Jain, the 'third son' heading Reliance Capital, forming hundreds of new companies in 1999 in a new coded 'matrix' of ownership. 'As each code had to be changed to hide the new reality, someone put an idea in Mukesh's head,' Srinivas wrote. 'What if the new configuration could be effected to his advantage? What if he could control the empire? What if he could build a new matrix that his younger brother, Anil, could never understand and, hence, could never break up the group?' The aim was not to rob Anil of his inheritance but protect it from his own possible follies.[6]

Around the same time, in 1999, Dhirubhai had signed a deed of partition that had broken up the Ambanis' 'Hindu Undivided Family', a customary entity recognised in Indian law as having corporate ownership, and dispersed its assets among the individual members. The family's main asset, its 34 per cent of Reliance, was held in the thicket of investment companies. Dhirubhai felt no need to leave a will, apparently confident that Anil would agree to work under Mukesh's leadership.

This was not at all Anil's attitude when Dhirubhai died in July 2002. He immediately proposed that Kokilaben assume the Reliance chairmanship, leaving the sons as almost equal executive directors. Mukesh rejected this immediately as 'giving the wrong signal' and was voted chairman at the end of the month by the other directors.

Talks about splitting the empire between the brothers began around November that year, with Anil talking to both Jain and Jhunjhunwala, but did not make any progress. Around this time, Anil learned about the reconfigured ownership web. 'When Anil got to know about the new matrix in 2002–03 he went berserk,' Srinivas said. 'It seemed to him that Mukesh had stabbed him in the back.'[7]

The issue simmered through 2003, with Anil occasionally reverting to his old role as the public face of the group. The Indian media occasionally hinted at a surrogate rivalry between the two brothers' wives. Nita Ambani, married to Mukesh, was emerging as a concerned and active corporate wife. She had supervised the planting of the green belt of mango trees around the Jamnagar refinery and the extension of drinking water to local villages from its seawater desalinators. In Mumbai she had handled the design and landscaping of the company's 'Knowledge City', ran the board of the new Dhirubhai Ambani International School and pursued educational programs for slum children, besides practising yoga and traditional dance.[8]

In various interviews after Dhirubhai's death, Nita had talked about her role as Mukesh's most frank confessor and adviser. In October 2002 the magazine *Society* headlined its cover story 'Mukesh and Nita Ambani – on turning Dhirubhai's dream into reality'. *Savvy* magazine talked of 'Nita Ambani's corporate avatar'. In interviews, Nita said she was the sounding board and the only one who could speak her mind to Mukesh, including on business affairs, such as what she called the 'premature' launch of Reliance Infocomm. 'People thought I came to Jamnagar as a rich man's wife to pass my time,' she was quoted as saying. 'Today I know what business is about. Today I understand and help Mukesh in execution.' Later this was portrayed, in at least one newspaper report quoting unnamed 'observers', as part of a campaign to replace Anil as vice-chairman of the company and as having 'driven a wedge' between the brothers.[9]

By the end of 2003 Anil's actions were bringing him into serious conflict with Mukesh. Anil was starting to use Reliance Energy, of which he was chairman and managing director, like an independent company, even though it was 51 per cent owned by Reliance Industries. He had also got closer to the Samajwadi government in Uttar Pradesh, which broadcast the 'news' that Reliance was going to build a huge power plant in the western part of the state, feeding the industrial belts close to Delhi. In January 2004 Anil announced that the plant at Dadri would be the largest gas-fired generator in the world, costing Rs 100 billion or $2.2 billion, and would take its fuel by pipeline from the Reliance discovery in the Krishna–Godavari basin.

It was not actually until two days later that the project came before the Reliance board, which agreed to commit Rs 35 billion, but withheld any commitment of gas produced in the Bay of Bengal field. After a Congress-led coalition with Manmohan Singh as Prime Minister replaced the Vajpayee BJP-led government in May that year and immediately announced plans to privatise the notoriously squalid Delhi and Mumbai airports, Anil jumped in again with an announcement that Reliance would join the bidding, without consulting Mukesh or the board. Mukesh was also resisting pressure from Anil for the company to 'adopt' a hospital in Mumbai and put Rs 180 million into the foundation that ran it (Anil was later to explain it was his mother's wish).

Mukesh's tolerance snapped on 16 June (only twelve days after the *New York Times* reported 'no obvious friction', although it had also noted Anil's absence from the Infocomm launch). He picked up the morning newspapers to read that Anil had accepted a nomination by the Samajwadi Party to occupy one of its allotted seats in the Rajya Sabha as an independent. Alongside him was Jaya Bachchan, actress wife of the 'Big B', Amitabh, who had apparently agreed to lend some of the family magic to Samajwadi in return for financial help arranged by Amar Singh from the Sahara group's Subroto Roy for his business activities.

Amar Singh flanked his two new stars as they were sworn in to their positions. Anil's required register of assets listed his wealth as comprising investments of Rs 1.6 billion, other assets of Rs 900 million and jewellery worth Rs 272 million, while his wife Tina's jewellery was put at Rs 650 million, giving a total of Rs 3.42 billion or about $77 million – meaning that the main Reliance stake in the investment companies was not being counted.

Mukesh was incandescent with anger at Anil's jump into politics with an opposition party, according to a family confidant. Soon afterwards he moved again to put Anil in his place. At a Reliance board meeting on 27 July 2004 the agenda included as its item no. 17 a motion blandly titled as being 'to approve constitution of a "Health, Safety and Environment" Committee and to confirm authorities hitherto delegated by the Board to Committees of Directors/Directors/Executives as also confirm such of those delegated authorities as are subsisting and to consider modifications, if any'. Tucked away as an annexure was a note setting out the functions of the chairman and managing director (Mukesh) and the vice-chairman and managing director (Anil) who would be under the 'overall authority' of Mukesh. The condominium was over: Mukesh was the boss.

Anil did not immediately twig to Mukesh's tactic. When he did, within a day or two, he began bombarding his brother and the company secretary with objections. It was neither in good faith, went one email on 30 July, nor in the spirit in which such matters had been handled within the company before, or the traditions set by Dhirubhai. It was a sorry state of affairs. The question had to be hammered out between the two brothers before coming back to the board.

The passage of the item remained in the minutes of the board meeting. Anil persisted with his objections, which were noted then rejected in a board meeting in October. The majority felt that Anil was overreacting and that the explanation of functions simply formulated the *status quo* of the company's leadership.

Not long afterwards it all broke out into the open. The spark was an entirely random and unrelated event. At a big function on the evening of 17 November 2004 attended by the 'cream of corporate captains' in Mumbai, Mukesh had introduced a talk on 'Unlocking Innovation' by the visiting chief executive of Microsoft, Steve Ballmer, who had been a classmate at Stanford University's School of Business.

After an effusive speech by Mukesh, Ballmer took the podium: 'I hope he [Mukesh] won't mind,' he said, 'but in our class in Stanford Business School, there were exactly two people who dropped out at the end of the first year, me and Mukesh.'

As Mukesh was to explain three years later, he had indeed not completed his master's degree. The young chemical engineer had won entrance to the prestigious school and quickly immersed himself in it. Then Reliance got its licence for the first polyester plant at Patalganga, and Dhirubhai told his son that work would start immediately. Six months short of completing the graduate program, Mukesh pulled out and returned to Mumbai.[10] Nothing wrong with that, and Mukesh had clearly got a lot out of his year at Stanford. But ever since his return in 1981, Reliance had been listing Mukesh as an MBA from Stanford, including this 'fact' in many of its corporate reports and statements. Ballmer's quip sent a frisson around the audience, many of whom were unclear whether it was a joke or the truth.

Possibly Mukesh was rattled too. As the event broke up around 10pm, he was stopped by a team from the television news channel

CNBC-TV-18 in which a Reliance subsidiary had a stake and which had sponsored Ballmer's talk. The reporter, Menaka Doshi, put the question in the most delicate way. 'There have been rumours about the Reliance group and the way the businesses are going to go in the future,' Doshi said. 'I don't think you need me to articulate any further. But can you, for your investors, tell us if there is ever going to be a likelihood of any split of any kind?'

After some minutes of blather about how Reliance was 'beyond one, two or three individuals, including myself' and was now run by professional talent, Mukesh came to the question. 'So, well, there are other issues which are ownership issues,' he said to the camera. 'These are in the private domain, but as far as Reliance is concerned, it is a very, very strong professional company.'

The channel put the interview in edited form to air that night, but it was not immediately noticed and Mukesh flew off the next morning to the United States. Only when the Press Trust of India put out a report in the afternoon did newspapers and the stockmarket wake up. There was an immediate plunge in the share prices of Reliance and all its listed subsidiaries and affiliates, including IPCL, thus bringing down the entire market index.

The Indian media began a feast of speculation and vaguely sourced reports, fed by anomymous sources said to be close to one or other of the brothers' 'camps'. Anil was said to have been sidelined from financial and investment activity after he had raised questions about the funds the parent company had been providing the Infocomm subsidiary. Mukesh had indicated that he was delaying by two years the commitment of Krishna–Godavari gas to the Uttar Pradesh power plant. Even the alleged intrusion of Mukesh's wife was raked up, amid the scanty public evidence available to explain the background of the 'ownership issues'.

One hard fact did emerge: that Dhirubhai had died intestate. Under the law of Hindu succession, the property of a man who died without leaving a will had to be divided among his wife and children. Property registered under the Hindu Undivided Family law had to be split between the wife, sons and unmarried daughters. But, as we have seen, Dhirubhai had nullified that undivided family status. Who actually owned the controlling 34 per cent stake held in the corporate web?

The *Business Standard* columnist T.N. Ninan found it 'astonishing' that Dhirubhai hadn't left a will, given all the evidence of bitter corporate rifts that had occurred after the death of various founders, like the division of the *Indian Express* group between the grandnephews of Ramnath Goenka.

> People with unusual success stories usually have a good understanding of human motivation and frailties … Both Mukesh and Anil Ambani are able, energetic and ambitious, and beyond a point no one company can have enough space for both of them, especially when the age difference is not great and there are family tensions adding to the complications. If this is obvious to most observers, surely it should have been obvious to Dhirubhai, who had few peers in his ability to size up people and situations. So why did he not plan an orderly succession?[11]

Mukesh returned to Mumbai late on the night of Sunday 21 November after a weekend of fevered speculation. In a written statement issued the next day (and later put out as a paid advertisement in major newspapers), he said he had been shocked at the way his remark had been 'torn out of context'. Citing only the first part of the question put to him – not the key part asking about the likelihood of a split – he claimed it was 'clear that I was responding to the query about the future businesses'

and that the 'ownership' referred to future initiatives. 'Placed in the context of the question put to me, it is obvious that my reply has nothing to do with the family ownership of Reliance,' Mukesh stated.

He also hit out at 'totally unjustified and tendentious comments' in some reports about his father. 'In keeping with the worldwide trend of transformation of family-owned businesses, Dhirubhai took, within his lifetime, all necessary steps to separate ownership from management and made Reliance a world-class professionally managed company. With his extraordinary foresight, he has also settled all ownership issues pertaining to Reliance within his lifetime.'

Mukesh concluded by hoping that 'all speculation on this issue will come to an end with this clarification'. But it didn't, and why would it? The television channel immediately started playing the full unedited interview, which contradicted Mukesh's claims about context. And 'market sources' were quoted asking that, if Dhirubhai had settled the succession issue in his lifetime, why was this not known either to family members apart from Mukesh or the stock exchanges and securities regulators?

Mukesh followed up his public statement with a message the next day to all the 85 000 Reliance employees, stating: 'There is no ambiguity in his [Dhirubhai's] legacy that the chairman and managing director is the final authority on all matters concerning Reliance.' That might have been the moment when the conflict was yanked back out of the public view. But, almost immediately, it burst out again.

Dalal Street, the stockmarket quarter, was perplexed that one of Reliance's longest serving directors, the lawyer M.L. Bhakta, chose that day to resign from the board, after serving on it since 1977. He had announced his decision after meeting Mukesh and several other directors earlier in the day. Was this the start of a board-level shake-out?

Bhakta agreed to reconsider his resignation within a day, at the announced request of Mukesh. Although a precise explanation of his initial decision was never given, it appeared to be a sign of anguish at the division between the brothers. Anil's camp, meanwhile, let it be known that the younger brother wanted to learn when exactly Dhirubhai had discussed the ownership issue with Mukesh and how Mukesh had gained control of the 300 investment companies holding the 34 per cent joint stake. On 25 November Anil seemed to be trying his father's old tactic of *bichu chordiya* – letting loose a scorpion – when six directors of his fiefdom Reliance Energy sent him their resignations. All were nominees of the parent company and significantly included the executive Amitabh Jhunjhunwala, an insider with intimate knowledge of Reliance finances and shareholdings.

Anil had been spending a lot of time with his mother, to whom he was loudly and repeatedly surrendering the decision on what should be done. Mukesh might have had all the biggest cards in his hand, but could he resist the mother's moral authority?

Mother and younger son had gone together to the Nathdwara temple near Udaipur to pray to Srinathji, the avatar of Krishna worshipped by their caste. Kokilaben was trying to get the family together. The two daughters had come to stay with her at Sea Wind. But the two sons were not in the same room. Anil later flew to Tirupati with his wife Tina, to pray at the famous temple to the deity Venkateswara for his help in 'preserving and enhancing the legacy of my late father, Dhirubhai Ambani'. Anil was reported to feel in a minority of one on the board, which was 'packed with family retainers and bureaucrats who had to be rewarded for past favours' and therefore unlikely to stand up to the chairman. He was also said to have changed his telephones from Infocomm to another carrier, for fear he was being tapped.[12] The following weekend, he went to Govardhan, to a temple near the spot where Krishna had appeared as a cowherd, and sped around its 21-kilometre *parikrama* or pilgrimage circuit (wearing runners, rather than assuming the normal bare feet). Kokilaben also widened her spiritual counselling, flying up to Bhavnagar in Gujarat to spend two hours at the ashram of a well-known guru who offered to hold a *katha* (a rendition of a holy text) at the Reliance complex in Jamnagar.

Around this time, the media started to receive a flow of revealing documents, from inside Reliance, aimed at putting one side or the other in a bad light. The first big leak was what seemed to be Anil's letter of complaint about the manoeuvre at the 27 July board meeting, whereby Mukesh had his supremacy confirmed in an annex to the item on the health, safety and environment committee. Within days, the media and various lawyers were chewing over the rights and wrongs of this incident.

But matters deteriorated sharply and quickly. As *Outlook*'s Alam Srinivas noted, the Ambanis had refined their skills in the arts of covert political warfare in their battles with Nusli Wadia and his Bombay Dyeing group and later in the messy attempt to take over Larsen & Toubro. Faxes on paper without letterheads were coming from public business centres and shops, containing the most riveting and damaging inside material. Journalists like Srinivas were getting leaks timed to meet their deadlines. One originator of emails purported to be 'Mohandas Karamdas Gandhi' – an inaccurate version of the long-dead Mahatma's name. The reporters were being summoned to coffee shops by Reliance executives, who handed over material put together by private detectives. 'Now the two brothers (Mukesh and Anil) were using the same against each other. Exactly in the same way their late father, Dhirubhai, had taught them to do against their rivals.'[13]

Inspired reports, intended to pressure Mukesh to reveal when and how his father had transferred control of what was now put at 362 shell companies owning the 34 per cent stake, drew the interest of the taxation and economic intelligence agencies attached to the Ministry of Finance. Adding to the murkiness, reports said lawyers searching regional offices of the Registrar of Companies from Ahmedabad to Chennai had found that, in most cases, the documents on ownership were missing.

Facing persistent press inquiries, Mukesh eventually replied in mid-December to the Press Trust of India on the ownership issue. 'The architecture of this ownership has been configured by Dhirubhai Ambani in a framework of companies,' he said via a spokesman. 'Given this configuration, it obviates the necessity of a will.' But sounding a little defensive for the first time, Mukesh said he would accept whatever his mother thought 'fair' in resolving the ownership issue.

Reports also began leaking some details of the Infocomm funding and ownership, suggesting that Mukesh had used the cash flow of the parent company to subsidise a personal holding in the telecom subsidiary. A document showed that Reliance Infocomm had issued 500 million shares at par value of one rupee to Mukesh in June 2000, giving him 12 per cent of the company. But this equity stake did not show up in Infocomm statements to its lenders until June 2004. By then, thanks to Rs 120 billion in funding from the parent company, Infocomm had developed into an operation valued at Rs 600 billion; Mukesh had thus gained a stake worth Rs 72 billion for just Rs 500 million. Through this and other holdings partly via an intermediary called Reliance Communications Infrastructure Ltd, Mukesh owned an estimated 56.5 per cent of Infocomm whereas Reliance Industries, which had put up 90 per cent of funding, had only 37 per cent and no nominee on the Infocomm board (the directors were Mukesh, as chairman, his wife Nita and his friends Anand Jain, Manoj Modi and Bharat Goenka).

According to one of the media recipients, Srinivas, this document had been faxed around by Amitabh Jhunjhunwala, who quit as the Reliance Industries treasurer on 20 December and thus placed himself firmly in the Anil camp. It read in part:

> There has been a mystery surrounding the ownership and management structure of Reliance Infocomm. This has been a source of great concern to the investors of RIL since the latter has pumped in more than Rs 12 167 crore [Rs 121.67 billion] for acquiring a 45 per cent stake in Reliance Infocomm. Every effort made in the last three years to get information about this aspect of Reliance Infocomm has been completely stonewalled by the Reliance group, headed by Mr Mukesh Ambani. Reliance Infocomm has now claimed that it is promoted not by the Ambani family as a whole but by Mr Mukesh Ambani personally.[14]

Mukesh had attempted to explain the par offer as typical 'sweat equity' given to risk-taking entrepreneurial founders, but this hardly applied to someone wielding the cash flows of a giant listed corporation. The stake seemed to have been sold to him cheaply around April 2004, when Infocomm was already up and running and over the worst. Where was his personal risk? On 23 December Mukesh backed off and announced that he would have the share issue annulled. The decision meant that the Infocomm ownership reverted to 45 per cent held by Reliance, another 45 per cent by companies associated with Mukesh and 10 per cent by employees.

To most observers, it looked like a hard blow delivered by Anil, which had come via another media note faxed by Jhunjhunwala. The alleged agreement for the 'sweat equity' in June 2000 had been 'an act of forgery and fraud', it said. It was never revealed to the Reliance Industries board, to shareholders meetings or in documents sent to investors and lenders. 'This so-called "sweat equity" agreement is completely fraudulent and forged – a feeble attempt by Mukesh Ambani to cover up the illegal and blasphemous mechanism in which he has clandestinely usurped the rights and hard-earned savings of RIL's 30-lakh [3 million] small shareholders to enhance his personal wealth empire.'[15]

There were more awkward questions. Before Dhirubhai died, the 45 per cent share of Infocomm was supposed to be a family stake; now, as Jhunjhunwala's first note pointed out, it belonged to Mukesh.

And if Mukesh had a personal stake in Infocomm, should he – as an interested party – have chaired most of the Reliance Industries board meetings that bailed Infocomm out of its shaky start in 2003, when customer defaults pushed its overdue accounts to Rs 35 billion? The parent company put Rs 81 billion into Infocomm from October 2002 via risky debentures and preference shares, with a face value of one rupee but a premium of Rs 49, while Mukesh was getting his for just the one rupee. At this time the fate of Reliance Infocomm remained in the hands of regulators. If they had not allowed fixed-line operators to offer CDMA cellular services, the enterprise would have failed. 'All those early stage risks were being funded through RIL, but it appears that RIL is getting a smaller part of the upside,' noted *Businessworld* magazine. Later, Anil's supporters claimed he had blocked proposals by Mukesh for the parent company to pay further premiums to convert these preference shares into full equity.[16]

In addition, Reliance Industries had put Rs 10 billion into the Flag Telecom acquisition and Rs 16 billion towards Infocomm's unified licence fee in January 2004. It had shelled out for some of the advertising and marketing expenses of the Infocomm launch, bought cell phone handsets for Infocomm, carried its overdue bills and given Rs 55 billion in financial guarantees.

At no time had the board been told the full and true ownership of

Infocomm, nor had any of the directors asked about it. In the accounts for the year ended March 2004, they had signed a statement saying: 'None of the transactions with any of the related parties were in conflict with the interests of the company.'

Then there were details of how funds invested or lent to Reliance Infocomm by the parent company or commercial banks had apparently been diverted into opportunistic sharemarket play in March 2004, allegedly for the personal benefit of Mukesh rather than the group. The vehicles were two small private companies, one linked by ownership to the shell-company web domiciled at 84A Mittal Court and having low-level Infocomm staff as dummy directors, and the other domiciled at the same address as a business run by Anand Jain's relatives. These two companies had managed to find Rs 16 billion for an initial public offering by the state-owned Oil and Natural Gas Corporation and a further Rs 15 billion for the initial public offering of the software house Tata Consultancy Services, grabbing the largest parcels of these floats. A lot of the shares acquired were sold for a quick profit, the rest some months later. Mukesh's side explained that these firms were subsidiaries of Reliance Communications and Infrastructure, the intermediary between the parent company and Infocomm that owned the nationwide optical-fibre network. Why it was 'stagging' the share issue of other groups, including a rival oil producer, was not really explained.

Anil also talked darkly of the 'chamchas [syncophants], chelas [devotees] and cronies' his father had warned him about. His camp suggested that Mukesh was unduly rewarding his closest executives and that they in turn were encouraging his estrangement from Anil in order to further their own influence. Chief among them were Anand Jain, whom Mukesh had known from primary school, and Manoj Modi, a former classmate at university. Many relatives of Jain held lucrative distribution and supply contracts with Reliance, while Modi's brothers ran the stockbrokerage used by the Reliance group.

With the Reliance share price sagging, Mukesh called a board meeting for 27 December to debate a proposal for a share buy-back offer, at a price slightly above the current market. Directors had not been available when Anil had called earlier for a meeting to discuss the question of undertakings to Reliance Energy and the newly revealed Infocomm funding, which had never been discussed by the board.

Although there was no blood on the floor and emotions were kept under control, the board meeting was a showdown. Anil arrived at the Maker Chamber IV building in Nariman Point for the 10am meeting. Although dressed in a dark grey suit, white shirt and yellow tie, he had the gait and grim face of a gunslinger in the American West walking into a bandit-held town. He told the waiting media that the buy-back was 'inappropriate, unnecessary' and that 'there was more than met the eye'.

Inside the boardroom, Mukesh introduced investment bankers from Morgan Stanley and Merrill Lynch and called on them to give presentations on the Rs 570-a-share buy-back, which was to cost just under Rs 30 billion, then recommended the board approve it.

Anil objected. The decline in Reliance's share price had little to do with its financial performance – it was all about the issues of corporate governance and ownership, which had not been addressed. If these were clarified, the price would rebound of its own accord. The manner of the buy-back was also suspect: it was proposed that the Rs 570 be a maximum, not fixed, and that the identity of sellers not be revealed under a screen-based transaction system. The suspicion would be that the company itself was bailing out and rewarding the interests close to

Mukesh, perhaps the ownership matrix firms, which had tried to prop up the share price by heavy buying in the weeks of dispute.

The other directors kept silent. Mukesh said his points had been noted, then asked for a press release, already drafted, to be sent to the Mumbai Stock Exchange. Anil demanded to see it. It said the buy-back resolution had been approved 'unanimously'. At his insistence, Mukesh ordered a change to note Anil's dissent, then rebuked Anil for his remarks before the meeting, saying he had raised issues where none existed and that his objections on corporate government were not made in a good spirit.

The board moved on to issues relating to the company's investment in Infocomm. It noted the conflict between the proposals made by the brothers. Mukesh had early pushed for conversion of the preferential shares at a premium. Anil suggested they be converted at the one-rupee par value, which would immediately raise the parent company's stake in Infocomm to 75 per cent. The board agreed to Mukesh's motion to refer the issue to a committee of the six independent directors, who would commission a fair valuation. With Anil leaving the room for the next item, the board passed a resolution requiring him to refer major decisions at Reliance Energy to the parent company board and assumed joint supervision over the Uttar Pradesh projects and the gas supplies. With Mukesh in the chair, the directors agreed that there was nothing more to be said about the way in which Reliance had supported Info-comm or the sweat equity Mukesh had annulled. The meeting broke up at 1.30pm, and Anil departed, quietly fuming. Inside the company, he was completely outgunned.[17]

A week later, Anil moved further away from Mukesh, resigning as vice-chairman and managing director of IPCL. He could not sit on the same board as Anand Jain, whom he described as the 'Shakuni' responsible for the family split. Shakuni was an evil character in the

Mahabharata, who had manipulated the Kauravas into the war with the Pandavas that destroyed them in the final battle at Kurukshetra, probably the bloodiest battle in all literature. Before that he had lured Yudhisthira, the Pandava king, into a rigged game of dice in which Yudisthira gambled away his kingdom of Indraprastra, his four brothers and their joint wife, Draupadi.

The two brothers were heading towards their own corporate Kurukshetra.

20

Mother India

The Reliance drama by now had almost every element of an Indian soap opera. It had wealthy tycoons, brothers fighting each other, sleazy political *neta* (patrons), clever financiers, angry wives, religious seers, a disputed inheritance, private eyes, allegations of forgery and phone-tapping, officials pretending to be active, frustrated investigators and a chorus of reporters besieging the main characters. Most important of all, it had the mother, respected and loved by all for her innate and unsophisticated wisdom, able to cut through to the main emotional issue.

Kokila had raised the four children with the help of a tutor while Dhirubhai spent most of his time on company business. She remained a god-fearing member of the Modh Bania, carrying with her from childhood a picture of Srinathji and going to worship at Nathdwara at least four times a year. Her husband was her other devotion: as they grew older and his health became fragile, she began collecting material and memorabilia about his life, which she was later to publish after his death.[1]

The rapid breakdown of the working relationship between Mukesh and Anil brought Kokilaben to the centre of things. Anil had quickly realised that Mukesh held nearly all the cards inside the company, but was it partly bluff? Family pressure offered him the best leverage with which to find out. By the end of December, Mukesh was being asked to show his main card: when and how had Dhirubhai handed him charge of the inner sanctum, the web of hundreds of companies 'acting in concert' to make family control of Reliance unassailable? He couldn't, or for some reason wouldn't, and was conceding too that he would abide by Kokilaben's decision.

After the showdown at the 27 December 2004 board meeting, Kokilaben had used family meetings the next day on Dhirubhai's birth anniversary to sound everyone out about where to go. Mukesh and Anil were still not speaking to each other directly. The older brother wrote privately to Anil three times over these weeks (on 30 November, 7 December and 18 January) offering to meet and work out an arrangement. On 20 January Anil had replied that he would meet 'only if there is an agenda and if all the family is present' and was reported to have said: 'We need two hands to clap, Mukeshbhai.'

But a division of the empire was already being discussed in the media, with lawyers and accountants giving their views on how it might be done. There were suggestions that Anil had been offered the companies he already ran, Reliance Energy and Reliance Capital, plus some cash, to go away. If so, he wanted a much more even split.

The problem was that so much of the group's value was concentrated in the core business under Reliance Industries. Dividing it would immediately remove the synergies and tax advantages of vertical integration, not to mention running roughshod over the interests of other investors. To try to clarify and split the ownership of the investment company web was also problematic. Dhirubhai had designed the matrix to be as opaque and impenetrable as possible, partly to lower taxes and quite possibly to aid insider trading in Reliance shares, but also to make it difficult for the holding to be broken up. His confidence in it was enough for him to feel no need to make a will and to dissolve the Hindu Undivided Family status. There were non-core group companies that could be surrendered more easily, but the biggest of them, Reliance Infocomm, was acknowledged even by Anil to be the pet project of Mukesh. Was it yet ready to be weaned away from the cash-cow of the parent company?[2] The day after the sad anniversary, Kokilaben called in one of the Mumbai financial community's best brains, an elder with a long and close relationship with the family. K.V. Kamath, chairman and chief executive of the ICICI Bank, had, as a junior officer of the government lending institution, approved one of the earliest loans obtained by Dhirubhai. Behind a cloak of secrecy and denials, Kamath got to work on the valuations of the different Reliance arms and the way in which they could be divided.

Meanwhile, the feud was dragging down India's rising image with international investors and reaching New Delhi, where both sons were putting their side of the story to senior leaders, including the Finance minister, P. Chidambaram, who said he had personally asked them 'to settle their dispute within the four walls of their house, Sea Wind'. But the fraternal war continued and the casualties mounted.

After his blast at the December board meeting, Anil sent a 'note' of no less than 500 pages to the other directors detailing what he saw as their failings of corporate governance and also sent a similar complaint focused on the buy-back to the Finance Ministry. The buy-back announcement had not mentioned that the Securities and Exchange Board of India was looking into trades made ahead of the announcement for possible insider trading and rigging. It hadn't mentioned that SEBI was still looking into Gurumurthy's complaint of three years earlier about the investment company matrix (although this was the first suggestion that SEBI had actually done anything about the Gurumurthy letter). Two 'unknown persons', Anil alleged, controlled this matrix, which he said held 29 per cent of Reliance shares – which would jump to 31 per cent with the help of shareholders' money via the buy-back.

As Sucheta Dalal noted, it was 'probably the first time in Indian corporate history that a vice chairman and managing director has written to the government demanding a investigation against a company while he continues to hold important fiduciary positions in top management'. As well as remaining on the company payroll, Anil had been part of top management at least until July 2004 and had been the public face of Reliance, presenting its financial results to journalists and analysts. He had even accepted a clutch of good governance awards on the company's behalf. 'That is why the sudden activism on behalf of shareholders rings phoney, although it is in the public interest.'[3]

In addition, an intriguing new aspect of the 2002 share issue by Reliance Infocomm had come to light in the *Asian Age*, which author Alam Srinivas listed in a general context as one of Anil's preferred channels for leaks. While the cash-cow parent company was being milked at up to Rs 250 a share, three small and obscure investment companies with fictitious addresses in Delhi and directors who seemed to know nothing about their business were shown to have received a total 10 million Infocomm shares at one rupee par, all on the same day in September 2002.

The newspaper traced their finance to ten other equally obscure shell companies in Delhi and found details for six of these. Their common address was used by a chartered accountant named Ashish Deora, who was close to the family of the former communications minister and BJP general secretary, Pramod Mahajan.

Deora, it emerged, had helped Mahajan out of a tight spot while he held an earlier ministerial post. While he was Minister for Information and Broadcasting earlier in the Vajpayee government, the state television network Prasar Bharati had entered a deal with a production company owned by Mahajan's wife and son whereby the company paid the broadcaster a fee to carry twenty-six episodes of a serial called *Truck Dhina Dhin*. The production house failed to pay all the fees and was left with an unpaid debt of Rs 65 million. In 2001 this was drawing unfavourable publicity and public interest litigation against Mahajan. Deora helped out via his internet company Indiaonline, which he had founded with Mahajan's son-in-law. Indiaonline borrowed from the Industrial Development Bank of India, ostensibly to develop its network, and diverted part of the funds to paying off Rs 50 million of the production company's debt.

Reliance Infocomm said the shares had been allotted because of Deora's great help in negotiating rights of way for its optical-fibre broadband cables around Mumbai and had been given under a lien related to performance from the 10 per cent of shares reserved for the company's staff. This lien had yanked the shares back in December 2004 when Deora had failed to meet his targets. But why such a generous reward in the first place, and why was it rescinded when Anil started airing the Reliance Infocomm linen?

Mahajan denied any connection, noting that the wireless in local-loop technology had been approved by his predecessor, Ram Vilas Paswan, and legitimised under the unified licences by his successor,

Arun Shourie. All he had done for Reliance was authorising the stamp commemorating Dhirubhai. 'If it's a crime then I am ready to pay a price for it,' he said.[4] A public interest petition later taken up by the Supreme Court of India alleged that, if the newspaper reports were true, the shares had been allotted for the benefit of Mahajan or at his instance and deserved investigation as a corruption case.[5]

In addition, a rather more lowly scandal was hitting Reliance Info-comm. In September 2004 the telecom authorities found the company was cheating the government-owned telephone companies BSNL and MTNL of large amounts of revenue from international calls, and their new minister, Dayanidhi Maran, had told them to take the company on. Reliance had allegedly used computer software to generate thousands of fake telephone numbers to mask the caller line identification for overseas calls and show them as local calls – avoiding paying what was called an access deficit charge to BSNL or MTNL. The telecom regulator ordered Infocomm to repay the two state utilities the revenues lost, which they claimed to total some Rs 5 billion and imposed a penalty of Rs 1.5 billion.

Reliance Infocomm lost its appeal to the Telecom Disputes Settlement and Appellate Tribunal on 4 March 2005, receiving devastating criticism from the bench for the 'rerouting' scam: 'The method Reliance Infocomm employed to camouflage an international call was certainly unprincipled and, if we may say so, unscrupulous.' By substituting fake numbers, the company had also put national security at risk. Infocomm had claimed that it kept records of the real numbers, which would have been furnished to intelligence agencies on request. But the judges said this was no use in an age of terrorism: 'When the security agencies want to monitor a call immediately/simultaneously that will be the crucial time to take action and not to wait for the records to be called, by which time it may be too late. With the spectre of terrorism and other dangers looming all over, even a second's delay could be disastrous.'[6]

Infocomm paid the fine, without accepting the findings of the tribunal, and announcing it would appeal to the Supreme Court. But by then the Criminal Bureau of Investigation and a police serious-fraud unit were looking at the case for possible criminal offences, raiding call centres in Chennai and Hyderabad to collect records. By early May 2005, with arrests in Hyderabad and several South Indian cities, a CBI chief in Chennai said that the laying of charges was near and a 'high official' of Reliance Infocomm had masterminded the scam. On 4 May Mukesh went to see the Prime Minister, Manmohan Singh, to express his concern about the investigation.

The flow of leaks intensified. Later that month, two newspapers got hold of an exchange of emails between senior executives of Reliance Infocomm and with Mukesh himself, which revealed an acute awareness that the rerouting exercise could be illegal and could rebound disastrously on the company, but that nevertheless it was decided to push the law to its limits and possibly suborn officials.

In March 2004, just before Infocomm began pushing a cut-price scheme for non-resident Indians to call home, Akhil Gupta, the chief executive for corporate development at Infocomm, had emailed Mukesh:

> I have reservations regarding the 12 cents per minute to all
> phones and not just [Reliance phones]. Here is the way I see the
> scenario unfolding. Within seven to ten days of our commercial
> launch, BSNL will know. It will clearly be established that we
> are violating in spirit if not the law and avoiding paying ADC
> [access deficit charge] to BSNL or government. I will be surprised

339

if TRAI [the Telecom Regulatory Authority of India]/other
government agencies do not move to reverse this. If we have to
reverse, how do we go back to consumers? We need to create a
softer image of Rel Info in NRIs' minds.

Mukesh appears to have asked another of his close executive circle,
Infocomm executive director Manoj Modi, to comment on Gupta's
reservations. Modi replied: 'With reference to my email sent last week
regarding concerns raised by Akhil Gupta I want to inform you that I
have personally spoken to the regulator PB today and have convinced
him of our intention. We are also ensuring that he's taken good care of.
Respectfully, MM.'

Modi, said to be deeply religious and apt to consult horoscopes and
celestial almanacs ahead of major decisions, evidently felt that the stars
and the powers that be in Delhi were favourably aligned. In an earlier
email to Mukesh, according to the leaks, Modi had also assured his
boss: 'The regulator could raise certain issues regarding rerouting of
these calls and changing of caller ID. However, we are very confident
that we will be able to handle the same using our good offices in the
government and other agencies. I assure you there is no cause for concern, please allow us to go ahead with our project. The risk-to-benefit
ratio is very high.' The chairman of the regulator (TRAI), Pradip Bai-
jail, said the emails were 'a fraud' and that he had not met Modi for a
year and had never discussed the rerouting issue with him.

Gupta continued to be worried. With his warning to Mukesh
ignored, he offered to resign and hand over his role in the expatriate
Indian marketing drive to Modi or another executive, B.D. Khurana.
'I have three to four weeks before we go on vacation. I would assist the
new sponsors during this time,' Gupta offered.

He was persuaded to stay on, with Modi taking responsibility for the
regulatory and legal issues in India and Gupta handling the marketing

effort in the United States. But when the rerouting was detected and put under investigation during September and October 2004, Gupta was disturbed to find that the rumour-mill was naming him as the mastermind behind it. In early December, as the 'ownership issues' conflict was escalating, Gupta emailed again to Mukesh:

> I have heard from several sources now that MM's office is spreading rumours that [I] was responsible for deciding to modify the caller line identification and not pay ADC. As you can see from my previous e-mail, I had opposed it and put my warning in writing. I do not know what the motivations might be in the current environment. Would you please help in stopping this unethical nonsense from spreading and set the record straight. It is very painful to see us paying huge penalties, spoiling our name and the person responsible gets to blame someone else. What a shame.

Shortly afterwards, Gupta resigned from Reliance and joined the American private investment fund Blackstone as its chief in India. Mukesh had now lost two members of his inner executive circle. Gupta had been a true insider, one of the few non-family members to live in the Sea Wind building. The defection of Amitabh Jhunjhunwala had become clear by then. He had resigned as Reliance treasurer and was suspected by the Mukesh camp of being the source of many leaks and the one who had tipped off the authorities about the rerouting tactic.[7]

In the background of all this, K.V. Kamath had been working on proposals for a settlement between Mukesh and Anil. He was aided in his calculation of corporate values by the Mumbai investment banker Nimesh Kampani, another of Dhirubhai's old intimate friends and business backers. On 9 March 2005 he had delivered his suggestions to

Kokilaben. While the brothers put up a barrage of leaks and rumour, they haggled over the details. Agreement was ready in the first week of June and, as hints of it leaked out, the Reliance share price gained steadily. Preceded by a flurry of trading late on Friday 17 June, which later led to calls for an insider-trading inquiry, the deal was announced the next day when Mumbai had settled into its weekend and the markets were closed. Instead of the normal corporate letterhead, it came on paper headed with the Hindi letter for the sacred sound 'Om' and giving the address as Sea Wind.

> With the blessings of Srinathji, I have today amicably resolved the issues between my two sons, Mukesh and Anil, keeping in mind the proud legacy of my husband, Dhirubhai Ambani. I am confident that both Mukesh and Anil will resolutely uphold the values of their father and work towards protecting and enhancing value for over three million shareholders of the Reliance Group, which has been the foundational principle on which my husband built India's largest private sector enterprise. Mukesh will have the responsibility for Reliance Industries and IPCL while Anil will have responsibility for Reliance Infocomm, Reliance Energy and Reliance Capital. My husband's foresight and vision and the values he stood for combined with my blessings will guide them to scale new heights.
>
> Kokilaben Ambani

Less than three years after Dhirubhai's death, his two heirs had divided the kingdom. But after the brawls of the previous eight months, India breathed a sigh of relief; at least its 15 or 20 million sharemarket investors did. The Sea Wind cloud hanging over India Inc. – the emerging industrial and knowledge economy that educated Indians knew was in them – had been dispelled. Both brothers could claim a victory. Mukesh had retained the core businesses and their mighty cash flows. But he had lost the business of the 'future', Reliance Infocomm, which he had created with a huge gamble.

Anil walked away with Reliance Infocomm and two of the other businesses that provided the essential linkages of the future super-economy: electric power and financial services. Kokilaben did not mention it, but Anil was also promised Rs 45 billion – about $1 billion – in cash. There was a promise of gas supply from Krishna–Godavari to his Dadri power plant at a cheap price – or so Anil thought. And he was given the right to use the Reliance name and flame logo. There was a five year no-competition agreement.

The next day Anil resigned his board positions at the parent company and announced the formation of his own outfit: the Anil Dhirubhai Ambani Group. On the evening of 20 June he and Tina went to dine in the most conspicuous restaurant in Mumbai, at the Taj Mahal Hotel near the Gateway of India. Then he went off to further pilgrimages, to Hindu holy places at Badrinath and Vaishnodevi.

Mukesh, equally characteristically, disappeared from sight, attending the wedding of the daughter of his friend Anand Jain in Goa. The press releases from his headquarters were insisting that Reliance Industries remained India's biggest private sector company by turnover, net profit and net worth. He had not resigned from his posts at Reliance Infocomm, and it was left unclear what Kokilaben had meant by 'responsibility' rather than control or ownership. How would be split be carried out? Sucheta Dalal, 'What this means: Anil's won a kingdom, now he needs to build fences and bridges' and 'Kiss and make-up time at Reliance', *Financial Express*, 19–20 June 2005.[8]

By the end of 2005, however, the group had a scheme of separation approved by a court, and during January and February 2006 the parent company carried out the demerger procedures, but with some testy public charges by Anil that it was dragging its feet. Eventually it floated four new emergent businesses: Reliance Capital Ventures, Reliance Communication Ventures, Reliance Energy Ventures and one that became Reliance Natural Resources. Anil and allied interests came out with stakes around 40 per cent, and 2.3 million existing Reliance shareholders were credited with proportionate allotments of shares in the new firms.[9]

The optimistic view among shareholders had been that India now had the benefit of two Ambani empires. But could they live with each other?

21

The Ambanis apart

There were now two Ambani empires. But had the entrepreneurial drive of Dhirubhai been dissipated? Each of the brothers set out to show the world that the spirit lay with him.

Mukesh had the core of Reliance Industries, with its oilfield to textiles vertical production chain. He sat in the old Maker Chambers IV corporate office in Nariman Point. He even got around in the same style of working clothes that Dhirubhai favoured: a white safari-type shirt (of a polyester blend) and dark-blue trousers. And there'd been a metamorphosis in the persona he showed to the world. In the struggle with Anil he had often seemed defensive – even depressed, to some close acquaintances – and reactive to Anil's tactics. But in the months after the settlement Mumbai, or at least an inner circle around the Ambani family, saw a more confident Mukesh emerge. He began giving extensive interviews, looking backwards to his upbringing and business apprenticeship under Dhirubhai, skating over the rift with Anil and giving grand outlines for the expansion of Reliance.

What struck many of his interviewers was his grasp of technical and market detail and an orderly mind setting out in direct, clear language the progress markers for this expansion in terms of funding and deadlines. Some began to look back at Dhirubhai's last years and reappraise Mukesh's role. Had much of what was attributed to the father – like the 'dream' of Indians making a cell phone call for the price of a postcard – actually been the vision of the son?

Along with this came some of the ambivalent perceptions of Dhirubhai. One acquaintance spoke of Mukesh as another 'Machiavelli' who continued the Reliance *modus operandi* established by Dhirubhai, including the 'dark side' of seeking out the weak points of rivals and potential obstacles that could be created for them – although Mukesh himself was to claim that this side of the business had been shed in the split.

More comfortable in himself, Mukesh spoke more of his own family and acted as host for social gatherings, bringing in his own Bollywood crowd (which notably excluded the Bachchans). He was seen dancing at his parties and generally shedding inhibitions about being rich and showing off his wealth. Construction began in 2007 of a new home, to replace his apartment in the old Sea Wind building. Set on a hillside on Altamount Road, the new building was named 'Antilla' after a mythical island and would rise the equivalent of sixty normal storeys or 173 metres, although its high ceilings meant it had only twenty-seven floors. It was to have a helipad, six floors of car parking, a mini-theatre and health club, and would house Mukesh's own family, Kokilaben and 600 guests and staff. Many reports said it would cost $1 billion, even $2 billion, although Mukesh insisted it would cost less than $100 million.

The initial building contractor, Australia's Leighton group, dropped out because of constant, costly modifications to the plans. In 2007 Mukesh bought an executive jet the size of a small airliner, an Airbus A-319, fitted out to accommodate up to twenty-two passengers instead of the usual 150, at a reported cost of $60 million. It seemed Mukesh was not afraid of the tax inspectors or underworld extorters, unlike many of the city's lesser rich.

Even before the split, Mukesh had begun work on a vast new project to increase the market share of Reliance's established petroleum business. Jamnagar was already the world's third biggest refinery. Talks had begun with the American industrial construction group Bechtel on a doubling of its capacity, to a total 60 million tonnes a year. In early 2006 Mukesh returned to a familiar path for raising capital. He floated a new Reliance Petroleum and went to the markets with an initial public offer to raise the Rs 150 billion or $3.4 billion required. The issue received a 'frenzied' response from everyone, from small retail investors to big institutions, and was oversubscribed by a factor of 51 times.

It was helped by two fortuitous pieces of news just before the share offer opened for subscription. The American oil major Chevron was going to take up 5 per cent of the new Reliance Petroleum, with an option to go up to 29 per cent, and was listed as a co-promoter of the issue. The Jamnagar refinery, it seemed, would fill an emerging shortage in Chevron's global refining capacity, particularly in the American market where environmental standards had deterred new investment. Initial reports had greatly exaggerated the Chevron investment, saying that the American giant was taking 29 per cent immediately.

Also, Reliance had made an oil find in the Godavari basin, near to its big gas field where it was pouring $2.75 billion into developing production wells and pipelines. At some stage, it was widely expected to move to fully take over and absorb the petrochemicals affiliate IPCL. Mukesh had also signalled a massive expansion into fertiliser production, using captive gas as feedstock and getting a far higher return for value added than by burning the gas for power. Mukesh's group was also feverishly extending its retail network, to end a dependence on the Indian Oil Corporation's nationwide chain of petrol stations for sales of its refined products. This deal had subordinated supplies from Jamnagar to IOC's own input and was due to end in March 2009. By the end of 2006 the group had built 2500 new service stations and was said to be planning 3400 more by 2009.[1]

But it was not just 'stick to your knitting' for Mukesh, who quickly announced plans for a massive diversification into urban development, agribusiness and biofuels on a scale that might have been dismissed as megalomanic – if it had not come from someone with his reputation for implementing complex projects and with Reliance's multibillion-dollar cash flow.

In January 2006 his group announced a large-scale move into retailing and food logistics, spending up to US$5 billion by 2011 on setting up a nationwide chain of supermarkets under the brand Reliance Fresh, with a supply chain of transport, food processing units and cold stores stretching back to farmers. Typically, the move showed Reliance jumping into a sector largely protected from international competition. Big foreign supermarket chains had been clamouring for a lifting of foreign investment controls, allowing them to set up in India. The rules had been relaxed, but only for single-brand outlets. None of the existing Indian retail chains had anything like the financial muscle to compete with Reliance. Mukesh was talking of opening superstores eventually in 1500 towns and cities, setting up eighty-five logistics centres and 1600 farm-supply centres providing advice, credit, seeds, fertiliser and fuel to growers as well as buying their produce. The network would create up to a million new jobs, as well as lifting farm incomes as much as ninefold and lowering consumer prices by cutting out the middlemen. Besides generating US$25 billion in annual sales, this 'Wal-Mart in India' could create US$20 billion in farm exports.[2]

As Mukesh explained it, the scheme had to be based on agriculture, on which 60 per cent of Indians depended, although it accounted for only 28 per cent of gross domestic product. India's fragmented farm holdings could be integrated into the national – even global – economy by a new generation of logistics. By getting cost-competitive, safe food to Indian consumers, it would be a natural leap to world markets.[3]

Throughout 2007 and 2008 Mukesh extended his retail plans. His group launched the first of a hundred 'Reliance Trends' shops selling modern international clothes from the new shopping malls springing up on the fringes of Indian cities. It announced plans to open fifty to sixty 'i stores' selling Apple computer products and another 150 'Reliance Digital' stores selling home appliance, consumer electronics and IT and telecom products.

Mukesh's second grand scheme was the development of two new satellite cities on the fringes of Mumbai and New Delhi, each with a population of five million people with average incomes of $5000 a year. This was enabled by legislation passed by the Indian parliament in 2005 under the Congress-led government, allowing private developers greater freedom to set up 'special economic zones' modelled on the coastal factory regions carved out by the Chinese communist leader Deng Xiaoping in the 1980s and 1990s.

Partly in partnership with a Maharashtra state agency, the City and Industrial Development Corporation (CIDCO), Reliance quickly moved to acquire 15 000 hectares of farmland and small settlements at Navi Mumbai, a district running from the head of the large bay lying to the east of the old city and extending down the eastern side of the bay. Plans were unveiled for new air and sea ports and a 20-kilometre bridge and tunnel link across the bay to connect it with old Mumbai. According to Anand Jain, the land was acquired at prices about a thousandth of those for sites in downtown Mumbai. With the city's 14 million people hemmed in by mountains to the north-west and dense settlements to the north, this south-eastern corridor was virtually the only way for India's financial centre and biggest port to expand.

Mukesh had gained the central position by buying out a fellow Gujarati entrepreneur, Nikhil Gandhi, from his company Sea King Infrastructure Ltd, which had won a tender to set up a joint venture development zone with CIDCO in 2003. The state agency had 4500 hectares of land but no funds. Sea King had won a 74 per cent share of the joint venture in an international tender, but opted to sell out to Mukesh around the start of 2005 rather than attempt to marshal the promised funds. After the new Congress government took power in 2004 and announced its special economic zone policy, Mukesh applied to set up a zone covering 11 000 hectares and adjoining the one covered by the CIDCO joint venture.

A fortuitous political change brought a friendly face into an important position in July 2005. A former Chief Minister of Maharashtra, Narayan Rane, quit the Shiv Sena party and joined the Congress-led state government and was immediately promoted to the key position of Revenue minister. By the end of 2005 revenue officials and the local administrator or collector were feeling top-down pressure to approve land acquisition. At central level, the Commerce minister, Kamal Nath, also gave Mukesh the development authority for 11 300 hectares, covering forty-five villages. However, by mid-2006 the central government's Ministry of Urban Development had misgivings about the requirement for compulsory acquisition of land from so many existing small owners. When the chairman of CIDCO raised the same objection, he found himself transferred out of his job three days later.

In Haryana, the wealthy farming state just west of Delhi, Reliance moved to acquire about 10 000 hectares of land close to the satellite town of Gurgaon, famous for its collection of call-centre and information technology businesses and, along with Bangalore, symbolising India's rapid advance into service and knowledge sectors. With investment of up to Rs 400 billion, this Reliance special zone would be another enclave of prosperity, with its residents engaged in knowledge industries and low-polluting manufacture. A smaller zone was also being set up in Gujarat, adjacent to the oil refinery at Jamnagar. The employment for these well-educated residents would be provided by international companies eager to utilise India's human resources but so far frustrated by the country's decrepit infrastructure and limited housing, according to Mukesh's vision.[4]

The third project of Mukesh was the Life Sciences Centre in Mumbai, focused on growing biofuels from cellulose and plants like jattropha on a commercial scale. He described this as aimed at engineering a second Green Revolution, an industrial fallback for a world in which petroleum prices are prohibitive. An associated activity was to pioneer usable biomass generators of electricity for dispersed farms and households. Mukesh wanted Indians to 'go wireless' for their electricity as they had for their telephones.[5]

For his part, Anil made a more direct, emotional appeal for the family legacy, naming his share of the inheritance the Anil Dhirubhai Ambani Group. His friends describe him as 'energised' by the split. 'He's got his freedom and he wants to show what he can do to the world,' one said. At the same time, he must have been aware that without the massive cash-flows of the Reliance petroleum and petrochemicals businesses, he had much less margin for mistakes than Mukesh.

His most spectacular early success was to carry through the launch of Mukesh's brainchild, the cellular telephone and data operation, now renamed Reliance Communication. India was fast gaining on China's spectacular lead in cell phone connections and by September 2007 had a total of 200 million subscribers, adding 7.6 million more every month. Although about three-quarters were on the GSM technology, Reliance and others operators like Tata Teleservices that had adopted the CDMA standard were offering their customers handsets that worked on both technologies. Anil was getting up to a million customers a month for special handsets made in China that his company was selling for less than $20, substantially below cost, in the drive for market share.

The younger brother also expanded the internet-based side of the business. Acquisitions helped expand the range of platforms and delivery systems. In July 2007 Anil agreed to pay $300 million for Yipes, an American company specialising in ethernet systems (technology that links local area networks by wireless data). He promoted a chain of internet outlets, branded as Reliance World, in which customers could access the internet and carry out financial transactions, including sharemarket trades or check their investment portfolios, and got the same facility installed at the fast-spreading Barista coffee shop chain, which was introducing Italian-style coffee drinking to the Indian middle class. And Anil's financial subsidiary, Reliance Capital, by dint of clever marketing of popular services, was becoming one of the biggest funds management institutions in India.

With his close Bollywood connections, Anil also pushed into content and distribution, acquiring the cinema chain Adlabs, which ran some of the best-known movie houses in Mumbai and other cities, with a total of 125 screens. His 'Big FM' radio network had stations operating in seventeen cities by mid-2007 and was reported to have licences for another twenty-three areas. Through Reliance Capital, Anil gained a 32 per cent stake in the cable/satellite media house TV Today, controlled by the India Today magazine group of Arun Purie. Anil also had interests in TV18, NDTV, Zee Enterprises and UTV Software. On the internet, Anil launched a gaming portal named Zapak.com and a social networking website called Big Adda. Towards the end of 2007 his group was also moving to launch a direct-to-home satellite broadcasting service called Reliance Blue Magic and an internet-based TV channel. If there was a logic to this spate of entertainment and news acquisitions, later grouped under the brandname 'Big', it was to gain a lock hold on content for his media channels.

Almost immediately, his venture into politics started to look like a liability. Anil's two biggest projects in Uttar Pradesh – the giant gas-fired power station at Dadri and a special economic zone at Noida, an industrial zone near Delhi – were hostage to the state's turbulent politics. In January 2006 several media groups in New Delhi were sent recordings said to be based on wiretaps of Amar Singh over a ten-week period. As well as picking up salacious conversations with young film actresses, the recordings contained conversations allegedly between the Samajwadi Party leader and Anil, in which business deals and favours were discussed in blunt detail. The Uttar Pradesh Chief Minister, Mulayam Singh Yadav, was also on record, purportedly, discussing an approach to a judge about a special economic zone at Noida.

Delhi police found that a private detective, Bhupendra Kumar, had gained the cooperation of Anil's own telephone company to carry out the interception on the basis of forged letters, one from a senior police officer requesting permission to run a wiretap and the other a faked response from a senior Home Ministry official, R. Narayan Swamy, giving consent. The letters were adaptations of real letters between the two officials on an unrelated matter. Kumar had been approached by a person identifying himself as a police officer and paid a 'handsome' amount for being 'used like a pawn'. Reliance Infocomm provided Kumar with a parallel line from Amar Singh's number to his cell phone. The operation went on until a company official realised it was the politician's telephone involved and told superiors. They passed the word to Mulayam Singh Yadav, the top Samajwadi leader and Chief Minister of Uttar Pradesh, who immediately went public, claiming a Congress conspiracy. In February 2006 Amar Singh sought and obtained a Supreme Court injunction barring the media from playing recordings of the alleged conversations, although copies on compact discs were in wide circulation.[6] In a rambling interview with NDTV, Singh said the tapping was orchestrated by Congress and a 'Mumbai-based industrialist'; that the recordings might have been patched together from innocuous conversations; and that the judge mentioned might not have been a sitting judge.

Anil resigned his Rajya Sabha seat in mid-2006, but his connection continued to dog him. In May 2007 the Samajwadi government of Mulayam Singh Yadav was voted out of office in Uttar Pradesh. The state's new Chief Minister, Mayawati (who uses one name only), immediately dissolved a state development council on which Anil sat, under the chairmanship of Amar Singh. She announced that clearances for Anil's Dadri power project would be reviewed. A dissident member of Samajwadi, Raj Babbar, and the old Ambani foe, former Prime Minister V.P. Singh, had raised grievances by local farmers during the election campaign. Mayawati's cabinet also asked the central government to withdraw approval for the special economic zone proposed by Anil's group for a 485-hectare site near the industrial zone Noida, adjacent to the national capital region. The request was made on the grounds that the area was bisected by a road when such zones had to be on contiguous land. Anil had some political spadework to do.[7]

Anil's biggest challenge was coming up with new projects. He was out of favour with the Congress party, which was in power at central level. On every opening, it seemed, he was coming up against the superior firepower and skills of his brother. As we have seen, Mukesh was not delivering on the promise that Anil, perhaps naively, thought he had gained of supply of natural gas from Krishna–Godavari at less than market price for the Dadri power station.

Anil lost out in bids for the modernisation of passenger terminals at the Delhi and Mumbai international airports, although not to Mukesh in these cases. In January 2006 Mukesh outbid Anil for a prime 7.5-hectare urban redevelopment site at Bandra–Kurla in Mumbai, which city authorities had zoned for hotels, shopping, offices and a convention centre. The price set a record for property outside the Raj-era centre of old Mumbai. But after contracts were signed in September that year, it emerged that Mukesh's group had been allowed double the floor-space ratio set in the tender, vastly increasing the potential profitability. In May 2007 Anil's Reliance Communications and Infrastructure launched a legal case against the Mumbai development authority in the Bombay High Court.

Anil's group also started litigation after being disqualified for bidding for Mumbai's planned new harbour crossing, a 22-km road-rail bridge from the old port district at Sewri to Nhava, the entry point for the Navi Mumbai area where Mukesh was planning his vast special economic zone. Mukesh's group was regarded as the most prospective bidder for this project. Among some other powerful consortiums, the two brothers were also likely to contest the tender for a new international airport at Navi Mumbai. The airport would be adjacent to the Reliance special zone, and winning the tender along with the harbour crossing would give Mukesh a dominating position in Mumbai's expansion.[8]

In January 2007 Anil suffered another big disappointment. The Hong Kong-based Hutchison telecom group wanted to sell its two-thirds stake in its Indian cellular telephone venture with Essar. Gaining control of this network would have instantly given Reliance Communications the top market share, as well as bringing kudos to Anil as a deal-maker. In the bidding, Anil was arrayed against powerful rivals, the British-based Vodafone, the Hinduja group and the minority partner Essar. Vodafone clinched the purchase with an offer of $11 billion, and the sale was approved by the government in April 2007 – against spoiling tactics used by disappointed bidders, as Vodafone's chief executive, Arun Sarin, revealed later. Speaking to a gathering of fellow Indian Institute of Technology alumni in Silicon Valley in July 2007, Sarin said he became aware of lobbying to 'crater the deal' at high level:

> I really did not expect people – the 'good and great' of India – to be calling cabinet secretaries, ministers, to say: 'You have to unwind this deal, because we want a piece of it' … The billionaire losers' club was trying to unwind the deal. What was fascinating was that there was absolutely no transparency to the process … What I didn't count on was that the bureaucracy would kick in with this kind of evil spirit from our competitors who had lost.[9]

After his remarks were picked up by a newswire and reported around the world, Sarin issued a statement praising Indian authorities for the 'speed and thoroughness' of their scrutiny, which he said was a positive example for investors. At no point did he specify which rivals he meant.[10]

As well as fighting each other and various business rivals, both Ambani brothers increasingly found themselves in the firing line of social protest. Their business activities were no longer at one or more removes from consumers. The size of their projects affected surrounding communities. Predictably, land provided the most volatile issue. The accusation of 'land grab' was flung around freely, and one petitioner to the Indian president, A.J.P. Abdul Kalam, even accused Mukesh of setting up an 'Ambani Desh' – an extraterritorial enclave of 'Ambaniland' inside India.[11]

In Haryana, some of the most powerful politicians based among its famous Jat caste of well-off farmers came out against Mukesh's special zone. Among them were Kuldip Bishnoi, son of the former Haryana Chief Minister Bhajan Lal, and Ajay Singh Chautala, both members of the Congress hierarchy in the state. They claimed that Reliance was getting a choice 688-hectare parcel of land near Gurgaon for Rs 3.6 billion when it was worth Rs 50 billion. As well as countering their litigation, Mukesh responded with a widely publicised 'corporate social responsibility' program, providing medical and dental services to villagers with mobile clinics emblazoned with the Reliance name.[12]

At Navi Mumbai, Mukesh was opposed by an embarrassingly wide array of public opponents. After the earlier opening of the Jawaharlal Nehru container port at the head of the bay, many of the port's associated professionals and businessmen in stevedoring, customs broking, logistics, warehousing and the like had seen the possibilities of setting up operations in Navi Mumbai and bought parcels of land there. The 26 000 residents of the region's forty-five villages became well aware of the risk of eviction with little compensation, and blocked attempts to survey their land. From time to time they held sit-down protests on roads through the area, although these were largely unreported in the mainstream Mumbai press. By early 2007 some ministers in the state government were getting nervous about the political risks and began quizzing Revenue minister Narayan Rane about the level of compensation for land.

By then there were seventy-two proposals for special economic zones in Maharashtra, but only seven were contentious, the Reliance project the biggest among them. In August 2007 the Shiv Sena party latched on to this discontent as a cause to help it return to power and to punish their defector, Narayan Rane. Its activists whipped up a large protest among farmers in the Raigad area, which turned into rioting in which scores of cars and buses were destroyed.[13]

In New Delhi, the Commerce Ministry began tightening up application of the rules on special economic zones, which were being proposed all over the country. It said it would extend and confirm approvals only for those coming within its 5000-hectare cap. Mukesh's two biggest zones, at Jhajjar in Haryana and Raigad in Maharashtra (coming under the name of a subsidiary called Gujarat Positra Port Infrastructure Ltd, but by now widely known as the Maha Mumbai SEZ), were both around 10 000 hectares. With in-principle approval for Navi Mumbai expired, Mukesh was given a year's extension but told to cut the size in half, to negotiate the consent of landowners to a sale and to keep the state authorities out of the process. However, within several months, the Commerce Ministry was going full circle, saying it was prepared to approve zones above the 5000-hectare limit on a 'case-by-case' basis.[14]

Facing a flurry of litigation from landowners, Mukesh and other developers applied for the Supreme Court to gather up all cases and hear them as a single matter, setting principles for land acquisition for the whole country, which Chief Justice K.G. Balakrishnan decided to do. By then Anil's proposed zone at Noida had been turned down by

Mayawati's Uttar Pradesh government. There was also legal disarray affecting Mukesh's two adjacent zones in Raigad. His partner in the original zone, the development agency CIDCO, was opposing its own government's move to notify the compulsory acquisition of 4000 hectares of land, affecting twenty-one villages. The agency took action in the Bombay High Court after being named respondent itself to public interest litigation (petitions to courts by civil society groups, not necessarily party to disputes) mounted by a farm activist, Datta Patil and others.

Mukesh's retail venture had also met some fierce reaction from traditional vendors feeling threatened by his large-scale, low-margin fresh food stores. In May 2007, at Ranchi, in the impoverished eastern state of Jharkhand, petty traders and vegetable shop owners attacked three of the five new Reliance Fresh outlets, smashing glass and pulling down shelves, and crowds began looting the shops. Warnings of similar protest came from left-wing politicians in nearby West Bengal. Four months later, Mukesh had to close his ten stores in Uttar Pradesh and lay off 870 staff in the face of threats.

Along with other oil refiners, his Reliance group was also subject to periodic allegations in parliament and the media that it was selling petroleum fractions like naphtha, benzene and toluene to non-industrial customers, to be mixed in with petrol and sold to unsuspecting vehicle owners. With two-thirds of all petrol stations and natural gas dealerships being owned by politicians and their families, described as a new class of 'petro-kulaks', scrutiny was lax. The more obvious suspects were the public-sector refineries rather than the private-sector giant.[15]

The power of the petro-kulaks meanwhile set back Mukesh's plans for a nationwide network of 5000 service stations. The rival outlets franchised by the public sector refiners continued to enjoy subsidies permitting retail prices of petrol and diesel well below cost, thanks to the political clout of the politicians and their friends who owned them. With world prices of petroleum spiralling in the middle of the decade, Mukesh was forced to halt expansion of his retail network once it had reached about 1300 outlets and, of these, about 200 were closed by late 2007.[16]

Anil's Reliance Energy was also a target of grassroots protest. In the Thane district of Maharashtra, local farmers were complaining that the company's 500MW coal power plant at Dahanu was turning their land into a wasteland, allegedly in part because the operators were switching off electrostatic precipitators in its smoke stack at night, allowing massive quantities of fly ash to be released.[17] In Delhi, electricity distribution had been given to private companies, known as 'discoms', in July 2002, about the time Dhirubhai died. Anil's company set up two discoms and soon began installing new electronic meters with its customers, replacing older electromechanical meters. By 2005 activists were claiming that the new meters were charging households more than the published rates, yielding high profits for the discoms without any great increase in supply; the activists were demanding independent testing of the meters. As one influential economist noted, the discoms had actually brought transmission and distribution power losses in Delhi down from a staggering 63 per cent to 50 per cent in three years; but customers were now only more sharply aware how some users were being slugged to make up for power thefts. A lesson for Anil was that 'it is not enough to make great presentations and wow everybody with financial deal-making. Running a business requires focus, sustained application, team-building and meeting customer expectations.'[18]

But the brothers' biggest enemies were each other.

On 3 February 2006, about seven months after Kokilaben's settlement of June the previous year, the two brothers signed an agreement between Reliance Industries and Reliance Natural Resources, setting a price and supply arrangement for natural gas to flow from the group's Krishna–Godavari field in the Bay of Bengal to Anil's planned new power plants at Dadri in Uttar Pradesh and at Patalganga, inland from Mumbai. They were soon fighting over its interpretation. Anil's group alleged that Mukesh's Reliance Industries was 'systematically violating every major commitment of the June 2005 settlement'. In particular, Mukesh's group was seeking to dishonour the agreement on gas supply at agreed prices (which were to be linked to the sale price Reliance had reached with the central government's National Thermal Power Corporation (NTPC), an offer not followed up by a firm contract as world petroleum prices spiraled higher.

In response, Mukesh's spokesman at Reliance Industries said the issues raised by Anil's group were 'an attempt to divert attention away from the shockingly petty acts of harassment of RIL employees at the Dhirubhai Ambani Knowledge City'. Things had indeed got very petty. Anil's Infocomm had cut off broadband connectivity to all of Mukesh's companies, causing an immense disruption to its routine business and requiring it to shift to another internet service provider. At the Knowledge City campus, the two groups had resorted to blocking each other's employees from using canteens, parking areas and banking terminals in their own locations. Even the Hindu temple on campus was reserved for the Anil group's staff.

The Petroleum Ministry, by then under ministerial direction by Murli Deora, the veteran Congress politician who had been Dhirubhai's colleague in his yarn-trading days, had also intervened in a way that upset the gas supply deal – in Mukesh's favour. It said the gas price was too low and had not been set through 'arm's-length' sales negotiation. The government was a party to the deal by virtue of its production-sharing contract with Reliance covering Krishna–Godavari. By the prevailing standards of domestic gas supply the price was far too generous to the buyer and less than half what Reliance was charging for gas from its older Panni/Mukti and Tapti gas fields in the Arabian Sea.

Anil's side countered by alleging that the Mukesh group had been 'deliberately misleading' the Petroleum Ministy in order to 'renege' on its gas supply commitment. The price had been set in arm's-length negotiations in the first half of 2004, the Anil group claimed – although how that could have happened when Reliance Energy was 41 per cent owned by Reliance Industries, which supplied its chairman and six other directors, was not explained. It was linked to the tentative deal signed around the same time between Reliance Industries and the NTPC, which had called open and international tenders for supply of gas for two new power plants in Gujarat. Reliance's offer for its Krishna–Godavari gas had won this bidding.

But it was not just Anil's deal that was in dispute. Mukesh was in dispute with NTPC. After signing the gas supply deal with the government generator in May 2004, Reliance Industries had dragged its feet and had been taken to court by NTPC in December 2005. The prevailing price of gas had doubled inside India, and obviously it was in Reliance's interest if its offer could be amended.

The ministry's intervention immediately put a spoke in Anil's wheel. Without an acceptable gas supply arrangement, the ministry was not going to give clearance for his group to start laying its Rs 160 billion ($3.6 billion) pipeline from Krishna–Godavari to the Dadri project, which would also supply domestic and industrial gas for numerous cities along its path.

In November, Reliance Natural Resources Ltd of the Anil group instituted a case in the Bombay High Court, asking it to direct Reliance Industries to implement the court order of December 2005 that enforced the demerger settlement, in which Anil claimed there was an agreement for the supply of gas to his Dadri and Patalganga plants. Thus a little more than four years after their father had died, and seventeen months after their mother laid down the family settlement, the two brothers were in litigation with each other in court.

The row over gas pricing was central to their rivalry. It put Murli Deora in an awkward position. Asked by Congress president Sonia Gandhi to be Petroleum minister, he had tried to refuse: better to stick to the familiar role of Congress fund-raiser. But to no avail. His main task was to adjudicate a national gas-pricing formula, with a decision rewarding either Anil or Mukesh. Anil was insisting on the low cost-plus price he believed had been promised. Mukesh was arguing for parity with the landed price of imported gas: world petroleum price, plus shipping, plus 30 per cent duty. The difference was billions of dollars in cash flow. The argument and the lobbying were internecine. 'It's all about the brothers,' officials were complaining to their confidants.

In August 2006 Manmohan Singh met Deora and at his request, so it was reported, decided to relieve him of the decision. The issue was handed to an 'empowered group of ministers' under the chairmanship of the External Affairs minister, Pranab Mukherjee, the same Congress veteran who had been so helpful to Dhirubhai in the 1980s.[19]

Furious lobbying began, with Anil marshalling the Samajwadi and Communist Party (Marxist) to oppose 'goldplating' of the Krishna–Godavari project, while Reliance warned that its delicately poised financing could be upset, creating a two-year delay in commencement of gas production.[20] The decision, announced on 12 September 2006, was interpreted as both a blow to the free market and a capitulation to Mukesh, since, as the Supreme Court later noted, it was based on a

363

formula very close to one suggested by Reliance. It set a price of $4.20 per million British thermal units, based on a five-year peg to an oil price of $60 a barrel, a hefty slug above the $2.34 that Anil claimed to have been promised, setting Mukesh in a position to dominate down-stream industries, including the vital sectors of power generation and fertilisers.[21]

Far from resolving the question, the ruling only intensified the rivalry between Mukesh and Anil and focused attention on the looming legal cases in Mumbai. The feud between the two billionaire brothers became a talking point in business circles worldwide.

The most obvious competition was to see who could lift the share prices of his group's companies the most and thereby increase his own paper wealth in the global rich lists put out by prestigious business maga-zines. In late 2007 the share prices of companies like Mukesh's Reliance Petroleum (the new offshoot set up for the expansion of the Jamnagar refinery) or Anil's Reliance Energy and Reliance Natural Resources shot up by multiples of the gains seen in the overall sharemarket index. At the end of October 2007 it was even reported that these high share prices had made Mukesh temporarily the world's richest man, his net worth on paper being estimated at $63.2 billion, above that of Micro-soft founder Bill Gates or the Mexican tycoon Carlos Slim Helu.[22]

There was speculation that both Reliance groups were using their many small investment companies to bid up the prices of these newer offshoots, either to solidify control of them or to list the share prices to raise more funds through share offerings. A large degree of hype and anticipation surrounded businesses that were still quite nascent.

At that point, Reliance Petroleum was still a year away from the start of actual refining in late 2008, and Chevron had yet to decide on exercising its option to buy a 29 per cent stake. Yet it was trading at twenty-five times the earnings per share expected in its first reporting year, putting it among India's fifteen biggest companies by market value. Anil's Reliance Energy had a share price valued at fifty times earnings per share, and his Reliance Natural Resources had a price-earnings ratio of 300 at one point.[23]

For his part, Anil's peak moment came in February 2008 with a much-anticipated share listing for a new company, Reliance Power, that took over the power generation assets of his Reliance Energy. Three months earlier, Anil's company had sent a letter to the Securities and Exchange Board of India complaining about a 'disinformation' campaign being waged against the initial public offering. The IPO's launch had been marked by a spate of anonymous emails and blogger comments claiming that Reliance Energy had illegally transferred assets to the new company without shareholder approval. Several politicians had become seized of the issue and had written to the SEBI questioning standards of corporate governance at Anil's group. Anil's group was said to have fingered Mukesh's organisation in its letter of complaint, although it declined to confirm this to newspapers. Mukesh's Reliance Industries said only that it was 'more amused than shocked' over the allegations.

In the event, the Reliance Power offering was oversubscribed by would-be investors by seventy-three times the $3 billion sought, even though this was then the largest amount of capital ever tapped in the Indian sharemarket. But Anil's exuberance was short lived. Within a day of listing, the share price had dropped 17 per cent below the issue price. There were reports that Anil's group blamed Mukesh's camp for somehow engineering the debacle.

Still, Anil had a massive injection of new cash, the party recovered in the Indian markets and soon Mukesh was looking defensive in his position as the richer brother. By the middle of 2008 Anil's paper wealth was only a billion or so dollars behind Mukesh's US$43 billion by some estimates.

Each played a constant game of one-upmanship against the other. When Mukesh bought the Mumbai Indians team in a new professional cricket tournament, the Indian Premier League, Anil was reported to be studying purchase of an English first division football club such as Newcastle United. When Mukesh announced bigger and bigger plans for his petroleum, retail and land divisions, Anil expanded his ties with the more glamorous worlds of communications, entertainment and media. His new venture, Reliance Big Entertainment, engaged a well-known lyric writer, producer and director of Bollywood movies, Amit Khanna, as chairman and a leading media executive, Rajesh Sawhney, as president, while the head of the Reliance Capital arm, Amitabh Jhunjhunwala, organised funding. During 2008 the new firm signed production deals with such Hollywood names as Tom Hanks, Brad Pitt, George Clooney and Nicolas Cage and took control of a cinema network across twenty-eight American centres. In October, in the midst of a global financial crisis, Anil replaced Paramount as partner in a joint production venture with Steven Spielberg's Dreamworks, with an investment of $550 million. The deal was said to make Anil 'one of the most powerful tycoons in Hollywood'.[24]

There was also a curious role-reversal. Mukesh had become the high-life socialite, with estimates of the cost of building his Antilla getting ever larger despite his attempts to downplay them. The perceived playboy Anil was portrayed as more ascetic, making frequent pilgrimages to Hindu shrines, even journeying on foot to circle the holy Mansarovar Lake and Mount Kailash in Tibet. He ran daily for kilometres before dawn and stayed in cheap business hotels instead of luxury suites on his travels. Communication between them came down to stiff press comments by spokesmen and a mounting number of court actions. However, both were said to put on a display of politeness at weekly breakfasts with their mother at Sea Wind.

In June 2008 Anil attempted a corporate manoevre that would have leapfrogged him in wealth far beyond Mukesh and possibly have made him the world's richest man in paper wealth. At a dinner hosted by Kokilaben, Anil reached agreement with Phuthuma Nhleko, chairman of the large South African cell telephone company MTN, to merge their businesses. The merger would combine India's second largest cellular network of 45 million subscribers with the 68 million subscribers of MTN through Africa and the Middle East, creating the world's fourth biggest cell phone operator with a base in some of the world's fastest growing emerging markets. The deal would involve Anil transferring his 66 per cent stake in Reliance Communications, in return for 35 per cent of MTN, then investing a further US$10 billion with the help of investment banks and Middle East sovereign wealth funds to gain effective control of the combined group.

Mukesh, who happened to be in southern Africa at the time, holidaying with his family in Botswana (entirely coincidentally, he said), immediately kyboshed the deal by writing to MTN and Anil to assert that, under the terms of the June 2005 division of their father's businesses, each brother had the first right of refusal in the event of any proposed sale of the assets by the other. The merger would therefore be challenged in court if it went ahead.

Anil immediately announced that if this were the case, he would object to the transfer of 5 per cent of Reliance Petroleum to Chevron. It was also mooted that Mukesh's action was insulting to Kokilaben, since she had seemed to bless the deal. But the deal was lost and eventually was offered to rival Bharti AirTel. By November 2009, India had 543 million cellphone subscriptions, an astonishing leap in less than a decade. Anil's network had more than 90 million customers, still behind Bharti's 116 million and with Vodafone Essar just behind with 88.6 million subscribers.[25]

Still, the unpredictable shifts of Indian politics were giving Mukesh some uncomfortable moments. Within a week of checking Anil's bold gambit, Mukesh had to rush to New Dehli to shore up his political connections. Manmohan Singh's government had pushed ahead with the agreement worked out with US President George Bush in 2006 that effectively lifted the Western nuclear embargo on India, in return for it separating its civilian nuclear facilities from its weapons-related ones and putting them under international safeguards. This had caused the Indian communist parties backing the Congress-led coalition to withdraw their support. Their place was taken by the Samajwadi Party, Anil's former group. The share price of the Reliance flagship dropped 6 per cent immediately on the news.

Amar Singh was back at the centre of power-broking and immediately announced that his group would be pressuring Manmohan Singh to introduce a 'windfall tax' on super-profits made by oil refineries from the then extremely high international oil prices and to stop Mukesh disrupting the MTN merger. Mukesh had urgent meetings with Singh and Sonia Gandhi to seek assurances.[26]

As the Mumbai court case over the pricing of Krishna–Godavari gas headed towards adjudication on the enforceability of the June 2005 assets split and its attached conditions, relations became even more acerbic.

Where Mukesh had cited Kokilaben's June 2005 settlement to foil Anil's attempted cellphone merger with the South African company MTN, his lawyer, Harish Salve, was now telling reporters outside the Bombay High Court that the agreement was a 'piece of trash' as far as the company was concerned, in that it was 'only between the two brothers'. In court he argued that the agreement was a 'ghost MoU [memorandum of understanding]' that had never been published and had no legal standing. Anil's lawyers argued that the agreement had force and got its presentation in court, or at least the parts relating to the gas pricing, although the text was not disclosed to the public. The Indian Government also entered the fray, seeking a lifting of a block imposed by the court on sale of Krishna–Godavari gas to customers other than Anil's Reliance Natural Gas, or to the government-owned National Thermal Power Corporation. The Petroleum Ministry's secretary, R.S. Pandey, argued that opening the flow of gas from the field in January 2009 was 'an issue of national importance'. (Mukesh himself said the full flow of oil and gas from Krishna–Godavari would save India about US$20 billion a year in energy imports.) Anil's side argued that this intervention showed the Congress-led government's partisanship towards Mukesh, even at the cost of damaging the interests of its own entity, the NTPC.[27]

So charged became the hostility and so high the economic stakes that the judges looked beyond the law for a resolution – to that icon of Indian society, the mother. In August 2008 the Bombay High Court bench suggested that Anil and Mukesh go to their mother again for a settlement, thereby making legal history.

The bitter dispute, with this rich flow of energy at its heart, threatened also to open up some of the more potentially embarrassing aspects of the Reliance story. An interview by Mukesh with the *New York Times* in June 2008 had got around to the 'dark side' of the group's activities. 'What most distinguishes Reliance from its rivals is what Ambani's friends and associates describe as his "intelligence agency", a network of lobbyists and spies in New Delhi who they say collect data about the vulnerabilities of the powerful, about the minutiae of bureaucrats' schedules, about the activities of their competitors.' Mukesh was quoted as saying that all such activities were overseen by his brother before they split and had since been expunged from his tranche of the company. 'We demergered all of that,' he said, breaking out in what was described as a 'belly laugh'.[28]

In August, Anil lodged a suit for defamation against Mukesh in the Bombay High Court, seeking Rs 100 billion for loss and damages. The *Times* and two Indian newspapers that published the interview were also named as defendants. Anil claimed the article was 'malicious' and that the defendants were 'part of a concerted conspiracy whose object is to damage' his reputation.

Once again, Anil was upping the ante in the feud with his brother. Indian business and political circles regarded the prospect of juicy court revelations with mixed glee and trepidation, as well as concern about what this dispute was doing to the 'story' of the new India in the outside world. Unfortunately, they were to be disappointed, as the brothers backed off. Mukesh said his remarks were made 'in jest', and Anil did not pursue the action.

The Bombay High Court action moved on appeal from both Mukesh and Anil from a single company law judge to a higher bench, which ruled in June 2009 that the family agreement prevailed, and that there was nothing in Mukesh's production-sharing contract with the government prohibiting the sale of gas to Anil at less than the price set by the formula approved by the government ministers. All three parties – Anil's Reliance Natural Resources, Mukesh's Reliance Industries and the Indian Government – appealed on various grounds to the Supreme Court of India.

The judgement handed down on 7 May 2010 was a victory for Mukesh and the Indian Government supporting the higher gas price. In different terms, two justices supported the argument of Mukesh's legal team, led by Harish Salve, and the government's lawyers that the production sharing contract required the private sector contractor in petroleum fields to obtain government approval on pricing and alloca- tion of gas or oil production. The inability of the government's NTPC to clinch its parallel deal with Reliance for Krishna–Godavari gas proved a fundamental weakness in Anil's position. The argument that Mukesh's evasions had robbed Anil of a 'bankable' supply contract to start building his power plants was rejected, given the huge sums Anil's corporate floats had raised.

The Chief Justice of India, K.G. Balakrishnan, who was about to retire four days later, lent his decision to the more moderately framed judgement, which ordered Mukesh and Anil to start negotiating a new gas supply agreement within six weeks and conclude it by eight weeks later. The judges observed that while the family agreement was 'not legally binding, it is a commitment which reflects the good interests of both the parties' and told the two sides to take it into account.

The minority judgement, by Justice B. Sudershan Reddy, was a more passionate tirade in defence of state authority, beginning with a Latin prescription by the Roman jurist Justinian that 'Public law cannot be changed by private pacts', and railing against the 'neo-liberal agenda' intent on stripping the state of power in order to benefit the rich few. 'Predatory forms of capitalism' organised themselves first and foremost around extractive industries to exploit natural resources. Sud- ershan Reddy said he was moved to these reflections by the petition of Anil's company "that it is entitled to receive, on account of a private pact between members of the Ambani family, vast quantities of natural gas, amounting to a significant portion of what would be available for the entire country, at a low price and for a long time, de-hors [*sic*] any policy made by the Government of India'.[29]

Anil, who had been sitting in the wood-panelled court to hear the judgement, went out to find the share prices of his power companies crashing. In a one-page statement Anil said he had no plans to file a review petition to the Supreme Court and looked forward to negotiating a new supply arrangement in the light of the court's finding that the family agreement had been the 'guiding force' in the division of Reliance. Mukesh did not attend.

On a Sunday two weeks later the brothers issued a joint statement proclaiming a rapprochement that would 'eliminate any room for further disputes' and that they were now confident of building an 'environment of harmony, cooperation and collaboration' between their groups. Yet, strangely, the substance that was revealed was a scrapping of the ten-year 'non-compete' clause of the 2005 agreement worked out under the auspices of their mother. The field of gas-fired power generation was the one exception, whereby the non-compete agreement was extended to 2022. This was initially hailed as an end of the feud, lifting shares prices of both groups. More sceptical observers thought it could be the prelude to more general warfare, now that each brother was free to enter the sector previously reserved for the other, although not under the Reliance name.

Anil was able to pull some chestnuts from the fire, thanks to the Supreme Court's order to negotiate a gas price in the spirit of the family agreement. The continued element of the non-compete agreement pointed to a merger or sale of Anil's power-generation business to Mukesh's group. Meanwhile, Anil was now unhampered by the 'right of first refusal' aspect of the non-compete agreement, which Mukesh had used to scupper the proposed MTN merger in cell phones. His Reliance Communications began entertaining approaches from foreign telecom firms for a 26 per cent stake, to recoup some of the heavy outlay in licences for 3G signal spectrum. Mukesh quickly launched a return into telecommunications, paying Rs 48 billion ($1.045 billion) for Infotel Broadband Services, a company that had won licences for wireless broadband across India. The move would require him to add another Rs 128.5 billion for the licences, and more than Rs 45 billion to build a network, but it put the new Reliance Infotel in prime position for when India embraced broadband in a big way, as it had done with cell phones in previous years.

The irony that the court's blow for the authority of the state was also putting extra billions in the coffers of one of the world's half-dozen richest men, as well as a lesser flow of royalties into government revenue, was not explored in the judgement. Nor did the judges reflect whether their 'resource nationalism' was in the best interest of encouraging more petroleum exploration for energy-short India. Private sector oil companies, Indian and foreign, were digesting the fact that their freedom to sell whatever they discovered was now greatly limited, subject to changeable and often murky government decisions. The price of $4.20 per mmbtu set by Pranab Mukherjee's ministerial team in 2006 for five years was a maximum price, based on what had become a subdued oil price at the start of this century. At times, the oil price had soared much higher. The prospect of great reward for great risk was diminished.[30]

Meanwhile, the Supreme Court noted in passing that gas from Reliance's older west coast fields (Panna, Mukti and Tapti) was being sold at a higher price, $5.51 per mmbtu, which was in fact the highest price allowed any of the listed private sector gas fields. The government's petroleum producers were continuing to supply gas to fertiliser factories and other customers designated as high priority for less than $2.

The final ruling on Krishna–Godavari had come from judges of India's apex court, respected for its high level of jurisprudence, incorruptibility and judicial activism. Yet the intervention of the Congress-led government had undoubtedly carried enormous weight. Once again, government policy had turned out to be tailor-made for the immediate needs of Reliance.

22

Goodbye, Gandhi

When the film *Guru* based on Dhirubhai Ambani's life appeared in 2007, distributed by Anil's company Adlab and with his Bachchan coterie involved, it seemed to show a new maturity in the Ambani camp about the mixed shades of the patriarch's legacy.

It certainly had a level of adulation that at least one of India's leading business chiefs, a Parsi himself, found too 'sickening' to keep watching the film when he flicked it on during a long-haul flight. But it included several of the clashes narrated in this book, ones that do not reflect too well on Dhirubhai. Guru falls out with Gupta when he tells the newspaperman about having 'one gold slipper and one silver slipper' with which to tap the recipients of his largesse, meaning that everyone has their price. He falls out with his original business partner after taking big decisions without consultation: an echo of his rift with

his first co-investor in the textile trade, Chambaklal Damani. There is
even an encounter with a central government 'minister' – shown from
behind, but having a profile and bald patch suspiciously like those of
Rajiv Gandhi – in which Guru mentions a 'small deposit' left with him
by the politician's late uncle and seeks instructions what to do with it.
The minister is soon agreeing to open Guru's newest factory. The coun-
terpoint to this protean myth is given by an investigative journalist,
clearly based on Gurumurthy. 'He doesn't just bend or break the law,
he buries it and builds a beautiful park on it,' Saxena says, recalling the
'first-class fountain' remark made by Dhirubhai about his early scrapes
with legality. Guru is the biggest hope of Indian industry, but 'he is a
disease, who should be locked up in jail and the keys thrown away,'
Saxena says. His growth rate is 400 per cent, 'but corruption and greed
have grown at twice that rate, thanks to his bribes'.

Here, in stark terms, is the essential debate about Dhirubhai Ambani
and the business approach he pioneered, although the film concludes
on the side of the self-serving myth. So does a collection of Dhirubhai's
managerial homilies – of the 'Dare to Dream' variety – compiled by
A.G. Krishnamurthy, an advertising man whose agency grew large on
the Reliance account. In a foreword, Mukesh Ambani offers the same
thesis as the movie presents.

> In India, such thinking was deemed to be heretical when
> Dhirubhai began to stride the corporate stage. This was an era
> of licences and quotas which caged entrepreneurship. But that
> did not dampen his ardour. He put to use the latest technological
> innovations and the most advanced management practices for the
> speedy expansion of his enterprise, which grew into an empire.
> In the bargain, he rattled pedigreed corporate houses, earned
> the ire of sections of the political class and the bureaucracy and
> attracted scorn and invective from powerful segments of the

media. What galled Dhirubhai's critics and detractors was his success in outwitting them at every turn. Not only did he dream bigger and bigger dreams but he also found novel methods to realise them. One such way was to ensure that ordinary citizens shared in the wealth he created. To the under-privileged and the un-empowered he showed by example how they could fulfil their hopes for a brighter tomorrow for themselves and for their children. No one doubts any more that such a vision brought about a paradigm shift in the history of Indian business ...[1]

Even one of the Western world's most illustrious business colleges, Wharton School at the University of Pennsylvania, signed up to this story when it accepted a multimillion dollar bequest from its alumnus Anil Ambani and named a new auditorium after Dhirubhai. 'He was a true pioneer in the development of the Indian economy, opening opportunity to thousands of his fellow citizens through his then-innovative public stock offerings,' declared Wharton's Dean, Patrick Harker.[2]

So what to make of Dhirubhai Ambani: revolutionary business guru or unsurpassed corruptor, or both? And how much of his legacy remains with the two business empires of Mukesh and Anil and more widely in corporate India?

Some analysts excuse the Ambani methods as an unavoidable – even just and necessary – riposte to a rotten and moribund system. 'Much of the criticism of Ambani is, in effect, of the Indian system of bureaucratic controls, state intervention, high but variable tariffs, industrial and import licensing, state control of unit trusts and life insurance,' wrote a respected Hong Kong-based authority on Asian business, the journalist Philip Bowring. 'To beat the system to get ahead, it was necessary to exploit the human frailties of its power holders. Everyone did it. Ambani did it more effectively.'[3]

Indeed, that was noted by some as a key strength, even the key strength. Reporting the first year in which Reliance actually paid corporate profit tax – 1997, nearly four decades after its beginning – *The Economist* noted that the Ambanis had built a 'strangely modern company' in an Indian business environment described as the 'Galapagos of capitalism'. In the same article, corporate analyst Manoj Badale saw the only common thread in the group's diverse activities (by then including telecommunications) as 'a focus on capital intensive industries in which success turns on the ability to get around regulators – and that, it seems, is what the Ambanis reckon is Reliance's core competence'.[4]

But it has to be said: this doesn't do justice to Dhirubhai's outstanding abilities and drive on so many fronts: as an innovative financier, an inspiring manager of talent, as astute marketer of his products and as a forward-looking industrialist. His story is also about the flowering of entrepreneurship from a traditional, isolated backwater like Junagadh; the accumulated ethic of centuries of business and banking among the Bania castes being transferred to modern corporations; the impressive numeracy of so many Indians from the poorest street traders to the high financiers; the way in which the age-old trading links to the Indian Ocean rim have been extended into Europe and North America by the past forty years of migration.

The energy and daring that showed itself in his early pranks, practical jokes and trading experiments developed into a boldness and willingness to live with risk that few other Indian corporate chiefs dared to emulate. His extraordinary talent for sustaining relationships and sometimes impressing men of standing, with much better formal education, won him vital support from both governments and institutions that was not always, or solely, based on mutual reward.

As for investors, as long as there was growth in the price of Reliance shares, they quickly forgot the episodes in which Dhirubhai played fast and loose with their trust. These were, notably, the mergers of subsidiaries at great advantage to promoters over ordinary shareholders; the unexpected private placements; the duplicate share and share-switching cases; the sustained pump-priming of share prices using the company's own funds or money raised for other purposes; the short-term investment profits reaped via the scores of 'trading and invest-ment' companies in the ownership 'matrix'. After his death, there was the issue of the 'sweat equity' cornered by Mukesh in the cell phone venture, later exposed by his brother.

Not so, say the critics outside the circle of political and financial contacts. They noted Dhirubhai Ambani's pervasive subversion of free press inquiry and commentary, via its tactics of bribery, selec-tive leaks, advertising power and marshalling of legal and regulatory obstacles.[5] They stressed the broad spectrum of government employees who became listed as Dhirubhai's people, plied with small gifts, their names put forward for favourable postings and made aware that deci-sions counter to Reliance interests could result in an abrupt transfer to a career backwater. Politicians learned that favours resulted in a talented team of Reliance government liaison staff pushing their advancement and helping with briefcases of campaign funds. Displeasure meant the same operatives digging for dirt or disadvantaged constituents and making sure the details were publicised in the least favourable light.

The dark side of Dhirubhai's abilities was an eye for human weakness and a willingness to exploit it. This gained him preferential treatment or at least a blind eye from the whole gamut of Indian insti-tutions at various times. Over decades in India, some of the world's best minds had applied themselves to building a system of government controls on capitalism. Dhirubhai Ambani made a complete mockery of it – admittedly at a stage when the system was decaying and partly corrupted already.

The Ministry of Finance and its enforcement agencies, the Reserve

Bank of India, the Central Bureau of Investigation, the Securities and Exchange Board of India and the Company Law Board, proved timid and sometimes complicit in their handling of the questionable episodes involving Reliance. Public financial institutions that held large blocks of shares in Reliance and had seats on its board were passive and acquiescent spectators, rather than responsible trustees for public savings.

Dhirubhai Ambani cautioned about the 'jealousy' inherent in the Indian business milieu. Reliance frequently, routinely, put any criticism or opposition to its actions down to motives of envy or a desire to pull down anyone achieving success. Throughout every crisis caused by exposure of alleged manipulations, company publicity took on a self-pitying victim's tone. But the record tends to show that it was Dhirubhai and Reliance that often made the first move to put a spoke in a rival's wheel, whether it was Kapal Mehra or Nusli Wadia, whose supporters blame hostile lobbying by Reliance for some of the financing difficulties encountered in Essar's efforts to build a steel, petroleum and shipping empire based on India's west coast.

Coincidentally with disputes with Reliance, various rivals were hit with government inspections, tax problems, unfavourable press reports, physical attacks and, in Wadia's case, a damaging forgery, a deportation order and, on the police case yet to be tested in court, an alleged conspiracy to murder him.

Reliance sought larger capacity clearances, lower duties on its imported chemical ingredients and higher duties on its finished products for itself – not for all players. It has been relentless in its use of monopoly or dominant market share. Many Indians took the effects of Dhirubhai Ambani's sustained cultivation of politicians and officials much more seriously than Mani Ratnam's film did. 'Ambani's hand in tarnishing the Indian state – in rendering dubious practice systematic – has dire consequences for ordinary Indians. Not everyone can afford the bribes for basic amenities and rights relentlessly extorted by a system made greedy by visionary local capitalists. And needless to say, it will be a very long time before ordinary Indians count among the beneficiaries of Ambani's economic revolution.'[6]

Indians love to tell the joke against themselves about the exporter of live frogs to the kitchens of France: he didn't need to put a lid on the crates, because as soon as one Indian frog tried to escape, the others pulled him down. The Licence Raj did indeed bring out a tendency to blow the whistle when someone makes a run for wealth or success. Jealousy can be strong in a crowded country with many qualified contenders for every opportunity and where growth of those opportunities is slow or static. But the opposition that Dhirubhai stirred up was not always or even mostly envy – quite often it was vigorous self-defence or a determination to extract the truth.

The disputes surrounding the rise of Dhirubhai Ambani also tell us something else about India: how it agonises over the morality of change, of success and failure, a syndrome explored by the economist Amartya Sen in his essay *The Argumentative Indian*.[7]

The snappy analogy made by the tabloid newspaper *Blitz* in 1985, comparing the erupting polyester industry battle to the epic *Mahabharata*, captured another aspect of this internal debate. On paper, the *Mahabharata* runs to millions of words and fills a dozen volumes, but the central story is a simple one. King Yudisthira is torn between his innate sense of rightness and his earthly duty as a ruler in which cheating, lying, intrigue and espionage are expected under the *dharma* (law and duty) of that role. Against his conscience and his personal inclination to withdraw from strife, Yudisthira allows his Pandava clan to enter a war of vengeance against the related but rival Kaurava house, culminating in the bloodiest fight of all literature at Kurukshetra, when millions are slaughtered on both sides – and a deception by Yudisthira turns the tide of battle. *Blitz* hesitated to assign the roles of Pandava and Kaurava between Dhirubhai and his textile rivals in the 'MahaPoly-ester War', a judgement also suspended by many investors and news-paper. Was not a certain amount of deception just part and parcel of the *dharma* of a businessman?

There perhaps the analogy ends. The questions raised during this story are not unique to India. What are the limits of ethical behaviour in a world full of surprise manoeuvres, innovation, inside connections and corruption? Unlike the *Mahabharata* and its relentless destiny, modern capitalism does allow a process of redemption in the life of a corpora-tion, over time. After all, opium-traders, slave-owners, black-marketeers and railway robber-barons have been able to transform themselves into pillars of corporate respectability, if they can survive scandals and the system's periodic crashes.

Has Reliance moved out of the shadows of its origins since Dhiru-bhai's death? In only five years, Reliance had divided, but each arm has grown bigger than the original parent company. Mukesh's part of the empire alone accounted for about 3 per cent of India's gross domestic product, and its activities extend into retail and urban development projects that touch on the lives of millions of consumers beyond the company's shareholders. With his successful float of Reliance Power in January 2008, Anil was treading close behind.

The two groups were moving into the international big league of business, attracting the attention of the world's main investment funds. Yet on home ground in India, elements of the 'dark' side of the old Reliance operating methods were widely seen as remaining. Both groups maintained large and active corporate affairs offices involved in manipulating politicians, government officials and public opinion towards their business plans. As noted earlier, Mukesh claimed in June 2008 that this manipulative side of the enterprise had been overseen by

Anil before the split and had been 'demerged' to him when the split took place in 2005, attracting a defamation suit from his brother. But only six months earlier it was reported that 'the brothers' shadowy presence in the political life of the country is unmistakable' and that they were 'often said to mould business-friendly policy behind the scenes', although much of the focus was countering the rival brother's moves.

> Journalists would jokingly call them plant managers, members of
> the Reliance Corporate Communications team. From reporters
> to editors, they all found the Reliance media managers handy,
> especially on a lean news day – they always had gossip up their
> sleeve, or a scoop, or a plant. They would land up at Reliance
> office at Meridien Towers in Delhi in the hope of picking up
> exclusive bits on things that ranged from hydrocarbon discoveries
> to defence deals to locomotive contracts to manoeuvrings in
> the corridors of power … Post split, Anil's men moved out of
> Meridien and engaged the media over coffee and smoked chicken
> lemon sandwiches at Barista outlets. Mukesh's propaganda
> shop was at the Taj Chambers; to begin with [its] main job was
> to counter anti-Mukesh stories. But Anil's men still rule the
> roost, ostensibly because they have a past master as boss who
> understands a journalist's mind like Beckham understands a
> free-kick.[8]

The legendary Reliance power to influence government policy and administrative decisions and to punish the uncooperative was also evident in recent property developments, especially those of Mukesh.

In May 2008 the head of Maharashtra state's Wakf Board, which administers property set aside inalienably for charitable or religious purposes under Islamic customary law, filed a petition in the Supreme Court for return of the Altamount Road site where Mukesh was building his Antilla mega-home, claiming that it had been sold on the understanding it would be used for an orphanage. Although the Wakf Board's petition was sent back to a lower court that had already blocked the case, its chief executive was transferred the next day.[9] The controversy, however, brought Mukesh's project to the attention of a shadowy Islamist terror group calling itself the Indian Mujahiddeen, which issued threats against him in mid-2008.

With Mukesh's special economic zones, government policy on the maximum permitted area wavered before coming down in his group's favour. As we have seen, a key Maharashtra official who tried to limit the compulsory acquisition of land was suddenly transferred to a far inland corner of the state. The small businessmen associated with Mumbai's seaport who tried to protect their own interests were constantly coming up against officials who benefited from past Reliance favours. There was an accumulation of cultivated goodwill towards Reliance. Many officials in revenue-collecting departments who were transferred into Mumbai were offered transition accommodation by Reliance for the usual six-month gap between starting their new job and provision of official housing. Certain key officials were also provided with cars on their arrival in a new post. The long accretion of gift vouchers given at Diwali to customs officials, on a graduated scale up to collector rank, created a pervasive sense of obligation in which officials bent over backwards to please Reliance. Often the mere production of a Reliance business card was sufficient for an executive to be waved through airport checkpoints without query or inspection.

In contrast to the swift clearances given to Reliance projects, other large and reputable companies complain privately of the inordinate delays even for uncontroversial works. It was not necessarily that Reliance had primed politicians and bureaucrats to work against rivals. In many cases, the projects subject to long delay were in fields in which

Reliance was not a competitor. It was simply that Reliance had set the bar so high that companies that tried to play by the book could not attract more than desultory attention to their paperwork.

Long after Dhirubhai's passing, some old vendettas were still being pursued – although it was unclear who, if anyone, was driving them from the top. One was against a veteran opponent of Reliance, the publisher R.V. Pandit. Pandit had used his close contacts with senior politicians like Manmohan Singh, Atul Behari Vajpayee and L.K. Advani to oppose attempts to take over what he saw as national strategic assets, from Larsen & Toubro in 1992 up to Arun Shourie's privatisations. Coincidentally, Pandit had been dogged by unusual official and police interest in a company called Frontier Trading, run by Pandit's only son, in which the father was also a shareholder. The company sold a Japanese-made therapeutic mattress whose embedded magnets were claimed to alleviate rheumatic pains. It had faced an action by customs for claiming a lower rate of duty for a medicinal product as against a 'luxury' one; but a more persistent case was the police allegation that an incentive payment to customers who introduced other buyers constituted a breach of India's law against pyramid selling.

In July 2007 the senior Pandit, then 76, was arrested in Chennai on the orders of a magistrate in the small town of Nalgonda in Andra Pradesh and brought to his court. Although only an investor in Frontier Trading, he was refused bail and held in custody. Friends including Nusli Wadia and a former Defence minister, George Fernandes, became alarmed that the jailing was an attempt to 'finish off' Pandit, who had a heart condition. They notified the Prime Minister, Manmohan Singh, who arranged for officials of the Intelligence Bureau (India's domestic security agency) to be sent down to Nalgonda to watch over Pandit. It took three weeks for Pandit's lawyer to secure him bail on medical grounds and get him back to Mumbai.[10]

The shortcomings of the state are often cited as the reason India has failed to fully exploit its potential for economic growth. In a widely read essay, Gurcharan Das, a former head of Proctor & Gamble India, argued that 'rather than rising with the help of the state, India is in many ways rising despite the state'. Like many other analysts, he sees the Indian government machinery as obstructors rather than enablers, although, like Amartya Sen, he concedes that a large part of the problem might be cultural: a 'bias for thought and against action', or that bureaucrats 'value ideas over accomplishment': 'What they [the founders of the Indian political system] did not anticipate is that politicians in India's democracy would "capture" the bureaucracy and use the system to create jobs and revenue for friends and supporters. The Indian state no longer generates public goods. Instead it creates private benefits for those who control it.'[11]

Yet what happens when private interests capture the politicians, along with many of the bureaucrats under them? One legacy of Dhirubhai Ambani was a dangerously suborned state. Years after his death this was reflected in the Indian parliamentary debates in late 2005 on the report by Paul Volcker on the Iraq Oil-for-Food scandals. As the Bangalore lawyer and activist Arun Agrawal detailed in a courageous book, speaker after speaker from both the Congress-led government and the BJP opposition, including former adversaries of Reliance, avoided even mentioning Reliance as the largest Indian recipient of oil allocations from the Saddam Hussein regime, let alone trying to probe the political circumstances in which the oil concessions were won. Agrawal also raises pertinent questions about the transfer of offshore oil and gas concessions from the state petroleum development sector to Reliance, including the Mukta, Panna and Tapti fields in the Arabian Sea and the immense Krishna–Godavari discovery in the Bay of Bengal.[12]

Mukesh Ambani's revealed thinking on his giant projects in urban development, distribution and retailing shows an almost contemptuous belief that such schemes are beyond the capacity of Indian governments to orchestrate. These are certainly the kind of sectoral developments that India needs, the generation of workaday jobs and communities that fill the gap between the vast subsistence and menial income group and the present tiny educated elite (in which the much vaunted IT sector employs a total 1.3 million people, about 0.1 per cent of the population and 0.2 per cent of the workforce). Yet can India as a whole develop if the most vigorous activity is nurtured in special economic zones exempted from many of the regulations and requirements that apply in the general community, almost like the East India Company's 'factories' in the Mughal era?

In his essay, Das concludes that 'the state cannot merely withdraw. Markets do not work in a vacuum. They need a network of regulations and institutions; they need umpires to settle disputes.' Das also observes that some of the most important post-1991 reforms succeeded because of the regulatory institutions established by the state. While India needs entrepreneurs like Mukesh Ambani, it also needs a much stronger state to regulate their excesses and prevent abuses. Businessmen will do what they can get away with, and the Reliance model shows a strong appreciation of the benefits of monopoly. A strong state would devote more resources to relevant and updated policies, better revenue collection and accountability and effective policing of rules, rather than persisting with so much effort in micro-managing affairs. It would strengthen its bureaucracy, not with greater powers but with better resources, education and discipline so as to be truly the 'steel framework' that Nehru envisaged, or the rule-keepers prescribed by Hayek.

Against those who tended to see the baleful influence of Reliance under every rock, however, it has to be noted that the brothers' feud opened up more space for public scrutiny of their businesses and family affairs. While some media groups had not known which way to jump in 2004, others had leapt into the fray on one side or the other, and both brothers felt the need to put their thoughts to a wide public.

While the brothers were separately richer, in paper wealth, than any Mughal emperor could have imagined and together formed the world's richest family, other billionaires were on the rise in India and provided some countervailing power. There were tycoons like Kushal Pal Singh, who headed the country's largest property developer, DLF, and Sunil Mittal, creator of India's largest mobile telephone operator, Bharti Airtel, each with assets close to $20 billion at the peak of the financial boom in the latter part of 2007. After building up a worldwide steelmaking chain, the London-based entrepreneur Lakshmi Mittal eclipsed Mukesh in personal wealth at the end of 2007. By then he had returned in a decisive way to his homeland, listing his group on local exchanges and making his plans to enter the petroleum sector very clear and competing for prospective oil leases. Mittal also displayed a new favour with Sonia Gandhi, while his son became close to her son Rahul, the fourth-generation heir apparent of the Nehru–Gandhi dynasty. Mukesh had a significant rival for political favour.[13]

The other great legacy of Dhirubhai Ambani was an unabashed flaunting of wealth. With dozens of new billionaires created by share-market floats, India saw an explosion of business and consumer power, with many of the new tycoons consciously modelling themselves on Dhirubhai. Indeed, the top four Indian billionaires controlled more assets than China's twenty top business people. In mid-2007 Manmohan Singh railed against the ever more lavish displays of wealth, in a speech to the Confederation of Indian Industry.

In a country with extreme poverty, industry needs to be moderate in the emolument levels it adopts. Rising income and wealth inequalities, if not matched by a corresponding rise of incomes across the nation, can lead to social unrest ... The electronic media carries the lifestyles of the rich and famous into every village slum. An area of great concern is the level of ostentatious expenditure on weddings and other family events. Such vulgarity insults the poverty of the less privileged, it is socially wasteful and it plants the seeds of resentment in the minds of the have-nots.[14]

Singh's warning met derision in the press. A large section of the intellectual elite had accommodated Dhirubhai Ambani and his sons within their approval. While both heirs paid a certain homage to the 'simple' personal life of their father, neither in his own lifestyle made any obeisance to Gandhian ideals. Anil's partying with the Bollywood crowd and Mukesh's erection of a modern palace in Mumbai and acquisition of a luxury corporate jet showed the final triumph of polyester over *khadi* cotton.

Sixty years after 'freedom at midnight', the moment of India's modern independence in 1947, the Modh Bania from Saurashtra named Dhirubhai Ambani seemed to portray the spirit of the new India more than the region's other most famous Modh Bania, Mohandas Gandhi.

$\mathcal{N}otes$

2 A PERSUASIVE YOUNG BANIA

1   N.A. Thoothi, *The Vaishnavas of Gujarat*, Longmans Green, Calcutta, 1935, pp. 357–8.
2   The following passage draws on H.V. Hodson, *The Great Divide*, Oxford University Press, 1962, pp. 427–40.

3 LESSONS FROM THE SOUK

1   Interview with author, February 1991. One lakh equals 100 000.
2   Charles Hepburn Johnston, *The View From Steamer Point*, Collins, London, 1964.
3   R.J. Gavin, *Aden Under British Rule 1839–1967*, C. Hurst & Co., London, 1975, p. 322.
4   Johnston, *The View From Steamer Point*, p. 55.
5   Gavin, *Aden Under British Rule 1839–1967*, pp. 318–51, covers the British withdrawal.
6   Letter to author, 1996.

4 CATCHING LIVE SERPENTS

1   Sucheta Dalal and Debashis Basu, interview with Mukesh Ambani, *MoneyLIFE* magazine, carried on rediff.com, 17–19 January 2007.

5 A FIRST-CLASS FOUNTAIN

1   Nitish Sen Gupta, *Inside the Steel Frame*, Vikas, New Delhi, 1995, p. 65.
2   Raj Thapar, *All These Years*, Seminar Publications, New Delhi, 1991, p. 249.
3   Ibid, pp. 337–8.
4   *Business Standard*, 11 April 1981.
5   *Organiser*, 12 September 1981.
6   Gita Piramal, *Business Maharajas*, Viking/Penguin, New Delhi, 1996, p. 34.
7   *India Today*, 30 June 1985.

6 GURU OF THE EQUITY CULT

1   Sen Gupta, *Inside the Steel Frame*, pp. 58–9.
2   *India Today*, 15 February 1983.

7 FRIENDS IN THE RIGHT PLACES

1   See *The Economic Scene*, September 1984.
2   Piramal, *Business Maharajas*, p. 6.
3   Sen Gupta, *Inside the Steel Frame*, p. 113.
4   *India Today*, 15 January 1984.
5   *Business Standard*, 29 August 1984.
6   Piramal, *Business Maharajas*, pp. 56–7.

8 THE GREAT POLYESTER WAR

1   Interview with author, November 1996.
2   'Nusli Wadia: Corporate samurai', *Business World*, 28 July–10 August 1993.
3   Inder Malhotra, *Indira Gandhi: A Personal and Political Biography*, Hodder & Stoughton, London, 1989, pp. 214–15.
4   Khushwant Singh, 'The new messiah', *Illustrated Weekly of India*, 15 November 1987; 'Loner', *Telegraph* (Calcutta), 15 January 1995; Prem Shanker Jha, *In the Eye of the Cyclone*, Viking/Penguin, New Delhi, 1993.
5   *Blitz*, 23 November 1985.
6   *Times of India*, 17 November 1985.
7   *Blitz*, 23 November 1985.
8   *Times of India*, 29 December 1985.

9 THE PAPER TIGER

1   Interview with author, February 1991.
2   *Illustrated Weekly of India*, 22 April 1990.
3   Interview with author, October 1996.
4   *Illustrated Weekly of India*, 22 April 1990.
5   Interview with author, September 1995.
6   This and other quotations in this chapter are drawn from Gurumurthy's twelve articles in the *Indian Express* between 22 March and 12 June 1986.
7   *India Today*, 15 August 1986.

10 SLEUTHS

1   Venkitaramanan commented that his closeness to Reliance was 'always exaggerated' (telephone conversation with author, February 1997).
2   Interview with S. Gurumurthy, October 1996.
3   *Economic Times*, 29 August 1986.

11 LETTING LOOSE A SCORPION

1   Prem Shankar Jha, *In the Eye of the Cyclone*, pp. 70–3.
2   *Illustrated Weekly of India*, 20 June 1986.
3   Vir Sangvi, 'The 40 Crore Question', *Sunday*, 13–19 March 1988.
4   *Illustrated Weekly of India*, 19 April and 23 August 1987.
5   *Sunday*, 8–14 February 1987.
6   Sangvi, 'The 40 Crore Question'.
7   Jha, *In the Eye of the Cyclone*, p. 74.
8   Singh, 'The new Messiah'.

12 BUSINESS AS USUAL

1   *India Today*, 15 March 1989.

13 MURDER MEDLEY

1   Nicholas Coleridge, *Paper Tigers*, Heinemann, London, 1993, pp. 234–5.
2   Madhav Godbole, *Unfinished Innings*, Orient Longman, New Delhi, 1996, pp. 168–73.

14 A POLITICAL DELUGE

1   *Indian Express*, 5 January 1990.
2   *Indian Express*, 2 January 1991.

3   A judgement on this case came only on 3 April 1997 when the Bombay
    Collector of Customs, S.K. Bharadwaj, ordered Reliance to pay Rs 401.4 million
    in additional duty. Reliance said it was appealing against part of the order. See
    Business Standard, 4 April 1997, and *Financial Express*, 9 April 1997.
4   *Financial Express*, 17 January 1990.
5   Interview with author, 1996.
6   Conversation with author, 1994.
7   Jha, *In the Eye of the Cyclone*, p. 98.
8   Godbole, *Unfinished Innings*, pp. 237–49.

15 UNDER THE REFORMS

1   *Economic Times*, 16 August 1991.
2   *BusinessIndia*, 19 August–1 September 1991.
3   Interview with author, 1992.
4   Interview with author, October 1996.
5   Debashis Basu, *Business Standard*, 20 and 21 July 1995.
6   R.C. Murthy, *The Fall of Angels*, Indus, New Delhi, 1995, p. 156.
7   Interview with author, November 1996.
8   *Business Today*, 7–21 September 1995.

16 HOUSEKEEPING SECRETS

1   *Economic Times*, 1 December 1995.
2   *Observer of Business and Politics*, 30 November 1995.

17 DHIRUBHAI'S DREAM

1   'The importance of being Balu', *India Today*, 23 November 1998.
2   *Indian Express*, 19 November 1998.
3   Raashid Alvi, 'Complaint to the government and its agencies regarding
    fraudulent misuse of large-scale public funds by Reliance Petroleum Ltd.' See
    'Reliance's smoking gun', *BusinessWeek*, 25 June 2001.
4   *Business Today*, 16 March 2003.
5   Sucheta Dalal, 'S. Gurumurthy on the warpath against Reliance again', 8
    February 2002, has a summary of Gurumurthy's accusations and a link to the
    Reliance response, www.suchetadalal.com.
6   Abhay Singh and Ravil Shirodkar, 'The feud menacing India Inc.', *Bloomberg
    Markets*, June 2005.
7   www.dhirubhai.net/dhcmshtml/2002.pdf.
8   Press Trust of India, 8 July 2003.
9   'Reliance didn't grow on permit raj: Anil Ambani', interview with Vir Sangvi,
    Star Talk, on rediff.com, 11 May 2002.

10   C.P. Chandrasekhar, 'The Dhirubhai legend', *Frontline*, Chennai, 20 July–2 August 2002.
11   Ibid.
12   Harish Nambiar, 'Dhirubhai Ambani: The Heathcliffe of Indian business', 15 July 2002, on www.chowk.com.
13   Paranjoy Guha Thakurta, 'Shourie's selective memory', www.rediff.com, 11 August 2003.
14   Ibid.
15   T.J.S. George, 'Can yesterday's vice become today's virtue?', 'Point of View', *Newindpress on Sunday*, 12 July 2003.
16   M.K. Venu, 'Shourie, Hayek and the Ambanis', *Economic Times*, 15 July 2003.
17   Edward Luce, *In Spite of the Gods: The Strange Rise of Modern India*, Doubleday, New York, 2007, pp. 7–8; Press Trust of India, *Indian Express*, 8 July 2003.

18 THE POLYESTER PRINCES

1   Sucheta Dalal and Debashis Basu, interview with Mukesh Ambani, *MoneyLIFE* magazine, on rediff.com, 17–19 January 2007.
2   Prabhu Chawla and Rohit Saran, 'The telescam', *India Today*, 23 April 2001; see also Rajni Gupta, 'India attempts to give a jump-start to its derailed telecommunications liberalization process', on http://arxiv.org/pdf/cs.CY/0109062.
3   V. Venkatesan, 'Seeking accountability', *Frontline*, 14–27 January 2006.
4   Virendra Kapoor, 'Poor Pramod', rediff.com, 1 February 2003; Satish Misra, *Tribune* (Chandigarh), 30 January 2003.
5   P. Vaidyanathan Iyer, 'Is Arun Shourie right?', rediff.com, 15 April 2003; 'Reliance's triumph angers mobile-phone competitors', *Economist*, 18 December 2003; Aravind Adiga and Meenakshi Ganguly, 'Families under fire', *Time Asia*, 16 February 2004; Sanjay Anand, 'Reliance Infocomm on the prowl', *Times of India*, 9 March 2004.
6   Ganguly, 'Families under fire'; Saritha Rai, 'A giant so big it's a proxy for India's economy', *New York Times*, 4 June 2004.

19 CORPORATE KURUKSHETRA

1   Sucheta Dalal, 'The Ambani dream and a mysterious absence', rediff.com, 2 January 2003.
2   Interview with Vir Sanghvi for *Star Talk*, carried on rediff.com, 11 May 2002.
3   T.N. Ninan, 'India Inc. and family squabbles', *Business Standard*, 20 November 2004; also on rediff.com.
4   Sumit Mitra, 'The network neta', *India Today*, 25 October 1999; Luce, *In Spite of the Gods*, p. 134; Christopher Kremmer, *Inhaling the Mahatma*, HarperCollins, Sydney, 2006, pp. 312–19.

5   Alam Srinivas, *Storms in the Sea Wind*, Roli Books, New Delhi, 2005, p. 139.
6   Olga Tellis, 'Anil to respond soon to brother', *Asian Age*, 28 November 2004.
7   Srinivas, *Storms in the Sea Wind*, p. 83.
8   Mira Kamdar, *Planet India*, Scribner, New York, 2007, pp. 205–8.
9   'Nita is cause of Ambani rift', *Asian Age*, 21 November 2004.
10 Sucheta Dalal and Debashis Basu, interview with Mukesh Ambani, *MoneyLIFE*, on rediff.com, 17–19 January 2007.
11 Ninan, 'India Inc. and family squabbles'.
12 Srinivas, *Storms in the Sea Wind*, pp. 7–8.
13 Ibid., p. 8.
14 Ibid., pp. 86–7.
15 Ibid., pp. 89–90.
16 Indrajit Gupta, Shishir Prasad, T. Surendar, 'Genie's out of the bottle', *Businessworld*, 20 December 2004.
17 T. Surendar, 'Showdown at Maker IV', *Businessworld*, 10 January 2005.

20 MOTHER INDIA

1   'Mom waited in the wings, kept flock intact', *Times of India*, 20 June 2005.
2   'Ambani vs Ambani', *India Today*, 29 November 2004; 'Dividing the Empire', *India Today*, 27 December 2004; 'Showdown at Maker IV', *Businessworld*, 10 January 2005.
3   Sucheta Dalal, 'Is Reliance rewriting rules of corp. governance?', rediff.com, 31 January 2005.
4   Srinivas, *Storms in the Sea Wind*, p. 105.
5   V. Venkatesan, 'Seeking accountability', *Frontline*, 14–27 January 2006.
6   *Hindu*, 6 March 2005.
7   Olga Tellis, 'CBI has email linking Mukesh man to "PB"', *Asian Age*, 22 May 2005; 'Call alert: Govt may refer Reliance Info case to CBI', *Times of India/Economic Times*, 20 May 2005; 'Rel info exec's e-mails under lens', *Times of India/Economic Times*, 19 May 2005.
8   Sucheta Dalal, 'What this means: Anil's won a kingdom, now he needs to build fences and bridges' and 'Kiss and make-up time at Reliance', *Financial Express*, 19–20 June 2005.
9   'Ambani brothers clash again – Mukesh refutes Anil's charges on non-transfer of business control', *Business Line*, 5 February 2006; Sucheta Dalal, *Financial Express*, 6 February 2006.

21 THE AMBANIS APART

1   Krishna Gopalan, 'End game', *Business Today*, 17 July 2005; Ron Moreau and Sudip Mazumdar, 'Bigger, faster, better', *Newsweek*, 17 July 2006.
2   Kamdar, *Planet India*, p. 226; Moreau and Mazumdar, 'Bigger, faster, better'.
3   Sucheta Dalal and Debashis Basu, February 2007 interview, rediff.com.

4   Ibid.
5   Kamdar, *Planet India*; Moreau and Mazumdar, 'Bigger, faster, better'.
6   'Amar Singh's telephone conversations recorded', 1 January 2006.
7   *Hindustan Times*, 24 May 2007.
8   Anjuli Bhargava, 'This airport is the cynosure of India Inc.', *Business Standard*, 31 August 2007.
9   Reuter News Service, 8 July 2007; Joe Leahy, 'Sarin lashes India's "vested interests"', *Financial Times*, 10 July 2007.
10 Ibid.
11 Ravinder Singh, Urgent e-petition to President, 14 June 2006.
12 Mukesh Bhardwaj, 'Land grab charge puts spotlight on Reliance's mega SEZ in Haryana', *Indian Express*, 13 June 2006; Sreelatha Menon, 'Reliance's CSR initiative in SEZ battles cynics', *Business Standard*, 3 August 2007.
13 'RIL deals directly with farmers for SEZ land in state', *Economic Times*, 15 January 2007; Renni Abraham, 'With foes like these, who needs friends?', *DNA*, 18 August 2007.
14 'Breather for SEZs with 5000-ha cap', *Business Standard*, 9 August 2007; *Times of India*, 4 December 2007.
15 'Petro adulteration scam: it can't be this crude', *Outlook India*, 11 April 2005.
16 John Elliott, 'Reliance hits gasoline and worsening retail road blocks', http://ridingtheelephant.blogs.fortune.cnn.com, 24 September 2007.
17 V.K. Shashikumar, 'Wetland to wasteland', *Tehelka*, 1 January 2005.
18 T.N. Ninan, 'Discom fever', *Business Standard*, 27 August 2005.
19 'PM sets up EGoM on Reliance gas price', *Hindustan Times*, 6 August 2007.
20 'CPM opposes gas price policy, RIL warns of two-year delay', *Economic Times*, 5 September 2007.
21 Manash Goswami and Dinakar Sethuraman, 'India caps natural gas price, may scare new explorers', Bloomberg news service, 13 September 2007.
22 Andrew Buncombe, 'Ambani overtakes Gates to become world's richest man', *Independent* (London), 30 October 2007.
23 Eric Bellman, 'In India, stock surge lifts Ambanis' riches to unfathomable high', *Wall Street Journal*, 24 November 2007.
24 Charles Ayres, 'Power shift in Hollywood as Steven Spielberg exits', *Times* (London), 6 October 2008; 'Reliance ADAG scripts Hollywood foray', *Business Standard*, 4 October 2008.
25 Telecom Regulatory Authority of India, press release 79/2009, 23 December 2009, at www.trai.gov.in.
26 Dean Nelson, 'India's $85bn Ambani brothers battle on', *Sunday Times* (London), 28 June 2008; Veeshal Bakshi, 'The Emperor strikes back', *Tehelka*, 26 July 2008.
27 'Sale of K-G basin gas: Govt to approach HC', *Business Standard*, 25 September 2008.
28 Anand Giridharadas, 'Indian to the core, and an oligarch', *New York Times*, 15 June 2008.

29 Supreme Court of India, Judgement on Civil Appeal No. 4273 of 2010 (accessible on www.supremecourtofindia.nic.in)
30 Cuckoo Paul, 'Court verdict disappoints supporters of free gas pricing', *Forbes India*, 7 May 2010, on www.moneycontrol.com/news/business.

22 GOODBYE, GANDHI

1   Foreword by Mukesh Ambani, in A.G. Krishnamurthy, *Dhirubhaism: The Remarkable Work Philosophy of Dhirubhai Ambani*, Tata McGraw-Hill, New Delhi, 2007.
2   'Wharton School names auditorium after Dhirubhai Ambani', India Abroad News Service, 16 May 2007.
3   Philip Bowring, Book review: *The Polyester Prince, International Herald Tribune*, 16 January 1999.
4   'Reliance on the wrong strategy', *Economist*, 25 July 1998.
5   'In invisible ink: missed scoop: the Ambanis can manage the media. On anything, anytime', *Outlook*, 30 November 1998.
6   Leela Gandhi, 'The mocking style of a capitalist folk-hero', *Age* (Melbourne), 13 February 1999.
7   Amartya Sen, *The Argumentative Indian: Writings on Indian Culture, History and Identity*, Allen Lane, London, 2005.
8   Shantanu Guha Ray, 'The press code: managing the media is another special Ambani trait', *Tehelka*, 29 December 2007.
9   Press Trust of India report in *The Hindu*, 5 May 2008.
10 'Delhi Confidential', *Indian Express*, 20 August 2007; George Fernandes, letter to *Indian Express*, 21 August 2007; Virendra Kapoor, 'Gloating over someone's troubles', Cybernoon, 27 August 2007.
11 Gurcharan Das, 'The India model', *Foreign Affairs*, July–August 2006.
12 Arun K.Agrawal, *Reliance: The Real Natwar*, Manas Publications, New Delhi, 2008.
13 'Mumbai tycoon Ambani a close second to steel magnate Mittal among Indian billionaires', Associated Press, *International Herald Tribune*, 15 November 2007.
14 Bruce Loudon, 'Pull your horns in: Singh sermon waves a red flag at India's bulls', *Australian*, 6 June 2007.

Index